Blessings

Rich
Jones

THE JOURNEY CONTINUES:
From Groaning to Dancing

RICHARD JONES

authorHOUSE

AuthorHouse™
1663 Liberty Drive
Bloomington, IN 47403
www.authorhouse.com
Phone: 833-262-8899

Published by AuthorHouse 01/24/2022

ISBN: 978-1-6655-4629-4 (sc)
ISBN: 978-1-6655-4628-7 (hc)
ISBN: 978-1-6655-4634-8 (e)

Library of Congress Control Number: 2022900538

Print information available on the last page.

Contents

Dedication

I dedicate this book to my partner in life and best friend for over 55 years, my precious wife, Helen. She has been at my side the good and the bad. We have learned *what it is to be in need, and what it is to have abundance...living in plenty or in want... and have learned to be content whatever the circumstances* (Philippians 4:11-12 NIV). I daily thank the Lord for bringing us together. What a great adventure we've had and continue to have. Special roses and confetti to you, my dear. She was a part of examining every page and gave me the freedom to spend hours in my study since retirement. I love you, Sweetheart!!

Acknowledgments

"In most cases, prayer consists more of groaning than of speaking, of tears rather than words. God sees our tears. Our groaning is not hidden from Him. He who made everything by a word does not need human words" (St Augustine). The more I write, the more I realize the truth of this, and the more I understand the "groaning," both in praying and in writing. And I have begun to discover the evolution from "groaning to dancing" in writing and praying as well.

I wish to acknowledge some special individuals who have been part of my "process," whether groaning or dancing, and encouraging me while bringing this work to completion. My grandson, Christian Schmidt, has served as my editor, spending many hours with me on this project. Christian is currently studying for the pastoral ministry at Trinity Evangelical Divinity School in Deerfield, Illinois. I gratefully thank all who have through the years influenced my life and my thinking—Warren and Patricia Jones, Opal Loehr, Alonzo and Edith Sims, Robert Green, Earl Wood, Marion Henderson, David Hargrove, Wayne Shaw, Robert Smith, Gene Fryar, Doug Weber, Donna Hale, Joyce Folk, Marisol Parr, and Roger Ash. Special thanks to my best friend of over 35 years, Greg Weiler (see entry of November 21), and special prayer partners of many years—Mike McDermott, Ben Mannix, and Alan Johnston. Thomas J. Watson (CEO of IBM, 1914 – 1956) said: "Follow the path of the unsafe, independent thinker. Expose your ideas to the dangers of controversy. And on issues that seem important to you, stand up and be counted at any cost." In my early years, I failed miserably in fulfilling that challenge. In these later years, the Lord has been teaching me to do a better job communicating my thoughts, controversial or not.

I am often asked what writers most have influenced me in my journey. While not exhaustive, the list would have to include Charles Swindoll, Oswald Chambers, C.S. Lewis, Robert Benson, Andrew Murray, Thomas Merton, Dietrich Bonhoeffer, Richard Foster, Henri Nouwen, Steven Brown, Lloyd John Ogilvie, Edith Schaeffer, Catherine Marshall, Anne Graham Lotz, Frederick Buechner, Madeleine L'Engle, John Piper, R.C. Sproul, Charles Colson, Walter Wangerin, Brennan Manning, Richard Exley, Fred Rogers, Jim Cymbala, Charles Colson, A.W. Tozer, and very recently, Sarah Bessey (Nouwen and Tozer, both as my influencers, weird, huh). At the end of this book is a list of authors that I have quoted. You might have noticed that it would be exceedingly difficult for you to pigeonhole me by way of my list of authors. That's good. If you know me, you know I hate to be placed in a category. These are MANY sources from men and women of various faiths and philosophical persuasions as well as from generations past. Contemporary Christianity, at times, tends to turn up its nose at sources such as these. I believe it to be arrogant to assume that only our generation or our era has anything valid to say to today's church.

And most of all, honor and glory to my LORD and Savior, Jesus Christ. May the rest of my years, however many He gives to me, be lived out in the spirit of John 3:30—*More of You, LORD; less of me.*

About "Random Thoughts for Today"

At the conclusion of most daily entries is a section entitled "Random Thoughts for the Day." In addition to scripture, some of these quotations are anonymous, some are my own, and many are words that I have jotted down in my journals through the years that have especially touched me. Perhaps there will be one or two each day that will minister to you.

Translations

All scripture quotations in this book (unless otherwise noted) are either the ENGLISH STANDARD VERSION or the NEW INTERNATIONAL VERSION. In scripture, when the word "Lord" is translated in lower case letters, it refers to the title for God—*Adonai*—kind of like President of the United States. You will note that many times in your Bible, all upper-case letters are used—"LORD." This is referring to the name of God—YAHWEH. LORD is His name; Lord is His title. In almost every case in this book, unless the word from scripture is *Adonai,* I have used all upper-case letters when writing the name of God—LORD.

About the Cover

The cover is a painting by Jacqueline Osborn, entitled "First Dance." Jacci says, "This was a painting I did of my son who came into my studio. I had some music playing, and he picked up his little girl who came in with him and started to dance with her" (See November 3 entry). Interesting side-note: this little girl recently got her driver's license. *(Painting used by permission)*

Ms. Osborn's website: jacci-osborn.squarespace.com

Foreword

It has been my privilege to have known Rick Jones for about three years, but in that short amount of time, I have grown to love and respect him for who he is and his commitment to living out his faith with genuineness and humility I have rarely seen in others who profess the name of Christ. Therefore, I am honored to be able to write a brief forward to his latest book, "The Journey Continues: From Groaning to Dancing."

In the introduction to his latest book, Rick mentions having more time to write in this season of his life. He spent eleven years since his last book ("Journey Through the School of Groaning") was written, serving God in a Christian school mentoring teenagers to follow Christ, both as a teacher and during his final two years at the school, as an administrator. He had planned to retire from the school ministry two years earlier but was asked by the school board to stay on for what ended up being an additional two years to serve as the interim administrator until a more permanent replacement could be found. That is an indication of his servant's heart and willingness to set aside his own agenda and desires in order to serve Christ. By his own admission, those two years were challenging. They required him to step outside of his comfort zone, but by "standing in the gap" for the school, he not only blessed the school but was also provided with new growth opportunities that undoubtedly found their way into this latest book.

As was the case with his previous book on prayer, his latest effort is filled with biblical integrity and sage advice from his own walk with God and that of many others he references in each daily devotional. Writing a book on prayer requires, among other things, both correct orthodoxy and orthopraxy. Rick writes with both viewpoints in mind. He simply doesn't write or talk about prayer. Rick is a practitioner of prayer as he daily pursues a relationship with God that has sustained him over the years.

On a more personal note, Rick's first book on prayer helped sustain me during my first year as the new administrator at Victory Christian Academy (VCA) in Valparaiso, Indiana, the school that Rick served at prior to my arrival on campus. The legacy he left at Victory, made my transition to the school much easier and certainly more pleasant. Thank you, Rick, for your friendship and support as my wife and I made the move to Northwest Indiana in 2019, after having spent the previous twenty-six years at a Christian school in Wichita, Kansas. May you continue to "dance" as you write, speak and serve Christ for many years to come!

David Funk
Administrator, Victory Christian Academy

Introduction

There are times when I am led to lay my prayer journal and lists aside and just "groan" before the Lord.

We struggle with prayer because it is not our priority.

Sometimes God responds to our prayers in a mighty way...Sometimes He just asks us to trust Him.

It is a pure pleasure for me to be writing again. Fourteen years of being involved in teaching and school administration have claimed most of my hours and focus. My desire to write turned into thoughts of "someday..." or "next year I'm gonna...". With departure from the business of the classroom, I once again have the freedom to commit myself to putting pen to paper (or I should say, "fingers to keyboard"). William Faulkner wrote, "It is the writer's privilege to help man endure by lifting his heart." That is my desire, and I appreciate your allowing me to be a small part of the "heart-lifting" process in your life. My first published writing, *Seasons of a Pastor,* came out in 2008, and my prayer devotional, *Journey Through the School of Groaning,* was published three years later. Since that last volume, I have had several requests to write a sequel (yes, another propaganda book), a second prayer devotional. A discussion with my late father around four years ago ended with a commitment to do so eventually. It is with pleasure that I honor that commitment. Like everyone else, I'm going to die. I love to write because what I write is a part of my legacy. Much of what I write is never seen by anyone but the Lord and me. But written words can live on as long as there are readers to see them. Michael Straczynski called it immortality by proxy.

What excites me most is that I am writing again in a new stage of my life. It's been over ten years since my last book. My journey has continued beyond retiring from pastoral ministry. I've spent fourteen years teaching in public and Christian schools and the last two years as an administrator, retiring in June of 2019. Now, as an official "retiree," I am still very busy, but busy doing what I want to do, including preaching on the weekend in a rural church of about twenty people. It's amazing how much you can grow and change in just ten years. My physical body is groaning more than ever, but my inner life is thriving.

I wrote this book during the worldwide COVID-19 pandemic. My writing will most certainly reflect that. There will be some entries reflecting the fears, disappointments, and struggles (some that became blessings) during this time of global chaos. This included a two-month lock-down of pretty much our entire country and a personal quarantine when Helen and I both tested positive for the virus. The blessing for me was a long period of being home-bound and being able to concentrate on this book, probably bringing it to completion at least six months ahead of schedule. As you read through this book, you will find some controversial topics included in these writings. I think that's a good thing. There have been many changes in my thinking and philosophy in life over the years, and I'm pretty sure there will be more changes in the years ahead. English writer Brian Aldiss said that there are two kinds of writers—"Those that make you think, and those that make you wonder." I hope that some of my thoughts will make you think, and some make you wonder. If you are pretty much a closed-minded individual and you have everything all figured out, this book may not be for you. My goal is not to necessarily give answers but to perhaps challenge conventional thinking. You don't pigeonhole me; I won't pigeonhole you.

Andrew Murray once said, "As we pray, our attitude should be one of silent expectation that the Holy Spirit will help in our weakness and pray for us with groanings that cannot be expressed." Here's an excerpt from the disclaimer (propaganda warning, if you will) from my first devotional—"Much of what I write in this book is meant to cause you to embrace prayer as I do. Prayer is not boring; it is an adventure. May you enjoy this journey in the days and months to come." David shares with us in Psalm 30, *weeping may endure for a night, but joy comes in the morning...You have turned for me my mourning into dancing; you have loosed my sackcloth and clothed me with gladness, that my glory may sing your praise and not be silent. O LORD my God, I will give thanks to You forever.* (Vv 11-12)

One poet said fill your paper with the breathings of your heart. I've prayed and labored to share those breathings with you. I hope that this volume will be a practical tool in helping spur you on to an intentional and growing prayer life. I am pleased to give you this latest chapter in my voyage, ***THE JOURNEY CONTINUES: FROM GROANING TO DANCING.*** So yes, it is a pure pleasure for me to be writing again. My aim is to share with you what I see and what I feel in the best and simplest way. How do I write? With the Lord's presence and blessing, one word at a time. The journey continues!!

Rick Jones (October, 2021)

We will not rewrite history…It is what it is…TRUTH MATTERS. (My personal philosophy in the study of history)

"We love because He first loved us." (The Apostle John)

January

"I wait for the LORD, my soul waits and in His word I put my hope. (Psalm 130:5)

January 1   Breaking Old Routines

I may be 77 years old, but I possess enough wisdom to know that breaking out of old routines is one of the secrets of staying young and energetic. But being a creature of habit, I have struggled with this. A brand-new year dawns, and I anticipate what the Lord has in store. One of the entries in my previous journal is a prayer – "My Lord God, I have no idea where I am going; I do not see the road ahead of me. I cannot know for certain where it will end. And I would continue that prayer by saying, "Even though I don't know the future...YOU do, Lord, and I fully trust in You." Psalm 130:5 continues to minister to my heart day in and day out—*I wait for the LORD; my soul waits, and in His word I put my hope.* Also, in a past journal, I came across an entry containing three prayers. They have become daily prayers for me within the last couple of years: <u>My prayer of faith</u>: "I believe; help me with my unbelief." <u>My prayer of hope</u>: "In YOU, I have hoped; let me never be confounded." <u>My prayer of love</u>: "Take away my heart of stone and give me a heart of flesh." Three marvelous prayers to begin any year. New year—A new chapter, new verse, or just the same old story? Ultimately we write it. The choice is yours.

Cast all your anxiety on Him because He cares for you. (1 Peter 5:7 NIV)

The person who says it can't be done should not interrupt the person who is doing it. *(Chinese Proverb)*

The grace of God never fails me; but I often fail the grace of God.

Keep on nudging me, Lord, in the direction you would have me to go in the year ahead.

Today is the first blank page of a 365-page book...Write a good one.

January 2   An Army of the Kind

Our world needs a new kind of army in the year ahead—AN ARMY OF THE KIND!! I never served in the military, and I am not close to being knowledgeable in principles of warfare or combat maneuvers. Still, I do know that one thing in short supply in our culture today is kindness. The late Dr. Harry Evans of Trinity College in Deerfield, Illinois had a sign in his office that simply read, "Kindness Spoken Here." I love that. The apostle Paul wrote in Galatians 5—*The fruit of the Spirit is...KINDNESS.* The term in the original language is *chrestotes,* a beautiful word for a beautiful grace. The Greek philosopher, Epictetus, said that a man had lost the very essence of manhood when he had lost his kindness. Even the heathen philosophers taught that kindness is that which makes man kin to God. I have lost track of the number of times I would have a student in my office with the counsel, "Hey, just be kind!!" I love the classroom rules that a first-grade student put on a poster she brought to class— "Be nice to everybody – Say nice things to each other – Just be nice." I can't help but think of Micah 6:8—*What is good: Do justice, love kindness, and walk humbly with your God.* About every other day, I find myself having to stop everything and remind myself of Micah's list. I need to read it aloud. I desire to not only mature in practicing kindness, but to love kindness as well. Do you genuinely LOVE kindness?

Random thoughts for today:

Be kind and compassionate to one another. (Ephesians 4:32 NIV)

When Jesus was my age, He went to church with a bunch of people and got lost...It happens. *(6- year old kid)*

Teaching should be filled with ideas instead of stuffed with facts.

Let His love fall on you so that your love can fall upon others around you...Love well.

The mind is like the stomach. It's not how much you put into it that counts, but how much it digests.

January 3   Seed Sowers

Have you noticed all the negativity around us in our world today? And it has permeated the church as well. It seems that we are defined more by what we're against rather than what we support. We seem to differ on just about everything from what constitutes godly worship music to our approach to the LGBTQ movement. No one is listening to anybody, because after all, I'm right so, why should I listen to you. I believe that honest, intelligent dialogue in the church has died, or at least it's very ill. My friend Nate Loucks once told me, "Christianity is not always complicated, but it is often very hard." Both the religious left AND the religious right have blown it. The church has elevated transitory issues of men when the core message of the gospel is to love God and to love others. I think it was Jesus who said that. The older I get, the more loving God and loving others becomes THE priority for me, and a lot of other stuff that used to be so important begins to fade. Isn't it interesting that all of our positions are "biblical," yet we disagree on so many things? Sincere Christians can disagree about the details of scripture and theology. Absolutely! But we cannot disagree on the command of Jesus to love God and love others. My youngest daughter, Becky, is a pastor. Yes, I know that both sides of the "woman-pastor issue" have "biblical" positions. In a message, some time ago, she said, "The love of God is the purest nourishment we can dispense to our world around us." If my motive is really to help (and to love), then I will find a way to speak the truth in love. Sometimes that may mean I need to approach others with an open ear to honest dialogue. Or I can join the majority in our world today (and that includes the church) and battle with personal insults and diatribes that may or may not be "biblical." You don't love people by hitting them over the head; that's assault, not love. That's a good thing for all of us to remember, whether we be conservative or liberal (whatever those labels even mean). In the words of one Christian author, I choose to spread "seeds of love." I think I want to be that kind of a "seed-sower" rather than a "crap-thrower!"

But those that wait upon the LORD will find new strength. They will fly high on wings like eagles. They will run and not be weary. They will walk and not faint. (Isaiah 40:31 NIV)

You change your life by changing your heart.

Since we are all naturally prone to hypocrisy, any empty semblance of righteousness is quite enough to satisfy us instead of righteousness.

People filled with the joy of the Lord seem to be more productive and helpful and likable and interested in others and friendlier and more resilient.

January 4   Be the Light

When we're praising God and celebrating good things in our lives, it's easy to be honest before the Lord...Not so much though in our times of hurting and confusion. Many times, in the New Testament, the apostle Paul refers to believers as *children of light*. The apostle John tells us that *light dispels the darkness.* One of my pastors tells us that a major fear of many people is fear of the dark. His solution: TURN ON THE LIGHT!! *You are all sons of light and sons of the day. We do not belong to the night or to the darkness* (I Thessalonians 5:5). My youngest daughter taught elementary school in Haiti for a year, and in the last few months she was without electricity. During that time, she told me that the contrasting metaphor between light and darkness in the Bible has weakened in our society since the advent of electricity. You have to imagine what it would have been like to live in a world without electricity and light bulbs to feel the impact of Paul's language. Have you ever noticed that most crimes are committed under the cover of darkness? Ever wonder why that is? Living in the light of Christ in you is like living in His brilliance. *Christ in YOU, the hope of glory!!* In Jesus Christ, YOU are the conductor of that light...How are you shining that light? How are you sharing that light? How are you spreading that light? There are already far too many who are busy spreading as much darkness as they possibly can. During what a lot of people are calling "dark days," be the one who turns on the light. Be that encourager who shines and shares and spreads that light to your family and neighbors.

Random thoughts for today:

Let your light shine before men, that they may see your good deeds and praise your Father in heaven. (Matthew 5:16 NIV)

Discipline my will, Father, that in hours of stress, I may honestly seek after those things for which I have prayed in hours of peace.

I think sometimes the accomplishment of my dreams is on the other side of fear.

Three things in human life are important: 1) Be kind 2) Be kind 3) Be kind

Thirty years of discipleship programs in the church, and we are still not discipled.

No doubt about it. The daily routine can get monotonous. Sometimes it seems that options of adventure are not on the horizon of today and probably not tomorrow. Why is it so difficult for our narrow minds to see greatness in small things and to think of our daily affairs in relation to the eternal? What does it take to jog our "ho-hum, same old, same old" spirits out of complacency and turn the so-called mundane acts that fill every day into sacred acts of worship? How many of us have days filled with small, routine tasks consisting of caring for others? Brother Lawrence talks about finding God in the commonplace of his monastery. I love that. He at one time had the nonspiritual task of washing dishes in his monastery. Through this experience he discovered some insights into spiritual disciplines. He said the most effective way to communicate with God is to do ordinary work. He didn't build as strong of a wall between secular and sacred as some of us do. Our daily lives are not divided into spiritual parts and secular parts. We should offer every activity to Him even before we do it, and then we give the Lord thanks when we accomplish something. Each morning I begin my day with this prayer: "Lord, come what may, I give you today and all that I do in this day. Walk with me, and may my choices be wise choices."

Random thoughts for today:

See, I have engraved you on the palms of my hands. (Isaiah 49:16 NIV)

May I continue to "glorify You, Lord, and enjoy You forever." *(from the Shorter Catechism)*

How to avoid criticism - "Do nothing – Say nothing – Be nothing." *(Aristotle)*

Kindness is difficult to give away because it keeps coming back.

People living deeply have no fear of death.

It is imperative that we teach our youth how to love one another.

Do not fight the thing in detail: Turn from it...Look only to your Lord...Sing. Read. Work*!!*

When life takes its ordinary course, it's hard to remember what matters.

January 6   Compassion is Not About Numbers

Compassion is not quantitative. Each year, my former church has an emphasis for Compassion International. Members of our church-community are encouraged to pray about "adopting" a child in a third-world country. The $24 a month commitment covers food, medical, and education. You have an opportunity to correspond with your child and receive periodic updates. Our family supported a little girl from Thailand some years ago when our daughters were in elementary school. We sponsored Bah Blue until she left the program at age 18. Today she is a fine Christian woman, married, and employed by Compassion. Often, I've heard individuals say, "What difference does it make? There are millions of kids in need in the world today. You can't help them all." This sentiment is laid alongside the "well-meaning" Christian who says, "Why have you made over 30 trips to Haiti. Don't we have enough poor people in our own country to help?" Certainly, it's true that there may be a million more equally entitled for every child that cries out in need. One writer said, "This is the poorest of all reasons for not helping the person whose cries you hear." All I know is that our family made a difference in the life of Bah Blue. Maybe you can't save millions, but you can save one. Each of us needs to be praying to make a difference and then respond by reaching out and getting involved in a life crying out to you. God will always lead you if you are listening.

Random thoughts for today:

Whatever you did for one of the least of these brothers and sisters of mine, you did for Me.. (Matthew 25:40 NIV)

We are still working on cures for AIDS. Malaria, etc. But we've already found a cure for hunger—It's called food.

Poor nutrition causes 8000 plus deaths (children under 5) per day. I don't see anyone changing their Facebook profile for that. *(Nate Loucks)*

New year? A new tradition may be an oxymoron, but that shouldn't prevent you from starting a new tradition you wish you had.

The most successful people I know have decided to become better, not bitter.

You stand for a just cause when you fight for truth.

I cannot help but wonder how many holy moments I've missed because I let all of the stuff that I "had to get done" keep me from that moment. God has so much to speak into my life. I believe that. I've been told that spending time alone with Him and devoting my attention to Him is vital to my spiritual maturing. Even Jesus often withdrew to lonely places and prayed *(Luke 5:16)*. You get the idea that this was important to Him, so perhaps it should also be important to me. Even though I know all of this, I've still struggled in past years to set that time aside. I know how vital that communication link between the Father and me is. In some ways, it's like the flow of blood through my body. I can say it's a priority, but making it my priority can be another story. I don't have all the answers, and I don't consider myself to be an expert on prayer, but I KNOW it needs to be daily. I KNOW it needs to be at a consistent time of day. And I KNOW it needs to happen in a place where I can be unrushed and undisturbed. It's a pretty difficult discipline to keep in our culture today, isn't it? If keeping a daily appointment with the Lord seems hard, it's because it IS hard. As one who has faithfully kept a detailed appointment book through the years, perhaps I need to start writing that time in daily. There's another thing I know...I KNOW that strong men and women of God through the ages have set time aside daily to be with the Lord. What's the answer? What's the secret? PRAY.

Random thoughts for today:

Pray continually. (I Thessalonians 5:17 NIV)

Priorities are a matter of the heart. We struggle with our walk with God because it's not our priority.

You stand for a just cause when you fight for the truth.

Do what you love.

Will your worries today matter next year?

Here I am this morning in the presence of my Father, doing nothing except sitting here in the presence of my Father.

January 8   Sold Out!

It's easy to get hung up on Luke 9:23. Most of us know John 3:16 by heart, but fewer have a handle on Luke 9:23. Jesus said, *If anyone would come after me, he must deny himself and take up his cross daily and follow me.* Two great verses, but there's a difference. John 3:16 emphasizes believing; Luke 9:23 emphasizes following. Hmm...*Come after me*...It's a phrase that was commonly used in the original language of a romantic relationship, a passionate pursuit if you will. In this context, following someone is pursuing someone you deeply love. It's all about abandonment, which is the heart and essence of success in our walk with the Lord. Jesus is inviting us to come to Him.—"I want you to become a part of Me and allow Me to become a part of you." He doesn't particularly care that you consider Him to be a cool guy or an insightful philosopher or an outstanding literary character. He wants to be Lord of your life. That means "in charge of." That means "the boss." And this directly relates to and affects our prayer life. Have you ever heard of a "pray-to-win mentality turned inside out." It's prayer that moves beyond trying to steer or manipulate God. Do we pray with that kind of abandonment—a product of a life that is sold out? Why do we keep being shocked at the radical life Jesus calls us to live out?

Random thoughts for today:

If anyone would come after me, he must deny himself and take up his cross daily and follow me. (Luke 9:23 NASB)

If God owns me (and He does), and if everything I have belongs to Him (and it does), then I need to honor Him with all that I have.

Owning a lot of things won't make your life safe. *(Jesus)*

We control our silences...We have to make time...We have an appointment with God.

We cannot pray in love and live in hate and still think we are worshipping God.

Grandparents are both our past and our future.

There's nothing I can do to make God love me more, and there's nothing I can do to make Him love me less.

January 9   Touch

Remember those electric bump cars at the amusement park. We just run at each other and smile and bump and go away." How often I think about this high-tech, fast-paced world of ours, passing hundreds of people every day without asking ourselves if they could use a compassionate touch. Let's not even talk about how those opportunities of touch are becoming less and less because of the hours we spend on our internet devices. Even when we do have personal contact, too often, we barely scratch the surface: "How are you doing?" "Great!" "How's everything going?" "Wonderful!" Some responses I have personally received from friends tell me nothing: "I'm just peachy!" "I'm better than I deserve." "Couldn't be better." And hopefully, my response to them isn't "I'll pray about that" (maybe). Then somebody slips out and dies inside a little more because there's no one to talk to. I've heard it said that genuine compassion is the capacity for feeling what it's like to live inside somebody else's skin. Our Lord looks with compassion upon His children; we are a part of His body. Should we do any less? How can I offer my personal touch of compassion to those that cross my path today? How much do we care?

Random thoughts for today:

We love because He first loved us. (1 John 4:19 NASB)

We shouldn't ask God to bless what we're doing...We find out what God is blessing and get on board.

Prayer is the most intimate activity I can share with God...In prayer, Jesus gives me permission to ask.

Evil cannot stand forgiveness!!

What a joy when I remove all the clutter from my life and discover that I just want Jesus.

By doing a little, day by day, we can accomplish much.

In what way do my actions today register my true "caring level"?

I read an interesting statement the other day about grandparents— Grandparents are both our past and our future. Quotations like this have become much more interesting to me since being a grandparent. I have the blessing of being a grandparent to five great young people, with two more soon to be added via upcoming summer weddings. My favorite trip as a boy was the four-and-a-half-hour journey to the home of my Grandmother, Maude Jones. She lived twenty miles from Muncie, Indiana, in a little town in Randolph County called Modoc. Many of my early lessons of faith came from Grandma Jones. Married to a Methodist preacher, she was widowed and left with four children when my father was just a little over a year old. My first impression of prayer came from my mother as she prayed with me each night at bedtime, but an impression that will never leave me came from my Grandma Jones. Sometimes when we stayed overnight at her house, my brother and I would sleep in the parlor next to her bedroom. On one such visit during my teen years, my brother was asleep, and I was wide awake watching the flame through the glass of the oil stove in the middle of the room. Suddenly, I heard my grandmother talking. I started to answer her, but then realized she wasn't talking to me. She prayed for close to an hour that night. She prayed for each of her children and their spouses, for each of her grandchildren by name, for her pastor and her church, her neighbors, and for missionaries she knew. I can still hear her quiet voice in my mind. I think the impression that penetrates my memory is what I learned from her about the work of prayer. I know that night meant more to me than any lecture in a prayer class ever could. As a grandparent, I pray that I might have that kind of impression upon my grandkids.

A good man leaves an inheritance to his children's children. (Proverbs 13:22 ESV)

Sometimes we ask God to change our circumstances, and all along, He simply desires to change me.

Common problem: We glance at the Word, but we do not feed upon it.

Prayer is the heart of my faith.

It's a wonderful thing to have a God to believe in.

January 11   Legacy

I've given a lot of thought lately about legacy and the difference between legacy and inheritance. One author has said, "Legacy encompasses how to live and how to die, the passing on of one's core values." What has been the theme of my life? I've discovered that inheritances can sometimes divide families, but legacies can bond them. This has led me to believe that leaving a legacy is much more important to me than leaving an inheritance. I leave the legacy I live. I can't expect anyone (my children, grandchildren, students, congregation) to treasure what I don't think is valuable enough to demonstrate in my own life. I need to live so that my children and grandchildren won't have to edit their heritage. Psalm 71 says, *even when I am old and gray, do not forsake me, my God, till I declare Your power to the next generations, Your mighty acts to all who are to come* (V 18). Our world is full of problems; it can be overwhelming. How can I make a difference? How can I leave my world a little better than I found it? What will the mention of my name bring to people's minds after I'm gone? What do others around me see that I'm all about? Have you ever wondered what your family will say about you in fifty years? One of my favorite people in the Bible is Enoch, father of Methuselah, in Genesis 5. His life is summed up with four words—*ENOCH WALKED WITH GOD!!* He walked with God. That's what I want on my tombstone.

Random thoughts for today:

I have competed well; I have finished the race; I have kept the faith. (2 Timothy 4:7 NABRE)

I believe the Lord delights in the good in my life even more than I do.

The past is safe because it's past, and we have survived.

It's not enough for a man to know how to ride; he must also know how to fall. *(Russian Proverb)*

The way we live is not found in a place or an event, but a Person.

Are we committed to leading our children to the place where they really don't care what society thinks, but who will be willing to stand alone and passionately say, "I want what God wants in my life"?

January 12   Follow or Flee

"Those who aren't following Jesus, aren't His followers. It's that simple. Followers follow. Those who don't follow aren't followers." (A quote I've used in my teaching many times; not sure where I first heard it) It is simple, isn't it? We focus on Jesus and hopefully get others to focus on Jesus as well. The reality is Jesus. It's the foundation of discipleship. And that reality is driven in our lives by our choice to either follow or flee. To follow someone is to pursue someone I love. Read Luke 9:23 and reread the thoughts of January 8. John Wesley said many times that if we're not walking in the way of the cross, we're not following Him. We like to live the comfortable life. Live safe. Nothing too crazy or radical. Give 10% to the church; help in the nursery occasionally, especially if we've been guilted into it. You know what? I really don't want to hear the Lord say to me at the end of my life, "Jones, you've lived the safest life you could possibly live." What have I done recently that has taken me out of my comfort zone? The more I read scripture, the more uncomfortable my comfortable life becomes. You mean I have to put others before myself? I have to love others no matter what? Turns out, following Jesus is a lot more than raising my hand and shouting, "Yea, Jesus!" Followers follow; those who don't follow aren't followers. Hmm...No middle road, huh? Of course, we know what happens to people who stay in the middle of the road...They get run over. Jesus says, "Take a stand...FOLLOW ME!!

Random thoughts for today:

"Come, follow Me," Jesus said, "I will send you out to fish for people.." (Matthew 4:19 NIV)

May my relationship to the Lord be founded upon His unconditional love for me, and not what He can do for me today.

The true measure of a man is how he treats somebody who can do him absolutely no good. *(Samuel Johnson)*

Don't let yesterday take up too much of today.

Who is Jesus? He's the One who makes clay, then adds powder, then shakes it all out and rubs it all around—And we become real. *(A Kid)*

When the student is ready, the teacher appears. *(Buddhist saying)*

January 13   Broken

I was reminded not too long ago that before 3,000 people were brought into the church on the day of Pentecost, the disciples had spent ten days in prayer, fasting, and spiritual travail. Now I realize that when the Lord said to Solomon, after the construction of the temple, "If my people...pray...then I will hear from heaven...", He was addressing Israel concerning their sin and repentance. But a principle is introduced here that is still valid today. I can't help but wonder if Christians would pray this kind of prayer for our world, that perhaps a time of peace might still be possible in our society today. I'm not sure that social media is the best place for evangelism (maybe it is, I don't know), but I DO know that it isn't the place for the church to be spewing their political opinions. C'mon brothers, and sisters, stop it!! I can't imagine Paul supporting a candidate, or a political party between writing *for me to live is Christ and to die is gain,* and *I can do all things through Christ who strengthens me.* I can vividly remember a specific trip to Haiti, and I can still picture a brother shaking his head and proclaiming, "This place is broken!" I see broken lives all around me, including my own. As I understand scripture, this breaks the heart of my Father more than mine. Years ago, I heard it said, "Does whatever breaks the heart of your Lord also break yours." Maybe if it did, I would pray that kind of prayer, and spend less time on Facebook. As a brother in Christ once prayed, "May my heart break with Yours, Father."

Random thoughts for today:

If my people...will humble themselves and pray and seek My face...then, I will hear from heaven. (2 Chronicles 7:14 NIV)

Help me to minister to the hurting as You have ministered to me when I have been hurting.

The best thing about the future is that it comes only one day at a time. *(Abraham Lincoln)*

Allow me to see the holy in all of life.

The biggest communication problem is we don't listen to understand...We listen to reply.

Be kind or be quiet!!

January 14   My Heroes

Henry Wadsworth Longfellow wrote, "Lives of great men... leave behind footprints on the sands of time." I think that our world has always been founded upon hero worship, but I believe that our definition of what makes a hero has changed drastically over the years. It appears that it has become more about being a winner in an ongoing popularity contest among athletes, musicians, Hollywood heartthrobs, and successful entrepreneurs. It would seem to me that our heroes should be examples of trustworthiness and integrity *in season and out of season.* In counseling with many high schoolers over the years, it troubles me how very few of them considered their mom or their dad to be their hero. Fred Rogers, of *Mr. Rogers' Neighborhood* fame, would do something before any public speaking event. He would ask his audience to pause and think about those who had a significant shaping influence upon their life. What a great exercise. I tried it. My dad is at the top of the list, followed immediately by my wife, Helen (yes, my wife is my hero). I heard on the radio the other day, "Heroes don't have to be famous—they only have to be heroic." What do you think makes a person heroic? Faithfulness? Truthfulness? A loving spirit? Our heroes become our role models. I think two critical questions for us to ask are 1) Who are we following? 2) Who is following us? The heroes in your life become your legacy to those who follow you.

Random thoughts for today:

Follow my example, as I follow the example of Christ. (1 Corinthians 11:1 NIV)

May I give the Lord praise and thanks during the humdrum days as much as I do in the midst of the "Yeeha" days of my life.

Loving God and loving others are often drowned out by our selfishness.

Instruction in youth is like engraving in stone. *(Columbian Proverb)*

There are two kinds of people—Those who do the work and those who take the credit. Try to be in the first group; there's much less competition.

I am a part of all that I have met. *(Tennyson)*

Many times, I flee silence because I don't want to be confronted with my hypocrisy and phoniness.

January 15   Random Journal Entries

I'm usually well organized in my thoughts, but today I want to share some random ideas that have come to me from various sources during my morning quiet time. I have subsequently put them into my journal.

- We frequently do wrong, and to make matters worse, we make excuses about it.
- It saddens me to see how easily I can blow off my sin... Sometimes I think about that when I partake of the Lord's Supper.
- Greed is the temptation that we will trade our humanity for 30 pieces of silver.
- How often are we asked to bind ourselves to a specific ideology or theology rather than binding ourselves to Jesus Christ?
- Christianity is not always complicated, but it is often very hard.
- We all have agendas, and they rarely coincide with God's.
- What are my greatest concerns? It's interesting how often they have to do with me.
- Christianity is, by its very nature, Christocentric...Jesus showed us how life is to be lived out.
- There are many different opinions but not many different truths—TRUTH MATTERS—Jesus said, *I am the truth,*

the way, and the life; no man comes to the Father but by Me. (John 14:6)

- The distinct characteristic of a free person is the presence of fearless love.
- I was still learning when I taught my last class.
- "Your will be done, Father" *(Jesus)* "Your will be changed, Father" *(Me)*
- Why am I just now learning major stuff about myself at 75 years of age?
- Does my participation in the "selfie" culture short-circuit loving and caring for others?
- Hasten unto Him who calls you in the silence of your heart.
- How often am I guilty of shrinking God's grace?
- JESUS IS AS GOOD AS I HOPED!!

LORD...Sometimes I think I need to get away from intellectual sophistication in my walk with You and just simply live out Jesus in my words, my demeanor, my attitudes, and my actions.

January 16   Biblical Nutrition

Everywhere I turn, I hear about good nutrition—what I should eat, what I should avoid, whole natural foods vs. processed foods. Medical reports abound about how my energy levels, my attitudes, and my mental prowess are all affected by the intake of the right foods (in regular and proper amounts, of course). The same is true when it comes to spiritual nutrition. Without regular biblical feeding, our inner lives begin to suffer the consequences. I believe the soul longs to be nourished and fed by scripture regularly.

Signs of spiritual malnutrition include becoming shallow, selfish, more demanding, less gentle, and reacting rashly and perhaps even angrily. I'm reminded of a quotation I used in my first book from A.W. Tozer—"The inadequacy of much of our spiritual experience can be traced back to our habit of skipping through the corridors of the kingdom like children through the marketplace, chattering about everything, but pausing to learn the true value of nothing." Spiritually there is a big difference between fast food and a carefully prepared meal from a fine restaurant. It's easy to be satisfied with skimming along the surface of faith instead of delving in and digging deeper. Too many in the church are still playing with blocks in the nursery instead of growing and maturing by diving into deeper truth. Are you struggling in your walk with the Lord? Perhaps Hebrews 5 gives you some answers as to why. *Someone who lives on milk is still an infant and doesn't know how to do what is right* (v 13). We don't have the skill *to recognize the difference between right and wrong* (v 14). If I'm not able to nourish my own soul, then I am a spiritual baby.

Random thoughts for today:

You are like babies who need milk and cannot eat solid food. (Hebrews 5:12 NLT)

True righteousness is doing the right thing for the right reason.

All I know is that when Jesus was my age, He behaved for His mom. *(A Kid)*

Have you had a kindness shown to you? Pass it on*!!*

Jesus is as good as we hoped.

More of You today, Lord...Less of me.

I caught myself humming a tune this morning. Then I realized it was *You Got a Friend in Me* from the movie *Toy Story*. My mother was right. She said, "If you can count your true friends on one hand, you're a lucky person." I have almost a thousand friends on Facebook...Or maybe not. I'm guessing we've got a lot of acquaintances, but not a lot of true friendships. I looked up "friend" in the dictionary, but it really didn't help me much. Then I read John 15:13—*Greater love has no one than this, that he lay down his life for his friends.* Jesus said that. I don't have many friends. But I DO have a few who I consider to be true friends. Why is my friend, my friend? Acceptance. Trust. He will stand by me, no matter what. He is someone with whom I can be myself. In his presence I can think out loud without fear. So I guess real friends aren't necessarily Facebook friends. So, my friend will help me achieve my goals. We walk the same path. We pray for each other. We aren't afraid to ask each other the hard questions. It's called accountability. True friends offer constructive criticism to each other (and receive it). I've known relationships where the participants would keep their mouth shut, even if they saw their friend involved in self-destructive behavior, "because I don't want them to be mad at me." That is NOT friendship! Do you have someone in your life who stirs within you a spiritual hunger and a desire for more of the Lord? Do you have someone to encourage you to move toward God and away from those things that would pull you away from Him? Do you have someone who prays for you daily, spurring you on to *love and good deeds* (Hebrews 10:24)? If not, start praying for someone like that. Maybe you need to begin today by seeking out a friend like that. Proverbs 27:9—*The sweetness of a friend gives delight.*

Lord, help me to recognize my true friends and to accept the ways You use them to make me a better person.

Random thoughts for today:

A friend loves at all times. (Proverbs 17:17 ESV)

A faint heart never filled a flush. *(Southern Proverb)*
A friend is a second self. *(Aristotle)*
A frightened world needs a fearless church.

January 18   Finishing Well

My dad often spoke to his children about finishing well. In the school where I worked, I've had the privilege to speak to graduating classes over the last few years. In each message, I would challenge these future adults to finish well. In the final days of the apostle Paul's life, he wrote these words, *I have fought the good fight, I've finished the race, I have kept the faith* (2 Timothy 4:7). Am I fighting the good fight? Will I be able to say when I have finished my course, "I have kept the faith?" We don't seem to hear many messages in our churches today about "hanging in there" or "keep on keeping on." There doesn't seem to be a lot of emphasis on finishing well. We're great starters, but not so much in the finishing category. The Church needs to offset the "I quit" mentality of our culture today. There have been too many people who have joined the path of faith and are not finishing the race they've started. Where are those who make a promise to the Lord and intend to keep it? (No matter what! No matter what it takes!)

In His last breath on the cross, Jesus uttered the words, *It is finished!* Three days later He climaxed it all at the empty tomb. You might say, "He finished well!" Hey guys...God didn't call any of us to drop out of the race...He called us TO FINISH*!!*

Random thoughts for today:

It is finished! (John 19:30 ESV)

I do not have the right to judge any man.

Sometimes I think I hear God say, "Rick, put your prayer lists away today and just talk to Me."

We struggle with prayer life because it's not our priority.

Only the ideals we live out are of any value.

When I have a suffering student, show me ways to comfort him, and lighten his load a little today.

We are what we repeatedly do...Excellence then, is not an act but a habit. *(Aristotle)*

January 19   Grasp His Willingness

Jesus said, *If you abide in me, and my words abide in you, ask whatever you wish, and it will be done for you* (John 15:7). What an exciting thing it is when God answers prayer. We like to quote the last part of that verse, *ask whatever you wish, and it will be done for you.* But how often do we quote the first part? *If you abide in Me...If My words abide in you.* Hmmm. Doesn't sound like carte blanche, does it? He does not always give us what we ask, but He does give us what we need WHEN WE NEED IT. God answers prayer!! Sometimes I wonder how many times God has responded to the Spirit's intercessory prayer for me that I didn't even know about. Lord, thank You for my great "prayer helper," the Holy Spirit, who intercedes for me daily. Your Abba Father wants to answer prayer. Are you sensing a blockage in your prayer life? Is there, for some reason, a gap between you and the Lord? Unconfessed sin? Is His Word remaining in you, in other words, are you allowing it to saturate your life? For that to be possible, you must spend time in the Word. God promises to answer your prayers. He is WILLING to answer...He LONGS to answer. So, I pray, "Father, I grasp Your willingness today."

Random thoughts for today:

This is the confidence we have before Him, that if we ask anything according to His will, He hears us. (1 John 5:14 ESV)

I really can't expect anyone to treasure what I don't think is valuable enough to demonstrate in my life.

I love the man who can smile in trouble, gather strength from distress, and grow brave by reflection.

Sometimes God responds to our prayers in a mighty way... Sometimes He just asks us to trust Him.

It is in the silence of the heart that God speaks.

It is especially difficult to ask when we need it most...Jesus gives us permission to ask. *(Matthew 7:7-11)*

Holiness is a lost concept. I remember a preacher saying years ago, "There is no fear of God in the land!" I realize that some will brand me as too "old school," but I believe that our churches are slipping further and further away from even knowing how to acknowledge the holiness of God. Perhaps this can at least partially explain why our churches are losing ground in America. Some time ago, I was sitting in the worship service of our church, and I was distracted. I know that I must share the blame for this, but I do get distracted. I noticed in the space of four minutes, five different individuals walked into the worship center carrying their Starbucks cups of coffee (or lattes, or whatever they were). I know that's not a mortal sin, but I guess I'm old school enough to have a problem with sipping my mocha while the congregation is singing, "Holy is the LORD." I noticed at least five or six people checking their email or texting (I'll give them the benefit of the doubt, perhaps they were playing "Words with Friends"). One woman in front of me answered her cell phone and responded, "I have to take this" and left the service. She was probably a doctor. Who knows? A friend of mine told me if I had been worshipping, I wouldn't have noticed all of this. I know that...I said I was distracted!! But I can't help wondering if I would be engaged in any of these activities if I were in the presence of the Queen of England or the President of the United States. Many times, to try and avoid such distraction, I try to picture the Lord on His throne up on the platform. I visualize those seraphim surrounding Him and singing, *Holy, holy, holy, is the LORD God Almighty, who was and is and is to come* (Revelation 4:8). How many times have I been in worship or whatever it was I was doing and hear the words of Jacob in Genesis 28:16—*Surely the LORD is in this place, and I wasn't even aware of it.* Heavenly Father, as I prepare to enter Your presence, may my spirit cry out, "Indeed, You ARE in this place." May my greatest desire at this time and in this place be to worship You!!

Random thoughts for today:

Worthy are You, my LORD and my God to receive glory and honor and power. (Revelation 4:11 ESV)

I've found that prayer and worship guard my heart and mind and bring peace out of chaos.

Great is the heart who has not lost his childlike heart. *(Mencius)*

What you do everyday matters more than what you do once in a while.

January 21   Just Show Up?

I recently finished a book on the qualities that move a believer to a disciple (translation: how I become a follower). There is a difference. Remember one of my favorite quotes, "Followers follow." (See January 12 entry) A few years ago, a slogan that became quite popular— "Just Show Up!" Many have used it but perhaps are not aware of its origin. It had political beginnings and was a part of a campaign to get young people out to vote. The tag line of the campaign was, "if you want to make a difference, show up." I'm not sure that is entirely true. There are a lot of folks out there who show up, who begin, but don't finish. A few years ago, there was a very popular national candidate who garnered a lot of excitement among college and older high school students. I visited with a few of them during Valparaiso, Indiana's huge Pop Corn Festival. It was an extremely enjoyable time for me; they were great kids with a lot of enthusiasm and excitement for their candidate. However, exit surveys from that election showed that while many of them did follow up their support by going to the polls, many never made it to the voting booth; some even forgot to register. As I read scripture, I get the distinct impression that God expects us to do more than just show up. The rich young ruler showed up, but he ended up walking away. One of my favorite radio preachers, Dr. James Ford Jr., said, "There are too many people in our churches who have not made the 18-inch journey from the head to the heart." One of my church leaders summed it up well— "Thirty years of discipleship programs in our churches and we are still not discipled" The world has not been reached or changed by believers...But it has been revolutionized by disciples (followers). Yup! Followers follow.

Random thoughts for today:

And Jesus said to Levi, son of Alphaeus, "Come, FOLLOW Me." And Levi rose and FOLLOWED Him. (Mark 2:14 ESV)

If I want to wear loyalty and kindness inside and outside of me, I must put them on every day.

No act of kindness, no matter how small, is ever wasted.

It's easier to cry against a thousand sins than to kill one of your own.

It's always the season for the old to learn. *(Aeschylus)*

If I don't understand, I trust and go on.

Many words have been written on prayer, and I have added to that verbose plethora on the subject. I've written about prayer techniques, formulas, postures, and of course, a tidy system of balancing praise, thanks, confession, petition, and intercession. I'm not saying that all of this is unimportant. It is. But through the years, I've also learned that silence is just as vital to times of prayer and that in prayer, my heart often follows my posture. "You may use eloquent words, deep theological truths…and none of this is necessarily bad if offered from the heart." (RWJ, *Journey Through the School of Groaning*) I continue to believe that there is no wrong way to pray. There is no official prayer technique. It's been said that technique alone is just an embroidered potholder. We live in a world where we can be passionate about cinema, sports, literature, or our careers, but we either grow silent or become offended when religious passion enters the scene. What is that unnatural movement of my soul that is the result of unconditional love without reason? Hard to define, isn't it? I know it when it takes over and consumes me, and I know what the lack of it feels like as well. Some of my more passionate times with the Lord have been during less structured prayer times. My preacher-daughter shared the story of 9-year old Joseph who drew a picture of prayer. (What would you draw? How do you draw prayer?) In addition to the sun and trees, he drew comic strip bubbles representing a conversation between himself and God. The conversation went like this—Joseph: "I love You, God." God: "I love you, Joseph." They repeated the words back and forth several times. No technique potholders here.

And being in agony Jesus prayed more earnestly; and his sweat became like great drops of blood falling down to the ground. (Luke 22:44 ESV)

It's interesting that so many people from your past know a version of you that doesn't exist anymore.

God's directions for living are not complicated, just challenging sometimes...Love God – Love Others – Love Well.

Be an advocate today for someone who needs it.

Why does God choose to work through my weaknesses? So that HE gets the glory. *(The apostle Paul)*

January 23   What Do You Expect?

So, you're having a time of prayer with the Lord this morning. What's your expectation in this time of prayer? None? No expectation whatsoever? Is it just a ritual? To quote one struggling writer in his journal, have you about decided that this is pretty much a "useless time." Another title for this section could be "What's Your Expectation Level?" I have previously talked about the difference between belief and following. That difference defines discipleship. A key to this transition is moving from belief to expectation. What do you expect? As you pray this morning (or evening, or whenever), what are you expecting from Him? I don't think belief is our major problem...I think it's expectation. Why are we so surprised when God moves? When the early church prayed, the building they were meeting in shook! We need to lean into the compassionate heart of God (He cares far more than we do). We need to rise above our doubts (and we all have them). We need to be more like Peter (after all, he DID get out of the boat). We need to act with the faith that we have and go with what's in our heart right now (no matter how small, like the mustard seed, it may seem). The ultimate foundation of miracle expectation is the absolute promise that we worship the God of miracles. What do you expect God to do in and through your life this week? Maybe you'll have a God-moment. Perhaps even a miracle-moment today!! Really, miracles? More about this unsettling subject later in the book.

Random thoughts for today:

For nothing will be impossible with God. (Luke 1:37 ESV)

It's better to know God than it is to know about God.

Love my enemies? Lord, how can I even call them enemies and love them? To which God responds, "Now you get my point."

Break my spirit, Lord, fill me with Your Holy Spirit!! *(King David)*

Recognizing my brokenness is absolutely the only way I can approach the Lord.

There is no shame in not knowing; the shame lies in not finding out. *(Assyrian Proverb)*

My relationship with the Lord isn't based upon emotionalism... But I can get pretty emotional about my relationship with my Lord.

There's a simple formula for leadership in the church. Leaders: Shepherd your people...People: Follow your leaders and figure out if you are a blessing or a burden to your leadership. I find two clear commands in all of the New Testament directed to members of the church concerning their leadership: 1) Pray for them. 2) Obey them. Now having said that, let me address the rest of this entry to the leadership. Leaders, are you a blessing or a burden to your people? I Thessalonians 2:1-12 gives a great checklist for spiritual leaders.

- Be gentle with your people
- Nourish your people
- Protect your people
- Guide your people

During his ministry in Nazi Germany, Dietrich Bonhoeffer spoke with great frustration over the leaders of the church for not shepherding their flocks. He basically said, "What good are you?" He went on to plead for spiritual leaders to fill the greatest need of the church—pastors/shepherds. Leaders, are you FOR your people? Do you LOVE your people? Would you be willing to DIE for your people? Remember, we lead by our example. *Follow me as I follow Christ.* (1 Corinthians 11:1) It is devotion and commitment to your task and to your flock, not perfection, that warms the heart of God. *And when the chief Shepherd appears, you will receive the unfading crown of glory.* (1 Peter 5:4)

Shepherd the flock of God that is among you... Not domineering over those in your charge but being examples to the flock. (1 Peter 5:2-3 ESV)

A husband's greatest privilege is to love his wife boldly and win her heart daily.

How does God test the heart? He melts it. The tests of life lead to a "molten" heart.

"Hey, Rick...Put your prayer lists away today and just talk to Me." *(God)*

Psalm 46:10—"BE STILL!"

January 25   Simplicity

There is simplicity in 1 John 4:19. It's a verse I've known by heart since I was in elementary school. Simple. Jesus said, *Unless you change and become like little children, you will never enter the kingdom of heaven* (Matthew 18:3). Young Rylee (age 7) prayed, "Dear God...I bet it's very hard for You to love all of everybody in the whole world...There are only five people in our family, and I can never do it." It's been said that a child's life ought to be a child's life...Full of simplicity. But yeah, we do struggle to love everybody. Loving God and loving others are often drowned out by our selfishness. Loving well is difficult for our selfie generation. As the body of Christ, we should want to love well, even when we sometimes struggle to know how best to do that. We have a role model. When I look at the cross and at my Lord dying for me, he shows me what true love is. Remember, the scripture says, *We love because He first loved us* (1 John 4:19 NASB). And I begin to realize the magnitude of what that love did and continues to do. I hear a lot lately about empowering people— "Power to the people!" That's not new. How about giving up power for the love of people? Why do we do what we do? Why do we serve? Why do we care? Because the love of Jesus Christ compels us to do what we do. Love needs to become an instinct. The love of God is the purest nourishment we can dispense to our world around us (My youngest daughter said that). Loving well always reveals the face of Jesus.

Random thoughts for today:

*...**but the greatest of these is love.*** (1 Corinthians 13:13 ESV)

It's better to do the right thing than it is to be "right."
Ask Him to fill your life until you overflow with His love—even for those you don't like.
If a friend is in trouble, don't ask if there's anything you can do...Just DO it!!
"Hate your enemy" is pretty easy to do...Jesus calls us to do the hard thing.
Love equals listening.

January 26   A Simple Living Eucharist

Many theologians have spent time analyzing and dissecting the Eucharist (communion) over the years because that's what they do. Is it symbolic, or is it transubstantiation? And we, the church, have spent much time through the ages arguing the fine points of the doctrine of the Lord's Supper because that's what we do. Do we partake daily, weekly, monthly, quarterly? And our gracious Father shakes His head and still loves us because that's what He does. It's quite simple. It's as simple as John 3:16. It's as simple as *God showed His love to us in that while we were yet sinners, Christ died for us* (Romans 5:8). Jesus says, "Remember these truths when you participate in this memorial meal." Simple. Sometimes I think we need to get away from the intellectual sophistication in our theology and doctrine and simply live Jesus in our words, our demeanor, and our actions. Do you know what the "secret" to living a simple life is? BE REAL. May the time you share in the Lord's Supper (whenever that time is), be a time that is real for you. You might be amazed at the impact it can have on the whole Eucharist experience as you commune with Him. Simple. Eucharist means, "Giving thanks." What should I do during this time? Thank Him. Clear your mind of the clutter and the stuff and focus on Jesus. Allow Him to look you full in the face. Confess your sin to Him; BE REAL. And remember what He did for you. Simplicity. It reminds me of what my Pastor Roger said to me once, "Take it...Participate...It's for sinners!"

Random thoughts for today:

...and Jesus took bread, and after blessing it broke it and gave it to the disciples, and said, "Take, eat; this is my body. (Matthew 26:26 ESV)

Authenticity is magnetic!!

Why do so many of us think that Jesus' command to love one another is optional?

One who wants a rose must respect the thorn. *(Persian Proverb)*

The fragrance always stays on the hand that gives the rose. *(Southern Proverb)*

True wisdom lies in gathering the precious things out of each day as it goes by.

God: "Focus upon My Word." Me: "Oh, so I don't get to edit scripture."

January 27   Image and Doubt

Biblical faith tells us that we are made in the image of God, whatever that means. I have studied the theology of creation and read many opinions from many scholars whose work I respect. I remember well a lengthy discussion in college on the subject in my Doctrines of the Church class (or at least I took some pretty good notes). After preaching for over 55 years, I can assure you that today I'm still not sure what it means altogether. I truly do believe that there is more to man than chemistry and the *dust of the ground.* How do we differ from the rest of created life on this planet? What transpired when God *breathed into the nostrils of man the breath of life.* Would it be doing violence to the Genesis text to say, THE BREATH OF GOD became a part of us? I don't think so. Being in the image of God means that we bear His mark upon us, which is difficult to define. One of my pastor friends said recently, "Grab the hand of the person sitting next to you. You are now touching someone that God has touched". Wouldn't it be a great time together just sharing what that might mean to us? What a delightful discussion we could have around a cup of coffee as we thoughtfully ponder being made in God's image. I long for those kinds of conversations. I know that this brief entry has clarified it all in your mind—No? Good! I have always struggled with doubts when I read of those who have their doctrinal packages all wrapped up with a big red bow on it. I freely admit I don't have all the answers. But this I KNOW with great confidence—I AM a child of God, and I AM made in His image. The Bible tells me so. His mark is upon me*!!*

Random thoughts for today:

Then God said, "let us make man in our image, after our likeness. (Genesis 1:26 ESV)

When did I stop listening? O God, forgive me my noise*!!*

Don't just pray when you feel like it...Make an appointment with the King and keep it.

There's no point at which you can say, "Well, I'm successful now; I might as well take a nap."

With the gift of listening comes the gift of healing.

I think a great lesson I have learned (and relearned) is that there is no substitute for paying attention.

January 28   Cancer and Peace

Jesus said, *I have said these things to you, that in me you may have peace. In the world you may have tribulation; but take heart; I have overcome the world.* (John 16:33)

In the Fall of 2019, we knew something wasn't quite right. My wife had been struggling with a number of physical issues for some time. Finally, after a visit to her primary physician, we were referred to a specialist who determined that a procedure with a follow-up biopsy was needed. The results confirmed our worst fears. Helen was directed to a gynecologist-oncologist in South Bend, Indiana, for the next phase of her treatment. This was a "brick-in-the-face" for us, coming out of nowhere. We have been blessed with good health through the years and have never really had any major physical problems. I have ministered to many through the years who have experienced battles with cancer in varying degrees and have conducted memorial services for many who have lost that battle. The words of Jesus *don't be afraid* became very real to both of us. The next months were filled with oncology appointments, CT scans, PET scans, consultations, a total hysterectomy, radiation treatments, and follow-ups. We were finally told that the prognosis was encouraging, and things looked extremely positive for the future. The ministry from many people from California to Haiti was overwhelming, and for this tremendous support, Helen and I are exceptionally grateful. But I am especially thankful for the Lord coming to us and making the above scripture a reality in our lives. The following is a prayer that I placed in my journal during these months:

The inner peace You provide, Lord, is unruffled and fearless, resting on the firm foundation of faith in You. It's a gift You left to Your followers— including me—for all time. I have learned that it is not like the circumstantial peace that the world offers based upon conditions of health or wealth or situation. Your peace is rock solid in EVERY

circumstance, good or bad. Please hold us in that gift of peace today and always.

Random thoughts for today:

Oh, Lord, forgive me when I whine...I'm blessed indeed, the world is mine. *(Opal Loehr, my material grandmother)*
Lord, encircle us with Your love, wherever we may be.

January 29   Go Cubs Go!!

You might say that I can get passionate about baseball. I played baseball as a kid, and my dad was the varsity baseball coach at our local high school. I even worked my way through college umpiring baseball. I've been a Chicago Cubs fan since I was four years old. My mom was a Cubs fan. My grandmother was a Cubs fan; oh yes, she was. I used to walk to her house (about two blocks away), and we would watch the Cubbies play most afternoons (Wrigley Field didn't have night lights back in those days). You can probably imagine that the Fall of 2016 was pretty exciting for me after not winning a World Series for 108 years. The Cubs actually won back-to-back series in 1907 and 1908, the first major league team to do so. It was kind of interesting. All of us die-hard Cub fans running around yelling, "We did it! We won! We finally did it!" Some of my friends went to the local sports store at 2:00 am to buy championship paraphernalia (yes, it was open). But in fact, WE didn't win the World Series. I didn't win the World Series. Anthony Rizzo, Ben Zobrist, Kris Bryant, Javier Baez, and their teammates can say THEY won the World Series, but I don't recall being on the diamond at Wrigley Field with a baseball glove fielding a double-play or slamming a 3-run homer. Having said that, I sure did reap the benefits of that victory celebration. Many times, since I've come to Jesus as my Lord and Savior, I've said, "I'm saved! I'm in Christ! I've been redeemed and won that victory over death!" But I don't recall ever being nailed to a cross or shedding any blood to purchase that gift of eternal life. Having said that, I certainly reap the benefits, don't I? Jesus has given me permission and the right to proclaim that I have won the victory!! Go Cubs Go!! No, not quite...But rather, THANK YOU JESUS!!

(I dedicate this entry to my favorite Cub fan, Ashley)

Random thoughts for today:

God showed His love for us in that while we were still sinners, Christ died for us. (Romans 5:8 ESV)

Are you in a spiritual or emotional desert? Perhaps God is in the process of making you thirsty for Him.

Once you feel the breath of God on your skin you can never turn back.

Most of us are umpires at heart...We love calling balls and strikes on somebody else.

God grant me tears. *(Old Welsh prayer...Part of my heritage)*

January 30   The Jesus Prayer

One of the lowliest of all prayers in orthodox Christianity is what church historians refer to as "The Jesus Prayer"—A single brief sentence— "Lord Jesus Christ, Son of God, have mercy on me a sinner." If this prayer is lifted to the Lord with passion and sincerity, it can be the beginning of real honesty and vulnerability in our prayer life. Praying this prayer many a morning has brought me to tears. Twelve words in English. In other languages it is even shorter—in Greek and Russian, it's no more than seven words. And yet around those few words, many believers over the centuries have built their spiritual lives. It's a prayer of stability and a prayer that places us face to face with God. I find it best to use my own words as the foundation of my prayers, but written prayers of mine or from others have also been helpful. And you certainly can't go wrong praying scripture. I have personally discovered that praying the Jesus Prayer over and over makes it a part of the foundation of my daily walk with the Lord. When I pray for myself, do I pray for perfection? I hope not. I always try to pray honestly as I come before God in my flawed understanding and with my faltering petitions. I happen to believe that God blesses imperfect and uncertain praying. *Lord, I believe...Help me with my unbelief.* Just as a happy child cannot "mis-hug" her daddy, the sincere heart cannot "mis-pray" to the Father. I'm not sure it's possible for a child of God to sincerely pray a lousy prayer, especially if the Jesus Prayer is at its center. How precious are those times alone with the Lord when you sense being washed over by the love of your Abba Father.

Abba Father, I belong to you.

Random thoughts for today:

...*God, be merciful to me a sinner.* (Luke 18:13 ESV)

Prayer is talking to God about what you are doing together.

Lord, help me to dissipate the fog...May my motives be clear and pleasing to you.

Great accomplishments do not come to those who yield to trends and fads and popular opinion.

If you knew Jesus was coming back tomorrow, what would you do today? THEN DO IT!!

I believe that God is love, but sometimes I come to the realization that my conception of love needs to be corrected.

January 31   Abba

The Hebrew term *Abba* is a descriptive term of family intimacy—a term more intimate than "father." It was an informal address used by little Jewish children toward their fathers and best translated "papa" or "daddy" in modern-day vernacular. It is a term that opens the possibility of intimacy with God, and was unthinkable in any other world religion to address almighty God as *Abba*. "He IS literally our heavenly Daddy, and I still tear up when I sing the lyrics of that chorus, 'Abba Father, I Love You, Daddy'"(RWJ – *Journey Through the School of Groaning*). The next chance you get, watch a child playing or talking with a loving parent, then think of your relationship with your loving heavenly Father. How often I've prayed the prayer, "Lord, keep the kid alive in me." My own father passed away in November of 2018 at the age of 97. His godly teaching in my life and our intimate relationship has been a major factor in my intimate relationship with my heavenly Daddy. In Mark 14:36, Jesus said, *Abba, Father, all things are possible for you. Remove this cup from me.* Paul writes in Romans 8:15—*You have received the spirit of adoption as sons, by whom we cry, "Abba! Father!"* Scripture invites us to approach God the way a child approaches his or her Daddy. If prayer depends on how I pray, I'm sunk! But if the power of prayer depends upon the One who hears the prayer, and if the One who hears the prayer is my Papa, then I have hope. My prayer begins with a heartfelt, "Oh, Daddy!" Forget greatness; seek childlikeness. Trust more. Strut less. It's hard to show off and call God "Daddy" at the same time. Perhaps that's the point. My heavenly Papa is low on fancy and high on accessibility. And you know what? In all honesty, there have been days in my life when "Daddy" was all I could muster.

Random thoughts for today:

Because you are sons, God has sent the Spirit of his Son into our hearts, crying "Abba, Father!" (Galatians 4:6 ESV)

Pursuing answers as to why God allows hard things has never given me the peace I want.

I want to learn to listen, not just to their words...I want to learn to listen to others' hearts.

The home marks a child for life.

When my concentration is on the Lord, my heart is light.

February

"Obedience is another word for love...
which is another word for Jesus."

February 1   The Romans Predicament

We Americans have a number of words and phrases to describe a predicament. My dictionary app says that a predicament is "an unpleasantly difficult, perplexing, or dangerous situation." If you're from the east coast, you talk about "being in a pinch." If you like to cook, you're in a "jam" or a "pickle." If you're from the south, you're "between a rock and a hard place." What is the most recent predicament you've had to navigate? Every once in a while, during a more contemplative time, I think about the predicament that affected us all. Have you ever spent any time thinking long and hard about the "Romans predicament"? Romans 3:23 says *we have ALL sinned and fallen short of the glory of God.* Yeah, we would all agree with that, but it is Romans 6:23 that brings the gravity of our situation to light—*The wages* (the payback) *of our sin is DEATH!* So, what's our response? WE have to do something, right? I've heard it said that God helps those who help themselves. That despicable saying doesn't come from the Bible. I've come to realize this is false teaching. The whole premise of scripture is not God helps us if we help ourselves, but rather it is GOD HELPS THE HELPLESS! As long as we're helping ourselves, who needs God? It's when we're at the end of our rope that we finally cry out,

"God, help me." And you know what? HE DOES! Scripture says, *Do not be afraid. Stand by and see the salvation of the LORD, which He will accomplish for you* (Exodus 14:13). Acts 4:11-12 tells us simply, yet bluntly, *JESUS...there is salvation in no one else, for there is no other name under heaven given among men by which we must be saved.* Did you notice that Romans 6:23 does not end with death? The Romans predicament becomes the Romans victory. Praise the Lord for the last half of that verse. *But the gift of God is eternal life through Jesus Christ our Lord.*

Random thoughts for today:

The wages of sin is death... (Romans 6:23 ESV)

When one loves, one does not calculate. *(St. Therese of Lisieux)*
Social media is the epitome of hidden pride...Prayer for this generation: "Put your phone down!"

February 2   Anthems and Flags

I need to begin this entry with a disclaimer so that I'm not instantly branded as a "left-wing, commie liberal," whatever that means. In eight years of teaching high school, my students worked hard to try and label me... "Mr. Jones, are you a conservative or a liberal?" And my response would be, "Depends on the topic of conversation. I'm a very conservative pro-lifer, and because I'm a conservative pro-lifer, I'm very "liberal" when it comes to the matter of the death penalty." I hate labels! First of all, I love my country. I've always tried to carry on the honor and legacy of my father, who fought in the Battle of Okinawa toward the close of

World War 2. I stand for the National Anthem with hand over heart and say the Pledge of Allegiance with pride. Without fail, I get emotional when I see one of those videos of a serviceman (or woman) coming home and surprising their kids in school after being gone for many months. I'm very much pro-American. Having said that, I found the hair standing up on the back of my neck when I recently read the following post from a brother on Facebook: "As for me and my house we will salute the flag, stand for the National Anthem, kneel before the cross, and serve the Lord." Hmmm, hopefully not in that order. Let me say it again: I love my country. But let us be cautious that we don't equate nationalism with faithful allegiance to Jesus Christ. I do not believe that God has called me to make America great again. That's not my mission. I am not called by God to save a republic. Our Father has not divided us into Americans and non-Americans. John 3:16 says *WHOEVER believes in Him should not perish but have everlasting life.* There's no nationality mentioned here. Spend some time meditating upon the goose-bump producing throne room scene of Revelation, chapter 4—A lot of Holy Spirit *ETHOS*, but no nationalistic *ETHNOS*. What is my position? Conservative or liberal? Label me as you please, but I strongly believe with the greatest of pride that all nationalistic allegiances must bow in reverence before the King of kings and Lord of lords.

Random thoughts for today:

There is neither Jew nor Greek, slave nor free, male nor female, for you are all one in Christ Jesus. (Galatians 3:28 ESV – Can I add "citizen or immigrant" to this?)

Our days can tend to suck the life out of us...Spending time with the Lord infuses life back into us.

There is no moment so commonplace that God is not present in it.

One of the clearest marks of a wise (or soon to be wise) person is an insatiable desire to learn.

February 3   Less is More

A high school student in central Indiana wrote out a prayer: "I'm me...I'm good...Cause God don't make no junk!" I found a little prayer on a wrinkled piece of paper stuck in one of my journals called "A Pocket-sized Prayer." It merely says, "Good Morning, Daddy...You are good...I need help...Heal and forgive me...They need help...Thank You...In Jesus' name, Amen." The simplest prayer I've ever come across is one I mentioned in a previous book attributed to Rich Mullins— "OH GOD!" Does our Father hear those kinds of prayers? Oh yeah, He does! No fancy language...No deep theology...No pretentiousness. I don't even have to speak in my "prayer voice." Something that's happened in my own prayer life the last few years has been a longer time with the Lord but with fewer words. I think a significant amount of my prayer time with God has evolved from *pray* (words) *without ceasing,* to *be still, and know that I am God.* I'm discovering that noise and activity have a way of siphoning my energy and distracting my attention, making prayer an added chore rather than a comforting relief. Another curious factor has been the shortening of my prayer goals. Ten years ago, I would have anywhere from 8 – 10 yearly prayer goals. Lately, my prayer objectives have been winnowed down to four: 1) To love well 2) To be a godly man 3) To mature

in wisdom 4) To leave behind a godly legacy. More of You, Lord...
And less of me. I can't get the words of one of my mentors out of
my head—Don't have long discussions about prayer...JUST PRAY!
I like that. Pretty simple.

Random thoughts for today:

***When you pray, go into your room and shut the
door and pray to your Father who is in secret.*** (Matthew
6:6 ESV)

Our goal is not to grow larger churches...It's to grow stronger
churches.

It's not what a man does that determines whether his work is
secular or sacred...Rather, it is WHY he does it.

Sometimes God's most meaningful touch upon my life comes
when I'm alone.

I don't want to live...I want to love first and live incidentally.

The greatest opportunity is right where you are.

February 4   The Lord's Prayer

In the Sermon on the Mount, Jesus said to His followers,
*Pray then like this: OUR FATHER IN HEAVEN, HALLOWED
BE YOUR NAME* (Matthew 6:9). Literally, that says, "Let Your
name be kept holy; let Your name be treated with reverence."
I'm not sure that we get that job done with our constant OMGs
throughout the day. One of my professors said, "As we look up
into the face of our Father in heaven, we commit ourselves to the
hallowing of His name." *Our Father in heaven* reminds me of

three things: 1) He loves us 2) He IS holy 3) He is power. I pray the Lord's Prayer (many refer to it as the model prayer) every morning during my quiet time. I got that idea from Brennan Manning when I heard him speak years ago. *OUR FATHER*. Isn't that great! Guess what? We're kinfolks! The prayer doesn't say, "Our God," it says, *"Our Father."* The Jews of biblical days had heard God referred to as Father before, but not very often. The idea of kinship was not developed until Jesus taught it. God is God, and people are people, but kinfolks have claims upon each other. We ask things of each other as kin. We say to our Father... Give us some bread...Don't hold things against us...Forgive us... Protect and defend us...Keep the devil away from us. Kinfolk is a good idea. Having said that, perhaps we need to ask ourselves some things as we pray this prayer.

- How can we say *OUR Father* if we are living only for ourselves?
- How can we say *FATHER* if we don't act like His child?
- How can we say *IN HEAVEN* if we lay up no treasure there?
- How can we say *HALLOWED BE YOUR NAME* if we're not striving for holiness?

We may know the words, but without His grace, we cannot understand the meaning. Your name...Your kingdom...Your honor...Your will. In true worship and prayer, the Father must be first. *Seek first His kingdom* (Matthew 6:33). It is a kingdom ruled by a King, and our King does not rule by the consent of His subjects. OUR FATHER IN HEAVEN...HOLY IS YOUR NAME. If we pray this way, we must of course, be prepared to live this way.

Precious heavenly Abba Father...May Your name always be honored and lifted up...May Your reign begin and may You accomplish Your will on earth as in heaven...Give us bread for our needs today...Forgive us the wrongs we have done as we have forgiven those who have wronged us... Do not subject us to temptation and rescue us from the evil one...For Yours is the kingdom and the power and the glory forever...Amen. (Matthew 6:9-13 – A paraphrase)

February 5   "Excuse" Me

I don't know if you realized it or not, but the church is not filled with perfect people. It's a hospital for those who KNOW they are sick and who want to be cured. We do, however, have plenty of folks who will be the first to tell you that they're "not worthy." "I'm not qualified; I'm not competent; I could never do that!" Helen and I are currently involved with two congregations (our home church and a little rural church where I preach on Sundays). I can say without hesitation that both of our churches are flawed. So, what are we supposed to do? Answer: Daily Double—GET OFF OUR EXCUSE!! Many of us say, "No," before God even has a chance to say, "GO." We're not saved by works, but we ARE saved by a faith that works. Living out our lives for Christ is counting the cost and then living out what scripture says. For example? Love your enemy (That's pretty practical). Forgive others (yeah, it's hard). Obey your parents. Begin living a selfless life. It's not about you... It's about Him. Where have we heard that before? Am I praying, "LORD, use me?" Yesterday we talked about the Lord's Prayer.

What does it say? *Your kingdom come; Your will be done.* As a follower, the kingdom of God demands my submission and my will and my life. It has nothing to do with my "qualifications." The most important thing in the world is to obey the will of God. The most important words in the world are "LORD, Your will be done." How much did it cost you to receive God's grace? NOTHING. What does it cost you to be a follower of Christ? EVERYTHING. You don't have to be certified or licensed to follow Jesus...Just committed.

Random thoughts for today:

For by grace, are you saved through faith, and that not of yourselves. It is the gift of God, not of works, lest any man should boast. (Ephesians 2:8-9 ESV)

There is a time for understanding...But sometimes it is just a time to trust.

Character counts more than appearance.

Maybe my Father expects me to do some stuff occasionally that I don't feel like doing.

Instead of spending our prayer time asking God for His will in our lives, we end up telling Him what we think His will ought to be.

February 6   Community

Paul writes in Philippians 2:1—*Make my joy complete by being of the same mind, maintaining the same love, united in one spirit, intent on one purpose.* The early church learned quickly that our survival goes hand-in-hand with what the New

Testament calls KOINONIA. That word in scripture has been translated "fellowship" – "partnership" – "community" – "sharing all things common." (Read Acts 2:42-47). Having a relationship like that calls for something that can't be accomplished at arm's length. It implies getting in touch, feeling the hurts of others, and being an instrument of encouragement and healing. Fences come down, and masks come off. One writer says, "Keys to the locks of our lives must be duplicated and distributed; bridges need to be lowered that allow others to cross our moats." I love that. When that kind of relationship occurs, it is then that we can authentically share our joys and sorrows. When I share my Christian walk with others, I can truly enjoy that walk. Certainly, there are facets of our faith that are personal, but the Bible doesn't zero in on those things so much. The New Testament talks primarily about community. Throughout his writings, Paul talks about how this kind of fellowship, Koinonia, if you will, is what brings true joy into his life. He declares, *It makes my joy complete!!* Let's make our Lord's joy complete this week as we commit to that kind of fellowship and sharing in our walk.

Random thoughts for today:

It is right for me to feel this way about all of you, since I have you in my heart. (Philippians 1:7 NIV)

God will not grow tired of you...He will not weary of your sins and weaknesses.

Lord, may I be willing to strip myself completely naked before You...Nothing hidden.

Thank You for quiet...Forgive me my noise.

One little word can light up someone's day.

Is my being right so important that I am willing to sacrifice fellowship over things that are not crucial and central to Christianity?

February 7 Living Loved

Ever hear the phrase, "Live loved"? It means to live like you are loved. One of my favorite verses (used several times in this devotional) is 1 John 4:19 NASB—*We love because He first loved us.* When I was a kid and using the KJV in Sunday School, the translation said, "We love HIM because He first loved us." But the "Him" isn't in the original text. The context of this verse certainly includes Him, but it goes far deeper. We DO love Him, but not just Him. WE LOVE...We love everyone. We love all. No conditions. That's the heart of this verse. We preachers are constantly telling people we need to love. We need to love more. "What the world needs now, is love, sweet love" But how do we pull that off? I understand more and more that I can't accomplish it apart from the power of God. 1 John 3:23 tells us that this is what God commands—*That we love each other.* OK. But how? How can I love and be kind to promise breakers? Or to those who are unkind to me? How can I be patient and loving to people who have the warmth of a vulture and the tenderness of a porcupine? How can I forgive the money-grubbers and the backstabbers I meet? How can I love as God loves, unconditionally? I want to. I long to. But how? BY LIVING LOVED, in his strength and by the power of His Holy Spirit. I love, because I am loved unconditionally by Him. It's what keeps me going every day of my life. It's what my walk with Him is all about. I love, because He first loved me. Oh yeah, I already said that. So, I'll say it again and again and again.

<u>Random thoughts for today</u>:

Beloved, let us love one another, for love is from God, and whoever loves has been born of God and knows God. Anyone who does not love does not know God, because God is love. (1 John 4:7-8 ESV)

What will the mention of my name bring to people's minds after I have passed from this earth? In ancient times a person's name represented his character.

Lord, help the church from our worst enemy...Us.

The true textbook for the student is his teacher. *(Gandhi)*

Better be alone than in bad company.

Love is a great beautifier!! *(Southern Proverb)*

February 8   Contentment

May I ask you an important question today? What if God says, "No"? Sometimes, the one thing you want can be the one thing you never receive. In 2 Corinthians 12:9 Paul shares the message he received from God—*My grace is sufficient for you, for My strength is made perfect in* (your) *weakness.* Paul had been asking God for a healing that He never gave to him. The concept I'm going for here is contentment. I love the following definition—"Contentment is a state of heart in which you would be at peace if God gave you nothing more than He already has." Wow. I need to stop and think about that for a while. If God says to you, "I've given you my grace, and that's enough," will you be content with that? Paul also writes in Philippians 4:11—*I have learned in whatever situation I am to be content.* I found an interesting entry in my journal that I had written down in 2016. It's entitled, "Prescription for Contentment."

1. Never allow yourself to complain about anything—even the weather.
2. Never picture yourself in any other circumstances or someplace else.
3. Never compare your lot with another.
4. Never allow yourself to wish for something or that things had been otherwise.
5. Never dwell on tomorrow...Remember that tomorrow is the Lord's, not ours.

Can you honestly pray today, "Lord, You have given me so much. Your grace truly IS sufficient for me. Thank You for what You've done in my life. I am content to ask You for no more."? Yeah, that's definitely the contentment I'm going for.

Random thoughts for today:

For the sake of Christ, then, I am content with weaknesses...For when I am weak, I am strong. (2 Corinthians 12:10 ESV)

May this be my Romans 12:12 day—*Rejoicing in hope... Enduring in troubles...Continuing steadfastly in prayer.*
Lord, I thirst for You...I long to be in Your presence.
Only the most mature of us are able to be childlike.
Jesus is God, only with real fingers and toes. *(A 6-year-old kid)*

I wish I had a fifty-dollar bill for every Bible study I was in, where someone would ask, "What does this verse mean to you?" Probably a more accurate question would be, "What did this verse mean to the one who wrote it?" I don't mean to say that there can never be dual meaning in a passage of scripture, but I DO mean to say that while there can be mystery in the Bible, a verse does not have a myriad of meanings comprised of a unique number of interpretations. "Well, I interpret this verse differently than you do." Have you ever heard someone say that? Perhaps we both need to pause and agree that one of us (maybe both of us) have misinterpreted the verse. My friend, Pastor Nate Loucks, says, "I believe that good, well-meaning Christians can come to separate interpretations of the text. So, be humble!" The problem is that many Christians (maybe most) have a "me"-centered view of the Bible. Christianity is CHRISTOCENTRIC, my friends. The center of the Word is NOT the Bible...It is Jesus Christ. Do we agree that Jesus is Lord? Do you give yourself grace to grow and even change your mind about some things as you mature? When in doubt about the meaning of a passage, do you default to following the grace and mercy of Jesus Christ? Are you a FOLLOWER of Jesus and not of a theological persuasion? Some scripture is extremely challenging to comprehend; it's complex. We need to realize that everything in the Bible can't be squeezed into a neat little package. I guess a bigger question in my mind is why are there so many church people telling me what the Bible says, but their lives don't reflect Jesus? But that's my interpretation!!

All scripture is profitable for teaching, reproof, correction, and for training in righteousness. (2 Timothy 3:16 ESV)

People who talk much will know little...A reading people will always be a knowing people. *(John Wesley)*

The Bible laying on the shelf is wasted ammunition.

God does not require that I be successful...He require me to be faithful.

If you don't have the time to respond to a tug on your pant leg, you are much too busy.

February 10   Discrimination

Proverbs 24:1-2 talks about wise discrimination—*Be not envious of evil men, nor desire to be with them, for their hearts devise violence, and their lips talk of trouble.* Discrimination has fallen into disrepute as a word in our culture. That's actually a good thing if you define discrimination as making a distinction based on whether a person is a member of a particular group, class, race, etc. rather than on individual merit. However, one thesaurus I used gave only the following synonyms for discrimination: prejudice, bias, unfairness, bigotry, intolerance. So, I guess there's no such thing as good discrimination. Or is there? What about the ability to make a fine distinction or differentiating judgment? Example: The artist chose her colors with great discrimination. We used to make a joke out of this in college with the flippant phrase, "I'm not judging you; I'm making a moral discrimination."

Where's the balance? Is there such a thing as wise discrimination? I believe there is. Sometimes prayer and wisdom need to be a part of that process, and that process should never be a judgment upon a fellow human being for whom Christ died. As I read Proverbs 24, I would certainly not want my children or grandchildren to be associating with the kind of person it describes. It is wise discrimination that allows me to be led to people of character and make it a point to associate with them. Wisdom also cautions me to avoid the company of those of question moral character (1 Corinthians 15:33). I guess the balance is between becoming all things to all people for the sake of the gospel and prayerfully making distinctions regarding ongoing relationships. A couple of the random thoughts below definitely urge me to proceed wisely when making those decisions. As one friend puts it, "If you see another in gross sin, beware of judgment. You do not know how long it may be until you fall."

Random thoughts for today:

Do not be deceived; "Bad company ruins good morals." (1 Corinthians 15:33 ESV)

The moment you put a label on another human being, you can no longer truly relate to that person.

Too many of us are seeking the hand of God rather than the face of God.

Grace is ours in Jesus Christ…Deny it or debate it, and we kill it.

The truth is not always the same as majority decision.

Want to know something really subversive? Love is everything it's cracked up to be.

I am human. Nothing human is alien to me. *(Terence)*

Isn't it interesting how many times words are our downfall? How well do I control my tongue? Am I careful with the words I say and how I say them? My Dad always told me that a person's character should be used to discern the value of his words. Proverbs says that a man who is careless with his words, or who spreads falsehoods about others is like a war club or a sword or a sharp arrow (25:18). My friend and former co-worker, Stacy Boyd, always used to say, "I'm from the South (you can tell that the moment she starts talking). In the South, we bless people's hearts and then talk about them." I had a discussion with one of my grandchildren a few years ago about profanity, and the statement was made, "They're just words, Grandpa!" Yup, they are, and I happen to believe that words mean something. One of the lessons I've tried to get across to my former students is just because it comes into your head, doesn't necessarily mean you have to say it...Probably a good lesson for our culture today. Proverbs 26:1 says *Like snow in summer and rain in harvest, so honor is not fitting for a fool.* Whenever I find myself surrounded by thoughtless decisions and excessive blaming and selfishness, I can safely assume a crop of fools has sprouted. I'm convinced that most of us would sin a lot less if we just got off social media. I'm tempted to start work on a new book—*A Planet of Idiots,* but Holy Spirit conviction keeps pulling me back from that idea. I propose that each of us take some time and read through James chapter three every day for a few weeks. *If anyone does not stumble in what he says, he is a perfect man – The tongue is a fire, a world of unrighteousness – It is a restless evil, full of deadly poison.* You're familiar with that teaching...And so am I. A Christian acquaintance of mine, who becomes Mr. Hyde every time he gets on Facebook, recently said to me, "I'm searching for new understandings for my life in scripture." Hmmm...How about practicing the precepts you already know?

Random thoughts for today:

A word fitly spoken is like apples of gold in a setting of silver. (Proverbs 25:11 ESV)

The humble are more pro-social, more helpful, tolerant, sensitive, and accepting of differences. *(Rebecca Crain)*

Grace is meant to be lived out to the fullest, not dissected and analyzed by those who would rather argue than eat.

A single sunbeam is enough to drive away many shadows. *(Francis of Assisi)*

The worst thing said about me has already been said about me—It's in the Bible.

February 12   Worship

"The perfect church service would be one we were almost unaware of...Our attention would have been on God." (C.S. Lewis) I've been spending a lot of time lately on that thought and allowing it to roll over in my mind (and hopefully in my heart). I have experienced many different styles of worship in many places. Quiet or noisy...Liturgical or very loose...Traditional or contemporary (whatever that means)... Structured or charismatic...English or Haitian (or Japanese, Chinese, Korean, Spanish). I've worshipped with bands, choirs, piano, organ, and acapella. I pretty much love all of them. I've learned that I can worship just about anywhere in any of these circumstances, with a few exceptions where the fog machines and strobes just distracted me too much. I've experienced worship where I could not stop the tears, even though I didn't understand a word being spoken. I remember a service in South Korea where people were speaking in tongues, and I found myself secretly hoping that one of the participants might all of a sudden start speaking in English. I've been in dynamic services that left me cold because my heart was cold that day. I've sat in "dead" services where I didn't have a clue what was being said or done, but God touched me. So, I guess the "perfect church service" depends upon where my heart is at that moment. In the same service, what might have been a beautiful time of worship for me might have been a dud for someone else. Maybe what Lewis is talking about is coming to Him with nothing except a surrendered heart and mind. First and foremost, I must be a worshiper. The God whom I could think up with my head, I will never get down on my knees to worship—Never. Wonder and mystery is the basis of worship. Is the pastor or priest or elder or worship leader really in charge of the service? I don't think so. One more question—When someone says, "Oh, I can worship God anywhere," my response is, "Do you?"

Random thoughts for today:

True worshipers will worship the Father in spirit and in truth. (John 4:23 ESV)

Love goes on forever!! *(1 Corinthians 13:8)*
God reserves the right to use people who disagree with me.
Happiness is someone to love, something to do, and something to live for. *(Chinese Proverb)*
If I get too serious in my praying, God might expect me to start living radically in my daily walk.

Have you ever been convicted so strongly that you were uncomfortable and might even have lost sleep over whatever truth or issue convicted you?

God: How do you feel about this issue now that I have convicted you?

Me: You've made me see things differently, Lord...It's complicated my life.

God: Good.

Me: Don't ever do that again!!

Truths or issues like:

- Would a stranger, after examining my life, conclude that I'm serious about my walk with the Lord?
- Am I doing better today in my walk than I did yesterday?
- God doesn't want my stuff...He wants me.
- May my words be evidence that I love You and treasure our relationship?
- Holy Spirit, give me insights that build up your people.
- The well-lived life in Jesus is not found in a place or an event, but rather in a Person.
- Am I living a well-lived life?

Read those bullet-points over again, slowly. OK...Too convicting...Let's move on.

Random thoughts for today:

If you abide in My Word, you are truly My disciples, and you will know the truth, and the truth will set you free. (John 8:31-32 ESV)

If love has an agenda, it's not love anymore...It's a program. God knows we don't need more programs in the church.

Dare to reach out your hand into the darkness to pull another hand into the light.

What we see depends mainly upon what we look for.

February 14   Valentine's Day

I love Valentine's Day...It's a special reminder to me about how blessed I am to have the beautiful gift from God that is Helen. Not that I don't thank Him for her every day, because I do. I'm feeling especially nostalgic today as my mind floods with so many great memories that make up the 55+ years we've been together. Both of us have had a tremendous legacy of marriage passed down to us from our parents (Helen's parents married almost 68 years; my mom and dad married almost 60 years). As each year passes, I realize more and more how blessed I am; and how much more and more I am in love with my wife. I think I've especially come to understand the preciousness of this gift these past few months as Helen and I are walking the journey of this "cancer thing" that's recently been a part of our lives. I came across this little ditty in my journal. It sums it up for me:

"Marriage means...
You are the other part of me
I am the other part of you.
We work through with never a thought of walking out.
Marriage means...
Two imperfect mates building permanently
Giving totally
In partnership with a perfect God.
Marriage, my love, means us!"

I believe with all my heart that marriage is not so much finding the right person as it is being the right person. You, my sweet Helen, ARE the right person!!

Random thoughts for today:

I found the one my heart loves. (Song of Solomon 3:4 NIV)

Think of the combined powerhouse of a wise woman coupled with a wise man.

Forgiveness is a strange thing...Sometimes it's easier to forgive our enemies than those we love.

I am the least difficult of men...All I want is boundless love.

February 15   Distraction

Sometimes I wonder if we're missing life right in front of us. In our efforts to become more efficient or more connected, are we becoming less intimate? Are we forsaking the opportunities for contemplation and concentration on the things that matter? I came across a convicting quote the other day in my journal. It came from a pastor friend of mine—"Today we're constantly clogged by a feeling that we should be elsewhere. Always on the go, we feel like we're in the right place at the right time ONLY when in transit, moving from point A to point B. Constant motion is a balm to an anxious culture." Convicting? What if busyness is the enemy of relationship and communion? Is the work of Christ in your life getting drowned out by the distractions of what's going on around you? I think of Jesus telling Martha that her sister Mary has *chosen the good portion* (Luke 10:38-42). Is our life structured to listen to the Lord when He says to us *Be still and know that I am God* (Psalm 46:10)? Have we made ourselves free enough to be able to dwell without distraction upon what is *true and honorable and just and pure and lovely and that which is commendable* (Philippians 4:8-9)? Has our culture and technology made it nearly impossible to bask in times of quiet, and yes, even silence? So yeah, I'm always busy. I'm engaged in living life and all of its activities around me. Sometimes I wonder if technology has exacerbated the problem. But let me propose my question one more time—Are you missing LIFE right in front of you?

Random thoughts for today:

Draw near to God, and He will draw near to you. (James 4:8 ESV)

Lovers of the Word seek to practice wisdom minute by minute. Nothing has a better effect on children than praise.

The truth is that I am enslaved in one vast love affair with my students. *(A Teacher)*

It's sad sometimes how much tremendous energy we spend to be "normal."

Be – YOU – tiful!!

February 16   Tested Love

Being a loving person doesn't mean you assassinate your thinking abilities. An educational study was done several years ago in which a group of people (100 to be exact) was presented a new concept none of them had ever heard of before. 50% of the group believed the new concept without thinking about it, just because they read it (kind of like "It's on the internet so it must be true"). 30% disbelieved without considering or studying it at all—"I just don't think that's true." 15% wanted to wait a little while before they made up their minds but didn't ask for any more information or clarification at all. Only 5% analyzed all the details before coming to a conclusion; in other words, they did their homework. SO, according to this study, one could say 5% of the population thinks, 15% think they think, and 80% don't even pretend to think. OK, it's a little tongue-in-cheek, but hopefully these statistics don't reflect the church as a whole. Unfortunately, I think it might. Paul writes in Philippians 1:9, *May your love abound more and more in knowledge and depth of insight* so *that you may be able to DISCERN what is best.* The original word for "discern" is *DOKIMOS*—"test with a view to approve." If an item (pottery, coins, metals) had *dokimos* stamped on it, it met specified standards; it was real, not bogus. It was kind of like a first-century Good Housekeeping Seal of Approval — "You can trust it!" Somebody did their homework before putting that stamp upon it. Paul exhorts in Ephesians, *teach the truth in love*. Love that does not act in knowledge and depth of insight of what is best, is love that is suspect; it may not be love at all. My love should be mature enough to differentiate between a genuine need that should be met, and a phony pitch should be exposed. Love should recognize the difference between crushing emotional stress, that I need to be reaching out to, and selfish egotism that should be rebuked. Reread Philippians 1:9. May your love mature in that way; a love that is tested and approved.

Random thoughts for today:

Love...rejoices with the truth. (1 Corinthians 13:6 ESV)

How many of us can say daily, "I've done my best"?

It is in that time of solitude that I discover that BEING is more important than HAVING.

Father, as a forgiven person today, I will forgive.

February 17   Life Verse

Proverbs 17:22 has been my wife Helen's life-verse since the early 1960s – *A cheerful heart is good medicine, but a crushed spirit dries up the bones*. She not only has quoted that verse since high school, but she also lives it. Her daily countenance through the years has been, "Don't take yourself so seriously...Lighten up and laugh with me." People who know me now and think I'm too serious (and there's some truth to that), wouldn't believe how different I am today from my high school and college years. My wife has transformed me. And I think maybe I've softened her down a bit as well. Marriage can do that. When I first started dating Helen, she was a first-class crazy and zany individual. I believe that the Lord brought her into my life because she was exactly what I needed to battle the chronic bouts of depression that I had experienced since early high school days. She's been a significant factor in helping me learn to relax when anxiety has me wrapped up in myself. I'm still a creature of habit, but she has led me into more spontaneity in life, which is not always easy for me. I also believe she has helped me develop a mindset that has freed me to enjoy my relationship with the Lord and to find out what He has planned for me to do. Through the years, I have (not without struggle) been able to find strength and real peace in the presence of the Lord. Finding peace in the presence of my wife has been a part of that journey. She has been a major reason why I can dance today. Thank you, sweetheart, for living out your life-verse in our home for 55 years plus.

Random thoughts for today:

Our mouth was filled with laughter and our tongue with joyful shouting. (Psalm 126:2 NASB)

Am I intentional in being an authentic person?
Listening, not imitation, may be the sincerest form of flattery.
I delight in learning so that I may teach. *(Seneca)*
How about giving up power for the love of people?
A lie doesn't become truth, wrong doesn't become right, and evil doesn't become good just because it is accepted by the majority. *(Booker T. Washington)*

Do you know what a cacophony is? It's a harsh discordance of sound; dissonance. In music, it is frequent discords of grating tones; a meaningless mixture of sounds. Sound like the world we live in? In her book, *Jesus Calling,* Sarah Young makes the suggestion that we learn to take mini-breaks from the world. I love this. It is a ritual that I have tried to practice over the years in my own devotional life. Here are a few suggestions that have worked for me; they are certainly not exhaustive.

- Sit by the fire (inside or out), just listening to what's around you in the quiet
- Take a 24 hour fast (or more) from the news and social media; listen to calm instrumental music while meditating upon scripture...Put your phone away
- Use Christian meditation apps (*Soultime,* and *Abide,* have been a particular blessing)
- Find a place where you can get away for a day or two; bring your Bible and perhaps a Christian author or two that have benefited you in your faith-journey...Make it your own personal retreat...Put your phone away
- Journal...Write out your prayers to the Lord
- Set a day where you concentrate on wordless prayers... Romans 8 announces we need not figure out how to pray; sometimes, we need only groan...As you go through the day, no words; allow the Holy Spirit to pray for you...Put your phone away (Thematic, huh?)

Tuning out the world is difficult, but if you plan and practice it, you'll get better at it. What works for one doesn't necessarily work for another. Use your own creativity on how you can best take a mini-break from the cacophony of the chaos around you.

<u>Random thoughts for today</u>:

The LORD will quiet you with His love, He will rejoice over you with singing. (Zephaniah 3:17 NKJV)

Even in our churches, confusion has replaced clarity and conviction.

I do not want merely to possess a faith...I want a faith that possesses me.

February 19   Noisy Grace

I have a small polished stone that I often carry in my pocket. It simply says, "GRACE." I love the sound of that beautiful word (Maybe because I have a granddaughter named Grace). I had an elementary Sunday School teacher who used to define grace as "needed, but not deserved." Benjamin Warfield used to preach it, "Grace is free sovereign favor to the ill-deserving." I am convinced that grace operates in a realm where my merit and my works cannot enter. *For by GRACE are we saved through faith* (Ephesians 2:8). Grace not only identifies the character of God, but I believe it gives us the freedom to NOT be silent. It is the foundation of *For God so loved the world that He GAVE His only Son* (John 3:16). I believe our churches across the land need to make noise about this incredible gift. We accept the idea of grace in theory, but so many times deny it in practice. I think there are probably three underlying reasons for this: 1) We are apathetic about it (we just don't get it) 2) We don't believe it 3) Deep down, we don't think we deserve it. Of course, there are those who believe that too much emphasis on grace, and not enough on obedience, will weaken the church. If my salvation depends upon my obedience, I've failed. When I embrace God's love and grace for me, He meets me where I am (no matter where that might be), and He doesn't leave me there. Grace is everything! To receive grace, we need only to love its Giver. When I feel self-criticisms over my failures, or when I hear the voices of doubt condemn me, I reach into my pocket and rub that smooth little stone as a reminder of God's truth and His promise to me. Sometimes I think I almost hear His voice; *My grace is sufficient for you* (2 Corinthians 12:9). Thank You, Jesus...I love You!!

Random thoughts for today:

I do not nullify the grace of God, for if justification were through the law, then Christ died for no purpose. (Galatians 2:21 ESV)

A handful of patience is worth more than a bushel of brains. *(Dutch Proverb)*

Lord, minister to my weariness today...Only in You can I be renewed.

Hard work beats talent when talent doesn't work hard.

Nothing is so strong as gentleness, and nothing so great as real strength.

Lord, help me to let go and rest quietly at Your feet in complete attention to You.

Please don't finish reading this entry and brand me a socialist. I am not. Socialism as an economic system that has and will fail, only because it depends upon the natural goodness of man to succeed. I do, however, understand why many young people today are filled with idealism (again, counting on all of us to do the right thing) and proclaim their belief in socialism over capitalism. I am very aware that capitalism certainly has many failings. There are some who would brand Jesus as a socialist and an advocate of income equality (whatever that means), but if you spend any time at all in studying scripture, you come to see that Jesus' "economic philosophy" is all about the economics of the heart. To have our goods available to others based upon the simplicity of *we love because He first loved us* (1 John 4:19 NASB), must come from an attitude of the heart. Forced or mandated sharing has never worked, anywhere! Jesus said, *...give to the poor, and you will have treasure in heaven...*(Matthew 19:21). The apostle Paul quoted Psalm 112:9 when he wrote, *He has distributed freely, he has given to the poor; his righteousness endures forever* (2 Corinthians 9:9). Paul states in Galatians 2:10 that the apostles have asked us *to remember the poor.* In 1772, Samuel Johnson said, "A decent provision for the poor is the true test of civilization." There's no doubt that Jesus has given us a directive for a heart philosophy of economics, and it goes far beyond our wallet. The heart of *we love because He first loved us* is what should motivate our wallet. One French author pondered that perhaps one function of the existence of the poor is to motivate our exercise of generosity. Maybe. So, if I tend to slightly slip into some "socialistic" tendencies, it's because my heart economics nudge me in that direction.

Random thoughts for today:

If I give away all I have...but have not love, I gain nothing. (1 Corinthians 13:3 ESV)

Trusting in the authority of God's word gives us wisdom and security in a changing world.

Those who would have nothing to do with thorns must never attempt to gather flowers.

The fire you kindle for your enemy often burns you more than him. *(Chinese Proverb)*

Jesus walked with people...I pray for people a lot...But do I walk with people?

February 21   God Whispers

Logan Pearsall Smith once said, "What I like in a good author isn't what he says, but what he whispers." He was the son of Hannah Whitall Smith. He was referring to the obvious vs. the not-so-apparent. Have you ever had an experience of sensing God's presence? And you just knew He was there, and that His "words" were comforting and lifting you up? Tis a mystery, isn't it? I've never experienced the audible voice of God, but I know I've heard Him in times of silence. There have been times that I have entered into a time of prayer, confused and befuddled, and walked away with confidence in direction. One theologian interestingly said, "Words. Who gives a hoot about words?" Sometimes words are important. At other times, we get an answer without words in those tranquil times of silence There's almost a sense of mystery there. Thomas Kelly calls it eternity's whisper. There is a haunting possibility that I've not heard the voice of God speaking in my life very often because I've been asking the wrong questions or making the wrong requests. Or maybe, I've been too busy talking to listen. We live in a pretty busy and noisy world. What God says to me in His word is vital. Absolutely. But how often do I miss Eternity's whisper?

> **O Lord...Teach me to seek You...Reveal Yourself to me...I know that I cannot fully seek You except You teach me...May You again and again turn Your countenance toward me and look me full in the face...Over and over and over again my I feel Your hand upon my shoulder as You allow me to lay my head upon Your breast.**

Random thoughts for today:

Be still and know that I am God. (Psalm 46:10 ESV)

The key to ministry is to desecularize the church and to emphasize its supernatural biblical foundation of Christ crucified for sinners.

I refuse to allow any manmade differences to separate me from any other person.

There can be a tendency, if we're not careful, to reduce prayer to a kind of magic formula that gets us what we want or what we think we need.

Do you want to be wise? Choose wise friends.

Prayer for this generation: "Put your phone down!" *(Heard that before?)*

Our culture proclaims it. How many times have you heard it? "Follow your heart!" Really? Yeah, just let your heart be your guide. Have you ever pondered; I mean, really pondered a scripture like Mark 7:21-23? Probably not. *For from within, out of the heart of man, come evil thoughts, sexual immorality, theft, murder, adultery, coveting, wickedness, deceit, sensuality, envy, slander, pride, foolishness. All these evil things come from within, and they defile a person.* What a fun passage. These are the products of following our hearts. Excuse me for being candid, but following your heart is a lie!! What's that old saying —"Let me not trust in the feelings of my heart." Proverbs 4:23 says *Above all else, GUARD your heart, for everything you do flows from it.* The heart is not a leader; it is designed to be led. Priority #1 becomes guarding our hearts. We must allow the heart to be steered. If we let our hearts direct us, we end up in trouble. I can give you many examples from my life to support this, as I'm sure you can as well. I've personally found the best way to guard my heart is to surrender it. I have often meditated upon Ezekiel 36—*I will give you a new heart, and a new spirit I will put within you. And I will remove the heart of stone from you and will give you a heart of flesh. And I will put my Spirit within you and cause you to walk in my ways* (Vv. 26-27). I remember a mentor of mine years ago saying to me, "Our world/nation needs renewed followers of Christ; our men and women in our churches need renewed hearts; and remember, Rick, only God can renew a heart!"

Random thoughts for today:

The heart is deceitful above all things and desperately sick; who can understand it? (Jeremiah 17:9 ESV)

The enormous wave of information brought to us by technology amazes us, but I'm pretty sure it hasn't helped us to grow in wisdom.

Rarely does quarreling have anything to do with the truth.

I'm not sure we can genuinely love anybody with whom we never laugh.

Instead of living in the shadows of yesterday, let's walk together in the light of today and the hope of tomorrow.

February 23   Pity Me

There are a countless number of pits into which any one of us can tumble. Perhaps one of the weightiest traps that many, if not most of us battle, is the hole of self-pity. That "slough of despond" in Bunyan's allegory, *The Pilgrim's Progress,* is a fictional, deep bog in which Christian sinks under the weight of his sins and his sense of guilt over them. I can remember how often during bouts of sadness that I battled to keep my head above water in that quagmire of self-pity. There was a time when I felt that I had no control over such bouts. This demonic snare was probably one of the greatest struggles in my life. Over time, and with the help of a counselor in college, I found that I could exercise some influence. There are several ways to protect yourself from self-pity:

- A consistent prayer life. I don't mean this as a cliché; I know it's difficult to pray when you're down, but you do it anyway.
- Occupy yourself with praising and thanking God for all things. It may be mechanical at first, but your Father will honor this. A grateful heart protects you from negative thinking.
- Memorize scripture. It REALLY does help. Maybe start with Psalm 46.
- Do a social media fast. You would be surprised how much this can improve your attitude (You might also quit listening to the news for a few days).
- Spend time in ministering to others who are hurting, maybe in the same way you are hurting. Pray for them. Call them. Go out for coffee, not to commiserate, but to lift and build that person up. Become prayer partners with someone who is struggling.

God is our refuge and strength, a very present help in trouble...Therefore we will not fear...Be still and know that I am God. (Psalm 46)

Random thoughts for today:

Let each of you look not only to his own interests, but also the interests of others. (Philippians 2:4 ESV)

How we measure intentionality is found in the way we follow Jesus—FRUIT.

Kind words can be short and easy to speak, but their echoes are truly endless *(Unknown)*

We need to be ready to allow ourselves to be interrupted by the Lord.

February 24   Powerless?

E. M. Bounds, who wrote eleven books (nine of them on the subject of prayer) before he died in 1913, said it plainly—The prime need of the church is prayer!! It impresses me how much the first church (read the Book of Acts) was immersed in the community practice of prayer. Acts 1:14 says that *they all met together continually for prayer.* Acts 2:42 tells me that they devoted themselves (literally, "tenaciously were clinging") to prayer. This is the church that began with a revival and had over 3,000 responses the very first day. It quickly grew to 5,000 and continued to grow exponentially from there. Acts 17:6 tells us that anti-Christians charged the believers with *turning the world upside down.* As long as the church maintained this character, it had the power to conquer. I wonder, as we have come under more and more influence of this world, if we have lost much of our supernatural strength and drifted from our mission? When was the last time your church had a meeting of prayer...Just prayer? When was the last time your meeting place was "shaken"? Do you want to know the secret of that early church? THEY PRAYED. Maybe each of us should pray for our congregations today; perhaps a prayer like, "Father, I pray for my church today, that it would be the prayer-filled, Spirit-led church You desire it to be. May it begin with me." *Devote yourselves to prayer, being watchful and thankful* (Colossians 4:2).

Random thoughts for today:

And when they had prayed, the place in which they were gathered together was shaken. (Acts 4:31 ESV)

We walk around pretty oblivious to our world around us...His Word helps me to pay attention to what God says is important. I think it's called priorities.

Don't need more strength. Don't need more knowledge. All I need is the will to do what needs to be done.

Love doesn't just sit there like a stone. It has to be made, like bread...Made all the time...Made new.

You can tell the size of a man by the size of the thing that makes him angry.

Jesus, are you convinced that I am crazy-in-love with You?

February 25   My Respectful Gandhi Page

Mahatma Gandhi was an Indian lawyer, anti-colonial nationalist, and political ethicist, who espoused nonviolent resistance to lead the successful campaign for India's independence from British rule. Gandhi's fame spread worldwide during his lifetime and only increased after his death. He was named Person of the Year by Time Magazine in 1930, and in 2007, his birthday, October 2, was declared by the United Nations as International Day of Non-violence. Although I'm certainly not a cheerleader for Hinduism (his family practiced Vaishnavism, a tradition within Hinduism), it's interesting to note that his faith was continually evolving as he studied other belief systems. Both the Bible and Tolstoy's analysis of Christian theology came to bear heavily on

Gandhi's concepts of spirituality. He was assassinated in 1948 in New Delhi, India. Although he never formally became a Christian, he often had things to say to the Christian community. Probably one of his best-known quotes was, "Jesus is ideal and wonderful, but you Christians, you are not like him" (from the mid-1920s). When missionary Stanley Jones met with Gandhi, he asked him, "Though you quote the words of Jesus often, why is it that you appear to so adamantly reject becoming his follower?" To which Gandhi replied, "Oh, I don't reject Christ. I love Jesus. It's just that so many of you Christians are so unlike him." I don't know about you, but that convicts me just a bit. I have long admired the convictions of this man and his place in history. I pulled all of my random thoughts today from Gandhi's quotations from my own journal. They are thoughts that have inspired me through the years, even "coming from a Hindu."

Random thoughts from Gandhi:

A small body of determined spirits fired by an unquenchable faith in their mission can alter the course of history. (Sounds like the Book of Acts)

Our greatness lies not so much in being able to remake the world, as in being able to remake ourselves.

Non-violence is not a weapon of the weak...It is a weapon of the strongest and the bravest.

Live as if you were to die tomorrow...Learn as if you were to live forever.

In a gentle way, you can shake the world.

I will not let anyone walk through my mind with their dirty feet. (One of my favorites)

Sarah Young shares, "We need to learn to rest in His presence and allow Him to take charge of our day; not bolting into the day like a racehorse suddenly released." This describes me, as a young man, struggling to turn off my brain at night and charging into the morning with things to do and places to go. Through the years, I've been taught (pretty sure by the Lord) to begin my day at a much slower pace; not hurrying to get through my prayer list or read my daily scripture. I've come to believe that you have to be disciplined to slow down. Deaccelerate!! Instead of going through a routine by rote, how much more refreshing is it to occasionally lay aside that prayer list and sit in the presence of the Lord and just listen *(Be still)*? Or perhaps you can meditate on a single verse of scripture instead of trying to plow through a section assigned by your read-thru-the-Bible-in-a-year chart. There have been mornings (sadly not a great many) where I have sat by the fireplace and not said a word. It's hard to do...We just have to talk, don't we? I really enjoy being with the Father in a wash of silence. I think in the latter years of my life, there have been fewer days of "groaning" and more days of "dancing"; in other words, more enjoyment in the time I share with my Father. I look forward to those mornings when I think I hear Him say to me, "Relax and enjoy the journey in My presence." And I do.

Random thoughts for today:

Who of you by worrying can add a single hour to his life? (Luke 12:25 NIV)

We can serve "the least of these" only when we know that WE are the least of these.

"I'm busy! What do you want me to do, Lord?"..."Be still and know that I am God!!"

When our memories exceed our dreams, we stop making a difference.

The things which hurt, instruct. *(Ben Franklin)*

If you're going to be standing firm, you can't be lying down. *(shared with me in person by Chuck Swindoll)*

February 27   Niebuhr's Prayer

My personal paraphrase of a prayer by Reinhold Niebuhr (1892-1971):

> O Lord, hear our prayers not based upon how weak our praise vocabulary or asking may be, but according to Your abundant grace. May our daily lives conform to what You desire to see in us.
>
> When our desires are inappropriate or awry, may they be vetoed by a power greater than ours, and by a mercy more powerful than ours.
>
> Grant us, Abba Father, Your kindness, that, seeing ourselves when compared to your purity, we may be washed of the pride and "show-off" airs which conceal Your truth.
>
> Knowing that we can hide nothing from You, may we recognize and challenge those pretensions and masks that we use to fool ourselves as well as those around us.

Lord, may we worship You in spirit and in truth, and in Your truth, may we see the truth.

Amen.

Random thoughts for today:

God is light, and in him is no darkness at all. (1 John 1:5 ESV)

Love is the chief hallmark of a disciple of Jesus Christ.
Each person must live their life as a model for others.
I don't need to know where my life is going tomorrow...I only need to know that He is leading.
If you all truly love one another, it will be enough. *(The aged apostle John)*
Character building begins with me, not a textbook.

February 28   Truth

Mrs. Fisher was recovering from surgery and got a card from her fourth-grade class: "Dear Mrs. Fisher, Your fourth-grade class wishes you a speedy recovery by a vote of 15-14." Hmmm...Truth. Jesus said, *I am truth*...With the power of the Holy Spirit, we are to be like Jesus. Are you a representation of truth? Remember the good old days and the "handshake" deal. Is your word as good as "your bond"? Are all your words true? Truth-telling seems to be a rarity in our culture today from the common man to the preacher to the politician to the celebrity. I'm told that the average adult lies at least three times in a fifteen-minute conversation. 39% of adults lie about their age; 97% of kids lie to their parents. Jesus said, in the Sermon on the Mount, *Your "yes" should be "yes" and your "no" should be "no"...All else comes from the evil one* (Matthew 5:37). Am I personally committed to absolute truth-telling? Are my actions and my words totally in sync? Josh Billings said, "It's better not to know so much than to know so many things that ain't so." Remember, knowing truth and loving truth aren't necessarily the same thing. Yes, Jesus said, *I am truth*...But people will not believe that we are a part of Christ if we don't tell and live the truth. Truth that is not lived out in our daily walk is dead truth (shades of the epistle of James). Don't just do righteous acts...BE RIGHTEOUS PEOPLE!! God forbid (pardon the old-school King James in me) that we should traffic in unlived truth.

Random thoughts for today:

...I have come into the world to bear witness to the truth. Everyone who is of the truth listens to my voice. (John 18:37 ESV)

Don't be impressed by money, followers, degrees, and titles... Be impressed by kindness, integrity, humility, and generosity.

Mature my capacity to respond to others always with a gentle wisdom.

Worry less – Worship more – Trust the Lord to lead you into victory. *(Michelle Thomae, fellow schoolteacher & friend)*

Better today than tomorrow morning. *(Irish Proverb)*

God does some pretty amazing things, but we should not labor under the notion that God is going to show up and tell us what kind of groceries to buy.

So, what about fasting? It's probably one more discipline that has slowly been lost to the church. I believe that the original purpose of the practice was to honor God and give thanks for what He has done for us. Perhaps the "absence makes the heart grow fonder" principle comes into play here. As I study scripture, it seems that there is an assumption that praying, giving, and fasting are all a part of the Christian walk. I believe that the key to ALL teaching in the New Testament is, "what does God say?" In other words, we don't get to edit scripture. In Matthew 6, Jesus assumes that people would fast, and what was needed was teaching on how to do it properly. I come to this conclusion because Jesus did not say, "If you fast" or "you must fast," but rather, "WHEN you fast." Unfortunately, Jesus had to address this because the practice had become a means to call attention to self—"Look at me!" Sometimes this still happens in our churches today. So why would I fast? Maybe a better question is, "Why would Jesus ask me to fast?" Fasting can simplify the compulsive and distracting nature of our appetites. When I fast, I begin to notice how little food I really need, compared to what I usually gobble down. I found a list in one of my journals on reasons for fasting; not sure where it came from:

- Fasting is good for health
- Fasting is good for self-discipline
- Fasting preserves us from becoming slaves of habit
- Fasting promotes the ability to go without things
- Fasting makes us appreciate things more (which I think may have been one of God's original purposes)

I think it's important to note that fasting is never encouraged in scripture apart from prayer—*Fasting and prayer.* The man of God in ancient times always joined prayer and fasting together. Some of my most meaningful times of prayer have come during times of fasting. Having said all this, the essential issue in understanding this practice is the whole area of motive. Why are you fasting? I like what one brother said, "I am fasting, because I feel the Lord has prompted me to fast for a specific reason or purpose." I believe positive outcomes will always occur when we are participating in denying ourselves.

Random thoughts for today:

The days will come, when the bridegroom is taken from them, and then they will fast. (Matthew 9:15 ESV)

Help me be a part of Your plan, Lord...Save me from self-absorption and self-sufficiency.

March

Sometimes our questions are as important as our answers.

March 1   How Do I Pray For You?

So how do I pray for you? I guess I'm talking about intercession. How do I pray for a friend for whom I pray daily? Maybe like, "Lord, I pray for you to bless my friend, Greg, and lead him; I pray that You will bless him richly." What does that mean? What does the word "bless" mean in our evangelical culture today? I think we'd probably all agree that it's quite overused. If Greg is a Christian and doing fairly well in his Christian life, how should I pray? We're not always quite sure what to pray, so we default to the word "bless." Translation: "Make things go well for him; make him happy," etc. I've often talked about prayer partners in my ministry. There are a few entries in my last devotional book concerning this concept. Perhaps I need to be praying something like, "Lord, Greg and I have been close friends for many years now. I thank You for that friendship. Forgive me for not praying for him as an intimate friend. Sometimes I'm not always sure how to specifically pray. Lord, how do you want me to pray? I want what You want in his life. I love him very much, but You love him more than I could ever love him. Continue to love him. Continue to guide him; draw him close to Yourself. May Your desires for Greg be his desires, and may those desires become a reality in his life, to Your glory!!" If

I am praying for my friend in such a way, I believe that could be called intercession.

Random thoughts for today:

I do not cease to give thanks for you, remembering you in my prayers, that the God of our Lord Jesus Christ, the Father of glory, may give you a spirit of wisdom and of revelation in the knowledge of Him. (Ephesians 1:16-17 ESV)

Sometimes I need to get away from intellectual sophistication in my faith and just let people see Jesus in me.

Timing is almost as important as truth when it comes to advice.

O love that will not let me go; I rest my weary soul in Thee. *(George Matheson)*

March 2   Balancing Act

Jesus said, *Judge not, that you be not judged. For with the judgment you pronounce you will be judged, and with the measure you use it will be measured to you* (Matthew 7:1-2). But what about when the Judge judges? If I am not the judge, does that mean I get to throw out all the laws of the land? I get to disregard all of the standards? If, as a law-enforcement officer, I give you a ticket for doing 65 mph in a 35 zone, that doesn't make me the judge. The standard has been set. So even though I have a lot of questions and puzzlement over this whole "judging" balancing act, I'm pretty sure that the command of Jesus for me not to judge doesn't mean that I disregard the standards of the Judge. Jesus has given us the standard (which none of us can measure up to, by the way), but many times if I share the standard of the Judge or try to live out that standard, I am accused of judging. Now I will admit that that accusation might be justly thrown my way because of my attitude of self-righteousness or condescension. I mean why doesn't everyone think like I do, right? If I am trying to live out those standards daily, hopefully without a condemning spirit, optimistically it's not me judging you, but rather the standard that has caused you discomfort. This passage from the Sermon on the Mount isn't talking about allowing God's standard to judge; it's all about a critical spirit in me. Maybe it's not up to me to use His standard to club you over the head. Maybe I'm not the Holy Spirit in your life. There have been times in my Christian walk that I have been convicted just by watching another person live out their lives according to God's standard. And to be honest, sometimes I felt like they were judging me. But you know what? They never said a word about my failings...They never put me down...And they never condemned me. And still, the Lord used them to bring about a change in my heart.

Random thoughts for today:

It is time for judgment to begin at the household of God... (1 Peter 4:17 ESV)

It is loneliness that makes the loudest noise...This is true of men as well as of dogs.

All human discontent comes from not knowing how to stay quietly in a room. *(Blaise Pascal)*

93

Do not go where the path may lead, go instead where there is no path and leave a trail. *(Ralph Waldo Emerson)*

Father, if it takes the blood of martyrs to reach my people for Christ, let me be the first to shed blood. *(A believer in Romania)*

March 3   Am I A Generous Person?

One thing I've learned this year is that owning a lot of things won't make your life safe. I had a pastor-friend about four years ago, or five, ask the question, "What is the well-lived life?" He went on to ask, "Have I brought more love and value to others rather than hate and anger and selfishness?" I came face to face with myself that day when he went on to say, "Generosity and greed are direct opposites—Generosity is a part of the well-lived life." Hmmm...I've never considered myself to be a greedy person, but perhaps the larger question is, "Am I a generous person?" I look at my world around me and have to admit that many of our lives are like one grand selfie. One of the most important things my dad taught me is that there are more important things than me. I read that poor nutrition causes approximately 8,000 deaths, to children under the age of five, per day. Americans will spend $465 billion this year on Christmas ($88 billion on Halloween). What Americans spend on cosmetics each year, is enough to provide basic education for all, worldwide. Hunger kills more people each year than AIDS, malaria, and TB combined. We're still working on cures on many diseases like influenza, and of course, coronavirus. But we already have a cure for hunger—It's called FOOD!! I can't feed the entire world, but I can generously be involved in the process. My relationship with God is part of my relationship with others. You remember—Love God – Love Others – Love Well. In her diary, Anne Frank wrote, "How wonderful it is that nobody need wait a single moment before starting to improve the world." Are you a generous person? Ponder that question. And this one too—Why are we generous? BECAUSE WE CARE!! (Hopefully).

Random thoughts for today:

For the love of money is a root of all kinds of evils. It is through this craving that some have wandered away from the faith and pierced themselves with many pangs. (1 Timothy 6:9-10 ESV)

Fallacies do not cease to be fallacies because they become fashions. *(G.K.Chesterton)*

Action springs not from thought, but from a readiness for responsibility.

When the fog comes into my life for a time, my Father calls me to walk by faith.

True humility makes me realize how small I am and how much I need the Lord.

Never assume that loud is strong and quiet is weak.

March 4   Miracle-Working God?

The dictionary defines a miracle as "an extraordinary event in the physical world that surpasses all known human or natural powers and is ascribed to a supernatural cause." May I begin by saying that I believe in miracles. Birth is a miracle, a meteor-shower is a miracle, some weddings I've performed over the years and the couple is still together, is a miracle. But I do not believe that supernatural miracles abound right and left as a daily occurrence in my life. You do not find such miracles on every page of scripture. If that were true, we'd call them "regulars," not miracles. Unfortunately, because of that reality, much of the church today discounts any kind of miraculous work of the Lord in the 21st century. That's regrettable. I have come to believe in a miracle-working God. My mother-in-law had an inoperable cancer when Helen was in elementary school. Just days after the elders of her church prayed over her, X-rays showed the cancer to have completely disappeared. She died at the age of 94. In Haiti, in 1991, another member of our mission team and I prayed over a 6-month old baby who was gasping for breath and not expected to live through the night. The next morning that child was well and feeding at his mother's breast. I come from a faith-heritage that does not accept those kinds of happenings. I was taught in college that miracles do NOT happen today. Why is that? We all get our theological ducks lined up in a row as to why or why not this is true. Helen and I broke our "rule" recently and watched a "Christian" movie. We usually don't do that because, quite frankly, most are very poorly acted and produced. That was true of this film as well. But the Lord convicted me. It was a story of a young boy (no church background) who came to faith in Christ by simply believing what the Bible said. He prayed for people, and they were healed. And my inner self said, "What's wrong with that?" How many limitations have we placed upon the sovereign God of the universe? Is He not able?

I have no silver or gold, but what I do have I give to you. In the name of Jesus Christ of Nazareth, rise up and walk. (Acts 3:6 ESV)

Sometimes I picture myself wrapped in His loving arms, with my head on His breast, and I can almost feel the warmth of His presence.

There are some things learned by the mind...But Christ crucified can only be learned by the heart.

Why do we fail in our walk with the Lord? We don't believe.

March 5   Miracle-Working God – Part 2

My personal study of miracles has led me to an "all things are possible" kind of faith for daily living. Fyodor Dostoevsky was right in saying faith does not spring from miracles, but miracles from faith. The Great Physician is still doing physical, emotional, and spiritual healings today through the Holy Spirit. Christ is the greatest miracle in history, and His incarnation, as the central miracle helps me to interpret miracles done today by Emmanuel, God with us. I worship a miracle-working God. I never demand miracles, but I believe in them. Have you ever meditated upon the first chapter of Colossians, specifically verses 16-20?

For by Him (Jesus) all things were created, in heaven and on earth, visible and invisible, whether thrones or dominions or rulers or authorities—all things were created through Him and for Him. And He is before all things, and in Him all things hold together. And He is the head of the body, the church. He is the beginning, the firstborn from the dead, that in everything He might be preeminent. For in Him all the fulness of God was pleased to dwell, and through Him to reconcile to Himself all things, whether on earth or in heaven, making peace by the blood of His cross.

Do you want to put any limitations upon that? What can't He do? Where do you need a miracle? What seems impossible to you? Bring it before the Lord. Our Lord Jesus said, *All things are possible for one who believes* (Mark 9:23). Yes, He is able!!

Lord, I do believe that You are a miracle-working God!!

Random thoughts for today:

I believe; help my unbelief! (Mark 9:24 ESV)

Forgiveness is a choice!!

Sometimes my heart needs to be opened more than my eyes do.

Give me honest-to-God honesty in everything...I want to be REAL with the Lord and for the Lord.

I've embraced all of Your gifts, Lord...But I forgot that my arms belong only around You.

When it's dark enough, you can see the stars.

March 6   It's Depressing

Proverbs 14:13 says, *Even in laughter the heart may ache, and joy may end in grief.* I have this piece of prose in one of my journals (authored by Robert Browning Hamilton):

"I walked a mile with Pleasure, she chatted all the way
But left me none the wiser for all she had to say
I walked a mile with Sorrow and not a word said she
But oh, the things I learned when Sorrow walked with me."

Another writer has said, "The haughty heart and the tearless eye should be foreign to the Christ-follower." As one who has battled depression through a good share of my life (beginning in high school), I write not theoretically, but personally. When Jesus speaks of one who "mourns" in the Sermon on the Mount, He's not talking about complainers or whiners, but rather those who experience an aching of the soul, and sometimes even a heart that is breaking. I related to John Bunyan when he said, "The best prayers have often more groans than words." Yeah, there are days like that. There was a stage of my journey that I prayed almost daily for God to remove the depression from me. He didn't, but through the years, He has given me the strength to live with it, and most of the time, to overcome it. You know the drill—*My grace is sufficient for you*. It's a continuing growth experience to realize that my most intimate times with the Lord are during these so-called "down-times." Psalm 34:18 says, *The LORD is close to the brokenhearted and saves those who are crushed in spirit.* It's true!!

Random thoughts for today:

Blessed are those who mourn; for they will be comforted. (Matthew 5:4 ESV)

99

Unless we are heroic or saintly persons beyond measure, each of us needs that one person (call him a friend) who we trust and to whom we are accountable.

Do the right thing...It will gratify some people and astonish the rest. *(Mark Twain)*

The distinct characteristic of a free person is the presence of fearless love.

Teacher Prayer: Help me on sleepy, overcast days to liven up my students' minds with colors of art and the sounds of music and laughter.

Don't tell me the sky's the limit when there are footprints on the moon.

March 7   Tribute to a Pastor's Wife

Women are amazing!! On my life journey, my wife Helen is right at the top of my list. I would never have been able to handle the years of ministry to which God called us without her at my side. The most valuable "tool" in my ministry bag is Helen. Proverbs 31 sums it up, doesn't it guys:

> *An excellent wife who can find? She is far more precious than jewels. The heart of her husband trusts in her, and he will have no lack of gain. She does him good, and not harm* (sounds like the Hippocratic oath), *all the days of her life...Strength and dignity are her clothing, and she laughs at the time to come* (actually, she laughs at most things). *She opens her mouth with wisdom, and the teaching of kindness is on her tongue...Her children rise up and call her blessed; her husband also, and he praises*

her: *"Many women have done excellently, but you surpass them all." Charm is deceitful, and beauty is vain, but a woman WHO FEARS THE LORD is to be praised. Give her of the fruit of her hands, and let her works praise her in the gates.*

She's been there when we lived under the state poverty level... She's been there when I have been attacked; "I got your back, Jack!"...She's been my up when I've been down...She nursed me through a month and a half of pneumonia...For 54 years, she has been my BFF. God bless you, my dear. And God bless all of you faithful pastors' wives. You are amazing!!

Random thoughts for today:

Let your fountain be blessed and rejoice in the wife of your youth... (Proverbs 5:18 ESV)

Treat yourself with loving-kindness...If you are gentle with yourself, you will be gentle with others.

Risk is always involved in following Christ...Sometimes doing the right thing can be risky.

The greatest conundrum of my life—Why can't everyone think like I do.

However long the night, the dawn will break. *(African Proverb)*

Maturity is the realization that it can be all too easy to mistake our emotions for God's voice.

One kind word can warm three winter months. *(Japanese Proverb)*

I have had people say to me, "Prayer just seems like such a useless waste of time; it's never done anything for me." It reminds me of that dear lady who said to me in my office years ago, "I've tried this Christianity thing for three weeks now, and I tell you it doesn't work!" I think of many examples of practices I've developed through the years—walking, talking, reading, writing, driving—just to name a few. How do I become a communicator with the Father, connecting effectively with Him? By doing it. Practice. I never took a course on how to pray, but I have matured in connecting with the Father by praying. I know it is often difficult to find time away from our busy schedules to spend quality time with the Lord. Yet it is so important to set aside a time and space to give Him our undivided attention. Many times, the way I become aware of His presence is that remarkable desire to return to my "place" each morning for that time of quiet of solitude. Because of the discipline and cultivation of these times, I realize how much these "useless times" hold me together. It is through these "worthless" times that I am truly completed. Brennan Manning comments that these times with the Lord help connect him with God, and he ends up listening more attentively to others and loving more unselfishly. He describes the joy of conscientiously "wasting time" with God. Once we have committed ourselves to spend time with the Lord like this, we begin to develop an attentiveness to God's voice in us. The psalmist talks about *deep calling out to deep at the roar of Your waterfalls, all Your breakers and Your waves have gone over me* (Psalm 42:7). What a beautiful description of the depth of our Abba Father calling out to the depth of our soul. There's only one way that is going to happen, and that is by spending a bunch of "useless" time with Him.

<u>Random thoughts for today:</u>

***Give ear to my words, O LORD; consider my
groaning. Give attention to the sound of my cry, my
King and my God, for to you do I pray.*** (Psalm 5:1-2 ESV)

Poor is not the person who has too little, but the person who craves more. *(Seneca)*

May I labor to be honest with the person I have most trouble being honest with—ME.

A friend is one who walks in when others walk out.

Don't forget that in a world of darkness, the Light will win.

March 9   Weird vs. Normal

Why is the body of Christ considered weird by most in our culture today? Think about it. Jesus never preached "normal." His message was counter-cultural; definitely weird in the eyes of His world. He never intended His church to be normal. It increasingly concerns me that I can't always tell the difference between what goes on in the church and what goes on in the world. I wonder how much of our labor in the church is geared toward normalizing Christ's message. His message wasn't normal. I mean, think about what Jesus taught:

- Put God first above all things
- Put others before yourself
- Have a servant's heart
- Money isn't that important
- Tell the truth, no matter what

- Sex is for marriage
- Stay married
- Be kind to others even if they're not kind to you
- Love your enemies
- Give away your money to feed the poor

WEIRD!! I look at the world around me today, and I say it again, these concepts are NOT normal.

Random thoughts for today:

You are a chosen race, a royal priesthood, a holy nation, a peculiar people... (1 Peter 2:9 ESV)

Never ruin an apology with an excuse. *(Ben Franklin)*

Isn't it interesting that we desire the blessing of the Lord before we've done what He has asked us to do?

I was still learning when I taught my last class. *(Retired schoolteacher)*

When so many are lonely, it seems inexcusably selfish to be lonely alone. *(Tennessee Williams)*

March 10   #1 Prayer Partner

In my first prayer devotional, I talked about the concept of prayer partners, dealing mostly with individuals within my congregation with whom I entered into prayer partnerships. In that discussion, I said, "The Holy Spirit continues to be my invisible prayer partner, as well as my Teacher in the school of prayer...Romans chapter 8 tells me that my God is praying for me.

It says that He is interceding for me and lifting me up (Romans 8:26-28). How's that for a prayer partner?" It is such a comfort and gives me confidence to know that the Spirit of God prays for me, even when my prayers are deficient or non-existent—The greatest prayer partner I could ever desire. I mean, think about it. The spirit of prayer IS the Holy Spirit. Jonathan Edwards said that when He intercedes for me, it is "God's breathing and panting" for me. Brennan Manning writes, "The Holy Spirit is the bond of tenderness between the Father and the Son; the indwelling Spirit bears the indelible stamp of the compassion of God." Romans 5:5 says *The love of God has been poured into our hearts by the Holy Spirit which has been given to us."* When this intercessory prayer partnership transpires, Manning continues, "the heart of the Spirit-filled person overflows with tenderness." Romans 8 says, *the Spirit intercedes for the saints according to the will of God.* If I pray incorrectly (and I know that I have), my number one prayer partner corrects it. Even though I continue to mature in my prayer relationship with the Father, I can rest in the fact that my prayers don't have to be perfect because, quite frankly, the Holy Spirit has my back.

Random thoughts for today:

...the Spirit himself intercedes for us with groanings too deep for words. (Romans 8:26 ESV)

You can't let God down...You were never holding Him up.
Without a sense of caring, there can be no sense of community.
One reason we have difficulty connecting with God is that we are way too noisy.

Do not seek love, but rather seek and find all the barriers within yourself that you have built against it.

Some people will never learn anything because they understand everything too soon.

March 11   Dirty or Stiff?

You may have caught on that one of my oft-quoted verses is 1 John 4:19 NASB—*We love because He first loved us.* I've spent a lot (and I mean a lot) of time contemplating the "why" of that second truth. Why did He first love us? Why should He love us? That's especially puzzling to me as I look at my journey with its many failures and wrong turns. It reminds me of a favorite comment from Steve Brown, "It's harder to hug a stiff kid than a dirty kid." Which one am I? I'll give you a hint—I have been both. Here I was, the dirtiest kid you'd ever want to see; I loved the mud puddles. Enter the Lord. I see Him, and I raise my arms and step toward Him for a great big hug. Not only did He hug me, but as we came together, He stripped me down and bathed me until I was clean. *Purge me with hyssop, and I shall be clean; wash me and I shall be whiter than snow* (Psalm 51:7). So how did this clean kid slowly evolve into a stiff kid? How did the stiffness of "I've got all the answers" - "My position is the right one; yours is wrong" – "My interpretation of scripture is the correct interpretation" creep slowly into my walk with Jesus? And how does this "I'm right all the time" stiffness affect my prayer life? How have I become so arrogant? I'm learning that the way we treat people we disagree with is a report card on what I've learned about love. I am so thankful that the Lord has been dealing with my stiffness over the last twenty years. And I'm sure that my having to be correct about every position from eternal security to which eschatological camp is the right one, was one factor in the high blood pressure problem and migraine headaches I struggled with in earlier years. I like what one sister in the Lord said—"If your devotional or Bible study group or conference is focused more on who you are and what your theology is than WHO JESUS IS, maybe it's time to pray about picking up another book or finding another group."

Random thoughts for today:

Love is not arrogant or rude. It does not insist on its own way... Not resentful... (I Corinthians 13:4-5 ESV)

Jesus is in the people we rub shoulders with everyday.

Am I authentic and courageous enough to pray for what is right in Your sight, Lord?

Fear is not a mind problem...It is a heart problem.

It is curious, but when one smiles, darkness fades.

March 12   Waiting

Waiting and trusting and hoping are tightly bound together as one...At least it seems that way to me. When I was involved in children's ministry at our church, we often sang a chorus, "I Will Wait Upon the Lord." With my propensity to impulsively move ahead in so many things, there came a time I found myself under conviction about singing it. "Jones, don't you think it's a bit hypocritical for you to sing that song, especially with so much gusto?" But waiting is a part of life, isn't it? I mean, I spend 50-60 hours a year waiting on stoplights. But what about waiting upon the Lord? Although I am not a patient driver (behind the wheel is where I sin most), I think I'm even less patient in waiting on God. Waiting upon Him is difficult because so much of my prayer life is based upon me. That's a polite way of saying that I'm selfish. I am so occupied with myself, my own needs, and my own efforts. Andrew Murray said, "In waiting upon God, our first thought needs to be of the God upon whom we wait." In other words, we need to discipline ourselves to wait on God until we know we are connected to Him. Prayer will then become quite different. Before you pray, sit silently before your Father, and remember who He is. Be still before Him. When we connect to our Abba Father, who is always faithful, even when we are not, we begin to sense the hope that is ours in a real relationship. We wait hopefully—with a hope that does not disappoint (Romans 5:5). Psalm 33:20 says *We wait in hope for the LORD; He is our help and our shield.* Why? Because we know that in His time and wisdom, He brings *all things together for good to those who love Him* (Romans 8:28). When I pray and live that out authentically, hope begins to become a reality in my journey. When I allow Him to fill me with His fruit of patience and his hope, then I can sing it with as much passion as I want—I WILL WAIT UPON THE LORD!!

Random thoughts for today:

Wait for the LORD; be strong and take heart and wait for the LORD. (Psalm 27:14 ESV)

I can't get too excited about prayer theology...But I can get pretty excited about talking to the Lord.

The key is patience...You get the chicken by hatching the egg, not smashing it.

Never underestimate the power of expectation.

The poet Kenneth Koch once said, "You aren't just the age you are; you are all the ages you have ever been." It's true. It's why I've prayed for many years that the Lord would keep the kid alive in me. Fred Rogers wrote, "The child is in me still...and sometimes not so still." Some of my favorite entries in my last devotional book were "Kids' Prayers"; I'll share a few more in this volume from my journal, the internet, and other sources. Enjoy.

> "When you pray, I think you're supposed to wipe your tears on Jesus' feet or something like that." *(Sam – Age 9)*

> "Jesus, Thank you for everything, except beer and drunk drivers." *(Ashley – Age 6)*

> "Dear God, please make my parents understand that if I don't eat salad I do better at school." *(Jeffrey – Age 7)*

> "Dear God, when will my sister stop being annoying, I'm down to my last patience." *(Susie – Age 10)*

> "You can always reach Him at dinnertime." *(7-year-old Adam, when asked how he talked to God.)*

> "Dear God, I wish you would not make it so easy for people to come apart; I had to have three stitches and a shot." *(Thomas – Age 7)*

What's interesting is the kid that's still in me relates to all of these petitions.

Jesus said, "Let the little children come to Me and do not hinder them, for to such belongs the kingdom of heaven. (Matthew 19:14 ESV)

Age is mind over matter...If you don't mind, it doesn't matter. *(Satchel Paige)*

You are braver than you believe, stronger than you seem, and smarter than you think. *(Christopher Robin/A.A. Milne)*

March 14   Justice?

May I begin with the disclaimer that I am a proponent of justice. I believe the scriptures are filled with God's teaching on justice. *Behold the days are coming, declares the LORD, when I will raise up for David a righteous Branch* (talking about the promised Messiah), *and He shall reign as king and deal wisely, and shall execute justice and righteousness in the land* (Jeremiah 23:5). Justice is paramount in biblical teaching, and yet it's interesting that the concept of justice God mostly talks about is the kind of justice we would just as soon avoid. If you recall the closing section of the Book of Jonah, you will remember his whining before the Lord because God didn't bring His justice down upon Nineveh as He told Jonah He was going to do. Jonah 4:1 says that this *displeased Jonah exceedingly, and he was angry.* So Jonah sulks under his homemade pity-shack because God didn't execute justice. It's called grace, Jonah. The prophet gets all spiritual—"I'm good; Nineveh isn't." This from a guy who had to be taught a "whale" of a lesson from God before he would even obey Him. God's response to Jonah is grow up! God asks, *Are you justified in being angry?* Jonah has no response to this. A mentor of mine years ago once said to me, "Beware of those who are constantly protesting and crying out for justice." I'm not anti-protesting; I have marched in anti-abortion protests. But what's my motive? I've learned when I have been treated unjustly or unfairly, my response can tell a lot about what's in my heart. What's that old Southern proverb—"What's in the well comes out in the water." I have an entry in my journal (not sure of its origin) — "Never look for justice, but never cease giving it." That statement pretty well sums up the essence of the Sermon on the Mount. Do I possess a "Jonah-heart" within me? Do I inwardly desire for God to "bring down His justice upon" any person or group of people that I know—a group toward which I have no positive thoughts or good wishes? I've discovered that the attitude of my heart can rob me of loving others as God has told me to do. It reminds me of a friend who, when asked, "How are you?" would respond, "Better than I deserve." Yup. It's called grace, "Jonah!"

Random thoughts for today:

(*) *You therefore must be perfect as your heavenly Father is perfect.* (Matthew 5:48 ESV)

In the depth of winter, I finally learned that within me lay an invincible summer.

We find no encouragement in the system of this world.

Loving others results in loss of freedom...That's why loving is always a risk.

**(*) Spend a little time meditating on this scripture...
Hmmm**

March 15   Beyond Myself

It's astounding how ignorant we can be about ourselves. We don't always recognize the envy, laziness, or pride within us when we see it. It's a complicated matter to look inward with courage. If there is any element of pride or conceit within us, Jesus has a real tough time teaching us much of anything. Years ago, I walked into a staff meeting at our school feeling pretty good about myself and recent accomplishments. During that staff meeting, our senior Bible teacher (my friend, Derek) told of a discussion his class had been having on proper attitudes, and those attitudes influencing our behaviors. Derek asked the question of the class, "How do you know if a behavior is appropriate or not?" One of his students replied, "If you can't do it in front of Rick Jones, you shouldn't be doing it." I was humbled that morning; I didn't know how to respond. This proud and flawed, imperfect "role-model" who has rebelled against the encouragements of the Spirit so many times this week has become the standard. God help us. Even now, when I realize that I have been showing disrespect for God, a compliment of this nature fills me with shame and humiliation for ignoring Him, or at the very least, not honoring Him. Genuine total surrender is a personal preference for Jesus Christ Himself. Total surrender, which we must be working toward daily, will always go beyond myself. So yup, I was humbled that morning. And once again, my sinful self, the real me unknown to most, is chastened, and I repent.

Random thoughts for today:

I desire to do Your will, O my God; your word is within my heart. (Psalm 40:8 NIV)

Behaviors have consequences.

When God brings a time of waiting into your life, don't fill it with busyness....JUST WAIT.

The real challenge for schoolteachers in Christian schools is to motivate those who have grown up in Christian homes.

We talk about victory over temptation, and yet never have the deep desire to give up that thing anyway.

Don't prove it to me...Show it to me. *(A dominant philosophy of the younger generation)*

Hope swells my sail. *(James Montgomery)*

March 16   Serving Jesus

I heard an interesting comment the other day—"All the holy men seem to have gone off and died. There's no one left but us sinners to carry on the ministry." So, what about our ministries, if in fact, they are ours. What about our "service"? Do you do what "you do for Jesus" because you have to or because you truly desire to do it? What are my motives for serving? How do you define service? Oswald Chambers said, "Sometimes we are fresh and eager to go to church but do we feel that same freshness for such mundane tasks as polishing shoes?" Being born again provides a freshness in thinking, talking, living—In everything! Freshness comes from the Holy Spirit...It gives new vision. I frequently ask myself, "Am I drawing my life from any source other than the

Lord Himself?" Do I ever draw life from the act of service itself? Hmmm. Beware of anything that competes with your loyalty to Jesus Christ. Sometimes it is easier to "serve" than it is to pour out our lives entirely for Him. The goal of the call of God is His approval, not merely that I should DO something for Him. The Son of God reveals Himself to others through my love for Him. How I specifically serve Him becomes secondary. Serving should become an overflow which pours from a life of love for Him; it becomes our way of life, rather than something that is always calculated or carefully planned out. It's almost like God saying to us, "Instead of trying to fit your ministry into what you think it should be, why not be on the lookout for what I'm doing and get on board." I love what J. Hudson Taylor said, "I used to ask God to help me. Then I asked if I might help Him. I ended up asking Him to do His work through me." Sounds like a great way to serve Jesus to me.

Random thoughts for today:

If I then, your Lord and teacher, have washed your feet, you also ought to wash one another's feet. (John 13:14 ESV)

Everyone must row with the oars he has. *(Southern Proverb)*

Does my faith give me room to wrestle, to struggle? Does it give me room to fail?

Let people around you see you laugh, and you let them see your heart.

Though there is no bone in the tongue, it has frequently broken a man's head. *(Irish Proverb)*

Why is it that my mind is always racing and thinking about what I have to do tomorrow or next week or even next month? Psalm 40:8 says *I delight to do Your will, O my God."* I seem to struggle in the "delighting in the Lord" part because of my anxiousness, and I hate it! How many times do we read in the New Testament the words of our Savior as He admonishes us not to be anxious, not to be afraid, and not to worry about tomorrow? What are my plans for next summer? I love what Anne Dillard has written, "I meant to accomplish a great deal today. Instead I keep thinking: Will the next generation of people remember to drain the pipes in the fall? I will leave them a note." What are you anxious about today? Jesus tells us not to worry about any of these things. Keep your mind stayed on Him because He has promised you so much more. *Seek first the Kingdom of God and His righteousness and all of these things will be added to you* (Matthew 6:33). Can you identify your greatest fear today? Can you bring it before your Abba Father and begin to allow Him to deal with it? If you keep it hidden within you, He can never cleanse it, much less use it to His glory. Offer your fears and anxieties to Him this week.

O God, who is willing to assist me, what grounds have I not to place my whole confidence in You, to throw myself into the arms of Your providence and wait upon You. *(The Book of Common Prayer—1979)*

<u>Random thoughts for today:</u>

Therefore do not be anxious about tomorrow, for tomorrow will be anxious for itself. Sufficient for the day is its own trouble. (Matthew 6:34 ESV)

There are those things that happen in life for which there is no satisfactory explanation or simple answers.

Are the doors of the church as wide open as the arms of the Savior? *(Nate Loucks)*

Refuse to be average or to surrender to the chill of your spiritual environment.

I never want to define You, God, for I cannot worship what I completely understand.

Always do the right thing...This will gratify some people and astonish the rest. *(Mark Twain)*

The church is not called to find cures, but rather to the ministry of listening, understanding, and spiritual consolation.

March 18   In the Midst of Chaos

As I write this entry today (March 18, 2020), our world is in the midst of a global pandemic (Coronavirus 2020 *). The number of cases worldwide topped 200,000 today. All schools, restaurants, bars, gyms, and churches (any gatherings over 50 people) have been closed by the governor of our state. New York City may be locked down by the end of the day, and the President just closed the borders between the US and Canada (He closed the Mexican border the next day). "Social-distancing" has become the new watchword, and grocery stores are dealing with shelves being emptied as soon as they are restocked (Six days later, the governor issued a mandatory stay-at-home order for the entire state). And all of this is hitting home in the middle of Helen's radiation treatments. We have to be screened at the door of the hospital just to enter. Is this the apocalypse? Probably not. But it's interesting to me how quickly priorities have shifted all around us. I liked a post on Facebook today—"Now, healthcare workers, grocery store employees, and truckers are more important than NBA players, actors, and famous musicians." I resonated with that sentiment. One comment said, "They always were essential!" In the first few days of our "voluntary" quarantine, it's been curious to see the balance between selflessness and selfishness. There are many examples of people going out of their way to help others, especially older people (we are one of the main concerns with COVID-19, although I'm not thrilled to be categorized as "older"). On the other hand, the hoarders and the price gougers continue to abound. My wife and I pray daily for our family, especially our oldest daughter, Chris, who works in a Chicago-area hospital, which I consider to be the firing-line. I pray Psalm 91 daily over our loved ones. In 2012, the Rand Corporation, in surveying international threats arrayed against the United States, concluded that "only pandemics posed an existential danger, in that they were capable of destroying America's way of life." Can this present threat seriously change America's way of life? Hmmm... Sometimes I wonder if that would be all bad. The headline of the Rand Corporation article read, "We Were Warned in 2012." Actually, when it comes to the spiritual side of things, we were warned a long time before that.

(*) On September, 2021, total worldwide cases were over 225 1/2 million)

He who dwells in the shelter of the Most High will abide in the shadow of the Almighty. (Psalm 91:1 ESV)

Lord, in the middle of the bad with You, it has never been so good. *(Student Prayer)*

The heart that loves is always young. *(Greek Proverb)*

March 19   The Language of Events

Immediately following Helen's diagnosis of cancer, we were called upon pretty quickly to make the transition from shock to plunging back into everyday life. In other words, living with a degree of routine in the shadow of personal crisis. John Claypool, in his book, *Tracks of a Fellow Struggler* said, "I have come to the conclusion that it is in the nature of God to speak to us in the language of events, and the nature of the church for men to share with each other what they thought they heard God say in the things that happened to them." I believe that. It may surprise you, but I think there are many portions of our lives that are a "dark mystery," in Claypool's words, "for which there is no satisfactory explanation." Between the Father's words, *Though I walk through the valley of the shadow...I will fear no evil for You are with me* (Psalm 23:4), and Jesus saying, *Peace, I leave with you; my peace I give to you...Let not your hearts be troubled, neither let them be afraid* (John 14:27), I find tremendous peace and comfort, but not necessarily answers. I do not necessarily subscribe to the "all things happen for a reason" school of thought, but I do know that we don't first get all the answers and then live our lives in light of that understanding. Insight many times comes not before, but through and after the experience. Specific answers and insights may never come in this life. We are not guaranteed to find "meaning" in our negative experiences in life. We are only guaranteed that the resurrection will be the final word over them all. Again, and I've said it often, "There are times that are not for understanding, but rather for trust." Trusting in the Lord is a moment by moment choice. Have I placed my full confidence in God Himself, or is it contingent upon whether I am experiencing trial or blessing? One day when I get to talk to the Lord about this, I might ask Him what this was all about. But probably not. Then, it won't really matter.

Random thoughts for today:

If I go and prepare a place for you, I will come again and will take you to Myself, that where I am you may be also. (John 14:3 ESV)

I don't want to be an expert on how we used to do ministry.

The Christian should be an alleluia from head to toe. *(St. Augustine)*

"As iron sharpens iron"...To be a "sharpener" of others is also to be an encourager. *(Luke Brechner)*

My ability to approach God depends entirely upon the cross of Christ (Period).

Praise does wonders for the sense of hearing.

Passionate people hang in there when things get difficult. Lord, I want to be passionate in my praying. *Men ought always to pray and not lose heart* (Luke 18:1). I want to persist. I want to persevere. I never want to lose heart. I never want to quit. I want to *never lag in diligence, be fervent in spirit, serving the LORD* (Romans 12:11). One of my mentors years ago told me that "this generation has yet to prove all that prayer can do for believing men and women." Am I a man of passion when it comes to my prayer life? Is prayer my priority? The early church took great delight in prayer. They had prayer meetings almost every day; they gathered together primarily to pray. The contemporary church gathers for dinner. The early church was fasting and praying, which may show the difference before us today. In Luke 18, Jesus tells the parable of the persistent widow. She is my role-model. I pray passionately and persistently until I receive an answer (either yes or no). I love what Paul says to the Corinthians—*But we have this treasure in jars of clay* (that would be us) *to show that the surpassing power belongs to God and not to us. Though our outer nature is wasting away, our inner nature is being renewed day by day...So we do not lose heart* (2 Corinthians 4:7; 16). Howard Taylor said of his father, Hudson Taylor, "For forty years the sun never rose on China that God didn't find him on his knees." Hudson used to say, "I have to exercise my prayer muscle." That's passionate praying.

Lord, I want to be passionate in my praying. Help me to lift my fervent prayers to You and to never lose heart.

Random thoughts for today:

**_For a righteous man may fall seven times and rise
again._** (Proverbs 24:16 ESV)

Lord, thank You for my great prayer partner, the Holy Spirit,
who intercedes for me every day.

I wasn't born with the "patience gene"...But it IS in my adoption
papers. *(Jeff Zigler)*

Sometimes my best action/option is to shut up and listen.

Thinking about my walk with the Lord helps me realize afresh
how much I am loved in the midst of everything.

Angry? Release your anger through forgiveness!!

March 21   Adventures

"Note to self: Where's the adventure? Or, as you age, are you
much more comfortable with your daily status quo? Perhaps
you don't get quite as excited about adventure as you used to be.
Why is that? You used to go canoe-camping and backpacking in
the wilderness. Remember when you had the 'Snow Train' out
of Sault Ste. Marie, Michigan drop you off in the middle of the
Canadian wilderness for a week? And if that weren't adventure
enough, you took a bunch of teenagers with you. Remember when
you went to Haiti two or three times a year (Over 30 trips in 30
years)? Where did your spirit of adventure go? Some would say
my starting a second career teaching school was an adventure.
Maybe. I wonder what adventures the Lord has for me in the next
ten years?" *(Excerpt from my personal journal – February 2009)*

I had been the lead pastor at a large church of over a thousand for close to 30 years. In 2005 I participated in a construction missions trip to Southern Mexico with some members of our congregation, when I began to sense a rather disturbing nudge that I believe came from the Lord—Resign!! What? And then what should I do? I was only 61 years old. I had no clue as to what the answers to those questions were, but the nudge to resign my ministry became stronger as the week wore on. Long story short, I met with my eldership later that summer and told them they needed to start praying and searching for a new lead pastor within the next year. I retired from the pastoral ministry the following summer, still with no idea of what was next. It was the end of the summer that I received a call from a member of our church (public school teacher) asking what I was planning to do now. Longer story shorter, that Fall, I began substitute teaching at the elementary level. Four years later I was still at it, working every day as a permanent sub for the corporation. What's next?

Random thoughts for today:

For you know the plans I have for you... (Jeremiah 29:11 ESV – I know Jeremiah is speaking to Israel here, but the Lord has put this verse on my heart a number of times)

The promise of sins forgiven is all or nothing...80% won't cut it.

Sometimes our idea of blessing has to do with stuff...Christ in me IS the blessing!!

If we had no winter, the Spring would not be nearly as pleasant.

So yeah, what's next? In the spring of my fourth year of subbing, I received a call from an area Christian school (an enrollment of about 300 students) asking if I might be interested in a full-time job teaching social studies. By the beginning of that summer, I was lesson preparing for five classes—High School History (twice), Middle School History, and Geography (twice). "So, Lord, what adventures do you have for me for the next ten years?" I had written that question in my journal many times before. I taught secondary social studies for the next eight years, finding new ministry and challenges with teenagers. Jump ahead to 2017, and I'm 72 years old. I received a call from the school board who was in emergency session. The new principal who had only been with us for a year, abruptly resigned with only seven weeks until a new school year started. "Mr. Jones, would you be willing to be interim principal for the next year?" One year turned into two years when the Lord finally opened the door for God's permanent administrator to join us. A godly gentleman from Wichita, Kansas, was led to become a part of our school family (actually, he has written the forward to this book). What's next? Yeah, that's the question once again. My wife and I prayerfully decided that this would be a good time to retire from teaching (Helen had retired a year and a half before). In the summer of 2019, the Lord opened a door for us to pastor a small rural church of about 15-20 people. What a blessing they have been to us. Because I am now "retired," my schedule has now opened up to spend many hours writing. What's next? I'm not sure of everything the Lord has in mind for us, but I'm sure it will be an adventure.

Thank You, Father, for adventures!!

<u>Random thoughts for today</u>:

For you know the plans I have for you... (Jeremiah 29:11 ESV)

What a great thing it is to be a kid with a loving Dad...Think of your relationship with your loving Abba Father...Lord, keep the kid alive in me.

The world has changed...The Word has not!!

Be yourself...Everyone else is already taken.

Don't just go with the flow...Take some dares through the rapids.

March 23   Depression

I mentioned previously my on and off battles with depression through the years. The following is an entry from my journal a few years ago:

"I wonder how much of my life has been spent in battling depression? Too much, I suppose. And yet, it is through depression that I know I am alive, for only material inanimate objects don't ever suffer depression. If I were not capable of depression, I would have no capacity for happiness and exaltation. I know that God doesn't chastise me for my depression, unlike some blessed saints who tell me Christians shouldn't ever go through things like this. I know He is not honored when I continually "bathe" in my unhappiness. I know that He does not will sadness in me. He desires so much more for me and would have me be lifted above any despair. And I think if Paul could sing and say, *Rejoice in the Lord and again I say, Rejoice* (Philippians 4:4) from a prison cell, then what the heck is my problem. Don't misunderstand me. I know clinical depression is real and devastating. I have never tried to belittle the reality or pain of depression or demean anyone else struggling with it. But I do know that when the Spirit of God is leading me to do something (whatever that might be), the moment I do it, the spirit of depression begins to lift. As soon as I arise and *get going* (Matthew 26:46), I begin to enter into a new plane of life. In the power of Jesus Christ, I try never to let the sense of past failure or any dark feelings in my inner life defeat my next step." (February 17, 2013)

Random thoughts for today:

You have turned for me my mourning into dancing; you have loosed my sackcloth and clothed me with gladness. (Psalm 30:11 ESV)

Envy and strife have overthrown great cities and rooted up mighty nations. *(Clement of Alexandria – AD 189)*

Before I rush to judgment toward another, I must ask, "Can I endure the scrutiny of the same standard by which I use to judge others?"

Wishing to be friends is quick work, but friendship is a slow ripening fruit. *(Aristotle)*

When we love someone, we accept him or her exactly as is—It's called unconditional love.

WORDS MEAN SOMETHING*!!*

#93% of our teens, aged 12-17, are online daily.

#190 million tweets a day are posted.

#89.5% of teens are on Facebook.

#61% of teenagers send private messages via social media.

#In one day, Facebook records over 2 billion "likes"; over 300 million pictures uploaded.

#I don't know if I've said this before, PUT DOWN YOUR PHONE!!

As a former teacher, I'd like to say we have a generation hooked on words, but that's not the case. Our words are incredibly important; they have power. I believe that we have lost the power of words. The universe came to be by words. Marriage was begun by words. The church is a community of the Word. As I have said before, WORDS MEAN SOMETHING!! Scripture says that we are to be held accountable for our words. We need to speak our words intentionally and realize that they have their origin in our hearts. What are you feeding your heart? Are you a thinker before you are a speaker (or I should say, "a poster or a tweeter"). How does your journey with the Lord affect your words? The more time I spend with Him, the more this will be reflected in my speech. How IS God revealed in your language? As I reflect on these questions, I consider THE Word—*In the beginning was the Word, and the Word was with God, and the Word was God* (John 1:1). Hmmm...I think that's talking about Jesus. So then, the example of how I should speak, is THE WORD.

Random thoughts for today:

When words are many, transgression is not lacking, but whoever restrains his lips is prudent. (Proverbs 10:19)

As I open my heart to God and step toward Him, I find Him already there with arms open wide.

If you're going to stand firm, you can't be lying down.

Children should be led into right paths, not by severity, but by heart-persuasion.

No creed or school of thought or experience can monopolize the Spirit of God.

March 25   Lessons from the Eastern Orthodox

Have you ever visited an Eastern Orthodox church? I think many of us have shied away from groups like this because of the term "orthodoxy," which basically means "right believing." Maybe that's why many people in the world today shy away from many of us as Christians. That visit can be an interesting experience. It is one of the largest Christian churches in the world, with approximately 260 million baptized members (3.5% of the world population). Roughly half of the Eastern Orthodox church live in Russia. By comparison, there are less than 400 Orthodox churches in America (little over 17,000 members). Faith and practice were defined by the first seven ecumenical councils, which includes the resulting Nicene Creed. After visiting a few of these congregations and having discussions with our local priest (their small building is about 2 ½ miles from my house), I have grown to respect this branch of the church. Our Eastern Orthodox brothers and sisters remind us of three major beliefs they hold dear.

1. <u>Mystery</u> – Mystery plays a vital role in our spiritual lives... *Great indeed, we confess, is the mystery of godliness* (1 Timothy 3:16). I think that much of the modern church has lost the mystery. When did we surrender the wonder?

2. <u>Christ doesn't hate you</u> – They place a lot of emphasis on 1 John, chapter 4...You know, *We love because He first loved us.* You've heard that verse, right? If we have to qualify God's love, we don't understand it.

3. <u>The sacred space of the church</u> – The church serves as a unique and peculiar place and dimension in this world. I'd like to think that all of our churches would embody that sacred space.

Actually, I'd like to believe that our churches would embrace all of the beliefs above.

<u>Random thoughts for today</u>:

He was manifested in the flesh, vindicated by the Spirit, seen by angels, proclaimed among the nations, believed on in the world, taken up in glory. (1 Timothy 3:16 ESV)

Lord, help me daily to be about YOUR business above my personal business.

Those whose faith and life rest on the Lord don't have to conquer the world...It already belongs to them.

The only real disability in life is a bad attitude.

Remember the account of the woman caught in adultery in John 8? The religious leaders drag this poor woman into the presence of Jesus, carrying their "woman-killing" sized rocks with them. It's pretty easy to see that they had staked out the Holiday Inn to catch her in the act. They had an agenda, and that was to trap Jesus in a no-win kerfuffle. Even though the lady was one of their own, they could care less about her as a person. A key question in the whole matter would be, "Where is the guy?" Why aren't they dragging him to Jesus as well? Last time I checked, it takes two for an act of adultery. Human beings are never more frightening than when they are convinced beyond doubt that they are right. Jesus responds with those words that even many unbelievers can quote, *Let him who is without sin among you be the first to throw a stone at her* (John 8:7). One-by-one, the religious dogmatists leave, dropping their stones on the ground. It's just Jesus and the woman now. *Woman, where are they? Has no one condemned you? She said, "No one, Lord."* (Right? – Parenthesis is mine) *And Jesus said, "Neither do I condemn you; go, and from now on sin no more"* (John 8:10-11). I love this account. Yes, she had sinned, but I love the fact that Jesus didn't kick her when she was down. We do that a lot, don't we? Like the old cliché of Christians shooting their wounded. Did we forget? Human beings judge one another by their external actions; God judges by the choices of our hearts." Matthew 12 talks about Jesus as a healer (on many levels). Matthew quotes Isaiah prophesying the Messiah—*A bruised reed He will not break, and a smoldering wick He will not quench, until He brings justice to victory* (Matthew 12:20). Jesus doesn't jerk out the bruised and struggling plant; He doesn't snuff out the smoldering candle flame. *In His name the Gentiles will hope*

(Matthew 12:21). I have a preacher friend. We went to school together and he stood up in our wedding. He used to keep a big rock on his pulpit; he called it "the first stone." He told me, "So far, no one's thrown it yet." May our churches today do away with our practices of reed-bruising and wick-snuffing. May we be known more by what we are FOR, rather than what we're against.

Random thoughts for today:

Behold my servant, whom I uphold, my chosen, in whom my soul delights; I have put my Spirit upon Him; He will bring forth justice to the nations. (Isaiah 42:1 ESV)

Lord, help me to keep my mouth closed today, and maybe I won't get in so much trouble.

Let's lay aside doctrinal and dogmatic arguments and formulas today, and just "heart-pray."

It's better to ask some of the questions than to know all the answers.

March 27   The Psalms and Me

I saw a posting on the internet earlier this year. It said, "My strength returns to me with my cup of coffee and the reading of the Psalms". This was posted by a Catholic activist for social causes such as unequal treatment of the poor and women's education. I relate to her coffee-Psalms jump start. The Bible contains many recorded models of prayer—the Lord's Prayer, prayers of men of God from Abraham to Paul, and of course, my favorites from the Book of Psalms. These prayerful songs are filled with calls for help, complaints, confessions of sin, depressions, celebrations, cries of hope and love, and undying commitment to the Lord. I confess that I haven't always been a Psalms-fan. I think my struggle with them had to do with my need to have my theological ducks all in a row. Certainly, in younger life, I had some definite ideas of what was appropriate and what wasn't in the practice of my faith. Frankly, some of the Psalms seemed to be rude, ill-mannered, and just not, I don't know—TIDY. I shouldn't be singing or praying about *dashing them to pieces* (Psalm 2:9) – Or *Breaking the teeth of the wicked* (Psalm 3:7) – Or other examples of the writer being outright mad at God. As time has passed, however, the Psalms have become, using the words of J. I. Packer, "the emotional world" of my prayer life. I connect with the passionate ups and downs of these writers. I have periodically used the Psalms as my prayers. During our present pandemic crisis going on, I regularly pray Psalm 91 over my family and loved ones. Billy Graham read five Psalms a day, which allowed him to go through the entire book once a month. I read from the Psalms each morning. I love what Thomas Merton said, "The Psalms are our Bread of Heaven in the wilderness of our Exodus."

Lord, teach me to make the Psalms my own.

Random thoughts for today:

How long, O LORD? Will you forget me forever? How long will You hide Your face from me? (Psalm 13:1 ESV)

Can we be like Jesus in anything unless we are like Jesus in everything?

Most of God's business that I am to be concerned with doesn't have anything to do with the church building.

I wasn't born with the "kindness gene"...But it IS in my adoption papers.

The man who moves a mountain must start by moving small stones. *(Chinese Proverb)*

March 28   Hoarding Manna

As I write this entry, we are still in the middle of the COVID-19 worldwide pandemic. On this date, we are fast approaching 100,000 confirmed cases in the United States (by Sept-2021, the number was over 41 million). I mentioned in my entry for March 18 that the hoarders were in full go mode and that many people had to deal with empty shelves. It's still next to impossible to find disinfectant wipes, hand sanitizers, and a challenge to find toilet paper. There is a concern over enough medical masks being available for health-care workers and first responders due to the hoarders clearing the stores of these products early on. I remember a number of years ago listening to a pastor in Jacmel, Haiti admonishing his flock on the subject of sharing with your neighbor—"If you have two loaves of bread for the table today, give one to your neighbor and trust the Lord to provide for tomorrow." How does that prayer Jesus taught us go? *Give us this day our daily bread?* Oh, yeah. During that same week in Haiti, our mission team gave a young boy a new shirt. One of our team members asked him if he would like to have another one. His response—"I have a brand new shirt. Why would I need another one?" E. M. Bounds wrote many years ago, "True faith is born out of present trials and present needs. Bread for today is enough. Bread given for today is the strongest pledge that there will be bread tomorrow." When the Israelites were in the wilderness, they were instructed by God to gather manna for their meals and only to gather what they needed that day, no more. Those who disobeyed and tried to hoard more than the daily ration found the food had spoiled by morning. Today's manna is what we need; tomorrow, God will see that our needs are supplied. Can you not hear your Abba Father calling to you—"I am your God who gives and gives and gives." Trust Him!!

Random thoughts for today:

Then the LORD said to Moses, "Behold I am about to rain bread from heaven for you, and the people shall go out and gather a day's portion every day... (Exodus 16:4 ESV)

There comes a time when the follower of Christ must stand on the truth of God and refuse to be shaken.

Help me to keep my eyes on the Lord and His working in my life...Even through the silences.

God fully knows me, and He fully loves me...The big mystery is why. *(Pastor Rebecca Crain)*

Today make me hear joy and gladness. *(Psalm 51:8)*

March 29 — God's Will?

The will of God. Quite a question, huh? For many, it's quite the conundrum. What is God's will for my career, my marriage, my ministry? And that's just the tip of the iceberg. A frequent question asked during my pastoral years was, "How can I know the will of God?" Years ago, my mentor would say to me, "Rick, we're asking God the wrong question. Not what is God's will in this particular matter, but rather what has God already told me to do that I'm not doing." I discovered through my journey that the best method of seeking the will of God is to daily be in the Word of God—Not questioning His will but seeking through His Word. It seems to be fruitless to pray for the Lord's will in a matter if I'm never studying His Word. Scripture plays an essential role in the salvation of men. The Bible is a divinely provided map of spiritual order. It contains directions and markings to guide a person not only into reconciliation with God but in so many other areas of life. The Bible can change not only a life (and it has) but an entire lifestyle. I can tell you of the many times in my own life that I struggled with a situation or decision that eventually became resolved through my study of the Word. To paraphrase St. Augustine, "If in scripture I come across anything that seems contrary to my understanding of truth, it is because of one of two reasons: there is fault in the translation I'm using, or there may be fault somewhere in my understanding." (In my experience, the latter is usually the case). Other books are given for our information. The Bible is provided for our transformation, and as I understand the scripture (with my limited knowledge), our transformation IS the will of God.

Random thoughts for today:

All scripture (is given) so that the man of God may be competent, equipped for every good work. (2 Timothy 3:17 ESV)

Leadership means duty, honor...It means character, and it means listening from time to time.

Abba Father, fill me with certainty in this world of uncertainty.

We're so busy saying we can do something that we never ask whether we should.

Let your anger set with the sun and rise again with it. *(Irish Proverb...Almost sounds biblical)*

March 30   Our Daily Bread

The following plaque can be found on an old inn in Lancaster, England:

> "Give us Lord, a bit o'sun,
> A bit o'work and a bit o'fun;
> Give us all in the struggle and sputter
> Our daily bread and a bit o'butter."

Not only has the Lord seen your need for salvation, but He also sees your day-to-day needs. In Genesis, after God provided the ram for sacrifice in place of his son, Isaac, Abraham named the location, *Jehovah-Jireh,* which translates, "the Lord will provide." He has promised to provide for us, and yet He still instructs us to pray, *Give us this day our daily bread* (Matthew 6:11). I wonder how many of us are living in the "land of Jehovah-Jireh"—Jehovah-Jireh churches, Jehovah-Jireh homes, "the Lord will provide" lives. I mean, am I still praying for God to provide my daily bread when my wife just went to the grocery store this morning and paid $2.19 for a loaf of all-natural 100% whole wheat bread along with other sundry food and household items? Is it really necessary to come to the sovereign ruler of the universe with the trivia of our individual needs? Do you ever ask yourself the question, why would God even care about you? I'm familiar with the old saying, "God gives us the ingredients for our daily bread, but He expects us to do the baking." I thank the Lord every day for my retirement income that makes it possible to buy that whole wheat bread—Yes, Lord, *give us this day our daily bread*. Our Jehovah-Jireh still bids us to come to Him for our needs. We're not as self-sufficient as we think we are. We daily worship Jehovah-Jireh and know that whatever we need, He will provide. J. Hudson Taylor wrote years ago, "God's work done in God's way will never lack God's supply."

Random thoughts for today:

Abraham called the name of that place, "the LORD will provide"; as it is said to this day, "On the mount of the LORD it shall be provided. (Genesis 22:14 ESV)

Good news is for everyone...If it's not for everyone, it's not good news. *(Pastor Becky Crain)*

You ain't never gonna break a horse if you stay sittin on a fence. *(Southern Proverb)*

If I want the Lord to be first in my life, I must first examine my attitude toward other things.

March 31   Simple Prayers

Two prayers recorded years ago in one of my journals:

"As a hand is made for holding and the eye for seeing, You have fashioned me for joy. Share with me the vision that shall find it everywhere: in the wild violet's beauty; in the lark's melody; in the face of a steadfast man; in a child's smile; in a mother's love; in the purity of Jesus." *(A Gaelic Prayer)*

"Lord, I want to be a spiritually simple person. I want to pursue spiritual wealth rather than material possessions. I want to have plenty to keep me busy but not let my job define me. I want my grandkids' smiles to be worth more to me than any amount of money. In other words, I want to keep it simple. Help me to stay focused on what matters. Help me never to be so busy that I fail to encourage those You bring into my life, especially those who silently cry out for my help and can do great things if someone believes in them. Let me live my life, so people will know that I am both simple and rich in Your Spirit." *(March 2012)*

In the words of Henry David Thoreau, "SIMPLIFY! SIMPLIFY!"

Random thoughts for today:

And it is my prayer that your love may abound more and more... (Philippians 1:9 ESV)

A room without books is like a body without a soul. *(Cicero)*
The best advice that can be given about prayer is to pray.
No one creed or school of thought or experience can monopolize the Spirit of God.
Thank You for tearing down the wall between the secular and the sacred and helping me to see that it is all holy when YOU are in it.
Religious folk didn't get what was happening on the cross that day, nor did they care.

April

If every word of God is true, He has said
some pretty amazing things.

April 1   Tribute to Teachers

Fourteen of the most challenging and exciting years of my life were from 2005 to 2019 as a schoolteacher and administrator. I dedicate this entry to my former co-workers in both the public and private school sector—Random thoughts from my journals during those years.

>Transform futures with adventure and creativity.
>Your smile could be just what your students need today.
>Allow your opinions to be enriched by the insight of others.
>Make understanding your priority before trying to be understood.
>If a great many of your students fail at some task, leave your pride at the door and look to yourself for the solutions.
>If a child lives with praise, he learns appreciation.
>See everything. Overlook a great deal. Correct a little.
>If you give up, you give up on your students...They deserve your perseverance.
>Your successes may not always show up in the classroom... Sometimes they show up when you expect them the least and need them the most.
>Little by little does the trick. *(Abraham Lincoln)*

A heart of compassion and belief can be the very thing that causes a student to make it.

Do not work so hard for Christ that you have no strength to pray...Prayer requires strength. *(J. Hudson Taylor)*

God gave some...to be teachers... (Ephesians 4:11)

God bless all of you teachers who give your kids something to take home to think about besides homework. Love you all. *(RWJ)*

April 2   Not the End

It was Easter weekend. My eldest daughter, Chris, was seven years old. We had just come home from our Good Friday worship service (after a stop at McDonalds, of course). I can still hear her voice as she asked me the question, "Daddy, why do they call it Good Friday? Jesus died on the cross!" Hmmm...from the mouths of babes. Why, indeed. It's not called "Bad Friday;" Black Friday is that thing after Thanksgiving. GOOD FRIDAY—Jesus on the cross; His body and blood given for us. We participated that night in the Lord's Supper. The bread and the cup. We gave thanks to the Lord for Jesus' body and blood being FREELY given for us. That's what Eucharist is all about, right? Jesus said, *It is finished,* but the cross certainly wasn't the end, was it? In Christ, we have hope. What we think is final is never final in Jesus Christ. The crucifixion was not good...But the result was very, very good. The resurrection three days later capped it all off and made it absolutely and awesomely good!! My pastor stated a straightforward truth a couple of years ago—"Without Good Friday, there would be no Easter. Yeah...GOOD FRIDAY. For the

Christian, it's all good in the end. And remember if it's not good...
IT'S NOT THE END!!

> "In the cross of Christ, I glory,
> Towering o'er the wrecks of time.
> All the light of sacred story
> Gathers round its head sublime." *(Sir John Bowring)*

Random thoughts for today:

Greater love has no one than this, that someone lay down his life for his friends. (John 15:13 ESV)

Message from the Lord: Trust Me one day at a time... Tomorrow is busy worrying about itself; don't get tangled up in its worry-webs.

The greatest note of triumph ever sounded in the ears of a startled universe—*IT IS FINISHED!!*

The paschal mystery—Suffering isn't unending – Death isn't terminal – Transformation is eternal. *(Nate Loucks)*

Faith comes to the heart as we elevate our conceptions of God.

April 3   Prayerlessness

Andrew Murray once asked, "What might be the sins which made the life of the church so feeble?" Pride? Maybe. I recently listened to a message that deeply convicted me. It centered on a pride that leads to perhaps the greatest sin in the church that has made much of what the American church does today so impotent—PRAYERLESSNESS. Nothing reveals the defective spiritual life in the pastor (the average American pastor prays less than 7 minutes a day) and the life of the congregation, which has led to a lack of believing in prayer. What has become of the intense times of prayer together in the church? Why don't we do that anymore? A congregation in Jacmel, Haiti, meets at 5:00 every morning for a meeting of prayer. I have attended those meetings and been strengthened. Christians in South Korea met every Friday evening, all night, for a meeting of prayer, which many credit to be a primary reason Christianity grew there exponentially in the twentieth century from 1% in 1900 to almost 30% of the population today. Have you ever attended an all-night prayer meeting? One church member said to me, "That would be silly!" And thus, the problem. As I mentioned earlier, when the early church prayed, the building shuddered. In 1971, I was privileged to attend an all-night service of prayer in Seoul, South Korea. The congregation there wanted to pray with me and over me as I was to preach the next morning. The service the next day was to be held in a converted Buddhist temple. Prayers were lifted through the night for many non-believers to come (if only to check out the Yankee in the pulpit). We prayed for many to come to Christ. It was pretty extreme, and keep in mind there is a lot about me that is not extremist at all. Pride is probably at the root of that, more so than wisdom. The next morning, an altar call was given at the close of the service. I confess that I don't even remember what I preached that day, but more than 100 individuals responded to the invitation to trust Jesus for salvation. The leadership was praying and counseling people for three to four hours after that service. How does that happen? Maybe a more pointed question is, "WHY doesn't that happen in our churches today?"

***There is no one who calls upon Your name, LORD,
who rouses himself to take hold of You; and you have
hidden Your face from us and have made us to melt in
the hands to our sins.*** (Isaiah 64:7 NIV)

To deny that God acts to give us moral and spiritual help is
implicit atheism.

Today I don't need band-aids...I need healing.

April 4   Shall Never Die

I begin every memorial service I conduct with John 11:25-26—
*He who lives and believes in Me shall never die. Do you believe
this?* Jesus asked that question. I contend that seeking the answer
to that question is the purpose of every funeral service, whether
realized or not. The word HOPE is used over seventy times in
scripture and most references are after the resurrection account
of Jesus. Our hope is not in something but in SOMEONE...GOOD
NEWS!! Without the good news of the resurrection, we have
nothing; we find ourselves caught in the middle of a hopeless
cause. Romans 3:23 says that *all have sinned and fallen short of
the glory of God* and Romans 6:23 says *the wages of sin is death.*
Problem. It sounds like we're the proverbial cooked goose. But
our God is the God of hopeless causes. Nothing is ever over until
God says it's over. Nothing is final when you are in Jesus Christ
until He says it's final. Because of the cross and the subsequent
resurrection, this goose has been rescued. Romans 6:23 also
says, *but the gift of God is eternal life through Jesus Christ our*

Lord. Ephesians 2:8-9 tells us *for by grace we are saved through faith, and that not of ourselves; it is the gift of God lest any man boast.* Good news*!!* Its message has not changed. On this Easter morning, as I reflect upon what Jesus has done for me through the cross and as I celebrate the resurrection this day, this is a reality for me. I praise my God that He did not quit on this hopeless cause (that would be me). *Do you believe this?* Yup...I sure do, with all of my heart. HAPPY EASTER*!!*

Random thoughts for today:

Don't be afraid, for I know that you seek Jesus who was crucified. He is not here, for He is risen as He said... (Matthew 28:5-6 ESV)

We are made well by Christ alone*!!*
The spirit of fatalism isn't the way of the church...The way of the church is RESURRECTION*!! (Nate Loucks)*
Easter is not Jesus just saying, "I got this." He is also saying, "I got you!"
Death may not be cheated...But death can be defeated.

April 5   Ah, These Women

One of my daughter's favorite authors recently stated that she grew up with mixed messages regarding a woman's worth; that her church taught that women were great in their place, but that place was pretty narrow. For years I've thought about the woman's position and how it has been such a controversial subject in our churches. It's always fascinated me what we argue about, but we often default into the old "descriptive" vs. "prescriptive" debate. Various scriptures that are used (by both sides of the issue) do seem to contradict each other, and I'm not always sure how to reconcile all the scriptures that both sides so easily quote. I personally don't think they do contradict, but that's another issue. Does the fact that I have two daughters (one who is a pastor), and three granddaughters have anything to do with my position? Maybe. I don't like the term "position," but that's just the foot-dragging of one anti-pigeon-holing individual. Stop trying to put me in a box!! Sorry, digression. I know that I wouldn't be the man I am today were it not for the women in my life—My mom (the greatest Bible teacher in my life), my two grandmothers, my great-grandmother, Helen's mother, and loving teachers both in school and in the church. The Old Testament talks about heroic women who stood for the Lord. The New Testament reveals women leading the church, prophesying, teaching, and co-laboring with men. Today women are getting the gospel out in Middle Eastern countries, many under threat of death. The underground church in China is flourishing, and a vital reason is because of the leadership of women. In the acknowledgment section of this book, you will find the names of women who have influenced me. I've written brief tributes in this volume to three women who have been my life (March 7 – May 10 – June 15). I guess what I'm trying to say is that women in the church are pretty amazing. That shouldn't be a surprise; they always have been.

Random thoughts for today:

Many women have done excellently, but you surpass them all. (Proverbs 31:29 ESV)

We're not puzzled about God's will nearly as much as we are stubborn and resistant to the One who directs our steps.

In need of grace? Don't forget to extend it to someone else as well.

If 50 million people say a foolish thing, it is still a foolish thing.

If I had to describe Jesus, I'd say He has lots of pockets...And when He takes his hands out of his pockets, they have scars in them. *(8-year-old kid)*

April 6   Ah, These Choices

I have said many times to my kids, grandkids, and students, "Life is filled with choices." Every day brings new choices. Each morning as I pray for my family and friends, I always say something like, "Lord, may they make wise decisions today." We are free to make any decision that we desire, but they can become difficult when it's a choice between where you should be and where you want to be. Much of the time our options are clear. Sometimes I wonder if there are times I don't follow my own advice to my loved ones. I mean, I can't fall if I don't take a stand. I can't lose my balance if I never climb. So I can either always take the safe route, or I can hear the voice of adventure...God's adventure. Nelson Mandela used to say, "May your choices reflect your hopes, not your fears." I suppose it's an almost daily decision. Do I build that fire in the hearth or in my heart? No, not almost. It IS a daily decision to follow God's impulses. Sometimes I think it's a matter of ignoring the noise all around me and just committing to following those impulses. I don't know how often I have prayed to make a difference in the Kingdom—deciding on those things that will make a difference. Safe? Probably not. But what is?

Random thoughts for today:

...Choose this day whom you will serve...But as for me and my house, we will serve the LORD. (Joshua 24:15 ESV)

People aren't hungry for fancy sermons or organizational polish...They just want to be loved.

Lord, help me to know my students by their hearts and not their reputations.

Some days I don't feel much like praying...But I do it anyway.

You are braver than you believe, and stronger than you seem, and smarter than you think. *(A.A. Milne)*

Too often we give youth answers to remember rather than problems to solve.

In the order of the Kingdom, love of God and love of our neighbor are inseparable.

Labor to keep alive in your breast that little spark of celestial fire called conscience. *(George Washington)*

April 7   Ah, These Rabbis

Born in 1907, Abraham Joshua Heschel was a Polish-born American and one of the leading conservative Jewish theologians and Jewish philosophers of the 20th century, as well as being quite active in the civil rights movement. He believed the teachings of the Old Testament prophets were a trumpet call for social action in the United States, working for civil rights for African-Americans and against the Viet Nam war. He received his rabbinical education in Berlin, Germany. In 1938 he was arrested by the Gestapo and deported to Warsaw. He made his way to London six weeks before the Nazi invasion of Poland. His sister died in a German bombing, his mother murdered by the Nazis, and his two other sisters died in Nazi concentration camps. He never returned to Poland or Germany. He once wrote, "If I should return, every stone, every tree would remind me of contempt, hatred, murder, of children killed, of mothers burned alive, of human beings asphyxiated." He finished his life as a professor of Jewish studies and ethics at the Jewish Theological Seminary of America in New York City. He died in 1972. He was a man who deeply believed in prayer. He said, "Prayer that connects is the microcosm of the soul. It is the whole soul in one moment." He contended that it was OUR component in the communication process with the Lord. If God doesn't have the power to speak to us (and of course, He does), how should we possess the power to speak to Him? Rabbi Heschel liked to say that the real issue of prayer is not so much our prayer, but rather the reality of God. "One cannot pray unless he has faith in his ability to accost the infinite, merciful, eternal God." Praise God that we DO have that ability and right to approach the living God of the universe because of our great High Priest.

Random thoughts for today

Let us then with confidence draw near to the throne of grace, that we may receive mercy and find grace to help in time of need. (Hebrews 4:16 ESV)

No man has a good enough memory to be a successful liar. *(Abraham Lincoln)*

We need to allow the Holy Spirit to grow us to the point that love is an instinct.

I delight in learning so that I can teach. (Seneca)

April 8   Why Wasn't He Healed?

Scripture tells us that *the prayer of faith will save the one who is sick.* I shared earlier in this devotional some personal testimonies of God's healing power (March 4). Exciting. But what about those times we prayed for a healing, and it didn't occur? Was God not around? Was He not paying attention? Was our faith not sufficient; our prayers not fervent enough? What's up with that, Lord? One of my favorite preachers tells the story of being called to the hospital to pray with one of his leaders who was in a coma. The family was told he wouldn't last through the night. The preacher prayed with the family for the peaceful passing of this brother. The next morning when he came back to the hospital he was surprised to see his friend sitting up in bed. He said, "Thanks Preacher for coming up to pray with me yesterday." The preacher's response, "Don't thank me. I prayed for you to die!" I love that account. What's my answer to all of this? My answer is I don't have an answer. I have concluded that it's fruitless to try to find a solution as to why some people are healed and some are not. Much of the happenings in this journey we are all walking (or should I say, plodding) will stay a mystery until we get to the "risen life" that scripture talks about. Even though prayer doesn't always give us the answer we desire or the "miracle" we want, we find the inner resources and sometimes the strength we didn't know we had. Prayer doesn't always change our circumstances, but it does change us. I'll say it again, "Sometimes it's not the time to understand; sometimes it's just time to trust."

<u>Random thoughts for today:</u>

And the prayer of faith will save the one who is sick, and the Lord will raise him up. And if he has committed sins, he will be forgiven. (James 5:15 ESV)

I believe it's possible to read my Bible, and yet not know what it means until I hear a voice in it.

It's a general popular error to suppose the loudest complainers for the public, are the most anxious for its welfare. *(Edmund Burke)*

My best friends are the ones who bring out the best in me.

It's easy to form an attitude about the poor, the addict, the immigrant when we have no contact with them.

Humility is an accurate assessment of strengths and weaknesses. *(Rebecca Crain)*

April 9   The Singing of Angels

Have you ever been in the middle of a day, or perhaps a season of life that is saturated with drabness and the commonplace? Maybe you were in a process of hurting, healing, or grieving. Then suddenly, the sadness and the grief are shot through with something that seems to touch you where you hurt, and somehow you feel lighter, and the wounds seem to lose some of their ache. I love the following thought I picked up years ago, "There must be always remaining in every man's life someplace for the singing of angels, some place for that which in itself is breathlessly beautiful." Have you ever had a "singing with angels" experience? Maybe it was a song heard on the radio or device that just plucked that heartstring of yours (and it may have been or not have been a Christian song). Maybe it was a passage of scripture or one verse that all of a sudden reached down into the depths of your hurting. Perhaps it was a single statement made by your pastor, and you're not even sure what the rest of the sermon was about. You could have heard the "angel-singing" while standing by a lake or walking through the woods. All you are sure of is that you heard or felt the Lord communicating with you, and you know that it was a genuine God-moment. You can't orchestrate them; they just come. The tears came, and you whispered, "Thank You, Abba Father." Despite all the chaos of life, despite all of its hardness, despite all the harsh discords of life, all is made better (perhaps it's happened more than one time on your journey) by the singing of angels. I've found it to be true. There are three rules for having a God-moment, and unfortunately, no one knows what they are. I've also found that to be true.

Random thoughts for today:

And suddenly there was with the angel a multitude of the heavenly host praising God and singing, "Glory to God in the highest, and on earth peace among those with whom He is pleased. (Luke 2:13-14 ESV)

It wasn't until quite late in life that I discovered how easy it is to say, "I don't know."

Even though I am most of the time, I've noticed that God is rarely in a hurry.

Why do you want to be like everyone else when you were born to stand out?

The tragedy of life doesn't lie in not reaching your goal, but rather in having no goal at all.

April 10   God's Politics

As I write this in 2020, it's a presidential election year, an extremely confusing election year. If I didn't think the memory of my Dad would come back and haunt me, I would be tempted not to vote. Since I've been old enough to vote, I've never missed participating in an election. When I take a close look at what I believe and what issues are important to me, I feel lost between being co-opted by the right and dismissed by the left. I disagree with the religious right who mistakenly claim that God has taken a side in this election and that Christians should only vote for _____. I do not believe God is a Republican or a Democrat, and I've never been a single-issue voter. So what's an "I will not be pigeon-holed Christian" to do? I recently came across an issue statement to be considered by voters who are believers. It doesn't try to tell you how to vote, but rather issues that Christians should think about:

- Poverty—caring for the poor and vulnerable—is a Christian issue
- The environment—caring for God's earth—is a Christian issue
- War is a Christian issue
- Truth-telling is a Christian issue
- Human rights-respecting every person on the planet is a Christian issue

- A consistent ethic of the value of life is a Christian issue
- The exploitation of our faith & congregations for partisan political purposes is a Christian issue

"You can't talk about religion and politics." Yeah, you've heard that one; maybe even uttered it. OK...Let's not talk about religion or politics. Let's, instead, stand up for truth and honesty and integrity and kindness and loving and respecting one another. Let's try that for a change.

Random thoughts for today:

I urge prayers and intercessions...for kings and all who are in high positions, that we may lead a peaceful and quiet life, godly and dignified in every way. (1 Timothy 2:2 ESV)

The liberty of the press consists in the right to publish with impunity truth with good motives, for justifiable ends. *(Alexander Hamilton)*

Without a sense of caring, there can be no sense of community.

One reason we have difficulty connecting with God is that we are too noisy.

April 11   Forsaking the Assembly

This Easter season (2020), combined with the ongoing COVID-19 lockdown all over the world, has brought about an interesting controversy. What about church services? Hebrews 10:25 tells the church *not to neglect to meet together as is the habit* *of some.* But the President of the United States and the Center for Disease Control has asked our houses of worship to shut down and that there be no assemblies of over ten people. Our governor, as well as most other state governors, have complemented that request with their own bans. That's not to say that the churches haven't been meeting. Thanks to technology, watch groups and worship chat get-togethers have been formed. Many churches across the country have recorded worship services and put them online for members of their congregations. Some churches in our part of the state have hosted "drive-in" services in their parking lots. I just recorded a message for a Good Friday service for our church broadcast over the internet. It's been exciting to see imagination and creativity come alive in bringing Christians together to worship. So, what's the controversy? Some pastors have openly defied the bans and insisted on holding their worship services. A number of these congregations have been good-sized churches with over a thousand meeting together at one time. A few pastors have been arrested for defying local bans and have stated that they are "taking a stand for the Lord." One pastor said, "Satan and a virus will not stop us!" Another leader said that Christians should be glad to sacrifice their lives (if they get the virus) defending their faith and their freedom of worship. Without getting into the whole "freedom of worship" discussion, I see a little problem here. I don't find any scripture admonition that says that I have to worship in an official church building with hundreds of people in order to honor the Lord. I look forward to joining together with our church family again(*), but in the meantime, I am not only free to worship, but I have been and will continue to worship my Lord. As one of the ancient writers once said, "What makes all the difference is WHO you worship, not how you worship.

(*)The little congregation where I preach reopened in June, 2020.

<u>Random thoughts for today:</u>

Singing psalms and hymns and spiritual songs, singing and making melody to the Lord with all your heart, giving thanks always and for everything to God. (Ephesians 5:19-20 ESV)

The prime need of the church is not men of money or men of brains, but men and women of prayer.

April 12   The Power of Touch

I confess it...I am a hugger! Even though it is no longer politically correct and considered by many to be inappropriate, I believe strongly in the power of touch. *And Jesus, moved with compassion, put forth His hand, and touched him, and said, "Be clean"* (Mark 1:41). I won't even get into the issue of the fact Jesus was touching a leper, which was uber-politically incorrect in his day. I have always communicated with touch—a hug, a squeeze of the arm, a hand on the shoulder—It's who I am. Because of the climate of our culture today, I have had to work hard to not do this, especially in my work in the schools (and I understand that). But when you see a youngster (or an adult for that matter) hurting or in need, it's difficult not to reach out. And then comes the "social-distancing" ethos of the COVID-19 pandemic. I hate to tell the CDC, but our nation has been practicing social-distancing for a number of years now, and it goes a lot deeper than physical touch. But I digress. So, no hugging, no touching, no handshaking, and stay at least six feet apart at all times. The first Sunday at my home church in LaPorte, after social-distancing was introduced by the CDC, it was weird. Hand sanitizers all over the building, especially at the welcome center. Waving, elbow-bumping, fist-bumping, everyone kind of joking about it all. At the end of the service, a man approached me in the foyer, and I could tell he was struggling. I have to confess that I didn't even know his name. With watery eyes, he said, "Pastor Jones, I know we're social-distancing and all, but can I hug you?" At that moment, I thought of Jesus and the leper, and we hugged. That was the last service before churches closed for a while. Today, in the midst of all of the news reports concerning the coronavirus (that was about all the news being reported), Dr. Anthony Fauci, physician and immunologist of the White House COVID-19 commission, made this statement—"When the pandemic is over the new normal will be compulsive hand-washing and the end of handshaking in our society." And that's probably the saddest thing I've heard all day.

Random thoughts for today:

For she said, "If I touch even His garments, I will be made well." (Mark 5:28 ESV)

You must be the change you want to see in the world.

Lord, give me ways to show others Your love today through my obedience.

We don't see things as they are...We see them as we are.

The difference between ordinary and extraordinary is that little extra!!

Sometimes I learn slowly; sometimes, wisdom comes hard. But through the years, I have learned some effective ways to praise kids. I think the Lord has schooled me through my experiences as a youth pastor, a children's pastor, a juvenile probation officer, a schoolteacher, an administrator, and oh yes, a dad and a grandpa. Here are some gems of phrases I've found to bring excellent results:

> That's incredible; great – Outstanding performance – I can't get over it – Unbelievable work – Phenomenal; excellent – You're special – Way to go – You've outdone yourself - Terrific – Fabulous – The time you put into this really shows – It couldn't be better – Exceptional – Fantastic work – Awesome (I think "amazing" has replaced this word today) – Keep up the good work – What an imagination – Stupendous – A+ work – Take a bow - Super job!!

In working with kids, I've kept a truth in mind that has driven me, for what seems like forever. It's a phrase I've kept in the flyleaf of one of my much-used devotional books.

<u>Right Living</u>

> "The dogged commitment to do the right thing in the face of a world which presents innumerable opportunities and overwhelming pressures to do the wrong thing." (*Unknown*)

You know, I just read over those above phrases again, and I think they probably will be just as effective with some adults you know as well.

Random thoughts for today:

...Do not provoke your children to anger... (Ephesians 6:4 ESV)

Any fool can criticize, condemn, and complain—And most fools do. *(Ben Franklin)*

Keep your mouth closed and you'll stay out of trouble. #Proverbs

Where is the knowledge we have lost in information?

LOVE—No specific rules...The most we can do is sign on as its accomplice.

Perfect vs. Flawed—A good garden may have some weeds.

April 14   Prayer in a Pandemic

The following prayer started circulating on the internet in April 2020. I don't know its origin. I do know that hundreds in our region of the country shared it.

"Eternal Father, You made the whole World stop spinning for a while.
You silenced the noise that we all have created.
You made us bend our knees
again and ask for a Miracle.

You closed Your Churches so we will realize how dark our World is without You in it.

You humbled the proud
and powerful.
The economy is crashing,
businesses are closing.
We were very proud,
we thought that everything
we have, everything we
possess, was the result of
our hard work.
We have forgotten that it was always Your grace and mercy that made us who we are.

We're running in circles looking for some cure to this disease, when in fact we need to humble ourselves and ask You for guidance and wisdom.

We've been living our lives like we will be here on Earth forever, like there's no Heaven.
Maybe these trials are Your
mercy in disguise.
Maybe this virus is actually
Your way of purifying us, &
cleansing our soul, bringing
us back to YOU.

Today as these words travel the internet, may all who see them join their hearts and hands together in prayer! Asking for forgiveness & asking for healing & protection from this virus... GOD just wipe it from the Earth!

Father You have been patiently waiting for us. We're so sorry for ignoring Your voice... and in our selfish ways, we've sometimes forgotten that YOU are GOD!

You only need to say the words and our souls shall all be healed. We ask these things in Jesus name!...Amen"

April 15   The Best at Being the Worst

"This is probably the most dangerous time in the history of our nation." No it isn't. "This is the most divisive time we've experienced ever." No it isn't. "But, Rick, the negativity in our culture is all around us. We've never been so divided." Yeah, today we think we're the best at being the worst. That seems pretty arrogant to me. Have you ever heard of the Civil War (1861-1865)? In the 1960s, kids protested; they hated their country, their school, their parents, and yes, religion. There were three major assassinations during the 60s, including the President of the United States. Since then, there were three attempted assassinations upon two Presidents and a presidential candidate (George Wallace). Interesting fact: a few weeks before the Wallace shooting, the same guy carried a firearm into an event intending to assassinate Richard Nixon but was put off by strong security (Sorry, this is the history teacher coming out). Unfortunately, fueled by conspiracy theories, partisan politicians, a media (right and left) not driven by integrity, and religious leaders driven by a convoluted interpretation of scripture, we are surrounded by those who believe it's never been this bad. "But, Rick, this whole pandemic is unprecedented." At this writing, approximately 200,000 have perished globally. During the 1918 Spanish flu epidemic, it's estimated that about one-third of the world's population was infected. The global death toll was around 50 million, depending upon what source you're using in your research. Whether you're listening to politicians, medical experts or whoever, we have become confused, and confusion leads to negativity. One modern-day columnist wrote, "I think this country has had enough of experts from organizations with acronyms, saying they know what's best, and getting it consistently wrong." Maybe. My favorite phrase continues to be, "It may not be a time for understanding; it may be one of those moments to trust." Much of the time, our understanding is limited, and we have to trust our Abba Father to know best. One old-timer said, "Don't worry; it can get worse." I think I prefer the words of the 91st Psalm ESV—*He who dwells in the shelter of the Most High will abide in the shadow of the Almighty. I will say the LORD, "My refuge and my fortress, my God, in whom I trust"* (vv 1-2). I don't know what next year will hold. I don't know what's coming tomorrow. But I do know the Lord has promised to walk with me a day at a time. That's security, my friend.

Random thoughts for today:

   ...and there's nothing new under the sun. (Ecclesiastes 1:9 ESV)

   God defines our "needs" a little differently than I define them for myself.
   You have a tell-tale heart; it lets everyone know by your actions whose needs you put first.

Luci Swindoll uses the phrase, "Don't edit your prayers." I really love that! She uses the example of a child blurting out his thoughts spontaneously when asking something of his mother. Sometimes I've found myself preparing the words of my prayers before the Lord. I see nothing wrong with using prepared prayers in some circumstances, but the danger is putting too much emphasis upon words and phraseology rather than the words of my heart. I've used it before, but I love the quotation of C. H. Spurgeon—"True prayer is measured by weight, not by length. A single groan before God may have more fulness of prayer in it than a fine oration of great length." Billy Graham said, "Remember, prayer is simply talking to God." Passion is not necessarily eloquence. The one great passion in the life of our Savior was His Father. Is the Lord my one great passion in life? When I am passionately talking to my Abba Father, do I prepare my thoughts ahead of time to make sure I pray correctly or to not say something that might be offensive to Him? No!! I know that my Father is much more concerned about my heart than He is my eloquence. My grandson, Christian, served as editor of this book to help prepare the pages to be published and presented to you. An editor is defined as "a person who edits, selects, and revises material for publication." I don't need an editor for my prayer time. Nor do you. Be honest, be real, be true to yourself, and pour out your heart to Him. It doesn't matter if the words don't come out right. He knows your heart. Once again, your prayer partner, the Holy Spirit, has your back.

Trust in Him at all times...Pour out your heart before Him. (Psalm 62:8 ESV)

Today the heart of God is an open wound of love.

Wisdom is what's left after we've run out of personal opinions.

Character is better than wealth. *(Irish Proverb)*

Lord, keep my anger from becoming meanness.

God's business is putting things right—Psalm 19:7

Two basic loves—The love of God unto the forgetfulness of self, or the love of self, unto the forgetfulness and denial of God. *(Augustine)*

April 17   Crises Crossroads

In the process of faith, doubts and crises must occur. I like what Paul Tillich says about faith. He says that doubt is not the opposite of faith, but rather one element of faith. I remember a college professor I had who made the statement, "There is faith in honest doubt." I can still hear his voice; those words still ring in my heart. I have learned that it is only through crises that my faith can grow and mature. For the term "crisis," the Chinese use two different characters—the character for "danger," and the one for "opportunity." There are those crossroads times in my life that demand choices—the crossroads of danger and opportunity. When we come to a crisis on our journey, are we confident in the midst of it as we trust in the Lord? Or do we regress to child-like prayers of panic that are no different than those who do not even know God? We reveal who we really are when we face a crisis. Tillich also says that it is doubt that eats away at our old relationship with God, but only so that a new one may be born. Remember, this faith thing is a process. As I was growing into adulthood, it was unsettling to me how many times the older generation would question my walk with Jesus. They seemed to be quite uncomfortable with my crises of faith, as if I shouldn't have any of those. My favorite proverb comes to mind—*Trust the LORD with all your heart and lean not on your own understanding. Acknowledge Him in all your ways, and He will make your path straight.* (Proverbs 3:5-6 NIV). At a crossroads? Keep your focus on Him...HE CAN BE TRUSTED!!

Random thoughts for today:

Why are you afraid, O you of little faith? (Matthew 8:26 ESV)

What a joy to discover what it means to live by grace and not performance.

On with the dance and let the joy be unconfined when there's any dance to dance or any joy to unconfine. *(Mark Twain)*

No failure, but low aim is the crime.

The primary purpose of prayer is not necessarily to change things, but rather to change me.

You cannot discover new oceans unless you have the courage to lose sight of the shore.

I sat in a class in my church this past year on the Book of Revelation. I've never quite understood the great interest of church people to continually study that particular book of the Bible. I've always shied away from such classes, but the teacher was a friend of mine whom I respect, and I thought to myself, "Why not?" Revelation studies cause me discomfort, not because I'm not ready for apocalyptic happenings, but because we "pre-millennialists" (I haven't decided whether that's what I am or not) like to give the impression that we have all our ducks-in-a-row and definitely have a handle on the end times. May I confess to you that I don't possess that kind of grip. I remember having some individuals leaving the church where I preached at one time because I wouldn't choose a millennial position and preach it with passion. Now, as a result of global crisis, conspiracy theorists are once again coming out of the woodwork touting "Christian" nationalism as they try to make symbols from Revelation match specific events in history. And let's not forget to throw Nostradamus into the mix. We are living in the midst of a time that is hyped-up for anxiety and fear. There is certainly no shortage of false prophets out there ready to pronounce their messages of doom. Is it possible that these "prophets" could be right in their assertions? Perhaps. Brennan Manning says, "The messianic bean counters and spin doctors may be correct in their dire ultimatum." But then again, Jesus said He didn't know the *day or the hour* (Matthew 24:36), so our modern-day prophet friends might be confused. This is my millennial position—The world as we know it will end – Jesus is coming back – We are to be ready and busy, not in spreading fear, but in sharing the hope of the Gospel. Kingdom work, my friends!!

Random thoughts for today:

Therefore, keep watch because you do not know the day or the hour. (Matthew 25:13 NIV)

You don't always need a plan...Sometimes you just need to breathe, trust, let go, and see what happens.

Silence can provide a haven and allow your own melodies to flourish.

In the long haul, we pray only as well as we live.

A well-timed silence can have more power than speech.

Intelligence without ambition is like a bird without wings.

April 19   Rights?

If there is one thing my culture has taught me, it is my right to fight for my rights. Hey, I'm a retired government and history teacher, and I know my constitutional rights to pursue life, liberty, and happiness (per the Declaration of Independence). And the battle for "rights" rages on!! I am guaranteed the freedom to choose. Freedom of religion, freedom of speech, and freedom to assemble. I demand the freedom to live as I please, and COVID-19 be damned. We are free in Christ, right? I do have a difficult time, however, picturing Jesus demanding His rights. He certainly did not do so at the cross. As a believer, the scripture teaches me _to love because He first loved me_ (1 John 4:19). James talks about the royal law of love in chapter two of his letter. I am saved by grace, and my life is to be guided by the Holy Spirit. But wait, am I not allowed to speak my mind? I have the freedom to share my political views, but what if I stir up fear and anxiety in those afraid of the future? Paul writes that we need to make sure the exercise of our so-called rights doesn't cause others to trip over that "freedom." He says, *Decide never to put a stumbling block or hindrance in the way of a brother* (Romans 14:13). He says that if we do hinder a brother, *we are no longer walking in love.* I sometimes wonder how many times the original hearers (or readers) of Paul's teaching were left wondering, "Are you serious?" Yeah, he really was. Lay down your rights today. How about encouraging others along in their journey? Let love guide you in all that you do. Hey, Church...Your words and actions impact others more than you know. I think today I will exercise my right, no wait, my responsibility to encourage you.

Random thoughts for today:

Take care that this right of yours does not somehow become a stumbling block to the weak. (I Corinthians 8:9 ESV)

Will Jesus make a difference today in my attitudes, actions, activities, ambitions, and associations? May it be so.

Keep me awake and sensitive to what is going on around me... Living in the present tense.

It takes a long time to become young. *(Picasso)*

Don't claim to be a representative of Jesus unless you are representing Jesus.

I often pray, "Lord, You see me as I am, right now. You see me at my blackest times, and you stand beside me. You are faithful, even when I am not." Surprise! All is not sweetness in our lives on a daily basis. It's easy to be happy (and hopefully honest) before the Lord as we lift our praises to Him, but it becomes a lot more challenging to be honest with God when we are hurting. Through the years, I have struggled with honesty in my prayer life because of the human tendency to repress the negative. I became quite good at that. I think that studying and spending more time in the Psalms in these later years has helped me toward a more honest relationship with my Abba Father. I guess I need to use David as a role-model. He let it all out when he talked to God, and you know what...God can handle it. I resonate with Eugene Peterson's comment, "We must pray who we actually are, not who we think we are, not who we think we should be." I love the old hymn by Thomas Obadiah Chisholm, written in the mid-19th century:

> "Great is Thy faithfulness Great is Thy faithfulness
> Morning by morning new mercies I see
> All I have needed Thy hand hath provided
> Great is Thy faithfulness, Lord unto me"

Lord, help me to give even my darkest times to You.

Random thoughts for today:

If I ascend to heaven, you are there! If I make my bed in Sheol (or "Hades"; literally, "place of darkness"), ***you are there!*** (Psalm 139:8 ESV)

Never doubt that a small group of committed people can change the world...It's really the only thing that ever has.

No one creed or school of theology or experience can monopolize the Spirit of God.

Keep a green tree in your heart, and a singing bird may come. *(Chinese Proverb)*

Even the toughest dogs can be afraid of vacuum-cleaners.

There is a God...And it is not me.

April 21   Writer's Block?

The last few years, I have been studying writers and their works. I've been taking a class that has been quite helpful in learning new lessons. This study has helped me on this journey we call life. For example:

If writing seems hard, it's because it is hard.

Christianity isn't all that complicated, but sometimes it's very hard.

Don't be a writer; be writing

Don't call yourself a Christian; live every day as a Christian.

You want to be a writer...You must write every day!!

You want to make a difference for Christ; live out the gospel every day.

A writer never has a vacation.

A believer never takes a vacation from living for Jesus.

And then there are those words of wisdom about writing that need no commentary; you can make the application without any problem:

Develop craftsmanship through years of discipline and practice.

Exercise those writing muscles every day.

Heart makes the eloquence.

And my favorite:

The author must keep his mouth shut when inspiration starts to speak.

Random thoughts for today:

You are our living letter, written on our hearts to be known and read by all…a letter from Christ…written not with ink, but with the Spirit of the living God… (2 Corinthians 3:2-3 ESV)

The more elaborate our means of communication, the less we communicate.

We get so much information overload that we lose our common sense.

Oswald Chambers often speaks of praying and living the ordinary. He says we have to be exceptional in the ordinary things. Colossians 1:27 ESV declares, *Christ in you, the hope of glory!* Paul refers to this as the "mystery" of the gospel. So there's no task too mundane or ordinary for the Lord in you, *the hope of glory.* In his book, *Practicing the Presence of God,* Brother Lawrence (known as Lawrence of the Resurrection) wrote about the spirituality of everyday tasks. This man, who never attained a position of pastor or priest, writes about his ministry of dirty dishes. Lawrence says, "The time of this business (referring to his dish-washing) does not with me differ from the time of prayer, and in the noise and clatter of my kitchen, I possess God in as great tranquility as if I were upon my knees before the Blessed Sacrament." This brother encourages me, not just because I've always disliked washing dishes, but because he reminds me of the deep calling on the lives of ordinary followers of Christ. We tend to not fully appreciate the greater percentage of people who do not work occupationally in the church but have a tremendous commitment to following Jesus. They are, excuse my repetition, followers because they passionately follow. Oswald sums it up— "We are not made for the mountains, for sunrises, or for the other beautiful attractions in life. Those are simply intended to be moments of inspiration. We are made for the valley and the ordinary things of life. That is where we have to prove our stamina and strength." Praise God for the ministry of dish-washing.

<u>Random thoughts for today</u>:

Whether you eat or drink, or whatever you do, do all to the glory of God. (1 Corinthians 10:31 ESV)

Many of us are wanting Jesus to look more like us rather than us looking more like Jesus.

I notice God is never in a hurry...I'm thankful for those times when I can just "drift along" with Him.

The key to good decision-making is not knowledge...It's understanding.

Give a little love to a child, and you get a great deal back.

Hope is the anthem. *(Switchfoot)*

April 23   Hope's Good

Seriously, how can any of us live our lives without hope? Someone has said, "We can live forty days without food, eight days without water, four minutes without air, but only a few seconds without hope." Give humanity hope, and it will be ready to suffer much. Give me hope, and I can smile on my worst day. One theologian said, "Hope is the parent of faith." Wait a minute, that might have been the author of Hebrews—*Faith is the assurance of things hoped for...*(Hebrews 11:1). In the midst of COVID-19, I personally believe that our media outlets have failed miserably by fostering more fear than hope. Starting each evening's broadcast with the current death count and with reporters wearing face-masks and portraying their "we're all gonna die" somber countenance, has not given people a whole lot of hope. There have been some bright rays of sunshine through all of this, however.

Actor John Krasinski put together his own broadcasts from home, SGN ("Some Good News"), highlighting some pretty cool things happening around the world, especially people doing cool stuff for each other. You know, stuff like being kind and helping one another, birthday parades and teacher caravans past homes, virtual church services and graduation ceremonies online, teachers going above and beyond for their students, people picking up groceries for the elderly or sick, individuals donating their government stimulus checks to others in need, and so much more. This past week in several of communities, there have been military flyovers to express appreciation and thanks to all the health-care workers who have ministered beyond what has been normally expected of them. One friend of mine expressed displeasure over the expense of such "idiocy" when we could use that money for something important. You know what? Spreading hope is pretty important. Hope is that extraordinary grace that God gives us to control our fears. You may remember that little kid in that old McDonalds commercial years ago when he stated, "HOPE'S GOOD!!"

> **O Lord, my God, when the storm is loud, and the night is dark, and the soul is sad, and the heart oppressed; then, as a weary traveler, may I look to you; and beholding the light of Your love, may it bear me on, until I learn to sing Your song in the night. Amen. (*The Little Book of Prayers* by George Dawson)**

Random thoughts for today:

Hope deferred makes the heart sick, but a desire fulfilled is a tree of life. (Proverbs 13:12 NIV)

We talked of hopes and dreams, watched the fire, and just enjoyed each other's company in the silence of the night. *(Journal entry about my grandson, Christian)*

April 24   Homework

How often have we been guilty of not doing our homework? I'm not talking about high-school stuff; I'm talking about life stuff. In the age of "fake news" and social media, it probably has become even more critical that we do our homework. We live in the era of Snopes, PolitiFact, FactCheck, and Hoax-Slayer. There has always been a need to double-check so-called "facts" presented by the experts, but thanks to the internet, we have witnessed the rise of the fact check website. Fairly often, I have had to gently remind friends and acquaintances to check their sources. "Have you done your homework?" Even though we pass along things about people we don't know personally, it is not automatically excusable to share "internet gossip." Bill Bullard (local politician on the west coast) says, "Opinion is really the lowest form of human knowledge. It requires no accountability, no understanding. The highest form of knowledge is empathy, for it requires us to suspend our egos and live in another's world." Thanks, Bill; I relate to that. And what happens every day in the media world has been happening in our churches forever. We have opinions, but often are short on facts—"Well, I know it's in the Bible somewhere!" Many Christians remain caught between ignorance and truth because we don't avail ourselves to the discipline of study. We don't do our homework. And it's not just intellectual. I had a prof in college that said we don't have enough formative reading in our churches, literally "form-receiving."

We may sing with passion and even have scripture memorized, but our lives remain unchanged. Have you ever pondered over a passage of scripture and allowed it to permeate your spirit? How often do you allow the Word of God to change your life? Have you ever read ideas that may differ from a position you've taken and held onto for years and tried to see where this "heretic" is coming from? Have you asked the Holy Spirit to guide you in your Bible study? It was a rabbi from Nazareth that said knowledge of the truth is what will set us free. I like the words of Alexander Pope— "Some people will never learn anything, because they understand everything too soon."

Random thoughts for today:

Now the Berean Jews were of more noble character than those in Thessalonica, for they received the message with great eagerness and examined the Scriptures every day to see if what Paul said was true.. (Acts 17:11 NIV)

We are the church...We are a bunch of "used-to-be" people.

A person's character should be used to discern the value of his words.

April 25   Wordless Prayers

How do I pray for a dead-end marriage where abuse has happened again and again? How do I intercede for a child diagnosed with terminal cancer? How do I talk to the Lord about Christians in the Middle East who are being persecuted, even to the point of gruesome execution? I know the frustration of not knowing how to pray; when the only words that come are, "Lord, I don't know how to pray!" How can I pray? What do I ask for? There are days that I can't open my prayer journal and start praying through my prayer lists. There are times that words themselves get in the way of my prayers. There are times that it is so hard to express what I actually feel. What words do I use to address my Abba Father? Maybe it's not so much about words; perhaps it's about communicating the heart. I've talked about it before, but occasionally our prayer-time becomes more of a groan-recitation than a praise-fest. Sometimes those simple phrases can focus your attention on God. My hour of prayer can and has become a succession of pleadings and phrases—"Oh, Lord" – "Abba, help me" – "Why, God" – "I don't know what to do" – "Please" – And sometimes, it's just the Lord and I sitting silently in the darkness of the morning. I can tell you that these moments can bring great peace and tranquility during times of confusion and uncertainty. And they have.

Thank You, Lord, for Your Holy Spirit who intercedes for me, even when I don't know what to pray. Amen.

Random thoughts for today:

...the Spirit himself intercedes for us with groanings too deep for words. (Romans 8:26 ESV)

I think when you pray, you're supposed to wipe your tears at His feet or something like that. *(A 9-year-old kid)*

Our lives begin to end the day we become silent about things that matter.

He will provide a way out of temptation...(1 Corinthians 10:13)...But many of us aren't looking for a way out.

Jesus is the lens through which we understand the Bible.

Many of us are willing to embark upon any adventure except to go into stillness and wait.

April 26   What's Next?

Have you ever really looked at the Parable of the Tenants (Matthew 21:33-46)? If you're not familiar with it, maybe you could read it right now before you go any further. Jesus tells a story; He was a story-teller, after all. He knew that a lot of times, without a story, we just don't get it. There's no doubt that this is a parable of the last days. The truth is, Jesus has promised to return. I believe that this is also a cautionary parable to the leadership of the church. It's a solemn responsibility to be a leader in God's church. I've said for years that our authority as leaders comes from our example. In writing to leaders, Peter says, *He who trusts in Him will never be put to shame* (1 Peter 2:6). But I also believe that this story is a "What's Next" parable. As I study it, I find myself asking, "As a follower of Jesus Christ, what IS my responsibility? What's next for me?" How I answer that question affects how I live the rest of my life. I only act upon the things I truly believe. We become like that which we truly worship. We may think we're calling the shots and running the show, but the Landlord is still in charge. A young man was visiting with his grandpa, and his grandfather asks him, "So, John, you graduate from high school this week. What's next?" John responds, "Well, I'm enrolled at Purdue University; start in the Fall." And the conversation continues—"That's great, John; what's next?" "I'm going to get my bachelor's in Economics." "Good; what's next?" "I plan to get my master's degree in business." "Then what, John; what's next?" "Well, I plan to get a job with a business firm and begin working my way up. Eventually, I'd like to start my own company and build it up." "Sounds like a plan, John; what's next?" "Well, I suppose I'll get married, have kids, and get involved in the community." "Good, John, good; then what?" "Well, I plan to retire; I want to have a great retirement fund so that I can live comfortably in my later years." "John, it looks like you've given a lot of thought to this; good goals. What's next?" To which John responded, "Well, grandpa—I guess I'll die." After a pause, grandpa smiles and says, "What's next?" Yup! The Landlord's still in charge!!

Random thoughts for today:

Finally, he sent his son to them, saying, "They will respect my son." (Matthew 21:37 ESV)

Why are there days when I can't seem to break through the clouds of my heart?

Father, give me confidence when You give me answers...Give me peace when You don't.

The greatest thoughts come from the heart.

I don't believe we can always define or label the experiences that come to us, good or bad.

They are one of my favorite couples at our church. Let's call them Jim and Cindy. Cindy is our church secretary, and she posted an interesting item on Facebook a few years ago. They were at the top of the observation tower at Washington Park Zoo in Michigan City—It's a landmark that's been around since the New Deal. Cindy's perspective of their long trek up the tower—"What a beautiful view!" Jim's perspective—"What a great sniper's nest this would make!" I should tell you that Jim is in law enforcement. I heard a radio preacher (can't remember who it was) say a few years ago, "We want God's perspective to be to place us as His number one priority; our perspective is to place Him as an optional priority." An interesting thing, perspective. So, what's your faith-perspective? When my wife and I were first married, we had a little saying that we would throw at each other, especially when the going got a little dicey. One of us would ask, "How big is your God? And the other would respond, "As big as your faith." It's been said that "faith is engaging in the deepest joy of heaven, knowing His unfathomable love for me as I walk through the desolate now" (Chuck Swindoll). In the account of the woman touching the hem of Jesus' robe to be healed (Mark 5:25-34), you have a throng of people pressing up against Jesus, bumping up against Him, rubbing shoulders with Him. Then there is this poor sick woman who touches the hem of his garment, expecting a healing. Perspective. Quite amazing when you think about it, jostling up against *the One in whom all the Godhead dwells*, and yet no one received a miracle, even though they touched and crowded Him. Isn't that like us at times? We walk into church, sing a few songs, raise our hands and hearts toward heaven, and pray and worship in His presence. Jesus did say that where two or three are gathered in His name that He would be in our midst. Yet we often only rub shoulders with Him, shake hands with our friends and go out the door unchanged. Another ho-hum Sunday...Let's have lunch. Isn't it incredible how we can be in His amazing presence and be so unaware of His mighty power; often too preoccupied to notice that maybe God wants to speak to us or move in our midst? Perspective. Perhaps you need that special touch from the Lord today. Has illness or trouble or circumstance overtaken you, and you are hurt, lonely, or hopeless? Is your spirit lacking peace? Are you living a faithless life? A life without faith is like driving through a fog. Don't be satisfied to "rub shoulders" with the Lord. Reach out and touch Him with a touch of faith. How big is your God? AS BIG AS YOUR FAITH.

Random thoughts for today:

"Daughter, your faith has made you well; go in peace, and be healed..." (Mark 5:34 ESV)

If 50 million people say a foolish thing, it is still a foolish thing.

If you think you're a servant, check your reaction the next time you're treated like one.

April 28   Animals

Francis of Assisi once said, "If you have men who will exclude any of God's creatures from the shelter of compassion and pity, you will have men who will deal likewise with their fellow men." Show me how a man treats animals, and I will tell you volumes about his character. In Genesis, chapter one, we read how God made all of these wonderful creatures, and for the first time in the creation account, the notion of "blessing" appears in verse 1:22. Scripture says that the blessing of these animals would be a delight for humanity. I can't speak to the theology of this, but I have a veterinarian friend who believes with all of his heart that animals will be in heaven. Why not? A few years ago, I was asked by good friends to come to their farm and speak at a "barn-blessing." Darlene runs a boarding stable for horses. If you know Dar, you know she has a passionate love for animals of all kinds. I think the last time I talked with her, she was presently boarding 30 plus horses. I love plants and flowers, but you can't spend an exciting, insightful day with a rhododendron bush, but you can with a horse. A horse has a mind and emotions and a will. I don't own a horse. I've ridden, but I am certainly no expert at it. When Helen and I go to the county fair, our first stop is always the horse barn. I think I will have always have a fascination with these animals because of God's promise to me as a faithful follower of Jesus, and that promise involves a horse. Revelation 19:11-16 says, *I saw heaven standing open and there was before me a white horse, whose rider is called Faithful and True...The armies of heaven were following Him, riding on white horses...On His robe and on His thigh He has this name written: King of kings and Lord of lords.* Remember the white horse...God's promise to us!!

Random thoughts for today:

Whoever is righteous has regard for the life of his beast... (Proverbs 12:10 ESV– Translation: "The godly man cares for his animals.")

Do we love the way Jesus loved? When people see this kind of love, they sit up and take notice...One way or another, they will respond.

Lord, may I be about Your business...It is that business that will matter 100 years from now.

Kindness begets kindness evermore. *(Sophocles)*

God made man in His own image and man returned the compliment. *(Blaise Pascal)*

April 29   What Fills You?

Pneumatology is what theologians call the study of the Holy Spirit. I have always struggled with practically trying to understand the Trinity as a whole, but there's no doubt that the Spirit has always been the least understood of the three members of the Godhead. Invisible, confusing, maybe a bit eerie. The Holy Spirit is often referred to as "it"; earlier generations called Him the Holy Ghost. Why can so many talk about the theology of the Spirit, but when it comes to the practical application of Him in our lives, we look like a deer caught in the headlights? I'll tell you why I think we struggle with the Holy Spirit. It's because dry theological facts apart from the power of the Spirit of God are boring. Why should I get excited in learning about the elements of the Holy Spirit when the evidence of His power are absent? Who cares if you can define His presence and His work in scripture if He's not working in your life? So what if you know He is the Paraclete if the fruit of the Spirit is not pouring out of you? There's a lot I don't know about the work of the Spirit, and I don't lose a bit of sleep over it, but here's what I do know:

1. When Jesus bodily left this planet, He left His Holy Spirit in charge.
2. When the church first started, it was the Holy Spirit that was the POWER.
3. When I gave my life to Jesus, I was given the gift of the Holy Spirit to guide me.
4. The Spirit lives inside of me today, but I must allow Him to FILL me daily.

My daily prayer is, "Lord, more of You; less of me." When He is filling me, I am able to live in the Spirit of God. Some of us may be full of it, but it's not the Spirit we're full of; that's been the case in my life many times. One of my pastors said, "Don't cheapen your life by the stuff you are swigging, but rather drink in the Spirit of God." What are you full of today?

Random thoughts for today:

And do not get drunk with wine...but be filled with the Spirit. (Ephesians 5:18 ESV)

A leader is a dealer in hope.
We need to work harder at finding joy in our days.
Ministry that costs me nothing accomplishes nothing.
Wherever I go, whatever I do, may the Lord be in the middle of it all.

It's easier to carry my Bible and say I believe it, than it is to live it. It's easier to talk about prayer than it is to have a prayer life. It's easier to theorize or get academic or debate the Holy Spirit than it is to live in the Spirit. I scratched the surface of this yesterday. *Be filled with the Spirit!* Allow Him to daily fill you with His life, His thoughts, His love, and His fruit. More of You, Lord, and less of me. I can remember talking to my eldest daughter when she was in elementary school about making the right choices in life. Her comment—"Daddy, you're really weird!" There was no way her little grammar school mind could comprehend how much I loved her, just as there is no way we can comprehend how much God loves us. Maybe we can think some of the words of our Abba Father are weird. Perhaps we wonder at times what our Father is doing. We question His work in our lives, and yes, sometimes His love. But then I hear His words—*I have loved you with an everlasting love* (Jeremiah 31:3). You know, Romans 5:8—*God SHOWED His love toward us in that while we were yet sinners, Christ died for us.* What can I say to that kind of emotion being poured out upon me? Note that the apostle Paul doesn't get into academic statements or theological treatises here. He simply explodes in gratitude with the truth of God's love. I remember talking to a classroom of teenagers a few years ago. It went something like this: "Your parents may blow it sometimes. Your teachers may tick you off sometimes. Your siblings may be ashamed of you. The world may dump on you. But within reach of our prayers is the Maker of the universe...OUR GOD REIGNS!! God is FOR you... Not may be...Not has been...Not was...Not would be...But GOD IS FOR YOU...Now – Today – At this hour. His loyalty won't increase if you're a better person, nor will it lessen if you blow it and really screw up. It's called grace. Read John 3:16; I mean READ it and embrace it. That's how God feels about you. Think about that the next time you're acting all cool and bad and tip-toeing around in your sin and foolishness." Because you are in Christ, because of the way Jesus has embraced you, is there anything that can get between you and His love? NOPE!! Paul says, *In all these things we are more than conquerors through Him who loved us.*

Random thoughts for today:

What then shall we say to these things? If God is for us, who can be against us? (Romans 8:31 ESV)

I strive to be a man of integrity so that my children and grandchildren will be blessed for it.

If we learn to be honest before God, it also helps us learn to be honest with each other.

May

What am I full of? What leaks out of my life?

May 1   Golden Rule

Have you noticed that so many lives today are like one grand selfie? One of the most important things my Dad taught me growing up is that there are more important things than me. That's what Jesus was getting at when he preached the Sermon on the Mount. And he sums it all up in a very few words (23 to be exact) God's law in a nutshell—*So in everything, do to others what you would have them do to you, for this sums up the Law and the Prophets* (Matthew 7:12 NIV). Treat others the way I want to be treated. In other words, Jesus teaches us to put ourselves in our neighbor's place, then conduct ourselves accordingly. Treat other people as though you were the other people. Interestingly enough, I've found similar teachings in the writings of Jewish rabbi Hillel, Socrates, Buddha, and Confucius. Still, as I compare what they wrote to Jesus' words, I find a fundamental difference. Essentially, these men state their "golden rule" in a negative approach—"Do NOT do to others what you would NOT have done to you." It's not a spiritual directive at all, involving nothing more than NOT doing certain things, refraining from specific actions or behaviors. You can sit and do nothing and keep the rule. You can slog through all of your years never doing injury to any man and still not live out the life Jesus talks about in the Sermon, still not live a well-lived life. Man's law compels me to obey the negative golden rule. The police officer compels me to obey traffic laws; I keep those laws for fear of getting a ticket and paying a fine. But man's law cannot force me to stop and help a guy along the road having car trouble. I can keep every city ordinance on the books (be a great law-abiding citizen) and never lift a finger or give a dime to feed a hungry person. But under the light of a positive golden rule given to us by Jesus, a new principle enters into our lives. This principle is at the heart of living out real Christianity.

Random thoughts for today:

You shall love your neighbor as yourself. (Matthew 22:39 ESV)

Jesus really can't teach us anything until we quiet our intellectual questions and get alone with Him.

The problem with most of us church people is not belief...It is expectation.

May 2   And Peter

One writer said it long ago – "Every great man or woman of God can point to a time of breaking in his or her life; a time of conflict, a time of pressure, or a time of decision that transformed them from an ordinary piece of coal into a precious diamond, pliable in the Master's hand." This could describe Abraham, Isaac, Jacob, David, Solomon, Jonah, Job...and Peter. All four gospels record his denial of Christ. He had the opportunity to stand up, but he blew it. What would you have done if you were Peter? You've just been caught. Do you try to get out of it? Deny it?! There will come a time when we all have to decide whether or not to stand up for Christ. And how do we respond to others when they blow it? Many a Christian has felt the wrath of an unforgiving believer. When your leaders blow it, how do you respond? Are you quick to bring criticism, or are you ready to bring restoration? No matter how solid our faith or conviction ("Lord, I'll NEVER deny You!"), no matter how beautiful the song from our lips or words from our pulpit, never forget, it can happen to any of us. The first step toward correction is not to act like we're invulnerable, because we're not. Not one of us can condemn Peter. When I think of Peter, I think of the gospel of the second chance. Do you remember the message of the angel at the tomb?—*He is not here; He is risen! But go and tell His disciples...AND PETER...that He is going before you to Galilee.* Two precious words that bring tears to our eyes as we read them...as we hear them. Why does the Lord single out Peter here? We know the answer as strongly as we see the sin in our own lives. Be sure to tell Peter that he's not left out; one failure doesn't make a total flop. Christ presents the gospel of the second chance, or third, or tenth, or twentieth. Go tell Peter that I love him with an everlasting love. Go tell his disciples...and Rick Jones...that I have loved Him with an everlasting love.

Random thoughts for today:

"Before the rooster crows twice, you will deny me three times." And Peter broke down and wept. (Mark 14:72 ESV)

Between the great things we can't do and the little things we won't do, the danger is we shall do nothing at all.

The people you disagree with are not your enemy.

Spiritual Scrabble of life—Play the tiles you get.

May 3   Talents

Several years ago, in a congregation I served, we tried a little experiment based upon Jesus' parable of the talents. Each member of the church was given an envelope with a twenty-dollar bill in it and was told to invest it in the Kingdom. A talent in biblical times represented a sum of money, sometimes paid in minted coins. The results of our experiment were quite fascinating. One member bought seed for her vegetable garden and gave the produce to a local food bank. An elementary student set up a lemonade stand and donated her profits to the Salvation Army. Another bought Bibles to give away. One young man took his money (plus some of his own) to Chicago to minister to the homeless. A college student used hers for advertising and set up a house-sitting business. A teacher bought materials and started a free tutoring service. Have you ever wondered why the Master entrusted different servants with different amounts? God holds a man accountable for what he has, not for what he doesn't have. He doesn't demand an "A" from a "C" student, nor is He satisfied with a "C" from an "A" student. And we note that that third servant was not condemned for not producing. He's called to account because he did nothing. Interesting side note: The first two servants each used sixteen words to report the result of their obedience. The lazy servant used forty-three words to alibi his failure. Likewise, the church is accountable for its faithfulness. Good word...Faithfulness. We're not called to be a cool or modern-thinking church. Our commission is not about talented musicians or good preaching or great programs for the church. It's not even all about being the friendliest church in town. No alibis...We are called to faithfulness. Are we faithful to our calling? Spiritual darkness comes because we do not intend to carry out the call of God. Do we emphasize blessing over faithfulness? The first two servants in the parable were commended because they were faithful. When my life here is finished, my desire is not to hear that I was a good preacher or teacher, or not that I was a generous giver. Nope. I desire to hear my Lord say to me, *Well done, good and faithful servant...Enter into the joy of your Master* (Matthew 25:23 ESV).

Random thoughts for today:

...and He will separate people from one another as a shepherd separates the sheep from the goats...And to sheep on His right He will say, "Come, you who are blessed by My Father, inherit the kingdom prepared for you from the foundation of the world. (Matthew 25:32-34 ESV)

In the end, we love people into belief...We do not argue them into belief.

Jesus knows the worst about me...Nonetheless, He is One who loves me most.

May 4   Centurion

Have you ever noticed the differences in the three gospel accounts of the Roman centurion at the cross of Jesus? In the Matthew version, all of the soldiers, including the centurion, were *filled with awe, and said, "Truly this was the Son of God"* (Matthew 27:54 ESV). The Mark account zeroes in on just the centurion. Mark 15:39 tells us that *the centurion stood facing Him, and when he saw that He had breathed His last, he said, "Truly this man was the Son of God!"* But the Luke account adds an interesting element. Luke 23:47 ESV—*Now when the centurion saw what had taken place, he PRAISED GOD..."* What's going on here? A change has obviously taken place. What happened to the heart of this hardened Roman warrior, a leader of men? The man had never heard or read John 3:16—*For God so loved the world that He gave His one and only Son...* He didn't need to. He had watched it unfold before him, his heart being guided and filled with the Holy Spirit. The centurion had seen other victims die of crucifixion. Unlike others, Jesus never cursed those who mocked Him and killed Him. In fact, by contrast to the evil words of the passers-by who ridiculed and belittled Him, He responded, *Father, forgive them, for they know not what they do* (Luke 23:34). What do you do with a centurion with a changed heart? Here was a man who could only see Jesus. I don't know everything that was going on inside his heart that day, and it doesn't matter. I do know that he experienced a profound spiritual experience and that his life could never be the same. I've often wished there was an account of what happened to him after this event. It's been said that only God can truly change a man's heart. As that centurion learned over two thousand years ago, you cannot come close to Jesus without being changed.

Random thoughts for today:

Jesus said, "Truly I say to you, unless one is born again, he cannot see the kingdom of God. (John 3:3 ESV)

Tell the truth...Sing with passion...Work with laughter...Love with heart.

Who dares to teach must never cease to learn.

We are more connected to the invisible than the visible. *(Novalis)*

There is nothing more artistic than loving people. *(Vincent van Gogh)*

May 5   Corporate Prayer

Three gospel writers, Matthew, Mark, and Luke, record the second cleansing of the temple, which took place during the final week of Jesus' life. In all three accounts, we read His words, *My house will be called a house of prayer.* After Jesus ascended into heaven, the Book of Acts tells us that the disciples went to the upper room and *devoted themselves to prayer* (Acts 1:14 ESV). Acts 2 says, after the birth of the church, the whole church *devoted themselves to the apostles' teaching and fellowship, to the breaking of bread and prayer* (v 42). Throughout Acts, we see the early church meeting for prayer again and again. We come across phrases like "the hour of prayer" – "we gave ourselves continually to prayer" – "Our prayers were made without ceasing" – "place of prayer together." Jonathan Edwards preached it years ago—"It is the expressly revealed will of God that His church should be very much in prayer for that glorious outpouring of the Spirit in these latter days." Does this describe your church? Is your church a house of prayer? One compiler of statistics reported that the average American church probably spends no more than 15-20 minutes a week in corporate prayer as a congregation. I don't know how accurately that reflects your church, but I suspect on average, it's probably true. Have you ever heard of the International House of Prayer in Kansas City? They made a commitment over twenty years ago to unceasing prayer and worship. On September 19, 1999, a prayer meeting began, which continues to this day, from dawn to dusk and through the watches of the night. By the grace of God, prayer and worship have continued twenty-four hours a day, seven days a week. Helen and I have a nephew who has been involved with this ministry for years. It's the real deal. Whenever I get to feeling a little cocky about my prayer life, I think about this ministry in Kansas City. I often wonder about what's happened to corporate prayer in our American churches. Are our houses of worship houses of prayer? Why are there no longer any regular meetings for prayer? As my friend, Steve Galloway likes to say, with a smile on his face, "What do you mean? Just get together for prayer? No singing, no teaching, no snacks? Just praying?" Maybe the Lord can use you to be a catalyst for starting a prayer ministry/meeting at your church. No? OK...Just a thought.

Random thoughts for today:

Pray without ceasing. (1 Thessalonians 5:17 ESV)

Praise from others is nice...But the ultimate is knowing that our Lord is pleased.

Advice is what we ask for when we already know the answer but wish we didn't.

A good listener is not only popular everywhere, but after a while, he gets to know something.

A young man, twenty-five years old or so, was sitting in a window seat on a southbound Amtrak. His nervousness and distress were evident to the older gentleman sitting next to him. He finally asked the younger man if he was OK. It was like the overflowing of a dam. "I'm going home," he said. "I haven't been home for almost six years. My father and I had a major falling-out, and I left the house shouting and cursing him, saying I would never come back. At that time, I hated him, or I thought I did. But the last year or so I've begun to really miss my dad. In the last couple of months, all I could think of was seeing my dad and talking to him. I finally made the decision to go home. I sent him a letter telling him how sorry I was for cutting him out of my life for the last six years and how much I loved him. I told him all I wanted to do was to come home and make our relationship right again. I have no idea if he wants me to come home or if he even desires a relationship. There's an old apple tree right next to the train station in my town. I suppose it's still there. I told him if he wanted me to come home, tie a white handkerchief in the tree. When the train pulled into the station, if there were no handkerchief, I wouldn't even get off the train." As they got closer to his destination, the more nervous he became. As the train pulled into the depot, the young man covered his eyes and almost whispered, "I can't look; you look. Can you see the apple tree?" Finally, the older gentleman blurted out, "Open your eyes, man; Look!" That apple tree was literally filled with white handkerchiefs! Have you read the parable of the Prodigal Son lately (Luke 15:11-24)? Your Abba Father wants you to come home. He has filled his apple tree with white handkerchiefs.

For this my son was dead and is alive again; he was lost and is found. (Luke 15:24 ESV)

It's just a fact—A good garden may have some weeds.

Your value is measured by your legacy, not your salary.

Prayer is bringing my soul before the Lord—No rules!!

Have my words or my actions this day contributed to the pain of the world around me or have they contributed to its healing?

May 7   Which Kingdom?

The account of the feeding of the 5,000 (John 6:1-13, as well as the other three gospels) holds a strong appeal to us as this sign shows Jesus to be the supplier of men's needs. He is the One who created the principle of the harvest from a few grains. Christ has always been the provider of our needs, and always will be. The question is, will we see our actual needs and look to Him to provide them? This account, when rightly understood, points to Jesus as the Messiah and to a heavenly kingdom. However, the problem was that the crowd, while very interested in having physical needs taken care of, were not enthusiastic about kingdom truths. Before the day was over, the crowd tried to take Jesus by force and make Him an earthly king. Ironic that they were attempting to make a king out of One who was already King. Sometimes I wonder if we don't have the same struggle. We want Jesus to be our king, a king who will always physically heal us...A king who will provide all of our physical wants and desires (shades of the prosperity gospel)...A king who will provide that raise in salary, a new house and a new car...A king that will solve all of our relational problems caused by our mistakes and misunderstandings—"Bless me, Jesus, no matter what I do!" It's not about what He does for us, but rather WHO HE IS. It's not about what He provides for us, but rather what He makes of us. *Christ in you, the hope of glory!* I'm reminded of that chorus we sing, "Lord, You are my daily bread. I'm desperate for You and lost without You."

Random thoughts for today:

Jesus then took the loaves, and having given thanks, He distributed to those who were seated, likewise also of the fish as much as they wanted. (John 6:11 ESV)

I think our first mistake is assuming that because it's in the Bible, it's in us.

As long as you live, keep learning how to live.

The church must counteract the "I quit" mentality of our culture.

Do not seek to follow the footsteps of the ancient fathers of our faith...Seek what they sought.

If there is a personal God who has made us and sustains us, He hears and responds to prayer.

May 8   Mary Magdalene and the Church

Mary Magdalene, sometimes called the Magdalene, was a Jewish woman who, according to the four gospels, traveled with Jesus as one of His earliest and closest followers and was witness to his crucifixion and burial. According to the texts, Mary was the first to witness the resurrected Jesus. She is mentioned 12 times in the gospels, more than most of the apostles. She was venerated by both the Roman Catholic and the Eastern Orthodox church. In some Christian traditions, she has been called the apostle to the apostles. Keep in mind that this was a time when women were not considered acceptable legal witnesses in any court proceeding. For many years, my wife and I sang the duet, "I've Just Seen Jesus" in our church on Easter morning. I tear up when I sing those words thinking of that conversation between Jesus and Mary in the garden. That's a whole bunch of writing to say what I want to say about beautiful women in the church. Ladies, you've taken a bum rap from the church through the years. No women preachers! No women elders! No women teaching men! *...the women should keep silent in the churches. For they are not permitted to speak...* (1 Corinthians 14:34 ESV). This text has proven to be much more than a little controversial over the years (do you think?). It is not my intention to get into this debate, and it can be debated scripturally on both sides of the issue. I don't have the end-all answers to this controversy in the body. I'm not sure there are end-all answers. I know my life has been influenced by godly women, some of them preachers. Billy Graham said that his daughter, Anne Graham Lotz was the best preacher in the family. I believe that speakers like Jennifer Hatmaker and Sarah Bessey have been used by God to bring renewal to women in our churches. I know that these women and others have had a transforming influence upon my daughter, who happens to be a pastor. God bless you, ladies!! May you continue to be a blessing to the body of Christ.

<u>Random thoughts for today</u>:

But the angel said to the women…Go quickly and tell His disciples that He is risen from the dead… (Matthew 28:5; 7 ESV)

Most of my time and effort is spent in battling judgmentalism… Mostly in me.

One of the best ways to persuade others is with your ears.

Surround yourself with those people who are going to lift you higher.

Happiness depends upon happenings…Joy depends upon the Lord.

May 9   Mom's Day

It's a literal truth and a cliché besides—None of us would be here without our mothers. Present or absent, good or bad, our mothers are the source of us all, and we forever circle the significance of that, especially on Mother's Day. On April 27, eighteen years ago, my mother passed from this life into the next. Psalm 3:5 ESV says, *I lay down and slept; I woke again for the LORD sustained me.* Sound familiar? How about, "Now I lay me down to sleep; I pray the Lord my soul to keep?" My first prayer was taught to me by my Mom. You would have liked my Mom. She loved the Lord, she was a scholar of the scriptures, and I have no doubt whatsoever that she belongs to Him. Maybe Mother's Day is the day we honor the real heroes of our world. It's a shame we honor you only one day a year. Hats off to every one of you! More than any statesman or teacher, more than any pastor or physician, more than any film star or athlete or author or scientist or politician or musician, you have the potential to be the most influential person in your child's life. Hey kids (no matter what your age), have you noticed that when your mother is in the "Mom-mode," she ends up doing stuff that is beyond common sense.

- Willing to nurse you when you're sick
- Help you with your homework when you're ignorant
- Comfort you when you're depressed
- Feed you when you're hungry
- Clean up after you when you're lazy

And with just a little thank you and a hug and "I love you" from you, they're all fired up and ready to do it again. Tony Campolo tells of how his wife responds when career women look down their nose at her and say, "And what do you do?" Her response? "I'm socializing two homo sapiens in the dominant values of the Judeo-Christian tradition in order that they might be instruments in the transformation of the social order, so that they might realize the eschatological potentialities of Utopia." Then she would look at them and ask, "And what do you do?" And they would answer, "Oh, I'm just a lawyer."

Random thoughts for today:

My son...forsake not your mother's teaching. Bind them on your heart always... (Proverbs 6:20-21 ESV)

A mother is a person who, seeing only four pieces of pie for five people, promptly announces she never did care for pie.

Hang in there, moms...No matter what your kids say or think, they cannot erase your influence.

I have already mentioned a couple of times that my youngest daughter is a pastor. Because of my background and my tendency toward legalism in my earlier days, this used to be a concern for me. It's an issue that I've wrestled with the Lord about, and one that has been resolved for me in these later years. Notice that I said, "for me." Please understand that I have no desire to jump into the pool of the pastor-gender debate. I love a friend of mine who said, "If we are all "biblical" in our various positions, why do we disagree so much?" If you believe there should be no female pastors or elders in the church, God bless you. I'm not going to invest any more time or energy into that controversy. All I know is, I have a daughter who was entrusted with a pastoral role in the congregation where she serves, and she has accepted that role with energy and a desire to follow the Lord she loves. She's an outstanding preacher and has the heart of a shepherd. Oh, and by the way, her mother and I are very proud of her. Many times when she preaches at her church, we're there. I have pages of notes from her sermons, and her teaching has continually blessed me. Even though it is still an area of disagreement in many of our churches, it was still quite hurtful to her when some members of her church left because she had been hired. Things like this shouldn't surprise me after being in the pastoral ministry for over fifty years, but there it is. 19th-century church historian, Philip Schaff, discusses what he calls the watchword of Christian peacemakers—"In essentials unity, in non-essentials liberty, in all things charity." Here are some favorite quotes from my daughter, Becky:

- "In order to discover our role in the kingdom, we must root our identity in love and belonging."
- "We must follow our own convictions no matter what; we must be true to our beliefs."
- "We are called to humility; true leaders are more powerful when they are humble."
- "Do we follow the Lord so we can be good, follow the rules, for reward?"
- "Your viewpoint isn't God...We plop our viewpoint down in the middle of our world, and our opinion becomes our understanding of the gospel."
- "Why are we so impatient to get to the end? Someone says, 'I can hardly wait to go be with the Lord.' No! You're with the Lord right now...Why are we in such a hurry to get to the end?"
- "We do light a great disservice when we underestimate the power of darkness."

Keep up the good work. ***Preach the word; be ready in season and out of season; reprove, rebuke, and exhort with complete patience and teaching.*** (2 Timothy 4:2 ESV) God bless you, pastor Becky.

May 11   Too Much Instruction

There have been times when I have prayed, "Lord, I want to be in a constant state of communion with You; I desire to make *pray without ceasing* a reality in my life, whatever that might be." Brother Lawrence of the Resurrection, a lay brother in a monastery in Paris in the 17th-century, is probably best known for his collection of writings, *The Practice of the Presence of God*. He writes, "Having found in many books different methods of praying, of going to God, of various practices of the spiritual life, I reckoned that so much instruction only puzzled me. Simply put, all I desired was how to become wholly God's." That absolutely resonates with me. I have attended numerous prayer seminars through the years, taught classes on prayer, read a countless number of volumes on the subject, and now have written two prayer devotionals. I have tried to mimic what others have written about what they did, used prayer acrostics (I suggested ACTS – Adoration, Confession, Thanksgiving, and Supplication in my last book), various prayer lists in my prayer journals, and several other notions with varying degrees of success. Is it possible to have too much instruction on how to pray? Yes, it is. I am exhibit A. I'm convinced that God isn't concerned with my wording or phrasing; I can't picture my Abba Father raising His eyebrows because I made a grammatical mistake in addressing Him. I've said it before that I don't think it's possible for a child of God to pray a bad prayer. Brother Lawrence also wrote, "There is not in the world a kind of life more sweet and delightful than that of a continual conversation with God." That kind of conversation has nothing to do with proper words or posture or technique. Thanks, brother Lawrence...I'm with you!!

Random thoughts for today:

I do not cease to give thanks for you, remembering you in my prayers... (Ephesians 1:16 ESV)

The Christian life is not found in a place or event, but rather in a Person.

You cannot protect yourself from sadness without protecting yourself from happiness.

If you miss the little things, you miss the vast majority of life.

Faith is the posture before God that receives grace and lives it out. *(Nate Loucks)*

When the church loses her first love, she becomes sick.

May 12   Bonhoeffer's Morning Prayer

Dietrich Bonhoeffer was a German evangelical pastor, theologian, anti-Nazi dissident, and key founding member of the Confessing Church. This was a movement within German Protestantism that arose in opposition to government-sponsored efforts to unify all Protestant churches into a single pro-Nazi Protestant Reich Church. Bonhoeffer's writings on the role of the church in our secular world have become widely influential, and his book, *The Cost of Discipleship,* is considered a modern classic. He was arrested in April 1943 by the Gestapo and imprisoned. After being accused of being associated with the plot to assassinate Adolph Hitler, he was tried, and along with other accused plotters, he was hanged on April 9, 1945, twenty-one days before Hitler committed suicide. Bonhoeffer was said to have prayed this prayer each morning:

> "I seek You in the morning, Lord, when the world is quiet, before the busy demands of the day. I turn my schedule over to You—Take my day and live Your life through me. Amen."

O LORD, in the morning You hear my voice; in the morning I prepare a sacrifice for You and watch. (Psalm 5:3 ESV)

Random thoughts for today:

For whoever would save his life will lose it, but whoever loses his life for My sake will find it. (Matthew 16:25 ESV)

The lowest ebb is the turn of the tide. *(Longfellow)*

Sometimes our prayer life lacks because we fail to understand that prayer is communication between a child and his Father.

What difference will *Christ in me, the hope of glory* make in me today?

Resist anything that leads to moodiness...Our prayer each day should be, May *the joy of the LORD be our strength.*

When there are no longer questions, answers are no longer bound by them. *(Lao Tzu)*

May 13   My Immigration Policy

I freely admit that the title of this entry is bogus; I have no immigration policy, and I have more questions than answers. Let me change that last statement—I have very few solutions to a very complex problem. So who do we go to for the answers? Where do we turn? We can get no consistency from political leaders. Both Presidents Bill Clinton and Barack Obama have made strong statements in the past concerning the need to stop illegal traffic at the border. Actually, some of their statements have surprisingly agreed with Donald Trump. And Congress has, in essence, done nothing. Both sides of the aisle have stated at one time or another, "It's a complex problem." Yeah, we already know that. It is an issue that has divided Christians. On the surface, it would seem that it is a division of right versus left, but I believe that's too simplistic. Scripture is not all that helpful either. The church has struggled to find appropriate guidance from the Bible for handling a very specific public policy. How do we apply the principle of Acts 17:2 ESV to immigration issues—*Paul went in, as was his custom, and on three Sabbath days, he reasoned with them from the scriptures.* Where do we find the balance between Romans 13:1— *Let every person be subject to the governing authorities,* and Matthew 25:35 ESV—*I was hungry and you gave me food, I was thirsty and you gave me drink, I was a stranger and you welcomed me.* Both the right and the left do damage to honest dialogue by oversimplifying the issue. And both sides HAVE oversimplified the issue. The authority God delegates to civil government focuses on justice, not mercy, whereas my conscience and my heart dictate me to apply mercy and grace to the problem. Biblical teachings of mercy generally apply to individual conduct and not to civil authority. Having said that, I firmly believe that God holds civil leaders accountable for their conduct. I've heard it said by some believers, "Let's just have open borders." It is evident in scripture that God DOES regard borders as meaningful and significant (Proverbs 22:28; Proverbs 23:10-11; Deuteronomy 32:8). I've heard other Christians say, "Well remember, Mary and Joseph were illegal immigrants. No they weren't. They broke no Egyptian laws when they fled their homeland. My heart doesn't take into account the major problems caused by any mandate that a society must welcome any and all foreigners presenting themselves at the border, without any regard to flooded borders, overcrowded school systems, and overtaxed medical facilities in the Southwestern states. Simple answers? Tell me what they are; I'm waiting. I won't even address the economic issues because my heart seldom takes into account economics. I'm not wired that way. And where does the so-called "Golden Rule" from the Sermon on the Mount factor in? We have to conclude, in the words of James R. Edwards, "It is questionable to construct an immigration policy for 21st-century America based upon a handful of scripture passages taken out of context or from particular instances of migration spanning centuries." How do you like all of my solutions so far? A word comes to mind...BEFUDDLEMENT!!

May 14   Laying Our Stones Down

Remember the old "Sticks and stones may break my bones, but names will never hurt me."— Another childhood myth. Why are we so quick to throw our verbal stones at each other? We look at people, size them up, pass judgment, and begin throwing our stones. An ancient writer said, "If we remember the wrongs which men have done us, we destroy the power of the remembrance of God." So, why do we throw them?

- Because we harbor hatred
- Because we hold on to bitterness
- Because our emotions are entangled with anger
- Because we seek revenge
- Because we won't let go of the things that upset us

Let him who is without sin among you be the first to throw a stone at her (John 8:7). Jesus said that. What are those actions that reveal sin in us? When we speak destructively. When we seek to create discord. When we stir up division. Forgiveness flows from the life of Jesus. It is empowered by His sacrifice on the cross and finalized by the triumph of the resurrection. What stones are you carrying today?

- Stones of bitterness?
- Stones of anger?
- Stones of hatred?
- Stones of prejudice?

Whatever stone you may be carrying, it is an unnecessary weight you bear; it's a pointless part of your life. Don't you think it's time for you to lay down that rock, to give that "weapon" over to your Abba Father? We had a service at our church a few years ago, where we had placed a rock on every seat in the worship auditorium. At the close of the service, we asked the body to take that stone in their hand and symbolically commit it to the Lord. We had an altar call, and everyone who participated brought their rock forward the laid it at the altar. The prayer given that morning was, "Lord, may we submit these stones to You, these stones that we would use to destroy. Take these stones, Father, and build something beautiful with them."

And Jesus said, "Neither do I condemn you; go, and from now on sin no more." (John 8:11 ESV)

Scottish theologian Archibald McBride Hunter wrote several years ago, "The Beatitudes are not so much ethics of obedience, as they are ethics of grace." In other words, they do not mean you must do these things in order to deserve and win the approval of God. God gives his blessings to those who claim no merit for themselves, but knowing their own needs of the heart, they are content to rest wholly on the mercy of God. The Beatitudes are qualities that describe what every Christian, by God's grace, ought to be. The Holy Spirit is concerned to work all of these graces within us. God is the gracious giver, and we are the humble receivers.

- Blessed are the poor in spirit
- Blessed are they that mourn
- Blessed are the meek
- Blessed are those who hunger and thirst after righteousness
- Blessed are the merciful
- Blessed are the pure in heart
- Blessed are the peacemakers
- Blessed are those who are persecuted (Matthew 5:3-11 ESV)

It's kind of like Jesus wanted to share some of the secrets of a well-lived life, so He gave us the Beatitudes.

Random thoughts for today:

Blessed are you who weep now, for you shall laugh.
(Luke 6:21 ESV)

I would rather feel compunction than know its definition. *(Thomas 'A Kempis)*

Children seldom misquote...In fact, they usually repeat word for word what you shouldn't have said.

Next time a wiser person offers me advice, I will dial down my pride and listen.

When our memories exceed our dreams, we will stop making a difference.

The way we worship becomes the way we believe.

That which is made forgets...The Maker forgets not. *(African Proverb)*

May 16   Let God Be God

Have you ever had someone say to you, "Well, my God would never do that!"? I came across a sentence in my journal this past week that stated, "God is not the way we say He is; God is the way scriptures say He is." I have spent a good share of my life (and ministry) battling pride and having too much confidence in myself. John Piper says that prayer is the antidote for the disease of ego and self-confidence. That little problem called ego can end up opposing what God wants to do in me. Piper defines prayer as "hanging out a help-wanted sign." I think that this is the underlying meaning of prayer. God will not surrender His glory to us, but He will work through us when we allow Him to be God in us. He exalts Himself by working through us as we wait upon Him. Keep your life so constantly in touch with God that His surpassing power can break through at any point. Live in a constant state of expectancy and leave room for God to come as He decides. Prayer is that essential discipline that does just that—acknowledging our helplessness and His power. The modern church has done a great job of fashioning their own god, which is nothing like the God of scripture. The more we drift away from the authority of God's Word, the more in danger we are of setting up a false god. There's a whole lot of that going on today. My admonition to the church of the 2020s...LET GOD BE GOD IN YOU!!

Today, Lord, I put out a "help-wanted sign" and choose to wait on You.

<u>Random thoughts for today</u>:

...The LORD our God, the LORD is one! (Deuteronomy 6:4 ESV)

He who knows himself well is not delighted when men praise him.

What wisdom can you find that is greater than kindness? *(Jean-Jacques Rousseau)*

If we were all "biblical" in our positions, why do we disagree so much?

Social Media = Too much diarrhea of the mouth and too little wisdom, kindness, and truth.

If I get discouraged today, I will take a break...Then I will get back to work...I will not quit.

When I communicate with my wife things are better...So it is with my relationship with the Lord.

One of the Wesley brothers was heard to say, "It cannot be that the people should grow in grace unless they give themselves to reading. A reading people will always be a knowing people." And of course, at the top of the list must be scripture. Whether you like it or not, we need to read daily. Henri Nouwen discussed how vital his reading was to his continued walk through life. He asks the challenging question concerning which words we would take with us in the hour when we have to survive without books. People who talk more than they read or study usually know very little. Nouwen says he does not want to end up "depending upon his own unredeemed ramblings and not have the Word of God to guide him." There are so many books available today that are helpful in our journey with the Lord. In addition to the Bible itself, I believe that reading other books have been a part of making me who I am. In my acknowledgment section at the beginning of this book is a list of writers who have influenced my thinking and my life. One of my mentors, years ago, said to me, "If you would be a writer, first be a reader." I've not forgotten that counsel. He also told to me, "Think before you speak and read before you think." I realize that some just don't like to read, or it is difficult for them to read. There are many things in life that we don't want to do, but we DO IT ANYWAY. Significant movements in the history of Christianity have always come from a reading people. Remember the words of that famous theologian, Groucho Marx—"I find television very educating. Every time somebody turns on the set, I go in the other room and read a book."

Random thoughts for today:

...*they received the word with all eagerness, examining the Scriptures daily to see if these things were so.* (Acts 17:11 ESV)

Many times the ignorance of people comes from having to have an answer for everything.

He who knows best knows how little he knows. *(Thomas Jefferson)*

In the long haul, we pray only as well as we live.

Reading maketh a full man. *(Sir Francis Bacon)*

The best and most beautiful things in the world cannot be seen or touched...They must be felt with the heart. *(Helen Keller)*

May 18   Deciding For Jesus?
                                          (Closet Calvinist?)

I was raised in a church tradition where we were taught from childhood that everything moves toward making a decision. It seemed that all of our childhood Sunday School days were built upon a progression that would ultimately lead to "deciding for Jesus." I'm not against this tradition per se, but I can't help but wonder if this emphasis upon MY deciding for Jesus might have placed the greater weight of the whole salvation process upon my shoulders, rather than upon Christ. *For by grace you have been saved through faith. And this is not your own doing; it is the gift of God, not a result of works, so that no one may boast* (Ephesians 2:8-9 ESV). Paul goes on to say in that passage that we are HIS workmanship. Although it is through my act of faith that connects me to Him, beyond that step, I have done nothing to affect my salvation. Scripture seems to teach that even my faith is a gift from Him. The phrase we hear so often "decide for Christ" is a concept in which our Lord never trusted. He never asks us to decide for Him, but rather to yield to Him—a very different thing altogether. In scripture, I see a much greater emphasis placed upon God seeking me out and drawing me to Himself, rather than seeing me doing anything at all to contribute to the process. Hmmm...Could I be a closet Calvinist? I don't think so. Do we decide for Jesus? In a sense, perhaps. But I praise my Lord daily that He decided for me long ago, like *before the foundation of the world* (Ephesians 1:4).

Random thoughts for today:

And I, when I am lifted up from the earth, will draw all people to Myself. (John 12:32 ESV)

Stay close to anything that makes you glad you are alive. *(Anonymous)*

Help me, Lord, to let the rays of Your love penetrate the clouds of my life and fill me with sunlight.

What soap is to the body, tears are to the soul. *(Jewish Proverb)*

You were born an original...Don't become a copy. *(Anonymous)*

May 19   Words That Remain

Those of you who know me are aware that I journal. My journal is with me most of the time. In my basement is a plastic tub with over thirty journals from past years. This practice goes

214

against the sage advice of the world, which tells us never to put anything in writing. For years I have asserted that journaling is a valuable discipline that clarifies our thoughts and even draws us to the Lord. As with my first two books, I have relied heavily upon my personal journals. I continue to glean thoughts and insights and perhaps occasional trivia, although I would never desire to *break you to pieces with words* (Job 19:2 ESV). In an age like ours, which is not given to letter-writing, we forget what an important part writing (letters, diaries, journals) used to play in people's lives and recording history. We lost much when we stopped writing. I was often saddened when a student would tell me that they hated to write. My personal opinion is that social media must share part of the blame for this; Facebook statuses and Instagram bios just don't cut it—but I digress. There's a Latin proverb that says, "A word that is heard perishes, but the word that is written remains." I've found journaling is an excellent way of slowing down this lunatic universe long enough to gather one's thoughts and clarify the "what's next" of life. I love what Phyllis Theroux has said—"To journal is a good way to go somewhere without moving anything but your heart."

"Why not seriously consider journaling. Get yourself a notebook—any size that's comfortable for you—and start writing down that which has spoken to your heart today. I can guarantee blessing ahead as well as a channel of expression for you not yet experienced. Try it...I think you'll like it." (*Journey Through the School of Groaning* by the author)

Random thoughts for today:

I write this with my own hand...the sign of genuineness in every letter of mine; it is the way I write. (2 Thessalonians 3:17 ESV)

The best gift anyone can give, I believe, is the gift of sharing themselves.

Thank You, Lord, for this new day, which is as a fresh new journal page for me.

I don't always trust myself...But I do trust in the grace of God.

A heart on the sleeve is so much more gripping than hate on a sleeve.

May 20   What a Wonderful World

It is my opinion that we spend way too much time in the church selling tickets to that grand prizefight between us and the world— secular vs. sacred. I realize that "this world is not my home," but I also know that I presently have a dual-citizenship that challenges me to a responsibility to this world in which I live. Perhaps there is more of the sacred in what we call secular than meets the eye. We spend a lot of time formulating and discussing our "world-view." What is our world-view of the world? I read somewhere, many years ago, that all the world is one great sacramental loaf. I'm not sure that the secular and sacred pigeon-holing game is of the Lord. We have worried too much about fighting the "world," rather than learning how to live life in it in such a way that honors God. That's my world-view. Either the world is holy, or it's not— God created it. I wonder how many time our own definition of "separation from the world" has ended up hemming in the Lord of the universe? Do we put barbed wire around our sacred places? Does our practice of holiness broadcast a message to our world around us that says, "Stay away from me"? I've had discussions with believers who won't celebrate Christmas because, "after all, it came from a secular entity." Guess what? I was a secular entity!! But the Lord came down and transformed that holiday into the holy just as *the Word become flesh* has transformed me into a sacred entity as well. Maybe that's why one of my favorite secular songs is Louis Armstrong's *What a Wonderful World*. Listen to the words. Does that reflect your world-view of the world? Wait a minute...Maybe it's not a secular song.

Random thoughts for today:

In the beginning, God created the heavens and the earth...And God saw that it was good. (Genesis1:1; 3 ESV)

A heart on a sleeve is so much more gripping than hate on a sleeve.

Success is not measured by our achievements, but rather by the lives we bless.

Someday I need to break through that wall that says I have no business before the throne of God.

I love friendly deeds better than fair words. *(Sir Walter Scott)*

May 21   Is Jesus Lord?

One of the major theological questions today is whether Christ can be Savior without being Lord. In a sense, that seems almost like asking if I can be a member of the Chicago Cubs without ever playing on the field (See January 29 entry). "I made the team, but I don't want to get involved in the game; I'm not sure I'll even suit-up today." George Gallup surveyed "born again" Christians and found that only ten percent considered their faith in daily decision-making. He indicated that 90 percent of us are nominal Christians. On those days that I find myself in a somewhat cynical mood, I think that percentage is a little high. Nominal Christianity is quite different from what Elizabeth Elliot (her husband, along with four other missionaries were killed in Ecuador while trying to evangelize Huaorani people in 1956) writes regarding lordship— "Until the will and the affections are brought under the authority of Christ, we have not begun to understand, let alone accept, His Lordship." "Jesus is Lord" is not my personal opinion. The Bible knows of no such believer who is saved without repentance. A disciple of Jesus Christ is a verbal, visible follower of Jesus Christ at the expense of all else. It's that serious. Lordship means that we bring every part of our lives under His authority—our home and family, our sexuality and marriage, our job, our money and possessions, our ambitions and recreations. If God is the Creator of the entire universe, then it must follow that He is the Lord of the whole universe. No part of the world is outside of His lordship. That means that no part of my life must be outside of His lordship. In other words, you don't make Him Lord. He already IS Lord. You just recognize it. Can Christ be Savior without being Lord? Sorry, that doesn't compute!!

Let all the house of Israel therefore know for certain that God has made Him both Lord and Christ... (Acts 2:36 ESV)

Christianity is not a cafeteria line where you say, "I'll have a little salvation, but no lordship right now.

Sometimes we worship God with open hands...Sometimes we have to pry them open.

Many church people haven't yet made the jump into this whole lordship thing.

May 22   Sabbath

Sabbath. What does that word mean to you? What comes to mind when you hear the concept of the Sabbath principle? I know what Sabbath meant to the Old Testament Israelite. I know what it means to the modern Jew today. Does it have any meaning to me, this old Gentile Evangelical Christian? The Sabbath principle was a thing of the past. Christians observed their Sabbath on the first day of the week instead of the seventh, but nonetheless, it was observed. I remember my Dad not allowing my brother and I to do any labor on Sunday ("You're not mowing the yard on Sunday"), a product of his early 20th-century upbringing. World War II changed all of that with the first wide-spread practice of seven-day-a-week, twenty-four-hour-a-day production. By the sixties and seventies, retailers were following suit. Not coincidentally, there was a significant increase in emotional dysfunction, juvenile delinquency, and divorce. Richard Exley talks about the rhythm of rest—silence, solitude, memory, mini-vacations, special friends, books that touch the heart, and the healing power of deep sleep—that rhythm that keeps us from unraveling at the seams—a personal Sabbath principle. One of the vital tools for keeping Sabbath alive in me is my resting in prayer. Prayer is Sabbath. It helps me daily to get off that anxious treadmill of worry and fear and being overwhelmed. There's nothing like spending quality time with the Lord to encourage my blood pressure to stop percolating and my mind to stop whirling like a hamster wheel. My daily time with God has become my personal *observing of the Sabbath and keeping it holy...* (Deuteronomy 5:12 ESV). Try it...You'll like it.

Random thoughts for today:

Remember the Sabbath, to keep it holy. (Exodus 20:8 ESV)

Help me never to forget that the trust of a child is to be cherished.

Love is not measured by what it gets, but rather by what it costs.

I used to admire intelligent people...As I grow older, I admire kind people.

I seek to rest from normal schedule one day a week. Revitalized, I find strength to battle new tomorrows.

It would seem that many of our problems emanate from our pride.

Do you have a special location where you regularly meet with the Lord? Of course, we can pray anywhere, any place, but a consistent location for your quiet time helps to build habit. Having said that, I believe that the key here is not necessarily the place, but rather the consistency. In the Book of Acts, we see many instances where the Holy Spirit came down upon the early church right where they were, and sometimes in the most common of places. I see a significant change from Old Testament to New Testament—an "amazing emancipation" in the words of E. Stanley Jones. Up to this time, religion had been associated with sacred places. Now in the Book of Acts, we see the center of gravity shift from places to persons. Religion was put where it belongs—in the human heart. The Holy Spirit comes upon people instead of places. There's no such thing as a holy place. A place has no moral qualities since it has no moral choice. Holy persons gather together to make a holy place, not the other way around. 1 Corinthians 3:16-17 ESV says, ...*For God's temple is holy, and that temple you are.* Holiness shifts from places to persons, and rightly so. I've met the Lord in simple church buildings, ornate cathedrals, prisons, the boundary waters of Canada, brush-arbor structures missing a roof, and, as I mentioned earlier in this book, a converted Buddhist temple. At different times in my life, I met God in different stations on my journey, and I might add, different levels of maturity. In each station, at each stopping point, it had absolutely nothing to do with a place...It was all about a meeting of the heart.

Random thoughts for today:

Where shall I go from your Spirit; where shall I flee from your presence? (Psalm 139:7 ESV)

Of what value is learning that does not turn to love? *(Anthony of Padua)*

In times of solitude, God can make us aware of those things we hide from others.

There is freedom in being honest with God that surpasses all other honesty.

Fearing the Lord means giving God proper place in our lives... If we don't, our knowledge lacks value.

It takes practice to become proficient at something...Practicing the presence of God will make us good at it.

May 24   Bitter Roots

"It's not fair!" I hear it often in our society today. I heard it many times in the classroom from my students. Sometimes life hurts, and we don't understand why some things happen. "Why me?" permeates our Western culture of entitlement. So many today are swimming *in the gall of bitterness* (Acts 8:23), that bitter bile secreted by the liver. How often do we find ourselves saying, "Where's my fair share?" – "I deserve" – "I ought to have." In these later years of my life, I have found myself responding to the "why me" cry, with "why not me?" How do I react when my journey comes to those inevitable crossroads and realities of our broken world? Our "why me" becomes "what now." As one grief counselor shared, "Not every illness is cured, not every relationship is mended, not every airplane comes home." Psalm 31:14 declares, *But I trust You, O LORD! You are my God!* Wow! I have a choice, don't I? I either fail to acknowledge the Lord in all things, or I put my trust in Him and His grace. Guess what choice will lead to what the scripture calls a root of bitterness? *See to it that no one fails to obtain the grace of God, that no "root of bitterness" springs up and causes trouble...*(Hebrews 12:15 ESV). Lesser-known professional baseball player, Leon Brown has described bitterness as a result of clinging to negative experiences. It serves you no good and closes the door to your future. Turning my back on the grace of God WILL cause that root to spring up and bring with it all kinds of trouble. So what happens when the "not supposed to happen" things run me off the road of my journey? I like what a Christian businessman said—"Am I going to become better or bitter?"

Random thoughts for today:

Let all bitterness and wrath and anger and clamor and slander be put away from you, along with all malice. (Ephesians 4:31 ESV)

Let's stand up for what we believe and teach those eternal truths to our children.

Father, I want to know You, but my coward heart fears to give up its toys.

Be kind whenever possible...It's always possible.

Two ways to be rich: 1) Acquire much 2) Desire little

Being honest with God helps me shed my carefully constructed façade.

A six-year-old boy prayed, "Thank You, God, for Your little boy, Jesus, and for Jesus' mommy...uh...uh...Mrs. Mary." He went on to explain the proper way to pray—"If you're Catholic, you gotta kneel down on boards. If you're regular, you just keep your eyes shut, and you don't open them until they say, 'Amen.'" Ah, the simplicity of a child. It is that simplicity, frankness, and naturalness which make the youngster so lovable, and sometimes so frustrating. I equate childlikeness with simplicity. One of the things that have complicated my prayer life from time to time is that I tend to make it too complicated. Like children coming to their parents, so we come to God. We bring our heart cries to our loving Abba Daddy. There is not only awe in that relationship, but there is intimacy. Our Father has said, *How often would I have gathered your children together as a hen gathers her brood under her wings...*(Matthew 23:37 ESV). I love what 9-year-old Eric prayed—"Peoples made cars and footballs and television and skateboards and clothes. So I just thank God for myself, cause nobody else could have made me." I have emphasized it in both of my previous books, and it's a regular part of my prayer time— "Lord, help to keep the kid alive in me." May we forever come as children to our loving Father in heaven who delights in giving and in forgiving. Have a great day, kids!!

Random thoughts for today:

The LORD is like a father to his children, tender and compassionate... (Psalm 103:13 ESV)

Today is mine...Tomorrow is none of my business. *(Paraphrase of Jesus' words)*

A simple lifestyle helps us to better share with those in need.

Two ways to live your life: 1) As though nothing is a miracle 2) As though everything is a miracle.

Life is about using the whole box of crayons.

May 26   God Can Fill A Purse

Charles Spurgeon proclaimed from the pulpit, "Faith can fill a purse, provide a meal, change a hard heart, procure a site for a building, heal sickness, quiet insubordination, and stay an epidemic." How I wish that all of us in Christ would believe in God as to lean upon Him in all the concerns of his life. Philippians 4:19 says, *And my God will meet all your needs according to His glorious riches by Christ Jesus.* It seems I must be continually re-educated in this principle. I doubt, or I forget, and God convicts me and causes me to remember His faithfulness to me through the years. God causes me to remember pulling into our first full-time ministry in Northern Michigan, which paid $75 a week plus parsonage. Our car had broken down in Grand Rapids, and I spent all of our auxiliary cash getting it fixed. We arrived at the parsonage with $1.04 to our name. After pulling into the driveway, I prayed, "Lord, I'm not sure what we're going to eat tonight, but we trust in You to provide." Not only was there a hot meal on the table, but the pantry and the refrigerator were stocked full. I remember six months later, when Helen gave birth to our oldest daughter (two months early). Not only did we live in one of the poorest counties in Michigan, but our flock only numbered around fifty people on a good Sunday. We had no health insurance. Helen and I prayed together in her hospital room. By the way, she had the baby in central Illinois while we were traveling home from her folks. "Lord," we prayed, "we got a pretty good hospital bill here, and we're not sure where the money's coming from, but we trust You to provide." He did. Periodically on this journey through life, God has to remind me that He IS in control and that He WILL provide. And He does. I could share story after story of His faithfulness to our family, and I praise Him for His faithfulness to me, even when I am not.

Random thoughts for today:

...if you have faith as small as a mustard seed, you can say to this mountain. "Move from here to there and it will move. Nothing will be impossible for you. (Matthew 17:20 ESV)

There's never a lane so long that it don't have some hills and curves. *(Southern Proverb)*

Help me not be so busy that I miss the small pleasures God has sprinkled throughout the day.

I can't understand why we fear new ideas...I'm frightened of some of the old ones.

A word once let out of the cage cannot be whistled back again.

I read scripture...Apparently, God believes our loving one another is extremely important.

"LIFE IS FILLED WITH CHOICES." Those who know me at all have heard me use that phrase again and again. And yet, how do these words that I've probably used thousands of times over the years, connect with my prayer life? Whether praying in church, in the quiet place of my home, as I drive or walk on the street, I pray many times throughout the day, "Lord, Your will be done." I think I pray this with the most intensity when I'm not sure what God's will is, and that is often. As I write this, I have two grandchildren preparing to get married this summer. I love the young man and young woman who will soon be a part of our family, but are they God's best for my special loved ones? I believe they are, and I have prayed daily, many years, for the will of God and His best in their seeking a mate. I have two godchildren. I pray daily for God's best in their lives, even though I have seen very little of both of them in the last few years; one lives out of the country. What do I know of God's specific will for their lives? There are some things I can pray on their behalf, no doubt, but mostly it's all about praying the Lord's will in their lives and the lives of their families—God's best. I've been preaching for a while in a little congregation of about 20 people. This church started shortly after the Civil War. Some think they should close their doors, but they want to continue on. What's God's will for this precious little flock? What does the future hold? The chairman of our board came to me after a Sunday service and said, "Rick, you should be preaching at a much larger church." My response—"Leon, I've been there and done that; I'm right where God wants me, right here, right now." The only thing I know at the present time is that God has placed Helen and me in the center of this small group as their pastor, and we're here to stay until God shows us otherwise. There are so many times that I don't know what's best for myself or for those I love. I just don't know. And when those many times confront me, I throw myself upon the will of my Father.

Random thoughts for today:

Since the day we heard about you, we have not stopped praying for you and asking God to fill you with knowledge of His will through all spiritual wisdom and understanding. (Colossians 1:9 ESV)

My LORD sends no one away except those who are filled with themselves.

Me: "I can't handle this!" LORD: "I know, but I can!"

Don't believe everything you think.

You are sowing the flowers of tomorrow in the seeds of today.

May 28   Flawed Praying

"We love You, Lord." I've noticed lately how often we use that phrase at the end of our public prayers. Nothing wrong with that. But to me, it seems that it is a phrase that has become kind of meaningless verbiage, like the "hey, how ya doin" many of us use with each other. Many times, I've publicly prayed, "We love You, Lord" as I was walking off the platform, closing my prayer. I DO love the Lord, but was it REALLY love for Him that was in my heart as I prayed? I ask these questions, not to judge the heart of anyone else, but to make sure my own motives are sincere. In my entry from a couple of days ago, I talked about the simplicity of the prayers of children. Have you ever listened to those brand-new

Christians pray? You know, those who haven't learned how to do it yet. And you are moved. They talk to God like He's their friend and may use street terms that are easily understood. They may stumble. They may even laugh or cry as they pray, but there's not a whole lot of meaningless verbiage. Beautiful!! And the Lord hears their hearts, as always. I often pray that the Lord will hear my heart and that He will hear my gratitude. One old preacher from the last century said, "How we have modernized and complicated and destroyed prayer in the public place." I hope I don't do that. Remember the Serenity Prayer? It's a simple prayer written by a theologian of all people.

> **God, grant me the serenity to accept the things I cannot change;**
> **Courage to change the things I can;**
> **And wisdom to know the difference.** (Reinhold Niebuhr)

Even a beginning believer can understand that. As a flawed person, pray today that the Lord will hear your heart.

Random thoughts for today:

So then, just as you received Christ Jesus as Lord, continue to live in Him, rooted and built up in Him, strengthened in the faith as you were taught, and overflowing with thankfulness. (Colossians 2:6-7 ESV)

We are dust filled with the breath of God.

I realize I am not in control and that there is Someone greater than me whom I must present my life, and I am humbled.

Jeremiah 23:23-24 ESV says, *I am a God at hand, and not a God afar off. If a man shall hide himself in secret places, shall I not then see him? Do not I fill heaven and earth?* Proverbs 15:3 ESV tells us that *the eyes of the LORD are in every place, keeping watch on the evil and the good.* I can know that God is present everywhere and that He hears and sees everything. Cyprian says that the Lord enters into our most hidden and secret places in His abundant majesty. Whether your prayer cries are noisy, or your words are disciplined with quietness and modesty, God enters into our remote places (speaking of both physical places as well as the places of our heart). In the stillness of our quiet time, we bring our requests before Him, and in the silence of our heart, we listen for His voice as His depth cries out to the depth of our soul (Psalm 42:7). A popular contemporary song in many of our churches today says, "In the secret, in the quiet hour I wait, only for You, 'cause I want to know You more." How often are you meeting Him in the secret places of your heart? How often are you allowing His "deep" call out to your "deep"?

It is in the secret place, Lord that I want you continue knowing You more and more.

Random thoughts for today:

Deep calls to deep in the roar of Your waterfalls; all Your waves and breakers have swept over me. (Psalm 42:7 ESV)

Everything that irritates us about others can lead us to an understanding of ourselves. *(Carl Jung)*

The way you travel through life is the most powerful legacy you can give your children.

My joy in learning is partly that it enables me to teach. *(Seneca)*

Encouragement is oxygen to the soul. *(George M. Adams)*

We need to zero in on who God is, not what we want Him to be. *(Rebecca Crain)*

My true peace is not the absence of tension or conflict...It is the presence of the love and compassion and joy of my Lord.

Well-timed silence hath more eloquence than speech. *(Ancient quote)*

May 30   Open the Door

If you grew up in a Christian environment, you've probably seen the famous picture by Warner Sallman of *Christ at Heart's Door.* Modern critics have said that this painting, as well as *The Head of Christ* by the same artist, is outdated and makes Jesus look too soft and too European. They also say that they don't relate to youth today. Maybe, but I like the pictures anyway. And you may have heard (or not) that the door upon which Jesus is knocking has no outside handle or latch. The latch is on the inside. Jesus says in the Revelation letter to Laodicea, "Behold, I stand at the door and knock; I will come in IF one opens it." Jesus never pushes the door open; he waits for us to open it. Our opening the door is not only true of our salvation encounter, but I believe it is just as true in our daily time with Him. Sometimes I can almost hear Jesus' audible voice, *Come away with Me by yourselves to a quiet place and get some rest* (Mark 6:31 ESV).

What an invitation! Right in the middle of a section of scripture full of action and movement, Jesus invites His disciples to rest with Him. Into the rushing, He calls us to slow, to listen to our breathing, and to focus on Him. Jesus is the rest our souls are craving. He knocks; we have to open the door. He knocks at the door of our prayer time. He knocks at the door of our study of scripture. We open the door of our heart and mind for Him to enter. And guess what? He will do just that.

Random thoughts for today:

Here I am! I stand at the door and knock. If anyone hears My voice and opens the door, I will come in and eat with him, and he with Me. (Revelation 3:20 ESV)

There is one happiness in life, to love and be loved.

So, Jesus took a towel and a basin of water and redefined greatness.

The struggles and problems you face today will become the means of God's glory tomorrow.

H.O.P.E. – Hold On, Pain Ends!!

God loves each of us as if there were only one of us. *(Augustine)*

The soul is never less alone than when it is alone with God. *(Samuel Chadwick)*

May 31   A Promise in Okinawa
                                A Memorial Day Tribute

The most severe and memorable battle of World War 2 happened in April of 1945, the battle for Okinawa. On Easter

Sunday, kamikaze planes filled the air diving for the ships on their suicide missions. My father's ship, the USS Edgecombe, dropped off troops near the beach then waited to retrieve the wounded. Each time this maneuver took place, the captain ordered their engine room to "make smoke." This maneuver was done to make their ship less visible to the kamikazes. The vessel next to my dad's was hit and sunk. Dad's ship stayed in position for five days. Although they were not a fighting ship, they did carry armament for self-protection. Dad has often said how aware he was that one cannot barter with God, but he has shared with us the tremendous felt need he had that week to talk with the Lord. This son of a pastor and Jesus had quite a meeting together aboard that ship. He committed to God that Easter week. He prayed to the Lord, "Father, get me home, and I will be Yours, forever!" During the Okinawa invasion, American casualties were over 49,000, including 12,520 killed. Over 110,000 Japanese lost their lives. 38 US ships were lost to kamikazes. On February 6, 1946, my dad came home to his wife and his eleven-month-old son (that would be me). My father honored his promise to the Lord made that day in the South Pacific. "I will be Yours forever!" He was...And he is.

(Thanks to my sister, Susan Crouse, for putting this information together)

Random thoughts for today:

Do not be afraid; do not be discouraged. Go out and face them tomorrow, and the LORD will be with you.
(2 Chronicles 20:17 ESV)

It's possible to teach math, science, and history without God...
It's also possible to teach the Bible without God as well.

We church people are terrible at being silent. *(Becky Crain)*

Kindness is a language that the deaf can hear and the blind can see. *(Mark Twain)*

I wonder how many of us living in this nation today truly take the time to REMEMBER. *(Memorial Day Address/2015 – Warren Jones)*

June

Love Does!!

Teach Me, LORD

Remember what the disciples asked Jesus before He taught the model prayer? "Lord, can you teach us how to pray? In my own experience, I believe there are three kinds of prayer:

1. <u>There is spoken prayer with a prepared text</u>. I shared with you earlier that I've used the Lord's Prayer on an almost daily basis. There are other special prayers, long and short, that can be effectively used on many occasions. And of course, there is the scripture itself. I have found it a blessing actually to pray scripture. I have no problem using a prepared prayer any more than using a manuscript when I preach or notes when I teach. My spirit has been lifted to the Lord many times praying in this way.

2. <u>There is spoken prayer without a prepared text</u>. This is probably the most frequent type of praying done in the church today. Spoken prayer can also be a part of your private prayer life. Speaking out loud has helped me to focus on my words without distraction. Sometimes, it can almost seem as if God and I are having an intimate conversation as if we were sitting together.

3. <u>Then there is prayer that is only in the heart</u>. Earlier in this book, I talk about those wordless prayers that are

silent and can bring rest to the body and soul. There are those times that words just don't get the job done; they can almost get in the way.

Lord, teach me how to pray. I am Your teachable student. Amen.

Random thoughts for today:

Lord, teach us to pray... (Luke 11:1 ESV)

Forgive me this day if I've done or said anything to increase the pain of this world around me.

The fact that I think I'm following God's will doesn't always mean I'm doing so.

Will I miss some of God's beauty today? Stop a moment...Look around you!!

June 2   Battle for "Rights"

I wrote an entry on April 19 about RIGHTS. That piece was written in the shadow of the COVID-19 surge and subsequent lock-down of our country. The issue of rights has once again come to the forefront, in an entirely different light. And the battle for "rights" rages on!! Over the last weekend, protests, rioting, looting, and destruction of businesses transpired across our country in the aftermath of the police-killing of George Floyd in Minneapolis on June 25 (2020). Closer to home, a peaceful protest in my city of Michigan City turned ugly for a few hours. 95% of the news, both national and area, has been video coverage of buildings burning, businesses being looted, and tense stand-offs between the police and various groups. It would seem, including in my town, that many peaceful demonstrations have been hijacked by people who have an agenda not related to peaceful protest. I've been studying the writings of Gandhi lately (see February 25 entry). His philosophy of non-violent protest is well-known, studied, and practiced by many including, Dr. Martin Luther King Jr. I've seen some social media posts this week that state that change will not happen without violent protest. That's not only false; it's not logical. There are a few exceptions in history, but very few. Violence begets only violence. Listening and dialogue don't happen until the violence has subsided. I think today I will exercise my right, no wait, my responsibility to encourage. I watched several video clips this morning of people encouraging people in the aftermath of the insanity of the weekend. A white policeman hugging a crying black woman. Black activists surrounding a white policeman, protecting him from a mob. A white policeman taking off his riot helmet, laying down his baton and supporting a group of protestors, who, in turn, invited him to march with them...He did. Our own police chief in Michigan City, standing in the middle of a group of protestors, dialoguing with them for a couple of hours. I believe he was the primary reason that no major damage was done in Michigan City. I went to bed last night with an agitated spirit, but I am lifted up today as I watch people encouraging people in our community and communities around the nation. *ENCOURAGE ONE ANOTHER DAILY* (Hebrews 3:13 ESV). Be an encourager today!!

Random thoughts for today:

Be kind to one another, tenderhearted, forgiving one another... (Ephesians 4:32 ESV)

When you finally learn that a person's behavior has more to do with their internal struggle than it ever did with you, you learn grace.

What am I truly authentic about in my life? In what areas am I NOT authentic?

How many people have you made homesick for the Lord?

June 3   What Racism?

I had a good friend ask me a question this past week, genuinely questioning the racism problem in our nation. He asked, "Do we believe that racism is as bad as people are saying it is in the country right now?" And therein lies the problem. We have several mindsets in our culture today. There are those who are NOT racist in any way, shape, or form; not many of those around. I sincerely believe that I am not a racist, and yet I pause when I read the words of one modern philosopher who said, "There's a bit of racism in all of us." Probably. Then there are those who are racist and are ignorant of the fact that they are racist. They think that they aren't, but they are. Some are racist and try to hide it. One citizen of the United Kingdom said this week, "Racism is a global disease. We have bigotry and discrimination in the United Kingdom, we just do a better job of hiding it." Then there are those who are unashamedly and categorically racist. They make no excuses, and many are passionately vocal about it (and sometimes violent). We can close our eyes and pretend it's really not all that bad. I've heard many say, "We've come so far; we're doing a better job as a country." I'm not sure we have. We do make advances, but then it seems we regress. A statistic that came out a couple of years ago reported that over one hundred unarmed blacks were killed by police. Symptomatic? Yes. Don't misunderstand me or unfriend me on Facebook yet. I am pro-police; I served for over ten years as a chaplain on the Michigan City police department. I passionately take a stand against looting and rioting, but all of this doesn't negate the fact that we have a problem. I'm tired of political activists accusing me of turning a blind eye to this problem or not thinking deeply enough because I refuse to justify anarchy in the streets. I weary of the constant put-downs, name-calling, divisive satire, and insulting memes that fill social media, especially from those I consider to be brothers and sisters in Christ. I've lived through three nation-wide racial conflicts. I cannot help but be cynical in thinking that political activism (no matter how well-intentioned) is going to change any problem in our society that has come from heart issues. I thank the Lord for our police chief, who is not only a black man but also an ordained pastor. We worked together when I was a chaplain; I prayer partner with him daily. I can and do try to be more involved in community issues for its betterment; however, I will never be able to change another's heart (see entry, May 4th). In the meantime, I will do my best to challenge the body of Christ to change mindsets and attitudes that stem from those heart issues. I will loudly proclaim, "C'mon, Church ...We're better than this." Yes, I'll say it, and not just as a cliché or a hashtag—"Black Lives Matter!" Let's rise up together and loudly proclaim our love for others...Choose life!! Choose love!!"

Have you not discriminated among yourselves and become judges with evil thoughts? (James 2:4 ESV)

June 4   More Journal Ramblings

From my personal journal: Some of my rambling thoughts gleaned from William Barclay, Thomas Merton, and Susan Muto.

> I have learned about power by experiencing helplessness.
> I have learned about victory through the admission of defeat.
> I have learned about goodness through the confession of my sin.
> I have learned about knowledge through the admission of my ignorance.
> I have learned about independence through my dependence upon the Lord.
> I have learned about freedom through servanthood.
> "Humility is a virtue, not a neurosis. It sets us free to act virtuously, to serve God, and to know Him. It sets us free to do what is really good."

Random thoughts for today:

For if you possess these qualities in increasing measure (the qualities listed in Vv 5-7), *they will keep you from being ineffective and unproductive in your knowledge of our Lord Jesus Christ. (2 Peter 1:8 ESV)*

Prayer is an ongoing conversation with God...All day long.

Correction does much...Encouragement much more!!

Judge people by their questions rather than by their answers. *(Voltaire)*

By learning, you will teach...By teaching, you will learn. *(Latin Proverb)*

SIMPLIFY!! SIMPLIFY!! *(Henry David Thoreau)*

Great works are performed not by strength but by perseverance. *(Samuel Johnson)*

June 5   Poor in Spirit

Blessed are the poor in spirit... (Matthew 5:3). There are moments in my quiet time that I come to the realization that "right prayer" (whatever that is) comes from a posture of great, genuine humility. When I am in the presence of God, I become vividly aware that I am not what I ought to be and often feel myself as a spiritual pauper before Him. When this sense overwhelms me, I find it much easier to be real with God—no pretense, no face-saving. I desire to see myself as God sees me. A time like this also makes me very teachable. 19th-century politician, Albert E. Day said, "My sins are as apparent as an ink stain upon the wall; my unlovingness is as visible as a broken bone in an X-ray photograph." That old, old gospel song sums up the real situation in sincere prayer:

> "Let not conscience make you linger,
> Nor of fitness fondly dream;
> All the fitness He requireth
> Is to feel your need of Him."

What's the last part of Matthew 5:3 ESV say? *Blessed are the poor in spirit, for theirs is the kingdom of heaven.* I love that.

<u>Random thoughts for today</u>:

None is righteous, no not one. *(Romans 3:10 ESV)*

Prayer is an ongoing conversation with God all day long. *(Brother Lawrence)*

We live our lives, not so that God will love us, but rather we live in such a way because He has already loved us.

Sometimes the most spiritual thing we can do is the practical thing.

Sometimes we don't need to understand...Sometimes we just need to trust.

Dear God...Hi...I'm crazy. Send help soon. *(Prayer of a friend)*

June 6   Hosea's Warnings to America
                                          (Oops, I mean Israel)

Have you ever studied the prophecy of Hosea? This prophet of God lived and served for 60 years or so in the final days of the Northern kingdom of Israel, which fell to the Assyrians in BC 722. The history of this man is fascinating as the Lord commands him to take a prostitute as his wife (her name was Gomer, no relation to Gomer Pyle). She is unfaithful to him and goes to other lovers; God subsequently tells Hosea to take her back again. Here are some of the themes the prophet shares from the Lord:

- No faithfulness or love in the land

- The many sins of the religious leaders of the nation
- The land referred to as "the house of wickedness"
- None of the national leaders are willing to call upon the Lord; rebellious
- It is a nation incapable of purity
- Sins of the people are many, and their hostility is great
- A deceitful people producing a "fruit of deception"
- A nation relying upon their military strength
- A refusal of the people to repent

On this 76th anniversary (when I wrote this) of D-Day in Normandy, I think about these things and our nation being so divided; some who claim to be "under God" and some who don't even pretend to be under Him. Despite the warnings of Hosea, the people of Israel remain entrenched in idolatry and rebellion. But the book of Hosea ends, as the Bible ends, with a great message of hope. There are days, even though I know better, when it seems that darkness is winning over light. But in the closing sections of Hosea, in the warnings of God's wrath, we read of life and hope and FORGIVENESS. *Return, O Israel, to the LORD your God. Your sins have been your downfall! Take words with you and return to the LORD. Say to Him: "Forgive all our sins and receive us graciously that we may offer the fruit of our lips"* (Hosea 14:1-2 ESV). Praise to the Lord...Always the promise of forgiveness.

Random thoughts for today:

I will ransom you from the power of the grave; I will redeem you from death. *(Hosea 13:14 ESV)*

I'm very disappointed, and I hate leaving the world feeling this way. *(Private Jack Port, age 97, on the state of our world today... He was on the beaches of Normandy, June 6, 1944)*

June 7   Meditation Prompt

Meditation is the activity of calling to mind, and thinking over, and dwelling on, and applying to oneself, the various things that one knows about the works and ways and promises of God. It is an activity of thinking consciously about the Lord in the presence of the Lord. I like the literal translation of Philippians 4:8 (scripture listed in Random Thoughts below). The last phrase says, "let your mind DWELL on these things." I've learned that prayer and meditation go hand-in-hand. Sometimes this happens during my regular quiet time in the morning. Sometimes it happens in the middle of the night when I wake up and have trouble falling back to sleep. That seems to happen more frequently as I get older. I think of Psalm 63:6—*I lie awake thinking of You, meditating on You through the night. I think of how You have helped me; I sing for joy in the shadow of your protecting wings* (NLT). Sometimes I like to sit out on my back deck or by a fire and listen to meditation apps (See entry of February 18 discussing mini-breaks). Journaling and writing out prayers and thoughts have also been a helpful tool. It can be a challenging discipline to master because our culture is all about "doing" something— anything. Most of us who are used to getting "drugged out" on activity struggle with this. TV, the internet, the cell phone, or work and school projects can become the enemy of meditation. Jean Crasset, a French Jesuit theologian, wrote in 1907, "It is meditation that leads us in spirit into the hallowed solitudes wherein we find

God alone—in peace, in calm, in silence, in recollection." So why not give it a try? Maybe you could start with a 3-5 minute period of time. Use a scripture or a daily devotional thought to get you started—kind of a "meditation prompt" (You know, like writing prompts in English class). Do nothing, except allow your mind to DWELL on Him!!

Random thoughts for today:

Finally, brothers, whatever is true, whatever is honorable, whatever is just, whatever is pure, whatever is lovely, whatever is commendable, if there is any excellence, if there is anything worthy of praise, think about these things. *(Philippians 4:8 ESV)*

It is well to give when asked, but it is better to give unasked.
Lord, help me to remember the importance of little things.
Sometimes life is about keeping our eyes open.
Often when I pray, I have to "grow down"...Don't let the world rob you of your childlikeness.

June 8   Articles 1, 2, & 3

FOR OUR LEADERS:

O Lord our Governor, whose glory is in all the world: We commend this nation to Thy merciful care, that, being guided by Thy Providence, we may dwell secure in Thy peace. Grant to the President of the United States, the Governor of this State (or Commonwealth), and to all in authority, wisdom, and strength to know and to do Thy will. Fill them with the love of truth and righteousness and make them ever mindful of their calling to serve this people in Thy fear; through Jesus Christ our Lord, who liveth and reigneth with Thee and the Holy Spirit, one God, world without end. Amen.

FOR CONGRESS:

O God, the fountain of wisdom, whose will is good and gracious, and whose law is truth: We beseech Thee so to guide and bless our Senators and Representatives in Congress assembled, that they may enact such laws as shall please Thee, to the glory of Thy Name and the welfare of this people; through Jesus Christ our Lord. Amen.

FOR COURTS OF JUSTICE:

Almighty God who sittest in the throne of judging right: we humbly beseech Thee to bless the courts of justice and the magistrates in all this land; and give unto them the spirit of wisdom and understanding, that they may discern the truth and impartially administer the law in the fear of Thee alone; through Him who shall come to be our Judge, Thy Son our Savior Jesus Christ. Amen.

(Taken from The Book of Common Prayer/Episcopal Church)

Father God, I lift our leaders to You today, as you have asked me to do. I ask You to guide and direct them. In all things, Father, I pray that Your kingdom would come.

Random thoughts for today:

Pray...for all in high positions, that we may lead a quiet and peaceful life... *(1 Timothy 2:1-2 ESV)*

The beginning is always today.

Grace is everything.

Do I have the wisdom to hear the truth from others? Do I get defensive when criticized?

Forgive and ask to be forgiven; excuse rather than accuse.

June 9   What Do You Want?

Lord, I want to see the fruit of the Spirit in my life. Good! But how much of it do I want? Do you remember the question Jesus asked a person in need? *What do you want me to do for you?* (Mark 10:51 ESV). My family gives me a rough time because I can never tell them what I want for Christmas (or birthday, or Father's Day). It's difficult to make a list when you really don't have any great needs. The usual conversation goes like this: "What do you want for your birthday, Dad?" "All I want is peace, love, and joy!" That exchange has gone on for many years now. The other day I was thinking about the Jesus-Bartimaeus exchange in Mark 10, and I wondered how often I respond to Jesus' question with a flippant "peace, love and joy" response? I could rationalize and say, "I don't want anything; I'm content." But is that contentment or complacency? Perhaps I don't spend enough time considering what the deep needs of my life are. Robert Louis Stevenson called it "the malady of not wanting." Young Solomon asked God for the wisdom he would need as king. As I look at my own life in light of Jesus' question, do I ask for things that have to do with my character? James writes in his epistle, *You do not have, because you do not ask* (4:2). Maybe when the Lord asks me, *What do you want me to do for you?* I need to seriously consider my response.

What I want for you to do for me, Lord, is to make me a loving, joyful, peaceable, patient, kind, good, faithful, gentle, disciplined Christian.

Random thoughts for today:

Be imitators of me, as I am of Christ. (1 Corinthians 11:1 ESV)

Humility is to put a seal on your lips and forget what you have done. *(Henry Drummond)*

Statistics are no substitute for good judgment. *(Henry Clay)*

Love does not define God...God defines love. *(Roger Ash)*

When you have only two pennies left in the world, buy a loaf of bread with one, and a rose with the other. *(Chinese Proverb)*

Make the best of what's in your power and take the rest as it happens. *(Epictetus)*

June 10   Just Shepherds

Have you ever stopped to think about the role of shepherds in scripture? We read through the Bible of many shepherds beginning with Cain. Many biblical figures were shepherds, among them the patriarchs Abraham, Isaac, and Jacob, the leaders of the twelve tribes, Moses, King David, and the Old Testament prophet,

Amos from Tekoa. The most famous psalm of all, of course, is the Shepherd's Psalm 23. And we can't forget the shepherds from Bethlehem who showed up at the manger at the birth of Christ and were the first worshippers of Jesus. Sheep are mentioned in scripture more than 500 times, more than any other animal, which would include our being labeled as sheep—*All we, like sheep, have gone astray* (Isaiah 53:6 ESV). A shepherd's responsibility was the safety and welfare of the flock. He would keep his flock intact, protect it from predators, and guide it into market areas in time for shearing. In the New Testament, one of the terms for the leadership of the church was shepherd. *To the elders...Shepherd the flock of God that is among you, exercising oversight...*(1 Peter 5:2 ESV). Church leaders today would do well to remember this charge. Some Middle-eastern flocks might include as many as 1,000 sheep. Domestic sheep cannot live without a shepherd; they are not capable of caring for themselves. And of course, Jesus referred to Himself as the Good Shepherd—*I am the Good Shepherd. The Good Shepherd lays down His life for the sheep* (John 10:11 ESV). In this chapter, Jesus sheds light on how He reigns, like a shepherd with a calming voice and protective hand and vigilance. I love the chorus we sing often in our church:

> "Gentle Shepherd, come and lead us, for we need You to help us find our way.
> Gentle Shepherd, come and feed us, for we need Your strength from day to day."

Random thoughts for today:

The LORD is my shepherd; I shall not want. *(Psalm 23:1 ESV)*

Genuine disciples don't get served...They serve.

The great opportunity is where you are.

I relate to the kind of people who think decorating consists mostly of building enough bookshelves.

I'm in a hurry, but God is not.

Sometimes the big miracles we're waiting on are happening right in front of us.

May the Holy Spirit help me to speak when the time is right, and to keep quiet when it's time to listen.

June 11   Catechetical Prayer

I have debated in my mind the value and effectiveness of catechetical learning. In my training as a schoolteacher, I learned many effective methods of teaching that have worked well for me (and hopefully, my students). I wonder how much of our preaching and teaching in the church is catechetical—in other words, the questions are taught together with the answers. I'm not saying that there isn't a place for this, but I believe that the charge against us that we rely too much on circular reasoning in our thought processes is sometimes true. An example of circular reasoning would be, "The Bible is true, so you should not doubt the Word of God" or "You must obey the law because it's illegal to break the law." You get the idea. Having said that, even though catechism isn't my favorite teaching method, I've discovered a truth in the Westminster Shorter Catechism that has been helpful to me. It defines prayer as "an offering up of our desires unto God for things agreeable to His will." I like this. It puts the emphasis where it belongs—on God and His will. No matter how sincere my desire might be, my prayer petitions are not really prayers unless God and the doing of His will are at the center of it. That makes sense to me. So, whereas circular reasoning may not be as effective in teaching or learning apologetics, it becomes quite a blessing to my prayer life. The study of objective apologetics has blessed me with an ability to reason in many areas of my faith. So yes, the Bible is true, so I should not doubt the Word of God.

Random thoughts for today:

Faith is the assurance of things hoped for, the conviction of things not seen. *(Hebrews 11:1 ESV)*

When there is food on my plate, I don't whine about mystery meat or my distaste for veggies...I'm just grateful that my belly is full.

What we see many times depends mainly on what we look for.

I work daily to stay fresh and keep my spirit out of a rut.

In the morning when I rise, just give me Jesus. *(From song based on old African melody)*...Nothing complicated—JUST JESUS!!

I didn't think orange went with purple until I saw the sunset You made on Tuesday night...That was really cool! *(Thomas, an 8-year-old kid)*

June 12   God Speaking

How does God speak to you? One writer says that sometimes He shouts, and sometimes He whispers; sometimes He speaks in the calm and the quiet, and sometimes He speaks through the storm. Henry Drummond wrote, "When God speaks, He can speak so loudly that all the voices of the world seem dumb. And yet when God speaks, He can speak so softly that no one hears the whisper but yourself." He can use the loud cacophony of the events in my life to get my attention, or He can, through the almost imperceptible rustle of a breeze through the trees, murmur my name. Without getting too mystical about it, I believe that God has spoken to me in a crowded room, and in the solitude of sitting by myself by a mountain stream. And when I talk about God speaking to me, it's not "God told me to tell you to give me a hundred dollars" speaking to me. It's an inner impression of confidence and trust in my Abba Father. Subjective? Yup... but very, very real. I've never heard an audible voice, but there have been times on my journey that His words were very much impressed upon my spirit—The evening before I was ordained to the ministry...The moment I saw Helen coming down the aisle to become my wife...When we miscarried our first child...At the birth of both of our daughters...At the bedside of my father right after he had passed. These are just a few special moments when I perceived the Lord whispering to my spirit—"I'm here; your Abba Father is here!" *Deep calling out to deep* (Psalm 42:7).

Random thoughts for today:

For God speaks in one way, and in two, though man does not perceive it. *(Job 33:14 ESV)*

Give away as much joy as you can, but never let anyone steal it from you.

You need to let the little things that would ordinarily bore you suddenly thrill you.

Christianity is not found in a place or an event, but rather in a Person.

Comforting truth—God can bless flawed and uncertain praying.

Be a fountain, not a drain. *(Anonymous)*

God doesn't want my stuff...HE WANTS ME!!

The degree of my compassion should run deepest for the suffering person.

June 13   Fruit of Obedience

Do you ever question God? Do you ever wonder WHY? Remember the account in Genesis 22 where God tells Abraham to go to the mountain to sacrifice his son, Isaac, to Him? Understand we're talking about a burnt-offering sacrifice. Why would He do that? There are so many accounts in scripture of God commanding certain things that just don't make sense—I mean, crazy things!! Moses, stretch out your staff over the Red Sea so that you can cross. Joshua, march around Jericho seven times, and you will conquer it. Gideon, smash a bunch of pottery and shout real loud, and you'll win the battle. Naaman, dunk yourself in that polluted river, and you'll be healed. Jehoshaphat, put your choir on the front lines of your army and get them singing, and you'll win the victory. These are just a few biblical examples. And how about, Jesus, even though you can call 10,000 angels down to protect You, I want You to freely give yourself over to be crucified. There is an ancient story of a monk who was told by his abba to plant a dry stick in the sand and to water it daily. So far away was the distance from his cell that he had to leave in the evening to fetch the water, and he only returned in the following morning. For three years, he patiently fulfilled his abba's command. At the end of this period, the stick suddenly put forth leaves and bore fruit. The abba picked the fruit, took it to the church, and invited the monks to eat, saying, "Come and taste the fruit of obedience." Maybe you're sensing a leading to do something for the Lord that doesn't make sense, and maybe that feeling isn't going away. Don't automatically dismiss it. Ask Him for direction and clarification. Begin where you are. Begin with what little obedience you're capable of, even if it begins with small steps. Aren't you glad that Jesus obeyed His father—*Father...Not as I will, but as You will* (Matthew 26:39)? Because he obeyed, this day, we taste the fruit of that obedience.

Random thoughts for today:

If you love Me, you will keep My commandments. (*John 14:15* ESV)

True Christians are grateful for the Word, even though they may have read it many times and still not grasped the beauty of all of it.

Whatever you're going through, whatever the storm, Jesus is the boat.

In a gentle way, you can shake the world. *(Gandhi)*

Loving well is the essence of true spirituality.

June 14   Does God Give a Hoot?

Have you ever had the church lay a major guilt trip on you about your commitment (or lack of it)? I was raised in the "old-school" of Christian thought that told me if I wanted to please God I must attend church two or three times a week (prayer meetings can be optional), read my Bible and pray every day, tithe, teach a class, show up for church workdays, support missions, and oh yeah, BE GOOD. Now don't get me wrong, all of these things can be good things, but they can also become negatives, depending upon our motives. Please understand that God does not demand all of this in order to please Him. God needs nothing and demands nothing. Paul writes, *Christ's love compels us...* (2 Corinthians 5:14). It is a life WITH the Lord that demands these things. Anne Dillard says, "God does not, I regret to report, give a hoot" about these things in and of themselves. She says, "You do not have to do these things—unless you want to know God." We do not do these disciplines or acts of service because we HAVE to do them; we do them out of our love for Him and our desire to grow closer to Him. Our motive—*We love because He first loved us* (Here we are again at 1 John 4:19). I don't serve or pray or study to please God; I serve and pray and study and whatever, because of what He has done for me. That's a debt I can never repay!!

Lord, let my body be a servant to my spirit, and both my body and spirit be servants of Jesus, doing all things for Your glory here. Amen.

Random thoughts for today:

Owe no one anything, except to love each other, for the one who loves another has fulfilled the law. (Romans 13:8 ESV)

The heart has her reasons about which the mind knows nothing. *(Blaise Pascal)*

Your greatest pleasure is that which rebounds from hearts that you have made glad.

I hope I'm never so stupid as to allow anything to come between me and the Lord.

Commitment is what transforms a promise into reality.

Trouble came knocking, but hearing laughter, hurried away. *(Ben Franklin)*

June 15   Tribute to a Nurse

John Ruskin once said, "Every time love and skill work together, expect a masterpiece." What a great definition of the nursing profession. In this time of the Covid-19 pandemic, our nation has honored essential workers as heroes in the midst of the storm. Nurses are at the top of that list. "Nurse" is just another word to describe a person strong enough to tolerate anything and soft enough to understand anyone. Nurses dispense comfort, compassion, and caring without even a prescription. They are there when the first breath is taken, and they are there when the last breath is taken as well. I spend a lot of time praying for the medical personnel in our communities, but I spend a GREAT amount of time daily praying for a special nurse to me—my oldest daughter, Christine Susan. She has been on the front lines this year in one of the largest hospitals in the greater Chicago area. Florence Nightingale said, "For the sick, it is important to have the best." I believe that Chris is one of the best. It's been said that the character of the nurse is as important as the knowledge she possesses. Chris has grown over the years in her faith and strong in character. Her mother and I couldn't be more proud. Am I prejudice in my opinion? You bet I am. My daily prayers for protection continue for her as she goes to work each morning, masked up, and attends to the tasks at hand for the day. So I write this tribute today to the third of three of the most important women in my life. Chris, keep your focus on the Lord...May your scrubs be comfy...Your coffee be strong...And your Mondays be short.

Care for one...That's love. Care for all...That's nursing.

Random thoughts for today:

I was sick and you looked after me. (Matthew 25:36 ESV)

True Christians have a sense of humor about the vanity of wanting to be noticed.

In what seems ordinary and routine, there is always more than meets the eye.

The people you disagree with are not necessarily your enemy... Even a legalist wants to do the right thing. (Nate Loucks)

Be patient towards all that is unresolved in your heart, and learn to love the questions themselves.

One of the secrets of life is that all that is really worth the doing is what we do for others.

Have you ever sung the old hymn, "Morning Has Broken?" It was first published in 1931 by author Eleanor Farjeon and set to a traditional Scottish Gaelic tune, "Bunessan."

> "Morning has broken like the first morning; Blackbird has spoken like the first bird.
> Praise for the singing; Praise for the morning
> Praise from their springing fresh from the Word."

A beautiful old song that reminds me of my summer mornings on my back deck. It's almost 6 am; the sun has been up for about a half an hour. My Bible is open on my lap turned to the Psalms. After a while I find myself gazing out over my backyard, watching and listening. The squirrels are active. So far I've seen cardinals, finches, wrens, chickadees, blue jays, nuthatches, and mourning doves at the feeder. *Look at the birds of the air: they neither sow nor reap nor gather into barns, and yet your heavenly Father feeds them* (Matthew 6:26 ESV). It's a fact they don't go hungry around here. A large woodpecker is at work on a tree about 50 feet from me, a chipmunk is eating from a dish on the deck three feet away from me, and I can hear the cry of a nearby catbird (for weeks I thought we had a kitty roaming the neighborhood). *You have given (man) dominion over the works of Your hands; You have put all things under his feet...the beasts of the field, the birds of the heavens, the fish of the sea...*(no fish in my backyard)*...O LORD, our Lord, how majestic is Your name in all the earth* (Psalm 8:6-8 ESV). Praise You, Abba Father, for another beautiful morning on my back deck.

"Praise for the singing; Praise for the morning!"

Random thoughts for today:

Ask the animals, and they will teach you, or the birds in the sky, and they will tell you. *(Job 12:7* ESV)

True Christians testify to the truth by the way they live.

We need to recover in the church today the spirit of love and compassion even in the face of major disagreement.

In this millennium of the church, have we become God's demanding little brats?

Tell the truth and run! *(Yugoslavian Proverb...I don't ascribe to this, but it made me laugh)*

June 17   Aaronic Blessing

A benediction that I have used often at the close of a congregational time of worship is the blessing found at the close of Numbers, chapter 6. *The LORD spoke to Moses, saying, "Speak to Aaron and his sons, saying, Thus you shall bless the people of Israel: you shall say to them"...* Following is what scholars through the generations have called, The Aaronic Blessing. I have prayed this blessing daily over my family. I have also prayed it over congregations, school chapels, in the classroom, and during class graduations. As I have studied it over the years, the original text as well as various devotional interpretations have helped to expand its meaning. I hope, in this expanded version, it will help to personalize it and make it more intimate for you.

May our LORD bless you and keep you

May our LORD make His face and His smile shine down upon you

May the LORD turn His countenance toward you, looking you full in the face

And may He give you peace

Why not pray this prayer over your family today. What a blessing!! A brother once share with me, "The sweetest time of the day for me is when I am praying for my family."

Random thoughts for today:

So shall they put my name upon the people of Israel, and I will bless them. (Numbers 6:27 ESV —This verse follows the blessing of Aaron.)

Yeah, we need to learn to be quiet, in many ways.

Grace meets us where we are, but it doesn't leave us there. *(Becky Crain)*

It's more important to proclaim what we are FOR, rather than what we're against.

Sometimes our first problem is not to learn, but to unlearn.

My value has nothing to do with my past decisions or achievements or lack of them...It has everything to do with *Christ in me, the hope of glory.*

When I approach a child, he inspires me in two ways: 1) Tenderness for what he is; 2) Respect for what he may become. *(Louis Pasteur)*

It's my job to keep all of our outside plants watered. I've tried to follow the advice of one crazy plant lady I used to know—"The cactus thrives in the desert while the fern thrives in the wetland; the fool will try to plant them in the same flowerbox (or something like that)." Every once in a while I'll notice a plant where both the leaves and the flowers are withering. Super-gardener to the rescue (I really am not)! Enter Jones with his water can. Within an hour the plant revives and begins to flourish. I'm so smart. Of course, if I were really that intelligent, I would have noticed much earlier that the soil was dry. Interesting parallel here. I know, and at times I must be reeducated, that PRAYER is the most effective means at my disposal to keep my soil from drying out and my fruit from dying out. Prayer is essential in the producing of fruit in your spiritual journey. There is no other way. Francis De Sales (17th century bishop) said that "prayer is like water that makes plants grow." He adds to his writing, "It also extinguishes fires." I have learned (or should say I am in the process of learning) to keep my relationship with the Lord as if I am growing the most beautiful sacred flower. I must keep watering it, keep tending its roots... Once you neglect your plant, it will die. My daily prayer time is the time for watering my garden. As one Egyptian philosopher said, "My mother is water." If that water is my prayer life, I agree.

Random thoughts for today:

So it towered high above all the trees of the field; its boughs grew large and its branches long from abundant water in its shoots. *(Ezekiel 31:5 ESV)*

We need to relearn that there is such a thing as a felt knowledge of God.

We accept the idea of grace in theory, but deny it in practice... Maybe because deep down we know we don't deserve it.

Love what you're doing, AND SHOW IT!!

Silence can be the difference between sight and insight.

Thank You, Father, for joy, in spite of ourselves.

June 19   Protevangelium

Have you ever bruised your heel? This type of injury affects the fat pad that protects the heel bone, also known as the policeman's heel. It can happen from a single injury or repeated trauma, such as the force of your foot striking the ground. A simply bruised heel can take one to three weeks to heal. If you've also bruised the heel bone, it may take up to six weeks to recover. Related, the development of plantar fasciitis, causes intense pain when you take a step. I struggled with this years ago and ended up having to wear orthotic inserts much of the time. Why would I share this with you? A scripture that the Lord brought to mind many times through the pain of my "heel infirmity", was Genesis 3:15 ESV —*I will put enmity* ("hostility; animosity") *between you and the woman, and between your offspring and her offspring; He shall crush your head, and you will bruise* (can also be translated, "strike") *His heel.* In Christian theology, this is called the protevangelium. The rest of scripture builds on this promise. It's a compound word of two Greek words, *protos* meaning "first" and *evangelion* meaning "good news" or "gospel". So the protevangelium in Genesis 3:15 is commonly referred to as the first mention of the good news of salvation in the Bible. It tells us that there will be one born of man who will crush the serpent's head—the first prophecy of the coming of the Messiah, Jesus Christ. I have always struggled with equating a bruised heel to crucifixion, but in the economy of the sovereign God of the universe, "bruised" wins over "crushed" every time. GOOD NEWS!!

Random thoughts for today:

The devil who had deceived them was thrown into the lake of fire and sulfur where the beast and false prophet were, and they will be tormented day and night forever and ever. (Revelation 20:10 ESV)

What's waiting for each of us out there, for all of us, is the love of God.

Help me to remember, Lord, that my life is in Your hands.

God didn't call me to drop out of the race...He called me to FINISH.

Just because something good ends, doesn't mean better won't begin. *(Ryan Shockey)*

Jesus Christ in me never says, "I love you, but I don't like you."

June 20   What Do I Really Control?

I was browsing through a volume entitled, *A House of the Soul and Concerning the Inner Life* by Evelyn Underhill. It amazes me how much treasure can be found in the pages of authors like her. Evelyn Underhill was an English Anglo-Catholic writer and pacifist born in 1875. She died in London in 1941. She talks about the wonderful world of life in which we exist, and that the key points of birth, growth, and death are never really under our control. Here are some of her thoughts that reached out and grabbed my spirit:

- Our anxiousness really doesn't change much
- Find out where your treasure really is
- Discern the substantive things in life
- Don't confuse your meals with your life
- Don't confuse your clothes with your body
- Don't lose your head over what perishes (which is nearly everything)
- Don't worry
- Don't mistake what you possess for what you are
- The simpler your house, the easier it will be to run
- If I have nothing, I possess all

Thanks, Evelyn...I needed that.

Random thoughts for today:

But seek first the kingdom of God and His righteousness, and all these things will be added to you. *(Matthew 6:33 ESV)*

The church needs to struggle with how we can be involved in creating good culture.

LIFE IS FILLED WITH CHOICES.

What you say and how you live reflects WHOSE you are.

The one who goes quietly, goes with health and goes far. *(Italian Proverb)*

There is always something to celebrate.

The chant begins as their beloved high school principal enters the gymnasium. "Warren Jones, Warren Jones, Warren Jones!" It is repeated over and over again. Another Elston High School pep rally has begun. "Is anybody here from City?" his voice booms. The mass of high school students roars, and the din does not die down soon. I sit among these students, my classmates, and my heart swells with pride. But this is not just my principal. This is my Dad. During the early morning hours of November 2, 2018, my father passed from this life into the next. Social media exploded by 8 am that morning and continued for days. Our community did an overwhelming job of proclaiming Dad's legacy in the school system and in Michigan City, Indiana. But the legacy our family knows and remembers is very different. His priorities above all else were faith and family. His memorial service in the old Elston school was exactly what he wanted; a memorial service that would honor the Lord. "Preach the good news of Jesus Christ," he told me. In the last weeks of his life, he would talk about going to meet the Lord and often would break into singing a hymn. He loved the Lord. He loved his wife. He loved his family. That was what Warren Jones was about. Just a few weeks before his death, we read a scripture together at his bedside—*Jesus said, 'I am the resurrection and the life; he who believes in Me shall live even if he dies, and everyone who lives and believes in Me shall never die* (John 11:25-26). The last part of that scripture is Jesus asking the question, *Do you believe this?* Yup! My Dad believed it. I'd like to borrow and paraphrase something Billy Graham said some years ago: "One day you'll open your newspaper and read in the obituaries that Warren Jones is dead. Don't you believe it. It will be a lie!" Rest in peace, Dad. I'm looking forward to seeing you soon.

Random thoughts for today:

Honor your father... (Exodus 20:12 ESV)

Quotes from Warren Jones:

Don't focus on the questions people aren't asking...Ask the Lord to help you focus on the right questions.

Set a good example with truth, pride, and enthusiasm.

Wear your citizenship to this great country with pride, and do your best to make it better.

Be a positive influence on others regardless of the circumstances.

June 22   Erasing History

Please bear with me today. I'm a retired history teacher, and I'm confused. I have been excited about the dialogue today taking place regarding racism in our country. Productive conversations are beginning to happen (we're trying to figure it out) in a way that I have not seen in my lifetime. Each year in my American history classes, I would introduce the course, and in that introduction, I would say, "There are many dark moments in the history of our nation; there is a dark side to the force. Our treatment of the native American and the despicable history of slavery are probably the two outstanding examples. We will study these periods and talk about them without censorship. We will not gloss over them or try to sanitize history. The old cliché, 'Those who do not study history will be doomed to repeat it.' We will not erase our heritage, whether good or evil." In the last few weeks, we have seen a trend developing across the country. Historical statues from Robert E. Lee to Jefferson Davis to Francis Scott Key have been toppled. Recently, statues of Ulysses Grant, George Washington, Christopher Columbus, and Theodore Roosevelt have been torn down or destroyed. Boston's mayor this week said it's time to remove a statue of Abraham Lincoln because it's racist. Again, I'm confused. What do these acts have to do with meaningful dialogue and uniting a nation split by racial bias? Erasing history is nothing new. One of the many tragedies that unfolded in the wake of the Islamic State (ISIS) is their smashing of statues and the destruction of ancient archaeological sites. Religious and historical statues, buildings, and valuable heritage in Nineveh, Nimrud, Hatra, and Palmyra fell in the rapid and terrifying advance of the IS. Both Stalin and Hitler were masters at erasing events AND people they disagreed with from history. Personally, my in-depth study of the Civil War era and the Jim Crow years have instilled within me an intense disgust and hatred for racism. My study as a historian of the Indian Removal Act of 1830, the Trail of Tears, and the massacre of Wounded Knee has also done its work on my conscience. As a student of American history, I stand confused, but I already said that. I continue to read books by black historians and scholars, trying to learn and be more informed. I have found that I can even learn from those with whom I disagree. I quote my youngest daughter in a recent post of hers on Facebook—"I will continue to HOPE because, as a person of faith, I have to hope. This is the way of Jesus, the way of love and life, the way of mercy and grace, and the way of newness and restoration."

Lord, in You I have hoped...Let me never be confounded...And when I think I'm right, help me not to be a jerk about it!

Someone close to me reposted a tweet on social media that asked the question, "What is your favorite scripture on your rights?" It was a question that gave me great pause. I'm assuming it was a tongue-in-cheek inquiry, or at least I hope so. Life, liberty, and the pursuit of happiness, right? Oh wait, that's the Declaration of Independence. I would have to say Luke 9:23 is my favorite Bible verse on my rights. Why do I do what I do? Why do I pray what I pray? If we are honest, we would have to admit that it has to do with our desires. Our greatest ongoing struggle in life is continual submission to the will of the Lord. It's amazing how many believers think that praying is urging our requests upon God, and answered prayer is God giving us what we desire. Thomas A' Kempis once wrote, "Can we refuse to submit to man for God's sake when God, for love of us, submits to man, even to his very executioners?" Do you remember the prayer of our Savior in the Garden of Gethsemane when He was deciding whether or not to go to the cross? He prayed, *My Father, if it be possible, let this cup* (of suffering) *pass from me; nevertheless, not as I will, but as You will* (Matthew 26:39). Here is a model prayer from our role-model. "I do this because You desire it, Lord...Abba Father, I want to be willing and obedient to do the things you ask me to do." I believe that prayer is the attitude of a person's spirit. The deepest expression of our prayer is not, "Do this, because I desire it, Lord," rather it is, "I do this because YOU desire it!" What is the attitude of your spirit as you pray? I'm speaking of that definitive decision about WHO sits on the throne of your life. Again, from Thomas A' Kempis—"I will therefore form myself upon the model of my submissive, dependent, obedient Savior."

If anyone would come after Me, let him deny himself and take up his cross daily and follow Me **(Luke 9:23** ESV**).**

Random thoughts for today:

Again, for the second time, He went away and prayed, "My Father, if this cannot pass unless I drink it, Your will be done." (Matthew 26:42 ESV)

Let them see you laugh, and you let them see your heart.

Sometimes it seems we've been fighting so hard to gain power in the wrong kingdom.

The less a man thinks or knows about his virtues, the better we like him. *(Anonymous)*

Extinguished hearth, extinguished family. *(Ancient saying)*

June 24   Remember the Journey

I read the Book of Micah this morning. This man of God prophesied in Judah during the reigns of Jotham, Ahaz, and Hezekiah, about the same time as Isaiah. The northern kingdom of Israel actually fell to the Assyrians during Micah's ministry (BC 722). Micah's predictions of future events are more specific than those of other prophets. I read in this prophecy about the fall of Judah to the Babylonians, the fall of Jerusalem, the destruction of the temple, the exile in Babylon, the return from captivity to peace and prosperity, and the birth of the Messiah in the little town of Bethlehem (5:2). *This was the word of the LORD that came from Micah* (1:1). As I read, I was almost nodding through passages about the judgment against Assyria, the eventual destruction of paganism, and the indictment against Judah, when a phrase instantly jumped off the page at me—*REMEMBER YOUR JOURNEY...that you may know the righteous acts of God* (Micah 6:5 ESV). I realize that this scripture is addressing the nation of Judah, but all of a sudden, it was speaking to me. I began to think back, years back—high school, college, early marriage, early ministries and congregations of fifty people, and later ministries of 1200 people. I remembered early adventures into my faith journey, mistakes, side-trips when I got off track, victories, joys, sorrows, and regrets. That time of reflection and meditation went far into the morning. I completed that morning with reading and praying over Micah 6:6-8 ESV —

> *With what shall I come before the LORD and bow down before the exalted God?...He has showed you, O man, what is good. And what does the LORD require of you? To act justly and to love mercy and to walk humbly with your God.*

May I encourage you today to remember your journey.

Random thoughts for today:

> *But as for me, I watch in hope for the LORD, I wait for God my Savior; and God will hear me. (Micah 7:7 ESV)*

I've discovered that time alone with God is a rock in my life...I wonder then why I don't spend more time with Him?

The truth God just revealed to me has complicated my life... Don't do that again!!

Truth knocks at the door, and you say, "Go away, I'm looking for the truth," and so it goes away, puzzling.

We're so impatient to get to the end!! Me: "I can hardly wait to go be with the Lord!" God: "You're with Me right now!" Why are we in such a hurry to get to the end?

June 25   Prayers That Are Short and Sweet

What does the word "simplicity" mean to you? (See January 25 entry). One dictionary defines it as "freedom from complexity, intricacy, or pretentiousness." I believe it is simplicity; freedom from deceit. It goes hand-in-hand with sincerity and naturalness and is an "essential discipline of the spiritual life. Where there is simplicity, words can be taken at their face value; no hidden or double meanings. One says what one means, and one means what one says. Where there is simplicity, there is no artificiality. This kind of praying requires no special formula. Many words are unnecessary; prayers need not be too long. Many words in our praying can come from the flesh if we're not cautious. *And when you pray, do not heap up empty phrases as the Gentiles do, for they think that they will be heard for their many words. Do not be like them, for your Father knows what you need before you ask Him.* (Matthew 6:7-8 ESV). What should my prayer contain? Read the next verse—*Pray then like this: Our Father in heaven, hallowed be Your name...* SIMPLICITY!! All that is needed is a movement of the heart toward the Lord; you need only to present your heart-desire to Him (See March 31 entry).

Dear Father, I'll keep my prayer short today. Thank You. I love You. I need You. Amen.

Random thoughts for today:

Love is patient and kind; love does not envy or boast; it is not arrogant. *(1 Corinthians 13:4 ESV)*

The unexamined life is not worth living. *(Socrates)*

Your faith should not stand in the wisdom of men, but in the power of God.

Humility must always be doing its work; without humility all will be lost. *(Teresa of Avila)*

As God leaves His fingerprints on me, I desire to leave my fingerprints upon whomever I encounter today.

Be sure to put your feet in the right place, then stand firm. *(Abraham Lincoln)*

God is most likely to speak to me in a gentle whisper rather than in a loud voice.

June 26   Memorization

Whenever I talk to people about memorizing scripture, I get the "seriously?" face! Why should I do that? The expression "to know by heart" already suggests its value. Psalm 119:11 ESV says *I have stored up* (treasured) *Your word in my heart, that I might not sin against You.* Psalm 37:31 tells us that when *the Law of God is in your heart; your steps do not slip.* I personally regret that I have not memorized more scripture through the years, especially the psalms and the prayers of the Bible. Learning scripture can be an extremely valuable component of meditation time with the Lord. Last year, good old COVID-2020 year, I have been working on memorizing Psalm 91 and the promise of God keeping the *deadly pestilence from my tent.* There is an account of a Methodist missionary using Psalm 23 and other scriptures to carry him through horrible hours in the Brazilian torture chamber, giving him peace at his darkest hour. Many of us have read testimonies of believers in countries where having copies of scripture was against the law and how one page of the Bible became a precious possession in the underground church. I often wondered how much of the Bible I could take with me in my heart and mind if I had to survive without scripture. Hopefully I would not have to depend upon my own wisdom to carry me through. If you would like to begin a discipline of memorizing scripture, Psalm 1, Psalm 23, and the Matthew 5:3-10 are great places to start.

Random thoughts for today:

How can a young man keep his way pure? By guarding it according to Your word. *(Psalm 119:9 ESV)*

Lord, Your sea is so great, and my boat is so small. *(Unknown seaman)*

He who would leap high must take a long run. *(Danish Proverb)*

Our culture has gone from ignoring His name to flippantly uttering, "O my God!"...That holiest, most precious, and beautiful name of the Lord.

Wherever a man turns, he can find someone who needs him.

The secret to teaching is to appear to have known all your life what you just learned this afternoon.

I am writing this entry on the eve of one of my wife's famous garage sales. We've been having a couple of these a year, and we get rid of a lot of stuff. Since retirement, I have also had an ongoing goal of decluttering my home. There are days I think we're winning; others, not so much. I recently read about a guy who selected two items in his house every day. Before he left his house, he would throw one in the trash, and the other in a box in his garage to give away. I've started that practice in recent days. I am convinced that I, along with the rest of our society, have a problem with stuff. A man could practice this for a thousand mornings, and there would still be a house full of stuff. One writer says, "It is not possible to keep abreast of the normal tides of acquisition." Our so-called acquisition goes on day and night. I heard one woman say that we have a "check-valve" in our homes that permits influx but prevents outflow. E.B. White, children's author, makes an interesting observation in one of his essays— "Goods seek a man out; they find him even though his guard is up. This steady influx is not counterbalanced by any comparable outgo." I realized as I was writing this that the only stuff leaving my house is paper trash and garbage; everything else stays, and as one decluttering expert says, "digs in." I am extremely blessed but well aware that I have a "stuff problem." I've stopped going to other people's garage sales and antique markets. I'm working to break my online shopping habit. I've been praying a lot lately for the Lord to help me simplify my life. There are several entries in this volume about simplifying our spiritual lives. I'm hoping to apply this to my problem with stuff. So, it's not about the stuff... It's about my heart.

For what does it profit a man to gain the whole world and forfeit his life? (Mark 8:36 ESV)

Do I seek the Lord with the longing of a lover? Do I crave His touch simply because it is His touch?

I wonder how often I miss the Lord speaking to me because my life is just too noisy.

In the Greek etymology, the word "enthusiasm" means, "God in us."

We seem to have so little tolerance in us for uncomfortable feelings. Is it possible that the Lord can to speak to us through these feelings?

June 28   Woe is Us

Woe to those who call evil good and good evil, who put darkness for light and light for darkness, who put bitter for sweet and sweet for bitter (Isaiah 5:20)! Man without God is a contradiction, a paradox, a drifting mess who sees evil in good and good in evil. What an accurate description of the chaos of our culture today. A well-known news anchor closed his broadcast recently with these words—"If you believe in one another and if you do the right thing for yourself and your community, things will get better in this country. You do NOT need help from above. The answer is within us!" I see many problems in that statement coming to fruition. The spirit of Isaiah 5:20 is alive and well in government, politics, educational philosophy, social media, and, unfortunately, in much of the church. If I say it, it might be true. If I read it, it's probably true. If it's on the internet, it's absolutely true! I don't even need to bother checking the facts. One acquaintance said, "Find an impartial, unbiased news source and ignore the rest." Seriously? That magical news source doesn't exist. And the point of just doing the right thing? In and of ourselves, that ain't gonna happen. Our newsman friend's final statement, "the answer is within us," can only be true if Colossians 1:27 is part and parcel of your life—*CHRIST IN YOU, the hope of glory!*

Random thoughts for today:

Woe to those who are wise in their own eyes, and shrewd in their own sight. *(Isaiah 5:21 ESV)*

All that I do, Lord—Be Thou my will. *(Anonymous prayer)*
I thank God for the lives of believers that impact me and make me want to be a better follower of Jesus.
Be slow in choosing a friend...Slower in changing. *(Ben Franklin)*
More and more, I've come to learn that LISTENING is one of the most important things we can do for each other.
I've learned that confession must always follow conviction.
Befriend faithfulness...Find safe pasture in the Lord.
Don't wait until tomorrow...Live today...Celebrate the simple things.

June 29   Tears in a Bottle

You have kept count of my tossings, put my tears in Your bottle. Are they not in Your book (Psalm 56:8)? Has anyone ever said to you, "God knows what you're going through?" It's true, He does. He knows your tossings and turnings; He keeps track. In beautiful metaphoric language, David says that the Lord even keeps our tears in a bottle. He wrote this psalm when the Philistines captured him in Gath. When no one else notices, mark it down, God notices. When no one else remembers, God remembers. Rewards will come for acts done in His name; maybe not today, maybe not tomorrow, but someday...God's long-term memory is excellent. He knows every thought you have, every ache you have in your heart, and he knows your every desire. He knows what you're going through, and if you just look to Him, He would confirm that for you. Sometimes, when we are at our lowest points, we think that God could not possibly care about us and our situation. So many things have gone wrong, and we feel that we are all alone. How could the Lord know what my struggles are? Hebrews 4:15 says *We do not have a high priest who is unable to sympathize with our weaknesses, but One who in every respect has been tempted as we are, yet without sin.* Does my Abba Father really care? Yeah, He really does!!

Random thoughts for today:

He will wipe away every tear from their eyes, and death shall be no more, neither shall there be mourning nor crying nor pain anymore, for the former things are passed away. (Revelation 21:4 ESV)

Those who are happiest are those who do the most for others. (Booker T. Washington)

We are not salesmen for Christianity...We are presenters of Jesus Christ.

Blessed is the man who, having nothing to say, abstains from giving wordy evidence of that fact. *(George Eliot)*

Let us not be satisfied just by giving money...Money is not everything...The world needs the work of our hands and the love of our hearts.

June 30   Critical Spirits

When you disagree with someone after you think you have discerned that they are wrong and you are right, do you turn that discernment into criticism or intercession on their behalf? I heard a preacher caution believers to be careful not to become a hypocrite by spending all your time trying to get others right before you worship God yourself. We can easily become criticism black holes instead of encouragers. A black hole is a region of spacetime where gravity is so strong that nothing—no particles, not even light—can escape from it.; the force keeps pulling you down. Physicists speculate that a person caught in a black hole would be shredded instantaneously. It reminds me of the fable of a bunch of crabs being caught in a large trap that didn't have a lid. Every time a crab tried to climb out, the other crabs pulled it back down. We can become concerned because someone else is not growing in the Lord or perhaps engaging in some activity of which we disapprove, but that does not legitimize a barrage of criticism from me. A critical spirit has rarely, if ever, changed anybody's mind, let alone their heart. Three thoughts come to me as I read Galatians chapter 6: 1) We are called to be free from sin. 2) Don't use that freedom as an excuse to serve the flesh. 3) Serve one another humbly in love. How have I been praying for this individual? It's called intercession. It is the most effective tool in our box to penetrate the hearts we can't open, teaching where we can't speak, comforting where our words have no power, lifting burdens that we cannot lift. God never gives us discernment in order that we may criticize, but rather that we might become servants of others.

Random thoughts for today:

Brothers, if anyone is caught in any transgression, you who are spiritual should restore him in a spirit of gentleness. Keep watch on yourself, lest you too be tempted. (Galatians 6:1 ESV)

God will always be much better than what we conceive Him to be. (Rebecca Crain)

We are called to faithfulness to our own convictions and empathy for other people, no matter what their convictions.

It takes troublesome work to undertake alteration of old beliefs.

No person is important enough to make me angry.

Let me cherish busy days with youth, happy to have a part in their world.

July

What Is The Good Of Experience
If You Do Not Reflect?

July 1   Foolishness

Years ago, a man was walking down the street with a sandwich board sign attached to him that said, "I am a fool for Christ. Who are you a fool for?" There are many kinds of fools (shades of Proverbs) that I do not desire to be.

- A prating fool shall fail *(Proverbs 10:8 ESV)*
- A fool utters slander *(Proverbs 10:18 ESV)*
- The fool rages on *(Proverbs 14:16 ESV)*
- A fool is perverse in his lips *(Proverbs 19:1 ESV)*
- Wisdom is too high for a fool *(Proverbs 24:7 ESV)*
- A fool utters all of his mind *(Proverbs 29:11 ESV)*

The summary verse of all of Proverbs is this—*The fear of the LORD is the beginning of knowledge; fools despise wisdom and instruction* (Proverbs 1:7). But there's another kind of "fool" that I do desire to be. I Corinthians 4:10 says that *we are fools for Christ's sake, but you are wise in Christ.* It used to be said of the boy-crazy teenaged girl, "she's in love with love." There is a part of my relationship with Jesus that is in love with love. The root meaning of "infatuation" derives from the Latin word *infatuus*— "to make foolish." In the eyes of the world, I am a fool. *The natural person does not accept the things of the Spirit of God, for they are folly to him, and he is not able to understand them because they are spiritually discerned* (1 Corinthians 2:14 ESV). I think that William Shakespeare got it right in this matter—"A fool thinks himself to be wise, but a wise man knows himself to be a fool."

Random thoughts for today:

A wise son makes a glad father, but a foolish son is a sorrow to his mother. *(Proverbs 10:1* ESV)

A small body of determined spirits fired by an unquenchable faith in their mission can alter the course of history. *(Gandhi)*

Guard your heart (Proverbs 4:23)—Everything you do flows from it.

Truth does not change according to our ability to accept it.

July 2   Jumping Through Hoops

Have you seen that TV commercial of the guy trying to get a loan at a bank? First, he has to jump through a hoop. The banker says, "OK, just a few more hoops to jump through," as he sets three or four more hoops on fire. The potential customer shakes his head and walks away. Have you ever wondered if the "hoops" of "church membership" have turned into barriers to seekers of the gospel? I'm not necessarily against church membership (whatever that means or does not mean). I have spent the majority of my life in churches where you "place your membership" at the appropriate time. In the last ten years, I've enjoyed being a part of a congregation that does not have membership. Basically, if you are a believer and fellowship with us, you are a part of our body. How often has the door been opened to those who came before, but they closed it behind them as they came in? Who are we closing the door to? Churches across the land have required various steps to be taken before you can qualify to be a member—interview with the elders, fill out an application form, write out your testimony, give your testimony in front of the congregation, be a probationary member for several of months, and I'm sure there are many more hoops (sorry, I mean steps) that could be added to this list. I wonder how many people who desire to fellowship with us in our local body end up shaking their heads and walking away. I am preaching at a little church of about 20 people (more about that in tomorrow's entry). Helen and I have been there for a little over two years. When an individual who has been worshipping with us indicates a desire to be a "member," we bring that person before the congregation and have them repeat their confession of faith—"I believe that Jesus is the Christ, the Son of the Living God; and I proclaim Him to be my savior and Lord." And by the way, the entire church repeats that confession right along with him. Sounds almost biblical, doesn't it?

Random thoughts for today:

And the Lord added (those who accepted the message) **to their number daily those who were being saved.** (Acts 2:47 ESV)

My father taught me, "If it's not honest, it's not useful.
To the Instagram generation—"Becoming like Jesus takes time." *(Nate Loucks)*

Life consists not in holding good cards but in playing those you hold well. *(Josh Billings)*

A lot of times, God wants you to be uncomfortable...This is the time we rely most on Him.

Patience is a bitter plant, but it has sweet fruit. *(Anonymous Proverb)*

July 3   Yet Another Adventure

This past couple of years, Helen and I have been ministering to a tiny flock (around 20 people; usually less, occasionally a few more) about 23 miles from our home. Community Church in New Carlisle, Indiana, was established a couple of years after the Civil War and flourished through the years as a Disciples of Christ denominational church. Presently, this is where I preach every Sunday, and Helen plays the piano. It started as a month's commitment, then the summer, and then the end of the year. Now, my "interim pastor" title has been dropped. This feisty little group has had an up-and-down history, nearly closing its doors. I think my attachment to this congregation partly comes from how much it reminds me of my first ministry in Pence, Indiana, in the mid-1960s. With Helen and I being the youngest people in the church (on most Sundays), there has been an extremely close bond that has developed between the congregation and us in the past year. This is a sweet group of people who have lovingly welcomed us with open arms. The ministry is evolving from a small group that had to find a preacher to keep the doors open, to an excited church that is ready for whatever the Lord has in mind. There is no doubt in my mind that this is where the Lord desires us to be, taking my place in a long line of over 20 pastors in a 154-year history. Helen and I have gone from interim preacher to a pastorate that we are willing to commit the next years of our lives. Thanks, Lord, for not putting us on the shelf.

*Helen and I are no longer the youngest people in the congregation.

Random thoughts for today:

Grace to you and peace from God our Father and the Lord Jesus Christ. *(Philippians 1:2 ESV)*

God is not the way we say He is...God is the way scripture says He is.

Is the cross still our priority message? Am I determined to preach nothing but Christ and Him crucified?

Will you miss some of God's beauty today? Stop for a moment and look around you.

Nothing is over until God says it's over.

We receive the blessing, but we forget the Blesser.

He is rich who is content with the least. *(Socrates)*

July 4   God and Country

Mark 12:17—*Render to Caesar the things that are Caesar's, and to God the things that are God's* (Jesus said that). Politics has always contained a potential for a negative response from Christians. We all seem to have an agenda, and it rarely coincides with God's agenda, but it is amazing how often it has to do with me. I find it interesting, during this presidential election year (writing this entry in 2020), to read many of the social media posts from my brothers and sisters in Christ. I guess a number of us think it's OK to lay aside the *be ye kind* scriptures when it comes to sharing our political opinions. It also disappoints me to see how often we don't do our homework or due diligence in ascertaining that what we post is actually true. But how important is that, really? Well, maybe as followers of the *truth, the way, and the life,* truth should be important to us. We do have dual-citizenship in this world. What does that mean for me? What it means, is centered in five biblical truths:

1. Pay taxes
2. Obey the law (unless it conflicts with God's Word)
3. Honor police/leaders/authorities
4. Do good to everyone
5. PRAY (especially for those in authority)

As I mentioned in an earlier entry, I love my country. It is my desire to respect my country with my words and my life. But more importantly than that, I desire to honor my Lord with all that I have and all that I am. HAPPY BIRTHDAY, AMERICA!!

Random thoughts for today:

Let every person be subject to the governing authorities. (Romans 13:1 ESV)

Lord, let me have no other gods before You, whether a nation, a party, a state, or church.

Great works are performed, not by strength, but by perseverance. *(Samuel Johnson)*

I don't want to become an expert on how I used to do ministry...
Lord, what do you want to do through me NOW.

I was still learning when I taught my last class.

July 5   My Opinion, Your Burden

Old Pharisees never die; they just multiply. A woman was knitting in a certain church, waiting for the service to start. She had been there for twenty minutes or so. A dear woman sitting next to her said, "Oh, honey, we don't do that in the house of God; here we read the Bible." As a reformed legalist, I have spent the better part of the last 40 years battling legalism, first within myself so as not to revert back to that disease, and second in the churches where I have served. Interesting, isn't it? Legalism has no pity on people. Legalism makes my opinion your burden, makes my opinion your boundary, makes my opinion your obligation. One of the more serious problems facing the orthodox Christian church today is the problem of legalism. The same was true in Paul's day...Same old, same old. During the reign of King Hezekiah, the prophet Isaiah warns the nation of Judah of their sinful ways. He gives a great definition of legalism—*So then, the word of the LORD to them will become: Do and do, do and do, rule on rule, rule on rule; a little here, a little there* (Isaiah 28:13 ESV). A few verses later, he says, *The bed is too short to stretch out on, the blanket too narrow to wrap around you* (V 20)— Short beds and narrow covers. Legalism makes a lousy bed and a miserable night's sleep; no rest for the legalist. Legalism robs the believer of his joy, so nothing is left but cramped, dull, and somber profession. S. Lewis Johnson wrote, "The Christian under law is a miserable parody of the real thing." Nothing will keep a Christian more immature than trying to keep a list. I'm reminded of the cartoon in *Leadership* magazine of a Pharisee witnessing—"Have you heard of the 4,973 spiritual laws?"

Random thoughts for today:

...to be ministers of the new covenant, not of the letter but of the Spirit. For the letter kills, but the Spirit gives life. (2 Corinthians 3:6 ESV)

Just to be is a blessing; just to live is holy. *(Rabbi Abraham Heschel)*

What is more natural and easier than talking with your Father? How could you not?

There are two ways of exerting strength: one is pushing down; the other is pulling up. *(Booker T. Washington)*

Every day may not be glorious, but there's something glorious in every day...FIND THE GLORY!

July 6   What Did God Say?

I don't want you to come away from yesterday's entry thinking I believe anything goes in our spiritual journey, or that all things ARE truly permissible (taking Paul's statement in 1 Corinthians 6:12 out of context). Let me encourage you to be cautious when differentiating between what my freedom in Christ truly is as opposed to my responsibility to obey the Lord when He has made His will clear. Rationalization can turn our so-called liberty into spiritual anarchy if we're not careful. It's not a debate between conservative or liberal, old school or new school, traditional thought or contemporary thought; it's about what God has said. It's about *Jesus Christ the same yesterday and today and forever* (Hebrews 13:8 ESV). Just because something's old doesn't mean it's out-of-date. And likewise, just because something's new doesn't mean it's necessarily heresy. That something new may not be new at all; it may be the Lord leading you to a new thought. But again, what does God say about it? King Saul offered worship to the Lord, but he lost his kingdom because he disobeyed God (1 Samuel 15). In 1 Kings 16, King Ahaz built a brand-new altar (1 Kings 16:10-18) to replace the original bronze altar prescribed by God in Exodus ("Let's just change what God originally commanded"). Sometimes a new approach IS better; sometimes not. Sometimes old is better, not because it's traditional or old school, but because God said so. I have tried to be open-minded when I hear an idea or thought that is contrary to what I have always believed. What I have always believed isn't the standard for truth. But we need to be vigilant when we change our thinking because of trends or the popular opinion of the world-system. Remember, it's not true because of majority rule; it's true because it's true, and it's true because God says it's true.

Random thoughts for today:

Behold, to obey is better than sacrifice. (1 Samuel 15:22 ESV)

May I be so in love with the Lord that I hear everything He says.

Finding time is a misnomer; if you want time, you must make it.

I find out more and more every day, how important it is for people to share their memories.

One of our tasks is to help others to realize how rare and valuable each of us is.

Experience is how life catches up with us and teaches us to love and forgive each other.

July 7   Kids' Prayers - 2

I love kids. And I love what kids read. I read all of the Harry Potter books because my grandkids and my students were reading them. My grandson introduced me to the Hunger Games series. When I taught 5th grade in the public schools, the girls in that classroom talked me into reading the Twilight series. Reading what kids read has been a great tool in relating to them. I like what Isaac Singer said, "Children read books, not reviews; they don't give a hoot about critics." Here are some more excerpts and remarks from kids.

> "It's hard to know what God looks like. When I pray to Him, I gotta use my imagination. He's indivisible." (Liam – Age 10)

> "I prayed for a boa constrictor, but I never got one. I think it's because my mom hates snakes, and she's prayed longer than I have." (Oliver – Age 9)

> "You want to know how long it takes for God to answer prayer? OK, I'll tell you. Nobody knows...nobody knows." (Emma – Age 11)

"Dear God, I just figured out it takes four years for You to answer prayer. I know, because I asked for a dog when I was three, and I just got one." *(Charlie – Age 7)*

"Dear God, You are a great person. You are greater than anyone or anything. You are infirmity and beyond!" *(Lucas – Age 8)*

"Dear God, I think I'm going to like it up in heaven because you can know lots of friends there. Down here, I hardly have any friends. *(Charlotte – Age 10)*

Oliver Wendell Holmes said, "Pretty much all the honest truth-telling there is in the world is done by children." I love the innocence, curiosity, and optimism in kids. I think sometimes they are, in short, everything I wish to be.

Random thoughts for today:

Jesus said, "Let the little children come to Me and do not hinder them, for to such belongs the kingdom of heaven. (Matthew 19:14 ESV)

Know that you can start over each and every morning.

Time spent playing (and praying) with kids is never time wasted.

As you've already surmised, I am very fond of the term, *ABBA*. I make many references in this volume to my *Abba Father*. I love the song we sing in our church: "I'm no longer a slave to fear; I AM A CHILD OF GOD." The New Living Translation of Romans 8:16 says, *His Holy Spirit speaks to us deep in our hearts and tells us that we are God's children.* Brennan Manning writes, "The prayer of the poor in spirit can simply be a single word: Abba." When we try to pray and can't, or when we attempt to walk the journey in a way that pleases the Father and we fail, God touches us tenderly anyway, because He is our heavenly Daddy. One ancient writer calls this the "Abba evocation." One repeats over and over again, the name, "Abba, Father." It's kind of like learning to type. Once learned, even if you have not typed for years, you can sit down and begin to type immediately. To make the name of Abba indelible in your mind and heart, is to be victorious over the plague of forgetting. The ancients would practice that prayer until it became second nature, and never forgotten.

Abba, Father, help me today to rest in Your love.

Random thoughts for today:

For you did not receive the spirit of slavery to fall back into fear, but you have received the Spirit of adoption as sons, by Whom we cry, Abba! Father! (Romans 8:15 ESV)

My walk with Jesus is like yesterday's cornbread—stale and dry. *(Southern Proverb)*

May you have warm words on a cold day, a full moon on a dark night, and a smooth road all the way to your door. *(Irish Proverb)*

The price of anything is the amount of life you exchange for it. *(Henry David Thoreau)*

CHANGE...Release the past – Value the present – Embrace the future

"Stay" is an excellent word in a friend's vocabulary.

The kingdom of Christ is to be a kingdom of grace, mercy, and of all comfort. *(Luther)*

In solitude and silence we discover what makes us feel alive.

July 9   Primary Purpose

What's your purpose? Socrates was considered wise, not because he knew all the right answers, but because he knew how to ask the right questions. Probably the question that seems to bug me the most lately is the question, "WHY?" Through the years, in several ministries, I've asked the query, "What IS the purpose of the church? Why, indeed, have we been called into existence? Why do we buy property and build buildings? Why do we sing? Why do we preach sermons? Why do we give our money? What's the deal with this missions thing? There are many, what I like to call, sub-purposes for the church—Pray, present the gospel to the lost, bring hope to the hurting, make disciples, teach the scriptures, social issues and action, and the list goes on. But what is our primary purpose? I believe the answer to that is found in 1 Corinthians 10:31—*So, whether you eat or drink, or whatever you do, do all to the glory of God.* I believe that is why we exist. The church's primary purpose is to glorify the Lord our God. *WHETHER...WHATEVER!!* The goal is God's greater glory.

Chuck Swindoll has said many times in his ministry, "Scripture virtually pulsates with the mandate—"Glorify God!" What a great motive checklist this gives to us, all encapsulated in that annoying question, "WHY?" Why do we do anything we do as the church? If it lifts up the Lord, let's do it. Let's accomplish it for His honor and glory and praise!!

Random thoughts for today:

But I do not account my life of any value nor as precious to myself, if only I may finish my course and the ministry that I received from the Lord Jesus, to testify to the gospel of the grace of God. (Acts 20:24 ESV)

Waiting silently is the hardest thing of all.

Everything full of life loves change...The characteristic of life is movement toward new goals.

To educate the mind without educating the heart is to educate a menace to society. *(Theodore Roosevelt)*

I can live for two months on a good compliment. *(Mark Twain)*

I am learning how difficult it is to dialogue with a person who considers it unthinkable that he/she might be wrong on any given subject.

July 10   According to St. Francis of Assisi

The Lord's Prayer

Your will be done, on earth as it is in heaven

May we love You with our whole heart by always thinking of You, with our whole soul by always desiring You, with our whole mind by directing all our intentions to You, and with our whole strength by spending all our energies in Your service. And may we love our neighbors as ourselves...

Give us this day our daily bread

In memory and understanding and reverence of the love which our Lord Jesus Christ has for us, revealed by His sacrifice for us on the cross, we ask for the perfect bread of His body.

And forgive us our trespasses

We know that You forgive us through the suffering and death of Your beloved Son.

As we forgive those who trespass against us

Enable us to forgive perfectly and without reserve any wrong that has been committed against us.

(The following thoughts are gleaned from Francis of Assisi)

Random thoughts for today:

And lead us not into temptation, but deliver us from evil. (Matthew 6:13 ESV)

When you get into trouble your friend will not walk away and leave you there.

You cannot discover new oceans unless you have the courage to lose sight of the shore.

It's not enough to have a good mind; the main thing is to use it well. *(Descartes)*

Practical apologetics: Quit trying to prove everything and start living it out because you know it to be true.

July 11   More Thoughts on Rights

Thomas R. Kelly regularly prayed, "In all that I do, Lord—BE THOU MY WILL!" Another way of praying the prayer of our Lord—*Father, not my will, but Your will be done* (Matthew 26:39). Abba Father, in everything I do, YOU are my will!! We Americans are continually talking about our rights. Our role-model, Jesus, never did. *Have this mind among yourselves, which is yours in Christ Jesus, who, though He was in the form of God, did not count equality with God a thing to be grasped, but made himself nothing, taking the form of a servant, being born in the likeness of men. And being found in human form, He humbled Himself by becoming obedient to the point of death, even death on a cross* (Philippians 2:5-8 ESV). The apostle Paul, speaking of his "right" to be supported by the church, wrote, *But we have not made use of this right, and we will put up with anything rather than hinder the gospel of Christ* (1 Corinthians 9:12). He says that technically he has this right, but...BUT... we will not put up any obstacle in the way of the gospel. A former co-worker recently shared a principle that left me with uber-conviction. She said that as a believer, my responsibilities are to LOVE GOD and LOVE OTHERS. What about my rights? My so-called "rights" are to be laid at the foot of the cross. Sounds pretty biblical. Why do I fight that principle so much? As one of my pastors prayed in a Sunday service—"Lord, today, as every day, I repent of who I am, left to myself."

In all that I do, Lord—BE THOU MY WILL!

Random thoughts for today:

...Your will be done, on earth as it is in heaven. (Matthew 6:10 ESV)

In heaven, you can play baseball and not be the last one picked for a team. *(9-year-old kid)*

Today I will embrace each detour and all of its possibilities.

Life is filled with choices every day.

Shall we make a new rule of life...To always try to be a little kinder than is necessary. *(J.M. Barrie)*

People don't realize how important it is to wake up every morning with a song in your heart.

July 12   It's All About Balance

In previous entries, I have alluded to the concept of BALANCE (February 2 and March 2). I believe in balance in almost every area of my life (except with the Cubs). I'm not talking about being "middle-of-the-road" on every issue. I made a statement earlier that we know what happens to people who stay in the middle of the road...They get run over. I have no problem taking a stand when a stand needs to be taken. I guess that when I apply the principle of balance, it makes it all that more difficult to pigeon-hole me (and you know how I feel about pigeon-holing). For example, on the pro-life issue, I end up with both a conservative and a liberal position (February 2). Again, it depends on the issue. As a member of overachievers anonymous, I have been a practicer for years of Richard Exley's rhythms of life. His philosophy is centered on the balancing of work, rest, worship, and play. My beautiful wife gave me a copy of his book when we were both in our thirties, and it has been a blessing to me (and to her because of it). Pressure in the ministry can be relentless—no time for family or friends or solitude or self. Even God can be crowded out. And the cost can be high—empty marriage, resentful children, burnout. I have tried to use this same principle of rhythm and balance in all areas of my life, although not always successfully I have to admit. I don't want to be remembered as a busy man, a conservative man, an evangelical man, an intelligent man, a preacher man, or a successful man. In other entries later this year, I want to talk about balance in the areas of theology, worship, prayer life, generosity, and maybe even civic responsibility. I can be content if I am known as a balanced man—in just about every realm, except faithfulness. In that area of my life, I'm glad to be called a radical any day.

Random thoughts for today:

Let me be weighed in a just balance, and let God know my integrity. (Job 31:6 ESV)

Everyone you will ever meet knows something you don't.
Speak when you are angry, and you make the best speech you will ever regret.
Free me from prejudice, Lord, that I may serve.
Too many church people believe in grace but practice law.

At the end of the game, pawns and kings go back in the same box. *(Italian Proverb)*

Each of us has his own alphabet with which to create poetry. *(Irving Stone)*

July 13   Change My Heart

The more and more we find out about Jesus, the more apparent becomes our great need for Him. And the more I realize this need, the more I know that I need to change. The word in the original New Testament text is <u>metanoia</u> = REPENTANCE. It is used over 90 times in scripture. Much of the fundamental church has preached a "get your act together, jerk, or you're gonna burn," repentance. That's not altogether untrue, however, it doesn't capture the depth of that word. It literally says, "to change one's direction." It is a prerequisite to a saving relationship with Christ. The emphasis in the New Testament is about a choice; as I've said before, life is filled with them. Repent or reject, there is no third option. When the Jews on Pentecost realized that they had crucified the Christ, they cried out, "What can we do?" Peter answered, *Repent and be baptized every one of you in the name of Jesus Christ for the forgiveness of your sins, and you will receive the gift of the Holy Spirit* (Acts 2:38). Change your direction in life, or it will not end well for you. Because of my realization of that underlying desperation for Jesus, my heart desires that change. Repentance is a part of the process of removing all of the garbage and junk, and when it has been removed, I discover that I just want Jesus!! And don't forget, ONLY GOD CAN CHANGE A HEART. We sing the chorus in our church often:

"Change my heart Oh God, make it ever true
Change my heart Oh God, may I be like You"

I tell you; but unless you repent, you will all likewise perish. (Luke 13:3 ESV)

When we come to end of ourselves, we come to the beginning of God.

Carry the spirit of the child into old age, which means never losing your enthusiasm.

Maybe today is a day for a little soul-cradling.

It's a funny thing: the more I practice, the luckier I get. *(Arnold Palmer)*

I wonder if an increasing anti-Christian sentiment in our nation is partially due to the practical atheism of too many Christians.

July 14   When Do I Graduate?

A little guy once asked his Sunday School teacher, "I have a perfect attendance pin for coming to Bible School for seven years...I'm wondering, when do I graduate?" As a boy, I can remember promotion Sundays at our church, where we would celebrate the completion of a year of Bible class and be bumped up to another year of Bible class. Our churches today have classes upon classes and studies upon studies. There's nothing wrong with that in itself, but I'm wondering, when do we graduate? 2 Timothy 2:15 tells us to be ready to *rightly handle the word of truth*— in other words, maturing in our competency with our use of scripture. Acts 17:11-12 ESV tells of the Jews in Berea who *were more noble than those in Thessalonica; they received the word with all eagerness, examining the Scriptures daily to see if these things were so. Many of them therefore believed...* Studying scripture brings good results, and that's great. But what enables us to graduate from Bible classes? What brings us from *needing someone to teach us again the basic principles of the oracles of God* to becoming a teacher of the word (Hebrews 5:12)? What transforms us from children into spiritual adults? We need to leave the elementary and go on to maturity (Hebrews 6:1). What will move us from believer to disciple of Jesus? One church I know of, structures their "milk to meat" (translation: discipleship) ministry in a very interesting way. New members are involved in a new believer class. Other classes are made available to the body, intentionally formed toward the maturing of the individual. Discipleship classes evolve into leadership classes (larger groups into smaller groups), and eventually into one-on-one mentoring. It's not the only way to do it, but it is one way to do it. The key result is to have baby Christians grow into mature spiritual adults, who, in turn, can grow others in the faith. 2 Timothy 2:2 ESV says, *What you have heard from me in the presence of many witnesses entrust to faithful men who will be able to teach others also.* Yeah. I guess what I'm talking about is a vital faith that moves from the classroom to living life.

Random thoughts for today:

Do your best to present yourself to God as one approved, a worker who has no need to be ashamed, rightly handling the word of truth. (2 Timothy 2:15 ESV)

The first duty of a man is the seeking after and the investigation of truth. *(Cicero)*

My Father in heaven is low on fancy and high on accessibility.

Encouragement is the oxygen of the soul.

May I pray today with my heart involved as well as my mouth.

July 15   Welcome Home!

Have you ever been a "minority?" Ever felt like you didn't belong? Many years ago, my wife and I were invited to attend a service in an all-black church in Michigan City. It was a concert on Memorial Day Eve, and the service didn't even begin until 10:00 pm. What a service; the music was fantastic! About a third of the way into the evening, the pastor had some announcements, welcomed everyone for coming out, and then, of course, that annoying part of the service (to some, anyway) when he asked the question, "Do we have any visitors tonight?" Instantly, about 150 eyes turned toward us, not surprisingly, as we were the only white people in the church. The pastor, and he was a giant of a man, smiled, stretched out his arms, and said in his preacher's booming voice, "WELCOME HOME!" I don't see how we could have been treated any warmer that night (at the time, I wondered if our congregation would have treated a visiting minority family that warmly). Know what? We've all been invited to this big banquet. Have you heard about it? Luke 14 and Revelation 19 both tell us to be ready. In Jesus Christ, we've all been invited. That's the good news because that's what the gospel is—GOOD NEWS!! We will all take our seats at the great banquet, all of us—rich and poor, CEOs seated next to trash collectors, men and women, black and white, Asian and European...Yes, even Democrats and Republicans. And we hear the voice of that angel—*Blessed are those who are invited to the marriage supper of the Lamb...Hallelujah! For the Lord, our God Almighty reigns...Let us rejoice and exult and give Him the glory, for the marriage of the Lamb has come, and His Bride has made herself ready* (Revelation 19:6-7). The Lamb of God who has taken away the sin of the world greets us and looks us full in the face...And He says, "WELCOME HOME!!"

Random thoughts for today:

And the angel said to me, "Write this: Blessed are those who are invited to the marriage supper of the Lamb." (Revelation 19:9 ESV)

I have seen enough of one war never to wish to see another. *(Thomas Jefferson – 1794)*

Good well-meaning Christians can come to differing interpretations of the text...So be humble. *(Nate Loucks)*

If you want to get warm, get close to the fire...If you want to get wet, jump into the water.

Our mind is not a vessel to be filled but rather a fire to be ignited. *(Plutarch)*

July 16   Pandemic Perspective

As I write this entry (2020), it would appear that our country is experiencing a surge, perhaps even a second wave of the Corona-19 virus. Yesterday, our county commissioners passed a resolution mandating the wearing of masks when out in the public domain. Our mayor also closed all local beaches starting tomorrow. Some states are even considering going back to the total lockdown status of this past spring. As I listen to various conversations around me and monitor social media (because that's always a reliable source as to what's going on), I've put together what I like to call, "Pandemic Perspective." Maybe you can see yourself in one of them.

- **The Pandemic Busters** – I ain't afraid of no pandemic! I ain't wearin no mask, either. I'll do what I want, when I want...This is America, and to the devil with everyone else (Kind of reminds me of a church member who snapped at an usher—"No one is going to tell me where to sit").
- **The Denier** – There is no virus; it's all a hoax! They just want to put microchips inside of me; you know, mark of the beast.
- **The Compliant One** – I will do what I'm told. I will accept whatever those in charge say. I will ask no questions (even though it's difficult to determine who is in charge).
- **The Fearful One** – I'm not leaving the house, and you can't come in. I'm in quarantine until the Lord comes, if need be. Living in fear? You betcha!!
- **The Caring One** – I will be sensitive to your feelings and your fears. If it means wearing a mask out in public to help protect you, I will. I will socially distance and do my best not to make you feel uncomfortable.
- **The Patrick Henry One** – "Give me liberty or give me death!" You're not taking away my rights; if I get COVID, I get COVID.
- **The Clueless One** – What pandemic??

My grandson shared a pandemic meme with me—"Stay inside and see what happens to everyone else." I'm not sure that's how the Golden Rule works.

<u>Random thoughts for today</u>:

He will deliver you...from the deadly pestilence.
(Psalm 91:3 ESV)

Don't confuse foolishness with freedom. Love your neighbor.
We can't solve problems using the same kind of thinking we used when we created them.

July 17   Social Justice

Micah 6:8 ESV tells us *what is good, and what the LORD requires of you—Do justice, love kindness, and walk humbly with your God.* The life and example of our role-model, Jesus Christ, would make social justice a mandate of faith and a fundamental expression of following Him. Social justice has its biblical roots in our Lord, who time and time again shows His love and compassion for the weak, the vulnerable, the marginalized, the disenfranchised, and the disinherited. World Vision calls social justice "a catch-all term that has gone through many seasons of being 'en vogue' and then going out of favor, often suffering from competing definitions and vastly different interpretations. It's like Silly Putty—that popular substance we used to play with as kids that can be twisted and contorted into whatever shape your heart desires." Many believers are more comfortable with the word "justice" than they are the word "social." Don't put yourself in a labeled box here. If Christ is indeed Lord over every aspect of our lives, then this must also include the social realm. Tim Dearborn says that social justice for the poor and oppressed is the decisive mark of being people who submit to the will and way of God. Our God is the God who said, *For I, the LORD, love justice* (Isaiah 61:8). Biblical references to the word "justice" mean "to make right." We're talking about loving our neighbor as we love ourselves, which is not only commanded but rooted in the character and nature of God. To my way of thinking, this would include human trafficking, economic exploitation, human rights abuses, infants dying needlessly from disease and malnutrition, and the list goes on. These ARE issues that need to be a part of what the church addresses. The Book of Common Prayer includes the following prayer for social justice:

> "Grant, O God, that Your holy and life-giving Spirit may so move every human heart (and especially the hearts of the people of this land), that barriers which divide us may crumble, suspicions disappear, and hatred cease; that our divisions being healed, we may live in justice and peace; through Jesus Christ our Lord. Amen."

Random thoughts for today:

Learn to do good, seek justice, correct oppression; bring justice to the fatherless, and plead the widow's cause. (Isaiah 1:17 ESV)

Abundance is, in large part, an attitude.
Nothing silences grumps like gratitude.
Tomorrow to fresh woods and pastures new. *(John Milton)*

During the reign of Ahaz of Judah, the southern kingdom, and just a few years before the fall of the northern kingdom in Assyrian devastation, Isaiah prophesies against Moab. In chapter 16:9-10, he says, *The shouts of joy over your ripened fruit and over your harvests* (abundance) *have been stilled. Joy and gladness have been taken away from the orchards; no one sings or shouts in the vineyards; no one treads out wine at the presses, for I have put an end to the shouting* (celebration). You've probably heard the expression, "the party's over!" Have you noticed how everyone seems to be angry about something today (some perhaps rightfully so)? So far, the year 2020 has given us an impeachment trial of the President of the United States, political partisanship, a pandemic complete with lockdowns and face-mask wars, racial division and unrest resulting in rioting and looting, not to mention the total disruption of sports (high school, college, professional), and you know how cranky that makes a lot of fans. That's my shortlist. *The Washington Post* published an article on June 30, 2020, interviewing experts who have tips for regulating our rage. *The Post* says, "Americans are living in a big 'anger incubator.'" No one shouts (celebrates) or sings much over things that are good today. Thanks to the help of social media, we only seem to be adept at shouting out our offenses. Honest dialogue has been relegated to the graveyard. "You're wrong; I'm right, and that settles it!" And, of course, we all claim that our anger is righteous anger. I wonder. We Christians say we love the Lord. Why not then, handle our anger HIS way?

Whoever is slow to anger has great understanding, but he who has a hasty temper exalts folly. (Proverbs 14:29 ESV)

A soft word turns away wrath, but a harsh word stirs up anger. (Proverbs 15:1 ESV)

Refrain from anger, and forsake wrath! Fret not yourself; it tends only to evil. (Psalms 37:8 ESV)

Make no friendship with a man given to anger, nor go with a wrathful man. (Proverbs 22:24 ESV)

Be angry and do not sin; do not let the sun go down on your anger. (Ephesians 4:26 ESV)

Forgive us our debts (trespasses), as we also have forgiven our debtors (those who trespass against us). (Matthew 6:12 ESV)

July 19   What a Fellowship

Have you ever played billiards? Actually, I'm talking about pool. Some professional pool players still use the term *billiards* to describe what's more commonly known as pool. We won't even get into English Billiards or snooker. I've played quite a few games in my lifetime, but I'm a terrible player. I know nothing of the skills needed to make those pool balls go exactly where I desire. This is probably a good thing because if I were really good, I'd want a pool table, and we don't have room for a pool table. One thing I'm learning a lot more about as I mature is relationship proficiencies.

I'm not talking Dale Carnegie here, but rather the skills that can emanate from the inner life, *deep calling to deep*. So many of our relationships with other people are like contacts, like one pool ball bumping up against another pool ball. One Catholic bishop said to his congregation, "We are like oranges in a box; we mingle with others externally but do not commune with them." 24/7 cable news keeps us buried with all the "late-breaking" stuff and lulls us into the belief that we are in contact with reality. My inner life is never given a chance to see myself as I really am. Why do all of my get-togethers tend to be business, ministry, church meeting, or social event related? Can I not spend time with an individual or a couple just to be together? Can we not spend time together because we enjoy each other's company? Do I have any relationships where I feel comfortable letting my guard down, you know, being authentic? We may have regular contacts in the church or our social circles but might be surprised as to how much we really don't know them. Why don't we try getting together with someone soon to have some honest time *in the light?* The Bible calls it fellowship, and it has nothing to do with coffee and donuts.

Random thoughts for today:

But if we walk in the light as He is in the light, we have fellowship with one another, and the blood of Jesus, His Son, purifies us from all sin. (1 John 1:7 ESV)

Rules for happiness—Something to do...Someone to love... Something to hope for. *(Immanuel Kant)*

Stay close to the Lord; don't spend too much time worrying about what other people think.

Prayer is the key to AM and the deadbolt to the PM. *(Matthew Henry)*

One does not "get an education"...It is a lifelong process.

July 20   When Did All This Happen?

Ecclesiastes 12:1 tells me to remember the days of my youth. Proverbs 20:29 ESV says that *the glory of young men is their strength, gray hair* (if you have any left) *is the splendor of the old.* And if I really want to be depressed, I finish reading Ecclesiastes 12—*the days of trouble and the years approach when you will say, "I find no pleasure in them"...Before the sun and the light and the moon and the stars grow dark, and the clouds return after the rain; when the keepers of the house tremble, and the strong men stoop, when the grinders cease because they are few* (that would be my teeth), *and those looking through the windows* (my eyes) *grow dim...When people rise up at the sound of birds but all their songs grow faint* (trying out new hearing aids this week); *when people are afraid of heights* (that would be me) *and of dangers in the streets; when the almond tree blossoms* (I wish mine would blossom a little more) *and the grasshopper drags itself along and desire no longer is stirred* (use your imagination)...*Then people go to their eternal home and mourners go about the streets... Remember him before the silver cord is severed...And the dust returns to the ground it came from, and the spirit returns to God who gave it* (Vv 1-7). So, when did all this come about? 9th-century Japanese poet, Ariwara no Narhira, wrote a poem for the not-so-young anymore—

"That it is a road which someday we all travel

310

I had heard it before, yet I never expected
To take it so soon myself."

I'm not sure when it happened exactly, but here I am in my so-called "golden years." Maybe that's why I love what Ben Franklin said, "Those who love deeply never grow old; they may die of old age, but they die young." My prayer continues to be, *Even when I am old and gray, do not forsake me, LORD, until I declare Your power to the next generation, Your might to all who are to come* (Psalm 71:18). I continue to honor and praise You, O Creator of the days of my youth!!

Random thoughts for today:

Even to your old age I am He, and to gray hairs I will carry you. I have made, and I will bear; I will carry and will save. (Isaiah 46:4 ESV)

Your struggles develop your strengths...When you go through hardships and decide not to surrender, that's strength.

Our culture today (even much of the church) says that the devil doesn't exist...Jesus, Peter, and Paul disagree.

July 21   Change My Heart - 2

Yup...Only God can change a heart. In the July 13 entry, I said, "Repentance is a part of the process of removing all of the garbage and junk, and when it has been removed, I discover that I just want Jesus!!" I know that as long as I am in the flesh, I will struggle with sin, and I know that God will never grow tired of me. It is real security, realizing that He will not weary of my sins. BUT... Repentance literally says, "to change one's direction." Contrition is not like the person who sent the IRS a check for $150 with the note, "If I can't sleep, I'll send you the rest." So even though I still sin, how do I know that I've changed direction? God has promised to forgive my sins, past, present, and future. But that promise is NOT license to sin. Let's say that I have been unfaithful to my wife, and I ask for her forgiveness. She says, "Yes, I forgive you." Then I go out and sleep with a bunch of women. That is NOT a change of direction, and obviously not genuine repentance. One young girl, perhaps best-defined repentance—"It's sorry enough to quit!"

Lord, change me. Sin is so ugly, so debilitating! Renew me until my heart belongs to you.

Yup...Only God can change a heart.

Random thoughts for today:

Repent, then, and turn to God, so that your sins may be wiped out, that times of refreshing may come from the Lord. (Acts 3:19 ESV)

Satan has a definite strategy, and it can be understood in one truth: HE LIES!

Sometimes love can be reckless.

Lord, give me the power to color my world with Your love.

Reject your sense of offense, and the offense itself disappears. *(Marcus Aurelius)*

We are more interested in absolution than accountability. *(Ryan Shockey)*

Never let me dishonor my love for Jesus by being cold or unkind or impatient.

Fall seven times...Stand up eight. *(Japanese Proverb)*

July 22   Memes, Clichés, and Snarkiness

"Oooooo, you got burned!" There's nothing like a great snarky comeback (Snarky is one of my wife's favorite words). I have cringed often at the comments and posts from church people who truly believe they are battling for truth. I could be wrong, but I believe if the Lord were giving us a grade on social media witnessing, it would be an F. We think we're winning the battle, but so many of our "take that, sinner" comments and comebacks are damaging our credibility. How about starting with a moratorium on quoting scripture out of context? My mother used to tell me, "Nobody ever wins a fight." I think that's especially true on the internet. Nonetheless, we continue on in our snarkiness. Here are some real-life examples I've gleaned off the internet.

- "When they kneel during the National Anthem, stop the music and say, 'Since we're kneeling, let's pray.'"
- "The problem isn't SKIN; the problem is SIN."
- It's not about RACE; it's about GRACE."
- "Bacon should be banned because it's offensive to Muslims."
- COVID-19 (substitute any other crisis)—This is God's wrath on a broken world."
- "Eternal life matters!"

- "They were warned, just like we are." (posted next to a picture of people drowning outside the ark)
- Some people think we should keep our mouths shut about politics. If Christians don't take a stand against all of this evil anti-American stuff going on right now and speak up, we ain't gonna have an America!"

You get the idea. Yeah, you burned em, but we will all learn someday that no one ever wins a fight. My personal philosophy in a fight is to not to fight at all. Do you struggle against the temptation to lash out and "speak your mind" in response to what you see on social media? Does the snarkiness win out within you? Maybe, just maybe, you need to take a break from social media. Here's a great principle in serving the Lord—Make sure your heart is right, then, offer your service to Him.

Random thoughts for today:

For though I am free from all, I have made myself a servant to all, that I might win more of them. (1 Corinthians 9:19 ESV)

What area of your life disgusts you enough to fuel change? *(Derek Chirch)*

July 23   14 Words

The story is told of a dream that Martin Luther had toward the end of his life. He stood before the Lord at judgment and Satan, the great accuser stood next to him, listing sin after sin after sin in his life. This went on for quite some time, until his "lawyer," the Great Advocate stood and began to speak. "Satan," said Jesus, "there is one entry you have ignored." "And what would that be?" responded Satan. "It is this," said Jesus. "The blood of Jesus Christ cleanses him of all sin." I love it. When the devil accuses, Jesus is ready to defend His own. The enemy of our souls loves to bring up all of our failures, our wrongs, and our disappointments. And if we continue to allow him to do this, it's extremely challenging to see and experience the joy of the Lord. As I've studied scripture through the years, there are a few things I've learned about the enemy—

- Satan lies and is the father of lies
- He is capable of blinding the minds of unbelievers
- He masquerades in costumes of light and righteousness
- He tempts people to sin
- He can snatch the word of God out of people's hearts

Fortunately, God has given us 14 wonderful words, which gives the secret to celebrating our life in Jesus. Paul wrote these words when he was in prison—

> *Forgetting what lies behind and reaching forward to what lies ahead. I PRESS ON...*
> **(Philippians 3:13-14 ESV)**

Random thoughts for today:

> *Therefore, if anyone is in Christ, the new creation has come: The old has gone, the new is here!* (2 Corinthians 5:17 ESV)

When people talk, listen to them; listen well...Most people never listen.

Help me not be so busy that I miss the small pleasures You've sprinkled throughout the day.

Lord, affirm what I'm doing right now or change what I'm doing right now.

Any "doctrine" that allows sin to be excused in my life if not pleasing to the Lord.

July 24   Blown Away?

When was the last time you were blown away, genuinely awestruck by the message of Jesus dying for you? When you read 1 Peter 3:18—*For Christ died for our sins once for all, the righteous for the unrighteous, to bring you to God,* how do you feel? What's your response to that? However you may interpret verses like that, or quibble over the theological nuances between penal atonement and substitutionary atonement, the fact remains that Jesus was on the cross because of our sin. Whether you accept the recapitulation theory, dramatic, mystical, or moral influence theories, and what church father you choose to follow in his interpretation, the fact STILL remains that Jesus died on the cross because of our sin. I think that it becomes difficult for us who have been Christians most of our lives, who have been raised on the "catechisms" of our denominations, and have been in Sunday school since childhood, to grasp and sense the passion of what happened in that Jerusalem Spring over 2,000 years ago. In a word, we have lost the wonder. How cool it is when I see a brand-new adult believer wrap his heart around *for God so loved the world that He gave His one and only Son.* Perhaps there is a connection between that lack of awe and wonder and the lack of servants today in the kingdom of God. More and more, I have come to realize that we will serve others with humility and wisdom and compassion only to the extent we are amazed that Jesus has died for us.

Random thoughts for today:

He Himself bore our sins in His body on the tree, that we might die to sin and live to righteousness. By His wounds you have been healed. (1 Peter 2:24 ESV)

Spiritual darkness comes into my life because of a command from God I do not intend to obey.

The deep root of all scriptural truth is this: absolute dependence upon the Lord.

It's not always wrong to say, "I don't know."

God not only orders our steps...He also orders our stops.

If you have one true friend, you have more than your share. *(Thomas Fuller)*

The Church: Do we really think we can join the family without being involved in the cause?

July 25   Purveyors of Opinion

I've been reading the Old Testament prophets lately; not always a fun thing to do. As a church leader, I get uncomfortable when I read—*This nation is the nation that has not obeyed the LORD its God. Truth has perished; it has vanished from their lips* (Jeremiah 7:27-28). Two chapters later, he calls them a *nation of liars*. I realize that he is talking to Judah, but I still get that "sounds more contemporary than I care to admit" feeling. Pontius Pilate asked the question, "What is truth?" How do we determine the answer to that inquiry? What IS our authority? As a young man, when I took the Word of God at face value without a pair of scissors in hand, I was much more stable in my journey. Don't get me wrong. There is always room for questioning and even sometimes doubting, but there has to be a firm foundation upon which to build. We have a tradition of a faith based upon the foundation of the Word of God. Orthodoxy is not a dirty word. Isaiah tells us, *My thoughts are not your thoughts, nor are your ways My ways* (55:8). We just don't get this. The way that I see it so many times is far different from the way God sees it. And guess what? The way God sees it, is the WAY IT IS. As one who has preached for over 50 years, I'm very concerned with the direction of the church today. Sometimes I feel that a lot of our churches are making it up as they go along. We are surrounded by too much spiritual diarrhea (a spiritual intestinal disorder caused by the poison food of compromise and false teaching) without any foundation of truth. Isaiah says, *The LORD has given me an instructed tongue, to know the word that sustains the weary* (50:4). Instructed tongues seem to be in short supply. I often pray, "Lord, do I have an instructed tongue today?" My opinions are my opinions; they are NOT necessarily truth. My opinion about Jesus doesn't change WHO He is (or what He taught). My prayer and challenge to the church today is for us to be committed to being proclaimers of truth and not purveyors of opinion.

Spare me, Lord, from the traps of my own opinions.

Random thoughts for today:

Beloved, do not believe every spirit, but test the spirits to see whether they are from God, for many false prophets have gone out into the world. (1 John 4:1 ESV)

Have you ever wondered what the faith of your family will look like 100 years from now?—It's called LEGACY.

My song today: "Lord, draw me near to You; never let me go."

A good heart is better than all the heads in the world. *(Anonymous)*

July 26   Amabilidad

I guess you can call this entry a follow-up (or I should say addition) to my May 13 entry on my immigration "no-plan." You may remember that I confessed to you I have few solutions to this extremely complicated problem. Through my confusion, and I am confused about many things these days, I have asked myself the question, "How do I feel about immigration into these United States of America?" I freely admit I don't have a plan, but I DO know how I feel. It's summed up in one word—AMABILIDAD. It is a word for KINDNESS, friendliness, gentleness, graciousness, sympathy, decency. That would seem to sum up the biblical attitude I should possess toward others, foreigner or not. It troubles me to hear and read many hateful diatribes and unkind opinions coming from those in the church. World-famous neuroscientist, Abhijit Naskar said it well—"Ayudar a los necesitados es no solo caridad, es cuestion de humanidad"**(*)**. Paul has told us that we *should have the same attitude as that of Christ Jesus* (Philippians

2:5). What did the prophet Micah say?—LOVE KINDNESS. Amabilidad. Proverbs 19:22 says that *what a man desires is unfailing kindness.* Peter teaches that we are to add kindness to our godliness (1:7). KINDNESS—amabilidad of my heart, of my mouth, and of my hands. I may not have a plan, but I DO know how I feel and what my attitude toward those in need ought to be. Don't forget the words and code of the Mandalorian (for all you Star Wars junkies)—"This is the way!"

(*) "Helping those in need is not just charity; it is a matter of humanity."

Random thoughts for today:

Do not oppress the alien... (Jeremiah 7:6) *Porque asi amo Dios al mundo, que el dio a su unico hijo, para que todo aquel que cree en el no se pierda, sino que tenga vida eterna.* (Juan 3:16)

Every truth we see is one to give to the world, not to keep to ourselves alone. *(Elizabeth Stanton)*

How often do I pray with sighs too deep for words?

You miss 100% of the shots you don't take. *(Wayne Gretzky)*

It's OK to say exactly what you think if you have learned to think exactly. *(Marcelene Cox)*

One who speaks the truth is always at ease. *(Persian Proverb)*

Never grow wise to the extent that you cannot laugh.

A Methodist preacher for over 40 years, confessed, "It is strange that one so involved in the life of spirit as I should be, is so turned off by 'religious' things." Me too. Like a sign at the entrance of a city park in a medium-sized city—"Jesus Park." Helen worked at a Christian bookstore for several years, and it always amazed me that the store sold more "Jesus junk" (a term we affectionately used to describe everything from Galilean Gummies to Bethlehem Monopoly) than they did books. I remember the sign I saw years ago on I-75 in northern Florida that read, "Jesus is Lord at Sheffields Catfish House—Best Catfish in the World." I'm imagining a cringing emoji. Jesus and marketing seem to be oxymoronic to me. I picture Him overturning tables in the temple courtyard. It seems that many are trying to make Christianity popular by marketing it as if it were a product on a store shelf. I confess that there have been times in my ministry that I have crossed the line in marketing the church. I have learned (sort of) and continue to learn that I do not desire to become "religious." If I may have the liberty of creating a proverb based upon Acts 8:20—"You are foolish if you think that marketing is the doorway to sharing God's gift." I become free in Christ and must continue to remind myself of that freedom. It is that freedom that leads me to faithfulness.

Random thoughts for today:

May your silver perish with you, because you thought you could obtain the gift of God with money. (Acts 8:20 ESV)

Men often oppose a thing merely because they have had no agency in planning it, or because it may have been planned by those they dislike. *(Alexander Hamilton)*

The true measure of a man is how he treats someone who cannot necessarily benefit him. *(Samuel Johnson)*

The older I get, the more I seem to be able to appreciate whomever I happen to be with at the moment.

We are what we repeatedly do...Excellence, then, is not an act but a habit. *(Paraphrasing Aristotle)*

July 28   My Anguish!

Have you ever been in "anguish" over anything? Anguish is a word used to describe being extremely distressed about something; severe mental or physical pain or suffering. Jeremiah 4:19-31 graphically pictures the prophet's anguish, which is the embodiment of God's anguish. With one voice, the prophet and God express their anguish over the people of Judah. *My anguish, my anguish* (V 19)! Literally translated, "my bowels, my bowels." In Hebrew, the bowels were considered to be the seat of all of our emotions. David Wilkerson once said that in order to have true passion for Christ and true revival in the church, we must be "baptized in anguish." I must agree that the American church today is blind to the lukewarmness that has crept into our churches little by little. This spirit is one of the least recognizable dangers in the lives of believers in our current culture. How many of us have committed to memory James 4:8—*Draw near to God and He will draw near to you. Cleanse your hands, you sinners, and purify your hearts, you double-minded.* Do I have the guts to honestly ask the Lord, "How often have I brought anguish to You? Show me where I have caused you anguish."

- Do I spend little or no time in Your word?
- Have I stopped laboring in prayer?
- Have I grown cold toward the body of Christ (Well, after all, there has been a pandemic)?
- Has my spiritual activity turned to passivity?
- Has my compassion for others decomposed into total apathy to what's happening around me?

Maybe I DO need a thorough "baptism of anguish." *My anguish, my anguish!* By the way, my editing check has informed me that I have way overused the word "anguish" in this entry. I know. It was purposeful!!

Random thoughts for today:

Be wretched and mourn and weep. Let your laughter be turned to mourning and your joy to gloom. (James 4:9 ESV)

When I am tired and weary help me remember that my rest and refreshment comes from you.

How busy we have become, and as a result, how empty.

July 29   The Problem With Language

Words are funny things. They can change meaning over time in ways that might surprise you. "Charity," of course, has changed culturally, and "gay" has a radically different meaning than it did 100 years ago. Did you know that "nice" used to mean silly or simple? "Silly" used to mean worthy or blessed. Here are a few more words we use and what they used to mean years ago:

- "Awful" – worthy of awe
- "Fizzle" – passing gas
- "Naughty" – you had nothing
- "Bachelor" – a young knight *(defined as a single man, post-Chaucer)*
- "Flirt" – flicking something away
- "Guy" – a frightful, evil person
- "Hussy" – housewife
- "Senile" – anything relating to old age

We love to play with words in creative ways. That's why language changes over time. Reuben Welch once wrote, "I perceive that some words like sanctification and holiness and redemption, which at one time were profoundly relevant, which were precious and beautiful life-words, have, for many people, lost their luster and much of their beauty and magnetism. At one time, these words had juice in them." Sometimes, wordiness can be a barrier to the gospel. I don't know if we can find new terms, new language, new lingo that would help us here, but I do know that there is still a heart-hunger in men, just as there is a heart-hunger in our Lord for His church. He STILL desires the salvation (once a beautiful and meaningful word) for the world and sanctification for His people.

<u>Random thoughts for today</u>:

A word fitly spoken is like apples of gold in a setting of silver. (Proverbs 25:11 ESV)

1 Peter talks about the devil as a roaring lion…Ironic, isn't it? We would run from a real lion, but we laugh about the devil!

We all have an agenda; it rarely coincides with God's agenda.

Give up trying to look like a saint; it'll be a lot better for everybody. *(Advice Brennan Manning's spiritual mentor gave to him)*

July 30   Counsel from a Pastoral-Intern

I heard my oldest grandson (*) preach his first sermon this past Spring. He did an exposition of Hebrews 12:1-9. You know— *Let us run with endurance the race that is set before us, looking to Jesus…* I'm jealous because his first sermon was better than my 20th sermon. It was a basic 3-point expositional message:

1. Look to the PAST
   - Who has gone before you, and what did they do?
2. Look to the PRESENT
   - What are you doing now?
   - Remove that which causes you to stumble
   - God shows you your sin through His Word
   - Endure suffering as a needed discipline to shape us
   - Why me? Because God disciplines those He loves
   - Do we praise God for our sufferings?

3. Look to the FUTURE
   - The result is the yield of the peaceful fruit of righteousness

His closing counsel:

If your faith isn't in Christ, what is it in? If you have stopped running the race, what's hindering you today? Are you tired? You are not alone. *We are surrounded by so great a cloud of witnesses.* PRESS ON!!

(*) Christian Schmidt, who is also editor of this book, presently interns at Christ Church in Lake Forest, Illinois.

<u>Random thoughts for today</u>:

Let no one despise you for your youth, but set the believers an example in speech, in conduct, in love, in faith, in purity. (1 Timothy 4:12 ESV)

The God of the Bible is the God of 2021.
Non-violence is not the weapon of the weak...It is the weapon of the strongest and the bravest. *(Gandhi)*

July 31   Peace in the Midst of Chaos

Life can often feel so chaotic. No kidding! As one guy posted on social media this past year, "2020, egads!! I think I'll just put up my Christmas tree and call it a year" (and this was posted in June). I confess to you that I have struggled with finding peace in my life through the years. It seems that the enemy has won many a battle with me and been able to plant many seeds of worry throughout the years. So here we are, still in the midst of this pandemic, racial unrest in cities all over the country, a presidential election that has divided the nation with great animosity, and a negative spirit that seems to permeate just about everything, even the church. And yet, I am at peace today more than I have ever been. Maybe the source of that peace has to do with my relationship with the Father, even in the midst of chaos. Thank You, Father for Your word.

PANDEMIC

- *Do not be anxious about anything, but in everything by prayer and supplication with thanksgiving, let your requests be made known to God. And the peace of God, which surpasses all understanding, will guard your hearts and your minds in Christ Jesus* (Philippians 4:6-7 ESV).

RIOTS, RACIAL UNREST

- *Repay no one evil for evil, but give thought to do what is honorable in the sight of all. If possible, so far as it depends on you, live peaceably with all* (Romans 12:17-18 ESV).

POLITICAL CORRUPTION AND CHAOS

- *Peace I leave with you; my peace I give to you. Not as the world gives do I give to you. Let not your hearts be troubled, neither let them be afraid* (John 14:27 ESV).

In the midst of calamity, plague, riots, unrest...*SING...BURST INTO SONG AND SHOUT FOR JOY!!* (Isaiah 54:1—My personal paraphrase)

<u>Random thoughts for today</u>:

Great peace have those who love Your law; nothing can make them stumble. (Psalm 119:165)

August

We Move Toward Each Other As
We Move Toward God.

August 1   Photocopier Love

There is an account of a sociology professor in a Midwestern university (this was in the late 1970s). He gave an assignment that was meant to be an experiment in sharing and giving. They asked each student to bring in a dollar. They said, "There are people starving in India; there's a plague there, and they really need your help. If you'd like to help, put a dollar in an envelope and write on it, 'India.'" The experiment wasn't over, however. "India is pretty far away. There are some people in a local ghetto, a family that needs groceries. If you want to help these people, put your dollar in an envelope and write, 'Poor People.'" The assignment continued. "Now, of course, we don't have a photocopier in the university student union. We need to get one for those of you who need to copy papers and manuscripts—and make it easily accessible to you. If you want to help buy a photocopier, put a dollar in the envelope and write, 'Copier' on it." 80% of the money went for the photocopy machine!!

Random thoughts for today:

In all things, I have shown you that by working hard in this way we must help the weak and remember the words of the Lord Jesus, how He Himself said, "It is more blessed to give than to receive." (Acts 20:35 ESV)

Make understanding your priority before trying to be understood.

What is my primary identity? I am the one Jesus loved.

What weight is holding you down and keeping you from flowing with the Spirit?

Don't miss the point of prayer—IT'S ABOUT RELATIONSHIP.

The way of Jesus is the way of invitation, not the way of manipulation...We are not called to manipulate people into making a decision.

Ignorance is not saying, "I don't know"...Ignorance says, "I don't want to know."

August 2   The Way I See It

To stay away from Christianity because part of the Bible's teaching is offensive to you assumes that if there is a God, He wouldn't have any views that upset you. Quite frankly, there are many scripture passages that upset me, and there are quite a few that I don't fully understand. I have a fundamental mistrust of those who seem to have all the easy answers to the hard questions. I've experienced many small group Bible studies, trying to dig in and get to the real meaning of a particular text. Then there is always that interruption by a group member who has not done any homework on the scripture being studied at all, say, "Well, this is my opinion; this is the way I see it!" Hopefully, our Bible studies are times of searching the scriptures together and participating in honest and open dialogue and not the sharing of ignorance. Years ago, we discussed Voodoo (in some parts of the world, it is spelled Vodou) in our group. One sister said she had just read an article on how many of our churches in Haiti had combined Christian music with Voodoo ritual to bring more into the faith. She thought that was a good idea. The next summer, I had an opportunity to spend a day with a Vodou high priest in Bombardopolis, Haiti, and I asked him about that. He smiled. His response—"At the very least, Vodou is controlled by Papa Legba, a Vodou deity, among other deities." Others I have talked to in Haiti who have come to Christ have shared with me that they believe Papa Legba is the devil. It's called syncretism. Syncretism in Christianity is when the Bible's teachings are blended in with culture or religious ideology that is not biblical. It happens in the church all the time. I guess that's the way I see it. I hope it's not an opinion born out of ignorance.

Random thoughts for today:

You will know the truth, and the truth will set you free. (John 8:32 ESV)

We are called to be in the ministry of lightening the burdens of others.

We love to communicate with those we love most..."Lord, teach me to pray!"

If you desire many things, many things will seem few. *(Ben Franklin)*

We cannot afford the great waste that comes from the neglect of a single child.

Those who bring sunshine to the lives of others cannot keep it from themselves.

I cry out to my Lord in the midst of a hostile world...And He is listening.

August 3   Nothing But the Truth

"What IS truth?" *(Pontius Pilate)*

Objective truth is not influenced by personal feelings or opinions; subjective truth IS. Biblically, the concept of truth comes from both the original Hebrew and Greek languages. The Hebrew (eh-MEHT) means "all-encompassing." The Greek (aletheia) means "full disclosure." So biblical truth, then, is all-encompassing full disclosure. The scripture immediately comes to mind—*I have hidden your word in my heart that I might not sin against You* (Psalm 119:11 ESV).

A Personal Prayer

Keep speaking TRUTH to me...It seems like there are times when Your truth, Your voice gets drowned out by everything around me, and I get distracted. There are fewer things more dangerous than to be distracted from truth...May I care more about the truth than what people think...May Your truth be an umbrella over my nation, my city, my church, and my family...Truth is not for or against

anything; it simply is...Truth is not a culturally driven direction nor a nostalgic concept of days past—It is truth...I work daily to focus on Your *still, small voice*...Keep sending Your message of truth in my direction...Ultimately, Lord, Yours is the only voice that makes sense...May this servant always BELIEVE truth, TEACH truth, and LIVE truth...In the name of my Savior who proclaimed that HE WAS THE TRUTH...Amen.

Random thoughts for today:

Your word is a lamp to my feet and a light to my path. (Psalm 119:105 ESV)

The act of acting morally is behaving as if everything we do matters.

A word of encouragement during a failure is worth more than an hour of praise after a success.

We are often asked to bind ourselves to certain ideologies or theologies rather than binding ourselves to Jesus Christ.

Make the mistakes of yesterday your lessons for today. *(Teddy Roosevelt)*

Time is the coin of your life. It is the only coin you have, and only you can determine how it is to be spent...Be careful lest you let other people spend it for you. *(Carl Sandburg)*

THEOLOGY = "the study of the nature of God and religious beliefs and theory when systematically developed." One theologian wrote, "It is the study of religious faith, practice, and experience, the study of God and God's relation to the world." I've been told that there are four types of theology: biblical studies, church history, systematic theology, and practical theology. I have no intention of delving into each of these and I am really not qualified to do so. I've taken enough courses on the subject to be dangerous. But you know what? God will always be better than our ideas of God. Contemplating the definitions above should be enough to reveal the problem. We're talking about the church who can't come together on free choice vs. predestination or once-saved-always-saved vs. falling from grace. Have you heard of the congregation that split over whether we should have our trespasses or our debts forgiven? Again, you see the problem. Throw in the difficulty of attempting to speak to our current age with our own language, and we run the danger of compromising the eternal message of the Gospel. Theology is not eternal. Only God is eternal, and no human mind or concept will ever capture that eternal reality. The ultimate test of a man's journey is not his theology but his life. Charles Haddon Spurgeon preached at the Metropolitan Tabernacle in London for decades, dying in his mid-fifties. Although certainly subjective opinion, many historians and theologians concur that he altered the city of London with his influence. On his deathbed, he said, "My theology has become very simple. It consists of four words: Jesus died for me."

<u>Random thoughts for today</u>:

In the beginning was the Word, and the Word was with God, and the Word was God. (John 1:1 ESV)

A diamond is a chunk of coal that did well under pressure.

Do we use the word of God as a club, or do we share it and live it in love?

The church should want to love well even when we're not sure how to love. *(Nate Loucks)*

A bit of fragrance clings to the hand of the one who gives flowers. *(Chinese Proverb)*

I wonder if many of us shy away from a growing prayer life with the Lord because we fear the intimacy.

August 5   Who Is My Neighbor?

Jesus taught that the second greatest commandment was *Love your neighbor as yourself.* Love God and love others has been a part of our church's mission statement for as long as I can remember. And you might remember the smart-mouthed question to Jesus from that religious leader, seeking to justify himself, *And just who IS my neighbor.* Jesus proceeds to tell the parable of the Good Samaritan, which translates, "Your neighbor is anyone who needs your help." WHO IS MY NEIGHBOR? The kid across the street from us who hit two golf balls into our front window. The family next door whose dog periodically pooped in our yard, or the neighbor whose dog barks for an hour at 4 am. The man who calls our home after midnight and asks if I have time to talk. The guy in our church who regularly drives me up the wall with his Bible interpretations. The arrogant pastor who used to know everything as a younger man, and still thinks he does. The rude clerk in a department store on Black Friday. The woman who encroaches on my space at Wal-Mart, even though we're in the middle of a pandemic. The homeless man on Michigan Avenue in Chicago. The liberal who hates conservatives. The conservative who hates liberals. The activist who trashes others publicly on social media. The evangelical who trashes others on social media. The kid who comes into your classroom when you're ready to leave and asks, "Can I talk to you?" The friend who disappoints you and leaves you with that feeling of betrayal. The list can go on and on. Jesus said, *Love your neighbor as yourself.* Hmmm. Maybe George MacDonald had it right after all—"A man must not choose his neighbor; he must take the neighbor God sent to him."

Random thoughts for today:

Which of these three proved to be a neighbor to the man who fell among the robbers? He said, "The one who showed him mercy." And Jesus said to him, "You go and do likewise." (Luke 10:36-37 ESV)

Give every truth time to send down deep roots into the heart. *(Francois Fenelon)*

Create an issue and make people afraid of it...Fear breeds misunderstanding and ignorance. *(politician's creed)*

Prayer can be a very dangerous business.

I will take some moments today to look at my world through childlike eyes...Maturity involves the ability to be childlike.

In John, chapter four, when the disciples told Jesus it was time to eat, He replied, "I've already eaten." Jesus said that His Father's work, doing His Father's will, was meat and drink to Him. Bob Benson says that in the church, there always seems to be the felt need of some for devising a new plan with a catchy title and slogan to enroll the saints in the Father's work. There's usually training involved and forms and cards to fill out. A few years ago, it was "Revive (you fill in your state)." No doubt about some of the results of Revive Indiana. Some churches found new life. Some Christians got excited about sharing the gospel (nothing wrong with that). There were some pretty well-attended worship services connected with the program (That's good). And the prayer effort behind this emphasis enlisted many across the state (and I'm for anything that gets people on their knees). One of the goals of the program was "to unite the church and pray alongside believers for revival." Now, in 2021, Indiana is still not revived. I've lived through the American Bible Society evangelism program of the 1960s, Evangelism Explosion of the 80s, "What Would Jesus Do" of the 90s, and various other programs and ministries to "revive" the church. After all the smoke has cleared, there has been very little change in local churches. The problem is that if love has an agenda, it's not love anymore. It's a program, and the church doesn't need any more programs. The Church exists for nothing else but to draw men unto Christ. At the end of the day, the biggest obstacle to evangelism is Christians who don't share the gospel. The simple definition of witnessing: those who know, telling those who don't. I'm all for lifestyle evangelism, but I'm also in favor of intentionality, where we seek out the opportunity to explain the gospel and why we believe it. No "Jesus Saves" signs, no banners, no "ichthus" bumper stickers...Just sharing what difference Jesus has made in my life. We may call it witnessing or evangelism. Jesus called it lunch.

Random thoughts for today:

Do you not say, "There are yet four months, then comes the harvest?" Look, I tell you, lift up your eyes, and see that the fields are white for harvest. (John 4:35 ESV)

Sometimes, doing "the best we can" may still fall short of what we would like to be able to do...Life isn't perfect.

Love well...Our love should always reveal the face of Jesus.

Cynicism is not courage...Actually, it is the height of cowardice.

August 7   What's the Question?

I'm sure you've heard the story about the Sunday School teacher who asked her Kindergarten class, "What's brown, has a bushy tail, and eats nuts?" A kindergartener responded, "Well, the answer is probably Jesus, but it sure sounds like a squirrel to me." My former high school students would have fun with me often. I would ask a question, and if they didn't know the answer, they would usually say, "Jesus." I've heard it so many times in my lifetime, from so many believers—"Jesus is the answer." Sometimes the response almost sounds like a flippant cliché. I had a prof in college who addressed this. He said, "OK, Jesus is the answer, but what is the question?" One student countered, "He's the answer to everything!" OK...but that isn't a satisfactory assumption to one who is honestly searching. What questions in your life does Jesus supply the answers to? One philosophy says that the three basic questions of life are 1) Who am I? 2) Why am I here? 3) Where am I going? Spoiler Alert = GOD KNOWS!! Jesus can answer all of those questions. He can bring purpose, and direction, and mission, and meaning to my life. He brings depth in answering that underlying question we all face, consciously or unconsciously—"Do I make a difference?" So yes, Jesus IS the answer, and I don't say that flippantly either.

Random thoughts for today:

Jesus said to them, "Who do you say that I am?" Simon Peter replied, "You are the Christ, the Son of the living God." (Matthew 16:15-16 ESV)

Money will buy a fine dog, but only kindness will make him wag his tail. *(Southern Proverb)*

May "the Lord provides" not just be a cliché; but rather a lifestyle in my daily walk.

Things can get stale pretty quickly in my life...We must work hard to keep our walk with the Lord fresh.

How bold one gets when one is sure of being loved. *(Sigmund Freud)*

Anything that keeps me from knowing God is my enemy.

Never lose the wonder!!

Not that the church needs any advice today, and what can these "old guys" from many generations past tell us anyway?

> MESSAGE FROM ST. BENEDICT - Halfway between Rome and Naples, was the first European abbey, Montecassino, founded by St. Benedict of Nursia in AD 529. It has a fascinating history if you care to look it up, including being bombed by the Allies during World War 2. The order at Montecassino was known for its loving and gentle countenance toward all, which was very much a part of the Rule of St. Benedict. There is one exception where Benedict spoke with vehemence; when he condemns the sins of murmuring—"If the heart is a quest to be a complete 'yes' to God in love, murmuring is diametrically opposed to this. Obedience with murmuring is a charade. It is obedience motivated by some intention not worthy of the human person. It is to miss the whole point of obedience."

I know we don't use the word murmur much today. In case you're unfamiliar with its basic meaning, its synonyms are muttering, babbling, grumbling, or complaining.

> MESSAGE FROM JOHN VIANNEY - He was a French Catholic priest (1786-1859) who is venerated as a saint and as the patron of parish priests. He was known as quite an evangelist and soul-winner. He was once asked the secret of his abnormal success in converting souls. His response—"It is done by being very indulgent to others and very hard on myself. There is a power in being outwardly

genial and inwardly austere, which is the real Christian temper. It can be achieved if courageously and faithfully sought, and there are no heights of love and holiness to which it cannot lead."

That's all there is to it. Thanks for the advice, guys!!

Random thoughts for today:

Listen to advice and accept instruction, that you may gain wisdom in the future. (Proverbs 19:20 ESV)

Church...Have we forgotten WHOSE we are?
LORD, keep changing me*!!*
If a student learns everything about the universe but nothing about their own gifts, what use would it be?

August 9   Hiding

I was doodling in my journal the other day. It's a sketch (and believe me when I tell you that I can't draw) of a guy peeking out of the door of his house. Right outside the door are conspiracies, viruses, riots and looting, fear-mongering media, anarchists, and false prophets. I put a title on my dubious artwork—"The Church Living in Fear." (Sub-title—"Please don't hurt us!") About a week and a half after the pandemic lockdown began (pretty much nationwide), my wife and I had not once been out of the house. Our daughters had almost forbidden it. Finally, I looked at Helen and said, "Put on your mask and let's go to the grocery store. After that, we'll go down to the lake (we live a couple of miles from Lake Michigan) and take a walk. I refuse to live in fear!" From that moment on, we have pretty much done what we want. We're not foolish, and we take proper precautions and follow the rules, but we refuse to hide in our house. Paul (in writing about Epaphroditus) says, *He almost died for the work of Christ, risking his life to make up for the help you were not able to give me* (Philippians 2:30). In AD 252, the plague broke out in Carthage, a seaside suburb of Tunisia's capital, Tunis. Most people in the city would throw their dead bodies out on the streets and would then flee the city in terror. Cyprian, a leader in the early church, and his followers gathered many in the church and set out to collect and bury all of these dead bodies. They also nursed many of the sick who still remained in the city. Some credit this group with saving the city, at the risk of their lives, from destruction and desolation. They became known as the *parabolani,* or literally, "the risk-takers." The church is always in need of risk-takers, willing to take the risk because as a believer, we know that we live forever in the presence and company of Christ. I don't know about you, but I'm pretty sure I don't want my legacy to be, "he hid in his house."

Random thoughts for today:

The LORD is my light and my salvation; whom shall I fear? The LORD is the stronghold of my life; of whom shall I be afraid? (Psalm 27:1 ESV)

Protect me, Lord, with Your salvation...Caress me with Your gentle ways.

Acceptance of prevailing standards of the day often means we have no standards of our own.

How many times have you noticed that it's the little quiet moments in life that seem to give the rest of life extra-special meaning?

August 10   Forgive Us Our What?

Suppose you recite the Lord's Prayer by memory with a group of people outside of your local church. Things probably go pretty smoothly until you get to the fourth line—*Forgive us our* _____? Do you say "debts"?—Presbyterian or reformed traditions are more likely to say that. Or do you say "trespasses"?— Anglican, Episcopal, Methodist, or Roman Catholic. A few churches, influenced by ecumenical liturgical movements, are more likely to say "sins," per Luke 11:4. Not too long ago, a friend of ours was visiting our little congregation for the first time. After the service, tongue and cheek, her comment was, "I'm sure glad you guys pray the Lord's Prayer the right way." I won't tell you which way we prayed; I have no desire to cause division in the church (OK...I changed my mind; we say "trespasses"). Where did that word come from? Well, part of the answer is tradition. Another possible answer is reading down two more verses in the Matthew account—*For if you forgive others their trespasses, your heavenly Father will also forgive you, but if you do not forgive others their trespasses, neither will your Father forgive your trespasses* (Matthew 6:14-15 ESV). Guess what? It's not about words. I couldn't care less whether you pray debts, trespasses, or sins. We get too caught up in etymology and miss the whole point. What Jesus does after reciting this prayer is to expound on the importance of forgiveness. Jon Bloom writes, "Jesus wanted us to understand sin in both the sense of owing a debt and the sense of trespassing into territory that doesn't belong to us." Jesus wants us to understand how vital forgiveness is to our spiritual well-being. Forgiveness is a renewal. For love to grow, it must be renewed every day. My pastor used to say, "To carry a grudge is to live in the past, to pitch your tent in the land of deceit." So which word shall you use when you pray the Lord's Prayer? Don't quibble over it. Don't lose sleep over it. Just sincerely pray it...AND THEN DO IT!!

Random thoughts for today:

Forgive us our debts, as we also have forgiven our debtors. (Matthew 6:12 ESV)

If you want others to be happy, practice compassion...If you want to be happy, practice compassion. *(Tenzin Gyatso)*

Difficult circumstances are often the ones that form our character and shape our lives.

I learn to appreciate inevitable mistakes and thank the Lord for the opportunities to learn.

Life is something that happens to you while you're making other plans.

There comes a time when one must take a position that is neither safe nor politic nor popular, but he must take it because his conscience tells him it is right.

August 11   Evolution of the "Sabbath"

Charlie Brown said, "Whoever enrolled me in the school of life didn't schedule enough recess." It reminds me of the Sabbath principle. Even though the command to keep the Sabbath holy was given to Israel's nation, the principle was given in Genesis 2, before the birth of the Jewish nation. Jews still observe their Sabbath on the seventh day, as does the Eastern Orthodox Church and the Seventh-Day Adventists. There are many discussions over whether Sunday has become the Christian "Sabbath." Are we obligated to keep the Sabbath, and what does keeping the Sabbath mean? I have no desire to get into all of that. My question is—Is the Sabbath principle still valid? Do we still have a day set aside to honor the Lord and break from the hectic busyness of the week? Well, Jones, every day should honor the Lord! Yeah, yeah, I know; good Sunday School answer. I've seen quite an evolution in our culture regarding a "day of rest." My father-in-law was a farmer. He took Exodus 34:21 literally—*Six days you shall work, but on the seventh day you shall rest. In plowing time and in harvest you shall rest.* In his lifetime he never once worked on Sunday; at one time he and his son farmed over 1500 acres. When I was in elementary school, churches were open, and all businesses were closed. God's command to Israel to rest on the Sabbath wasn't about just taking a break. He knew they would be tired and worn out from their labor. He knew they should set aside time to worship. He knew they needed quiet hours with their families. The seventh day of rest forced each one to remember the true source of everything they needed—God Himself. I don't have all the answers or specifics on how to "keep the Sabbath" in our crazy, high-tech world, and I have no desire to be a legalist. But it seems to me that our culture, especially our churches, have either lost or chosen to ignore the principle altogether. Who has time to honor the Sabbath today anyway? C'mon, guys, we're busy people!!

<u>Random thoughts for today</u>:

Remember the Sabbath day, to keep it holy. (Exodus 20:8 ESV)

If you are careless with small matters, you cannot be trusted with larger ones.

The more I study, the more I discover my ignorance...It was a lot more fun when I knew everything.

It is more rewarding to watch money change the world than watch it accumulate.

Without the Lord, nothing else really makes sense.

August 12   Last Days Question

This year has been one of many conspiracy theories and prophecies of the end of the world. That's not all that new, is it? Many in the church are convinced that the Lord is returning, like, any moment. I can't dispute that; scripture does say that as believers, we are to be expectant and ready for His return at any time. I'm good with that. Be that as it may, I am not prepared to put on a white robe and sit on my rooftop to wait for the rapture. Paul was addressing that mentality when he wrote his second letter to the Thessalonians. The study of the end times can be fascinating, but it shouldn't become obsessive. In years past, I've had members of our church leave the fellowship over prophecy and millennial-position issues (Pre – Post – or Amillenial). In a recent study of Jeremiah, I came across a scripture that helps solidify my personal position. In the middle of the Babylonian siege of Jerusalem (which lasted two years before its destruction), Jeremiah shares a gem. He's referring to the destruction of Jerusalem and the exile of His people. Still, I believe the principle goes beyond that event. He says, *The LORD will not finish until He fully accomplishes the purposes of His heart* (Jeremiah 30:24). I think that thought blends beautifully into the words of Jesus in Matthew 24:36—*But concerning that day and hour no one knows, not even the angels in heaven, nor the Son, but the Father only.* So then, when is this day of His returning? In past generations, dates have been set and proclaimed, books have been written about it, sermons have sounded the trumpet, but the fact remains that the Lord will return when the Father has fully accomplished the purposes of His heart. I guess that makes me a "purpose-millennial." When You're ready...Come Lord Jesus!!

Random thoughts for today:

So you must also be ready, because the Son of Man will come at an hour when you do not expect Him. (Matthew 24:44 NIV)

If I truly loved my neighbor as myself, what a difference I could make.

Love makes your soul crawl out from its hiding place.

Time is what we want most, but what we use worst. *(William Penn)*

Jesus was a great story-teller...Many times, without a story, we just don't get it. *(Rebecca Crain)*

The scriptural teaching on the power of the Holy Spirit has convicted me more than ever lately. Romans 8:14 says that the true children of God are those who let God's Spirit lead them. There are times in my life where you would think I didn't believe that. What do I actually believe about the Trinity? I talk about the Father and the Son, but it would seem that I am confused at best and apathetic at worst when it comes to the Holy Spirit. Does this last statement sum up where the church today finds itself? Perhaps we have drifted into apathy in our understanding of the Spirit because there are so many around us (in the church) working very hard to tell us what the Spirit can't do. Perhaps we need to simplify things a bit. The Holy Spirit is the presence of my Abba Father in my life, giving me power to do what Jesus wants me to do. The Spirit helps me (that's why He's called the "Helper") in three directions:

> Inwardly – He grants me the fruits of the Spirit (Galatians 5:22-24)
>
> Upwardly – He prays for me; my prayer partner (Romans 8:26)
>
> Outwardly – He continues to pour God's love into my heart (Romans 5:5)

Maybe I need to quit trying to dissect the Spirit and stop getting into debates about the Holy Spirit, and allow Him to fill me daily.

> "God is moving by His Spirit
> Moving in all the earth;

Signs and wonders when God moveth,
Move, O Lord, in me." *(Written by Lillian Edith Sims, my mother-in-law)*

<u>Random thoughts for today</u>:

And do not grieve the Holy Spirit of God, with whom you were sealed for the day of redemption. (Ephesians 4:30 ESV)

A brother may not be a friend, but a friend will always be a brother. *(Ben Franklin)*

A sense of gratitude transforms any situation from a grudge to a gift.

Your heart of compassion can be the very thing that causes someone else "to make it."

August 14   God's Holy Word

One of my pastors said, "It's easy to fall for the lies of Satan when we're not students and followers of the Word of God." It's my understanding that we are called to speak to the culture of our day. Do we influence our culture, or does our culture influence us? Are we willing to accept that something is OK, just because our society says it's OK? How do we follow Jesus in a world that doesn't honor marriage or sexual purity or the sanctity of life? When we eliminate God from the equation, how do we determine good and evil, right and wrong, or morality and immorality? Take the Lord out of it, and you end up with *everyone doing what is right in their own eyes* (Judges 21:25), even in the church. Isn't it interesting how easy it is to fall for the deceit of the enemy when you don't know the voice of the Father? Today, many churches need a good dose of truth-conviction, and then the courage to stand up for that truth. I can't help but think of that old pledge we used to recite in Sunday School:

"I pledge allegiance to the Bible, God's holy Word.
I will make it a lamp unto my feet and a light unto my path
And will hide its words in my heart that I might not sin against God"

American culture is becoming increasingly anti-Christian these days. Part of that is a result of our terrible witness. Perhaps it is also a reaction to the practical atheism that exists in our daily lifestyles. How about reading Isaiah 59:21 two or three times before you sleep tonight. GOD'S WORD DOES NOT CHANGE.

Random thoughts for today:

Your word is a lamp to my feet and a light to my path. (Psalm 119:105 ESV)

The passions of a revolution are apt to hurry even good men into excesses. *(Alexander Hamilton)*

Character may be manifested in the great moments, but it is made in the small ones.

The things that make me different are the things that make me, ME.

We can become so preoccupied with trying to model Christian virtues that we lose touch with the real message of the gospel, the good news that God loves us as we are.

What you find in your mind is what you put there...Put good things there.

August 15   Introvert

Pastor Becky (that would be my youngest daughter) confessed from the pulpit last year, "I am a closet introvert." That wasn't a shocking statement to me. Since then, I've thought a lot about that and concluded that Jesus was also a closet introvert. His love for people went deep, but if He had the choice between being with lots of people or just a few people, He would choose the latter. He had His twelve disciples. That narrowed down to his inner circle of Peter, James, and John. And of course, His favorite fellowship group was time alone with His Father. Jesus didn't relish the crowds; often, He sought to sneak away from them. I mentioned that I wasn't shocked to hear my daughter make that statement; she comes by it honestly. I, too, am a closet introvert— An interesting trait for a pastor. I would choose to be with a few people over many people. Spending dinner and conversation with another couple is my favorite kind of "recreation." My most memorable recollections of the ministry, where I served for almost 30 years (1200 people in 3 worship services), were when we were a body of 50 to 150 people. I am thoroughly enjoying my present pastorate, preaching and pastoring a congregation of twenty people. And I too, most enjoy that time alone with my Abba Father. So yes, I, like my daughter, am a closet introvert. And I guess that's one of the few traits I share with the Lord.

Random thoughts for today:

Now when Jesus saw a great crowd around Him, He gave orders to go over to the other side. (Matthew 8:18 ESV)

It's a horrible travesty to practice Christianity without holiness.

Sometimes, Lord, You need to help me undo my assumptions.

It's good to embrace a hope. *(Ovid)*

Wonder is the desire for knowledge. *(St. Thomas Aquinas)*

Lord, help me keep my anger from becoming nastiness and callousness.

Praise isn't just for sports fans, artists, and lovers...It's for all of us who know we owe our blessings to Someone else.

August 16   Philippians 2

If you have any encouragement from being united with Christ, if any comfort from His love, if any fellowship with the Spirit, if any tenderness or compassion, then make my joy complete by being like-minded, having the same love, being one in spirit and purpose. Do nothing out of selfish ambition or vain conceit, but in humility consider others better than yourselves. Each of you should look not only to your own interests, but also to the interests of others. Your attitude should be the same as that of Christ Jesus. **(Philippians 2:1-5)**

I find myself preaching the second chapter of Philippians often. It resonates with what I perceive our calling as Christians to be. THE ATTITUDE OR MIND OF CHRIST. What was important to Jesus? What were His objectives? What principles did He cherish? He made His choices based upon what? What brought Him joy? What broke His heart? What made Him angry? All of these issues that were important to Him should be important to us. You could write all of these questions down in your journal or notebook and spend the next three to four weeks searching your heart in giving specific answers to them. What a great beginning to taking steps toward being more like Jesus. What a super exercise to beginning the attainment of Paul's goal when he proclaimed, *I WANT TO KNOW CHRIST...* (Philippians 3:1).

Random thoughts for today:

He made of Himself nothing, taking the very nature of a servant...He humbled Himself and became obedient to death—even death on a cross. (Philippians 2:7-8 NIV)

My life changed when I realized God was for me.

What greater gift can we give to the republic than to teach truth to our young.

Many people would rather die than think...In fact, they do. *(Bertrand Russell)*

Take care of this moment.

Miracles sometimes happen, but more often life is made of faith and wit and hope and imagination, to say nothing of sweat. *(Tom Waldman)*

In the Psalms, I read prayers from God's people with phrases like, *Break their teeth with a rod of iron, LORD – Answer me, LORD, right now – Dash my enemies to pieces – Why are You so far away from me, LORD – How long are You going to forget me, LORD.* These writers were certainly honest with God. I've been collecting unusual prayers and writing them down in my journal. Some are crazy, some are silly (in my opinion; perhaps not God's), some are thought-provoking. Here are a few:

> "Open my eyes to see that Jesus is with me no matter what I go through, unlike the disciples that had the Son of God with them and didn't know it."

> "Thank You, Lord, for my smokin' hot wife tonight... Thank you for this race (invocation prayed by a pastor at NASCAR)...Boogity, boogity, boogity...Let's do it in Jesus' name."

> "Dear Lord...As your humble servant, let me prove to You that winning the lottery won't change me."

> "Please don't let my husband be home when all my online orders arrive. Amen."

> "Lord, as I go through my day, please keep your arm around my shoulder and your hand over my mouth."

> "Oh, God!" *(The most honest prayer I ever prayed—Rich Mullins)*

"When the world has gotten me down, and I feel rotten, and I'm too doggone tired to pray, and I'm in a big hurry, and besides, I'm mad at everybody, even You, Lord...HELP!!"

Definitely some unusual praying. I'm not sure I would be comfortable praying all of these prayers in public, but perhaps it does point out that we need to loosen up a little bit when we talk to the Lord. Are you honest when you communicate with the Lord?

Random thoughts for today:

Before a word is on my tongue you, You, LORD, know it completely. (Psalm 139:4 NIV)

Little is much when God is in it.
"Struggle" has become a Christian code-word today for postponed obedience.

August 18   The Oath

I shared earlier about the little congregation Helen and I have been attending the last year. In July (2020), I officially became their pastor. As I mentioned before, they are a small flock of precious people struggling to keep their doors open. It's been over 15 years since I pastored a church, so I wondered if I might be a little rusty. I guess old shepherds never die. I'm sure you've heard of the Hippocratic Oath, taken by men and women when they enter into their chosen field of medicine. One of the promises within that oath is "to do no harm *(primum non nocere* – Latin translation from the Greek) or injustice" to their patients. While we have no such oath in pastoral ministry, I remember a charge that was given to me when I was ordained in 1967—*Preach the Word; be prepared in season and out of season; correct, rebuke, and encourage—with great patience and careful instruction* (2 Timothy 4:2 ESV). Scripture calls me to be a leader and a shepherd after God's own heart. There is no point at which I can say, "I've pastored over 50 years; I might as well take a nap." In the early years, of my ministry I came across a scripture that has become a part of my pastor's creed, so to speak. Isaiah 57:14 says, "Remove the obstacles out of the way of my people...Build them up!" Who said this? *For thus says the One who is high and lifted up, who inhabits eternity, whose name is Holy* (Isaiah 57:15 ESV). Remove obstacles out of the way of the people...Build them up. Hmmm...Sounds like the pastoral call TO DO NO HARM.

Lord, give each of us as pastors a servant's heart...
May we desire to be leaders after God's own heart.

<u>Random thoughts for today</u>:

Keep watch over yourselves and all the flock of which the Holy Spirit has made you overseers. Be shepherds of the church of God, which He bought with His own blood. (Acts 20:28 NIV)

To love what you do and feel that it matters—How can anything be more fun?

In the kingdom of God, pride must be crowded out with love... Through no doing of our own, God loves us.

Timing is almost as important as truth when it comes to giving advice. *(Proverbs 24:11 NIV)*

356

You don't stop laughing because you grow old; you grow old because you stop laughing.

You are that which you are seeking. *(Francis of Assisi)*

August 19   Unlightenment?

Enlightenment has been defined as a state of serenity achieved through mindfulness, yoga, and meditation. Here are some responses from some who have tried the discipline of enlightenment:

> I love routine, until I'm bored, then I love excitement, until I'm overwhelmed, then I love routine.

> My three lists: "To Do Today – To Do Soon – Who Am I Kidding? I'll Never Do This

> I tell myself exactly what I need to do to be healthy. Problem is, I hate being told what to do.

> I'll live in the moment when I have time.

I've done some study on Eastern meditation and enlightenment, but I've never been able to relate. I frequently engage in what some would call Christian mediation (See entries, February 18 and June 7). I've experimented with some practices over the years (February 18). Again, I refer to this as taking a mini-break, and I don't say "OMM" over and over. I'm all for enlightenment, but it all comes down to how you define that term. I believe scripture is the key to any extended focus or "mindfulness" (again, whatever that means). The time I spend in the word of God has a lot to do with my ability to keep my mind stayed on Him. As opposed to junk reading, junk TV, junk video games, and junk whatever. Like the old cliché—"Junk in; junk out!!"

Random thoughts for today:

His delight is in the law (instruction) of the LORD, and on His law he meditates day and night. (Psalm 1:2 ESV)

Today me will live in the moment, unless it is unpleasant...In which case me will eat a cookie. *(Cookie Monster)*

I'm just enjoying God's gift of life...Try it, you'll like it.

Nothing can make our life or the lives of others more beautiful than perpetual kindness.

I'm just enjoying God's gift of life...Try it; you'll like it.

August 20   The Eternal Now

As a former teacher of both American and world history, I've always advocated protecting the truth of the past. That's not an easy task. I'm also an opponent of rewriting or erasing history (See entry, June 22). "How can we learn lessons from our history if we don't KNOW our history." George Santayana is credited with that original statement. My philosophy of teaching history has always been, "It is what it is; truth matters." I am, however, not naïve enough to believe that just because we know our history, we will be immune from repeating the disasters of our history. I see similar dangers in the church. Our churches are filled with experts in biblical studies and history but are not consistent practitioners of what scripture teaches. We don't always do that great of a job living it out. Just because you know all 66 books of the Bible in order and have a myriad of verses memorized doesn't mean that you are maturing in your walk with Jesus Christ. It is the Spirit of the living God that makes me alive and vibrant and excited about Jesus. As important as the written page of scripture is, it is the *Spirit that gives life!* Jesus said that (John 6:63 ESV). It's not the Bible in me, the hope of glory...It is CHRIST IN ME, the hope of glory!! Don't get me wrong. We absolutely need to be in the Word of God. But the Word has to become more than just history to us. The love of our Eternal God must break through to us into this time—NOW!! The personal, intimate presence of His love.

Random thoughts for today:

You yourselves are our letter ("epistles"—KJV), ***written on our hearts, known and read by everybody.*** (2 Corinthians 3:2)

Stop a moment, cease your work, look around you.

That which is striking and beautiful is not always good, but that which is good is always beautiful.

It's all a matter of keeping my eyes open.

My life is my message. *(Mohandas Gandhi)*

Courage is what it takes to stand up and speak; it is also what it takes to sit down and listen.

Accepting God's grace frees me to pray prayers that are honest and authentic.

I am passionate about authenticity! Truth means everything to me as well as living a genuine life. As much as I abhor phoniness, it may surprise you to know that I am an imposter. If we dig deep enough, we realize that we are all imposters. Brennan Manning talks about "the imposter in me." I relate to that. That kind of confession can begin to bring about true freedom in our walk with God. Titus 2:7-8 tells us to *show yourself in all respects to be a model of good works and in your teaching show integrity, dignity, and sound speech that cannot be condemned so that an opponent may be put to shame, having nothing evil to say about us.* Why is it that every time I read this scripture, I am convicted of that lack of authenticity that keeps rearing its ugly head in my life? Why do we struggle so much to be real? I hear it in the church—"We gotta keep it real!" But we don't. That hypocrisy virus finds its way into all of us and continues to threaten our spiritual health. I've learned that dealing with inauthenticity in my walk is a constant battle. Each morning I begin a daily surrendering process, and daily, this is something this imposter must do. Many mornings I sing the words of Israel Houghton—"I surrender all, I surrender all. All to Thee my blessed Savior, I surrender all." Day by day...Hour by hour...Minute by minute...I surrender my imposterness to You, Father. Alright! I just made up another word.

Random thoughts for today:

I am reminded of your sincere (authentic) *faith, a faith that dwelt first in your grandmother Lois and your*

mother Eunice and now, I am sure dwells in you as well. (2 Timothy 1:5 ESV)

Many in the church are willing to do almost anything, as long as it doesn't require self-denial.

We are shaped and fashioned by what we love. *(Goethe)*

Be an advocate for someone who really needs it.

The will of God is more important to me than my comfort. *(Written on the wall of the art room at Victory Christian Academy)*

God's discipline is not punitive, but neither is His grace unconditionally acceptant of a sinful lifestyle.

The older I get, the more I realize that just keeping on in the Lord is what life is all about.

August 22   Accountability

You may have seen that commercial of the little guy quickly responding to his dad, "I didn't do it!" It's pretty obvious he did. Exodus 20:5 says that the Lord your God visits *the iniquity of the fathers on the children to the third and the fourth generation.* Memorize that if you ever need to throw your parents under the bus. My recent studies in Ezekiel contain one of the most explicit passages in all of prophecy for personal accountability. The heart of his message is *the soul that sins is the one who will die* (Ezekiel 18:20). He discounts any notion that it's somebody else's fault. I've read that accountability is the willingness to accept responsibility for one's actions. Accountability in my journey includes responsibility to the Lord and to others. Daniel Webster said, "The greatest responsibility that can occupy my mind is my accountability to God." Recently I came across a list entitled, "Four Things Necessary for Spiritual Growth." Here they are.

1. Right attitude
   My attitude, not the attitude of my parents or "everybody else."
2. Right spiritual food
   My diet, not someone else's diet
3. Training
   My disciplines – My stewardship of time and effort
4. A servant's heart in whatever I do
   Not my parents' service, not my pastor's heart, but MY heart.

OK...We're not just talking about accountability...We're talking about PERSONAL accountability. And you know what? We are all responsible for what we do or say, even if those behaviors occur in extremely stressful times.

Random thoughts for today:

But everyone shall die for his own sin... (Jeremiah 31:30 ESV)

When you are offended at any man's fault, turn to yourself and study your own failings...Then you will forget your anger. *(Epictetus)*

The will to succeed is important, but what's even more important is the will to prepare.

Why is it that so many are always getting ready to live and yet never really living?

Live well...Laugh often...Love much.

We all seem to have a soft spot in our eating habits for comfort food. Comfort food can be different things to different people. What's your comfort food? High carb or sugar content? Meals that you associate with childhood memories of home cooking? One chef says, "it is food that provides consolation or feelings of well-being." Mine is a good steak or pizza, or my wife's chili on a cold winter night. Philippians 3:14 ESV says that we are *to press on toward the goal for the prize of the upward call of God in Christ Jesus.* Often I pray, "In all things, Lord, help me keep my focus on You...You are my priority, You are my prize...May I continue to press on toward the prize today." What's important to you? What's your "comfort" food? What do your loyalties breathe through? Your work, hobbies, golf, your boat, your yard? How about your pastoral work, preacher? What upsets you more? The fact that your prayer life has waned or that your cell phone went on the fritz today? We don't like our comfort zones to be messed with, do we? Jesus tells us in Matthew 6:33 that our focus is to seek first the Kingdom of God. Our focus on seeking the prize must take priority over absolutely everything. If anything else takes priority, it becomes idolatry. Have you ever known someone who's life comes apart because their breakfast coffee was cold? I had a preacher say to me once, "If you prefer to give priority to secondary loyalties, you will not disturb your regular pattern of life in any way." No wonder Jesus can find no place to be at home in our world. I think that there is a place for spiritual "comfort food" in my life (a special song or favorite scripture or author), but I know that I need to spend more time wrestling with those things that DO disturb the regular pattern of my life. All comfort food in my diet does not lead to good health. Periodically, I think my routine DOES need to be disturbed.

Random thoughts for today:

Then I will give you shepherds after My own heart, who will feed you on knowledge and understanding.
(Jeremiah 3:15 ESV)

Are you fleeing, fighting, or flowing with the Spirit of God?

No one rises to low expectations.

Far too many of us have very little humor or laughter in our lives. Carpe Smilem.

When you're finished changing, you're finished. *(Ben Franklin)*

When you're offended by any man's fault, turn to yourself and study your own failings...You will then forget your anger. *(Epictetus)*

August 24   Powerlessness

Have you ever been consumed in attempting to minister comfort to a grieving spirit? You know what I'm talking about. You pour yourself out to a brother or sister who is absolutely devastated and grief-stricken over the loss of a loved one; they are inconsolable. You search your heart for the right words, even though deep down you know that the most effective thing you are doing is just being there with them. Ultimately you end up sitting at their side, weeping with them. You feel no real power in your ministry today, and yet, maybe that's not true. There have been occasions when praying with these precious friends that I have simply wept through my prayer. If there was one word to describe my feelings in this moment it would be powerlessness. My first experience with this was with a family in our church whose three-year-old son drown in their backyard pool. I had nothing to say or share with them that would bring comfort. I know I was filled with this desire to bring her son back to her—"Lord, if I could just give this family back their son; if I just had the faith to raise him from the dead." In ministering to this family I found myself asking "why" right alongside these hurting parents. My ministry that day lay more in powerlessness than in power. I could only give my tears.

Random thoughts for today:

Rejoice with those who rejoice, weep with those who weep. (Romans 12:15 ESV)

True, loving charity musts cost us.

Am I the "salt of the earth?" Am I seasoning the lives of those around me?

Lord, may I leave fingerprints on those You bring into my life.

If you want to go quickly, go alone...If you want to go far, go together. *(African Proverb)*

Education is not knowledge of facts...It is knowledge of values.

The more rules...The more offenders.

Prayer is not what you offer...It's what you receive.

We accept from the Lord what we may not understand...That is the dynamic of faith.

August 25   Imposter - 2

I just talked about this four days ago (August 21), but as I said, dealing with my "imposterness" is a daily chore. I think it will always be a struggle in this lifetime. My daughter gave me an inscribed glass at my retirement party that said, "The Legend has retired—2019." Pretty cool. Last week I preached chapel services at my former school. When some of the students heard I was coming, one remarked, "You mean Rick Jones, the Legend!" Yeah, that would be me. That encouraged me, but it also puffed me up a bit. And the imposter in me rises up again, only to shrink as I am convicted (again) of the "brilliant vice of my alleged virtues." John 8:44 says that Satan is a liar and the father of lies. You would think that after all these years I would be on to him, and yet I can still get sucked into his lies. I believe that genuine followers of Jesus Christ have a good sense of self-esteem, but also don't hesitate to admit their vulnerability and faults. I think authentic believers really listen to others and prefer deep conversations. And then there is an area with which we all struggle. Too many of us imposters are driven by our surroundings rather than an inner voice. It's too easy to allow the majority to feed the imposter within and believe our own "press clippings" rather than respond with what we know is right in our hearts. Thank You, Lord, for your daily reminder.

Random thoughts for today:

Show yourself in all respects to be a model of good works, and in your teaching show integrity, dignity. (Titus 2:7 ESV)

The crucifixion was how God fixed everybody up. *(8-year-old kid)*

In what ways today will I show my reverence and awe to God?

The true secret of happiness lies in taking a genuine interest in all the details of daily life.

You don't lead by hitting people over the head...That's assault, not leadership. *(D.L. Eisenhower)*

For every mean and hateful act we hear about on the news, there are a thousand kindnesses that go unreported.

Character is a by-product of walking with Jesus.

I really have no business being satisfied with mediocrity.

August 26   Yes, Way!

Jesus tells us in John 14:6—*I am the way the truth and the life. No one comes to the Father except through Me.* In my younger years, I had a mentor who shared with me, "Jesus is not many ways, He is THE way; Jesus is not many truths, He is THE truth. And He is THE life." Paul tells us in Colossians, chapter three that our lives *are hidden with Christ*...that Jesus Christ *is our life* (Vv 3-4). The world says, "No way!" Jesus says, "Yes, WAY!" When Jesus said He was the way, he meant more than just a direction to the Father. In His teaching He also tells us a way to think, a way to act, a way to react, a way for all of life.

> I came across this prayer from my journal of a few years back—**"Each day I am finding out how not to live. I run into many ways that leave me frustrated and exhausted and hurt. Help me to find THE Way. For in finding the Way I shall find You. Thank You for Jesus...He is our way and truth and life. Amen."**

We live as maturing believers when we live as people seeking the Lord. That process does not end until we are ushered into eternity. What can we do but worship Him and love Him and obey His word? What can we do but give Him our life? This week, pray that you will truly be in the Way.

<u>Random thoughts for today</u>:

But if you seek the LORD your God, you will find Him with all your heart and with all your soul. (Deuteronomy 4:29 ESV)

What do we live for, if it is not to make life less difficult for each other? *(George Eliot)*

Commitment is what transforms a promise into reality.

We can't always build the future for our youth...But we can build our youth for the future.

Let Your love, Lord, shape my life.

If your motive is truly to help, you'll find a way to speak the truth in love.

August 27   Advice from a Prison Cell

I've been preaching through Philippians. What a great letter from the apostle Paul with a theme of predictable joy in an unpredictable world. The unpredictability of life is due in part to the unpredictable situations we encounter, the unpredictable people we meet, and the unpredictable problems we face. While it would be impossible for scripture to give us specific step-by-step instruction to apply to every single situation, it does give us guidelines, principles that tells us how to cope with crises, people, and problems that come our way. You won't find specifics about what to do if your toddler flushes a toy down the toilet, or you burn the dinner, or your co-worker drives you nuts, or your teenager just drove the new car through the garage door. There are an infinite number of variations possible when it comes to the unpredictability of situations and people and problems. The first seven verses of chapter four of this letter gives us some great advice.

> How to greet every situation: *Rejoice in the Lord always, and again I say rejoice* (V 4).
> How to treat very person: *Let your gentleness be evident to all* (V 5).
> How to meet every problem: *Don't be anxious about anything. In everything, by thanksgiving, present your requests to God* (V 6).

And the result of taking this advice? *The peace of God, which transcends all understanding, will guard your hearts and minds in Christ Jesus* (V 7). Too simplistic? I seem to recollect that Paul gave us this advice from a prison cell.

Random thoughts for today:

Have this mind among yourselves, which is yours in Christ Jesus. (Philippians 2:5 ESV)

Today I will not focus on my age spots or new wrinkles... Instead I will seek out new adventure or opportunity for growth.

Trouble came knocking, but hearing laughter, hurried away. *(Ben Franklin)*

If I don't have faith in what the Lord has done, how can I really have faith in what He can do through me today?

As the true King, our powerful God has a deep concern for the powerless.

When you have exhausted all possibilities, remember this—You haven't!

August 28   Balanced Worship

In 2 Chronicles, chapter twenty, we find an interesting account describing the power of the song (or the power of worship and praise). The Lord says to King Jehoshaphat and the people of Judah, when you go against the enemy, *You will not have to fight this battle; the LORD will be with you* (V 17). Read the whole chapter. Seriously, read the whole chapter. Did you ever wonder why God appointed the choir to be on the front line? Maybe because of all of the feistiness in church musicians? I'm not sure. To go against the enemy, the choir is to lead the soldiers against the enemy and sing, *Give thanks to the LORD, for His love endures forever* (V 21). For too many years, it seems that the worship and praise ministry of the church has become the war zone. A few years ago, many Christian leaders coined the term "worship wars." Why is that? The enemy is attacking the church on a daily basis. Worship and praise is to be our weapon against these attacks. Is it possible that Satan causes division and tension in the worship ministries of our churches so that worship leaders cannot effectively lead the church into battle? Balanced worship is really not about having all kinds of worship styles (contemporary or hymns, etc.) in our weekly service. It's not about style or preferences or musical abilities at all. As I pray for balanced worship in our congregation, this is specifically what I pray for in the lives of our worship leaders:

- For each one to have a servant's heart
- That each one would first and foremost be a servant of Jesus; secondly a musician
- That all could say with Paul, *Imitate me as I imitate Christ*
- That everyone's priority in this ministry would ALWAYS be for the glory of God and for the good of the church
- That if any have an issue with another member of the team, he/she would go to that person to work it out and pray together
- That each member of the team would commit to make to make worship and praise a holy thing for the Lord

When all the above happens, worship and praise leadership are ready to take the body into the battle.

Random thoughts for today:

Worship the LORD in the splendor of His holiness...
(Psalm 96:9 ESV)

The choice of evil over good is a deliberate choice...The devil makes us do nothing.

I don't know what to say to You right now, Lord, so I think I'll just sit here and be with You.

In the midst of life's struggles, I see miracles everywhere.

August 29   True Freedom

It is difficult for a self-conscious person to be an individual and not be at the beck and call of the crowd or conventional wisdom. I've heard it said that it's so difficult to be yourself because we live in a world that is constantly trying to make us something else. One definition of maturity is a new lack of self-consciousness. I believe that maturity and freedom are linked together. God created man to be free and responsible. Dag Hammarskjold, second Secretary-General of the UN said, "Don't be afraid of yourself, live your individuality to the full—but for the good of others." In other words, I'm all for being yourself. I think it's extremely healthy in that walk toward the authenticity we've discussed. But I need to be cautious that my "I gotta be me" spirit doesn't segue into "even if it means trashing you." We have tried to raise our two daughters with independent spirits. We're proud of the way they have grown in thinking for themselves and being themselves, and at the same time being filled with a compassion for others around them (See entries—May 10 & June 15). Jen Hatmaker says, "There is no typecast in humanity." We come from a creative God; we are not all the same. You are you and I am me (that's pretty deep, isn't it?). I come down pretty strong on being the self that results from *Christ in you, the hope of glory.* Hammarskjold also said, "He who places himself in God's hands stands free vis-à-vis men." That's true freedom, my friends.

Random thoughts for today:

Be steadfast, immovable, always abounding in the work of the Lord, knowing that in the Lord your labor is not in vain. (1 Corinthians 15:58 ESV)

I'm going to spend the day today looking for God-things.
Men learn while they teach. *(Seneca)*
If we are all "biblical" in our positions in the church, why do we disagree so much?

We rarely have time for everything we want to do in life, so we need to make choices.

What would happen if we declared our churches, our social interaction, our work-places, and our homes as gossip-free zones?

I'm spending the day today looking for God-things.

August 30   Unborn, but Present

Even as a teenager, one of my favorite passages was a portion of Psalm 139 ESV—*For you formed my inward parts; you knitted me together in my mother's womb. I praise You, for I am fearfully and wonderfully made* (Vv 13-14). It was a passage I prayed over my wife as she carried both of our daughters. And it was a prayer Helen and I prayed together when she miscarried a third. I recently read a statement from a contemporary Christian writer that was pretty confusing to me. She stated that she was both pro-life and pro-choice. As I spent time reading various writers as to this position, I discovered varied definitions of both pro-life and pro-choice. If we keep changing definitions, it becomes easier to talk out of both sides of our mouths. The late Rachel Held Evans talks about her embarrassment by the pro-life cause, illustrated by those conservative bumper-sticker Christians with a "Choose Life" sticker on one side, and a "You'll Have to Pry My Gun From My Cold Dead Hands" on the other. I agree. Wouldn't it be cool to see a "Choose Life: Abolish Abortion" on one side of the bumper, and "Choose Life: Abolish Capital Punishment" on the other? When will the church realize that forming political alliances with the right is not going to change anything. Nor is forming political alliances with the left, by the way. Putting more conservative justices on the Supreme Court so that Roe v. Wade can be reversed will not stop abortions in our country any more than "Just Say No" will eliminate drug abuse among our kids. We've elected a number of so-called conservative Republican presidents over the past years and Roe v. Wade remains intact. The church becomes more and more involved in politics, and less and less with the matters of the heart and yet many women are still seeking abortions. I believe that the church needs to dialogue this issue and how we can be involved in reducing the number of abortions being performed in our nation. All of the factors that might contribute to her decision to terminate her pregnancy don't seem to matter much to the pro-life cause. On the other hand, one pro-choicer said, "It's not ALL about the baby!" Well, even though there are many issues that may surround your pro-life/ pro-choice philosophy, abortion is pretty much about the baby. So I read Psalm 139 again. Regardless of how I justify it in my head, I can't justify it in my heart. I will not condemn or judge you in your position. Please don't judge me in mine. It's possible, that we may both have error in our opinions.

Random thoughts for today:

My frame was not hidden from You, when I was being made in secret, intricately woven in the depths of the earth. Your eyes saw my unformed substance; in Your book were written, every one of them, the days that were formed for me, when as yet there were none of them. (Psalm 139:15-16 ESV)

Yes, it's true...Babies do cry in the womb. *(The Discovery Channel)*

Around the time of the first Earth Day in 1970, a number of predictions were made by various scientists around the world.

- Civilization will end within the next 15-30 years (Harvard biologist)
- The death rate will increase until at least 100-200 million people per year will starve to death during the next 10 years (German ecologist)
- The greatest cataclysm in the history of man will result in famines of unbelievable proportions by 1975 (German ecologist)...Other experts feel this won't happen until the decade of the 1980s
- By 2000, there will be no crude oil (National Academy of Science)
- In 25 years, 75 to 80% of all living animals will be extinct (Smithsonian Institute)

It's a phrase I hear almost every day in the middle of this pandemic; interestingly, more from politicians than scientists—"Follow the Science!" A close friend of mine, who IS a scientist, shared with me, "A lot of what we are being asked to follow today is NOT science." Recently I had a former student send me a dollar bill with the phrase, "In God We Trust" altered. He had scratched out "God" and substituted the word, "Science." Hmmm. Which science? Meteorology (there's an exact science) – Psychology – Psychiatry – Climatology – Ecology – Nutrition – Economics (yes, economics is considered a science)? How about physics? I am NOT anti-science. One of my side-projects this year is trying to understand more about the world of physics. I'm presently reading *The Universe in a Nutshell* by Stephen Hawking. I recently read an article by a Nobel-prize winning physicist who said that theoretical particle physics is definitely a dead subject. They went on to say that many areas of study seemed to have reached an era in which theory is virtually unconstrained by experiment. This is way above my pay-grade and I'll have to leave the physicists to battle this out. I remember studying the Scientific Theory in Jr. High School, and today find quite a bit of conflict and confusion between its tenants and what people mean when they say, "Follow the Science." Michael Andrew Gove, former journalist and Secretary of State for Environment, Food, and Rural Affairs of the United Kingdom, recently stated, "I think people have had enough of experts from organizations with acronyms saying they know what is best, and getting it consistently wrong." Dr. Tony Campolo said some time ago, "What if science and scripture conflict? My advice is to go with scripture and science will eventually catch up." But then again, Tony is not a scientist. What does he know?

> *For the wisdom of this world is folly with God. For it is written, "He catches the wise in their craftiness," and again, "The Lord knows the thoughts of the wise, that they are futile."* (1 Corinthians 3:19-20 ESV)

September

Life Is Short And There Will Always
Be Dirty Dishes, So Let's Dance.

September 1   When Did All This Happen? - 2

Here's a sobering (but true) thought—I am now as far away from the 1980s as the 1980s were from the 1940s. There's a drawing in my journal of an older couple sitting on the park bench holding an umbrella over their heads. They both are wearing hats—one to cover a bald head and the other to cover a gray head. The caption says, "You're still my everything." Forty years ago it would have been cute and quaint to me. Today it is reality. Helen and I have shared a lot of memories during our days of pandemic quarantine—mourning memories...dancing memories. How fast time passes. I remember looking into the crib of my 6-month old daughter, and eight to ten years later (at least it seemed) I was walking her down the aisle. We have memories of vacation trips to the mountains, to the ocean, to the Northern Lights boundary waters of Canada, to the Appalachian Trail...So many memories. And yet, scripture tells me that all of these memories, as precious as they are, are but shadows. Shadows that grow dimmer as each year passes. And as the doctor says, "I don't have a pill for that." But it's OK. Oh man, the holidays that await us. In the words of C.S. Lewis, "We are far too easily pleased." Yes, we are. Inwardly, we thrive in that desire for that far off country—Aslan's Country.

The day is coming that the fading shadows will become reality. *We don't yet see things clearly. We're squinting in a fog, peering through a mist. But it won't be long before the weather clears and the sun shines bright! We'll see it all then, see it all as clearly as God sees us, knowing Him directly just as He knows us* (1 Corinthians 13:12 ESV—The Message). Praise God!! Aslan IS on the move.

Random thoughts for today:

He who dwells in the shelter of the Most High will abide in the shadow of the Almighty. I will say to the LORD, "My refuge and my fortress, my God in Whom I trust." (Psalm 91:1 ESV)

Teach us delight in simple things. *(Rudyard Kipling)*

Maturity breeds the confidence to have no opinion on many things.

September 2   Before My Day Begins

Heavenly Father, as this new day begins and calls me to the work You have for me, I pray that You may enable me to do what You desire me to do. May I do it as a servant of Christ, doing Your will from my heart.

I believe that the validity of my prayer life can be seen in the ways that I act and speak and live. In my own life, that emanates from how I begin my day. I personally find it helpful to begin the day by silently committing that day into God's hands, whatever it will bring. Francois Fenelon, writing in the 17th century, said, "The men who have done the most for God in this world seem to be those who have been early on their knees. If God is not first in our thoughts and efforts in the morning, He will be in the last place the remainder of the day."

In the morning, Lord, I seek Your face. In the early hours You will hear my prayer.

As you begin each day this week, how about asking God to help you see the tasks of your life, not as opportunities for advancement or as stepping-stones to some future work. May you instead see them as places where you have been called to serve today, and that you might do them gladly.

**"God give me the work
Till my life shall end
And life
Till my work is done. Amen."** (On a Yorkshire tombstone)

Random thoughts for today:

And rising very early in the morning, while it was still dark, He departed and went out to a desolate place, and there he prayed. (Mark 1:35 ESV)

The will, like an absolute sovereign, reigns over the body. *(John Flavel)*

A good heart is better than all the heads in the world.

Return to the old watering holes for more than water; friends and dreams are there to meet you. *(African Proverb)*

Lord, I've found that to keep in touch with my own childlike spirit is simply to spend time with children.

September 3   Hitlahavut

The Oxford Dictionary of the Jewish Religion introduces the word, *HITLAHAVUT.* In Hasidism it is defined as enthusiasm; the profound joy in God. It carries with it the idea of the soul of the worshiper being on fire. It is going out of myself to *taste and see how good God is* (Psalm 34:8) right now, in the moment. In other words, the joy of NOW moments. As the ancient rabbi prayed, "Teach me to rejoice at THIS MOMENT." It does no good to be so busy planning to earn bread for next week that I cannot enjoy what I'm eating now. Hitlahavut is the ecstasy of enjoying the Lord right now. I do not allow tomorrow to rob me of the pleasure of today. We spend too much of our lives in anticipation of a time that is to come and miss the joy of the present. Another rabbi states, "Begin to celebrate breath and water and food and NOW!" I came across an entry in one of my journals, written some time ago:

> Don't wait until tomorrow
> Live today
> Celebrate the simple things
> Don't wait until all the problems are solved or the bills are paid
> Live in the now

Random thoughts for today:

Praise the LORD! Praise the LORD, O my soul! I will praise the LORD as long as I live; I will sing praises to my God while I have my being. (Literally, "where I am and what I'm doing right now"—Psalm 146:1-2 ESV)

Wasting a little time is definitely a part of time management.

How good are you at welcoming children into your life?

I struggle with my prayer life—Let's just say that I'm glad that God accepts my looping scrawls of crayoned passion.

Acting upon truth is a vital principle for us in our daily walk.

September 4   I Am A Rich Person

Yes, I'm talking about money

I've known for some time that I am a rich person. So are you. While the average wage in the United States is $66,000, the annual per capita salary in Haiti is $350 ($2130 in India and $540 in Afghanistan). These figures may vary some, depending upon your source. If you care to do the research, you can find per capita earnings from every country in the world. Just be cautious that you don't allow your research to cause you to slip into your "Oh well, what can I do about that" mode. At this present writing, my wife and I are living on Social Security and a small wage from the little church where we're serving. All of that, to say this: I am a rich person. I've heard Christians say, "Well yes, in Christ we are all rich!" That's true, but I'm not talking about spiritual wealth; I'm talking about per capita financial wealth. I'm rich... So are you. In these latter years of my life, I am becoming more and more convicted concerning sharing that wealth with those less "wealthy"—food banks, hospitals, third world agricultural projects, organizations dedicated to stopping trafficking, adopt-a-child groups—You need to work through your own convictions. Every once in a while, during my quiet time and scripture study I come across words that deeply trouble me. I generally don't come into my quiet time to be convicted. I'm not looking for passages like these, but there they are. Let me share one of them, without comment. Just read the words...And pray about them.

> *Woe to all who are rich, for you have already received your comfort.*
> *Woe to you who are well-fed now, for you will go hungry.*
> *Woe to you who laugh now, for you will mourn and weep.*
> *Woe to you when all men shall speak well of you, for that is how their fathers treated the false prophets.* (Jesus – Luke 6:24-26 NIV)

Random thoughts for today:

Like a couple of prunes, as time goes by, we're gettin' wrinkled, but a whole lot sweeter. *(Southern Proverb)*

Today we are not preparing for life...We are to be living.

He who knows best knows how little he knows. *(Thomas Jefferson)*

What dreams has the Spirit given you? Beware the dream squashers and vision stealers.

The title of this entry can be a little fuzzy. Am I talking about the length of our prayers? Dr. Dixon Edward Hoste, director of China Inland Mission (successor to Hudson Taylor), counted it his first responsibility for the mission to pray four hours a day; it was also his custom to walk as he prayed. I had professors in college that enjoyed challenging us with that kind of information, although I think it ended up being discouraging for many when we failed to meet that standard. I don't want to make an excuse for the pathetic prayer lives of the average 21st-century believer, but I don't believe that my Abba Father starts a stopwatch when I begin my prayer time. It DOES concern me that the average congregation in America probably doesn't spend more than 15-20 minutes per week in community prayer together. I understand why most in our busy lives would have difficulty praying hours a day. That became clear to me after my official retirement (I didn't have to be at work at 7:30 every day), and my personal time with the Lord at least doubled most mornings. I've been a lot more reluctant to lay guilt trips on members of our flock who are still working 40 hours or more a week—"How much time do YOU spend in prayer each day?" I still don't believe God records the length and number of my quiet times. When I think of balanced praying, I think mostly of WHAT I pray. It's interesting that over 80% of the local church's prayer requests are for sickness and physical infirmity. In my time with the Lord, what is the percentage of time I spend praying for myself, instead of others? How much time do I spend "talking?" How much time do I spend in silence, just listening? I have attempted to vary my prayer times through the week between concentrating on my prayer lists and laying aside those lists, and sit in the quiet with an open Bible on my lap. It is during those "open Bible" times that I do most of my journaling. There have been days that I haven't uttered a word; I just spent time with my Father. What am I trying to communicate here? BALANCE your prayer times with God. Get out of the rut. VARIETY! And quit worrying about whether you're doing it right or not.

Random thoughts for today:

But truly God has listened; He has attended to the voice of my prayer. (Psalm 66:19 NIV)

A truth that is told with bad intent beats all the lies you can invent. *(William Blake)*

How many of us are involved in doing "small things" to the best of our ability?

Accept what you can't change...Change what you can't accept.

September 6   The Ministry of a Broken Heart

As I read through 2 Kings, 2 Chronicles, and the prophets, especially the final days of the southern kingdom of Judah, I realize again that nations do not come apart overnight or in a single generation. Spiritual disease and disintegration happen slowly throughout many generations and during the leadership of many "watchmen."

In my study, I find many of Judah's national characteristics ultimately brought her downfall.

- Leaders do evil in the sight of the Lord

- The people become stubborn and rebellious
- Less and less turn to the Lord
- God's message is mocked; the Word of God is despised
- Detestable practices by both the people and their leaders
- More and more of God's people become unfaithful
- Men of God not teaching truth

Concerning these things, Jeremiah shares *My heart is broken within me* (Jeremiah 23:9). Scholars estimate that this was written around BC 599. Jerusalem fell in BC 586. Does the "weeping prophet" give any encouragement whatsoever? You bet! In the midst of all of this, a Messianic prophecy is given—*I will raise up a righteous BRANCH, and He shall reign and deal wisely, and shall execute justice and righteousness in the land* (Jeremiah 23:5). Verse 6 goes on to say that He will be called *The LORD is our righteousness.* Merry Christmas!!

Random thoughts for today:

This is the nation that did not obey the voice of the LORD, their God and did not accept discipline; TRUTH has perished; it is cut off from their lips. (Jeremiah 7:28 ESV)

See, the thing is, we gotta live with people!!
Hover over my students...And if any need my help, let me be an approachable teacher. Amen.
Today...LIVE LOVED!! *(I John 4:19)*
Don't postpone joy until you've learned all your lessons...Joy may be the lesson.

The piece of pie you pass up is the piece you'll never get. *(Southern Proverb)*

There is a wacky kind of arrogance maintaining everything is right, when it's wrong.

September 7   Tribute to Teachers - 2

Labor Day is over...School is in session (many have been in session for 3 or 4 weeks). Some schools are meeting in person, some virtually, and others in various hybrid modes. Here's another page with some of my journal excerpts for my precious teacher friends:

Be an advocate today for someone who needs it.

No act of kindness, no matter how small, is ever wasted. *(Aesop)*

Tell the parents the positive first...It makes the negative more palatable later (Actually that's pretty good advice in ALL relationships).

Give your students a chance, and they might make you proud.

Never underestimate the power of expectation.

Let your students see you laugh and let them see your heart.

Sometimes we need to take the attitude of a student— Never be too big to ask questions and never know too much to learn something new.

Is your classroom a safe place to dream?...Allow individuality in your students; only then will they discover their potential.

Students need models rather than critics.

The best teachers teach from the heart, not from the book.

Some days, in the classroom, the problems are small, and the solutions are fun and easy...Thank You, Lord, for those days. Amen.

The secret of genius is to carry the spirit of the child into old age, which means never losing your enthusiasm. (Keep the kid alive in me!)

Lord, so many children come to school hurting...Let me be a comfort in their lives.

Not many of you should become teachers...for you know that we who teach will be judged with greater strictness. (James 3:1 ESV)

Lord, let me cherish busy days with young people, happy to have a part in their world...Help me learn to slow down and relax in my teaching. Hover over my students today, and if any need my help, let me be an approachable teacher. Amen.

September 8   Community of the Reconciled

Forgiveness is a concept of renewal. For our love to mature, it has to be renewed every day. To walk around carrying a grudge is counter-productive in so many ways. It is living in the past and allows bitterness and disappointment to be the thermostat of your life. This brings with it too high a price to pay. Ernest Boyer tells the story of a 9-year old child who was out the door to get his brother a Christmas present he had been saving for when he discovered that his brother had just broken one of his favorite toys. He immediately flew into a rage. I know of many relationships that have been shattered over much less. "What were you doing with it?" screamed the 9-year old. "You didn't even ask me if you could use it. And why weren't you more careful? Just for that, you can never play with my toys again. And also, I've decided that I'm not going to buy you a Christmas present this year." And with that, he stomped out of the room. A few minutes later, he returned to the kitchen and slipped on his coat. "I'm going, Mom," he said in a voice that in no way suggested the anger of a moment before. "Going where?" his mother asked. "To buy the present." His mother couldn't hide her look of surprise. "Well, he is my brother, isn't he?" Yup...He is my brother...Or my sister. I've learned that to live in the cloud of refusing to forgive a brother, and somehow thinking that's OK, is like camping in the woods of deception. Reinhold Niebuhr said, "Forgiving love is a possibility only for those who know they are not good, who feel themselves in need of divine mercy." It's been said, "We pardon in the degree that we love." We are the community of reconciliation...A community of the forgiven!!

Random thoughts for today:

Be kind to one another, forgiving each other, just as in Christ God forgave you. (Ephesians 4:32 ESV)

There is no better relationship than a prudent and faithful friend. *(Benjamin Franklin)*

It is the preoccupation with possessions, more than anything else, that prevents us from living freely and nobly. *(Bertrand Russell)*

Some people look for a beautiful place...Others make a place beautiful.

Let's make America kind again. *(Posted on social media)*

September 9   Truth - 2

Jesus taught us as His followers that we were not to swear an oath—"Cross my heart and hope to die; stick a needle in my eye." He said, *Let what you say be simply "Yes" or "No"; anything more than that comes from evil* (Matthew 5:37 ESV). Every word you speak is spoken in the presence of God (See February 28 entry). If I always speak the truth, and nothing but the truth, and everyone knows that this is a fact of my life, I have no need to swear any kind of oath. Dietrich Bonhoeffer said, "What matters first and last in this matter of truthfulness is that a man's whole being should be exposed when he speaks." Unfortunately, we live in a world that hates that kind of honesty and resists it with all its might. That's why they persecute and crucify it. I think that it is only because we follow Jesus that we can be genuinely truthful. The Cross is God's truth surrounding us and is the only power which can make us truthful. Untruthfulness destroys fellowship; truth establishes genuine brotherhood. Proverbs 12:19 assures me that *true lips endure forever.* I have learned that knowing the truth is not the same as loving the truth. It is a constant struggle with the flesh to make love of the truth a consistent priority. In the counsel of Bonhoeffer, "A disciple of Jesus must always be a light, even in his words." I desire that I be known as one who always tells the truth.

<u>Random thoughts for today</u>:

If you abide in my word, you are truly my disciples, and you will know the truth, and the truth will set you free. (John 8:31-32 ESV)

There seems to be a glorious and victorious side of Christianity that few Christians experience.

Use what gift you possess...The world would be very silent if no birds sang except those who sang best. *(Henry Van Dyke)*

One person can make a difference, and every person should try.

The greatest compliment given to me is when someone asks me what I think and then actually listens to me.

I strive to do that which I cannot do, in order that I may learn how to do it.

A pretty good lesson for life—BE REAL!!

September 10   Shotgun Praying

Have you ever prayed a "shotgun prayer?" The psalmist tells us *Call on Me in the day of trouble; I will deliver you, and you shall glorify Me* (Psalm 50:15)—Literally, "I will rescue you and You will honor me." Quick and to the point praying—Help now, please! Sometimes you don't have time for a long conversation with God. It's like the Rich Mullins prayer at the bottom of this page and elsewhere in this volume (See August 17). Rick Warren calls this SOS kind of praying, a "microwave" prayer. He says, "Remember, heaven has a 24-hour emergency hotline." In my first prayer devotional, I called them ejaculatory prayers. My prayer shotgun blast goes out immediately—BOOM!

<u>Examples of Shotgun Prayers</u>:

"Come, Holy Spirit"

"Father, not My will, but Your will be done!"

"Jesus Christ, have mercy on me, a sinner!" *(See entry on January 30)*

"I'm afraid...I put my trust in You."

"Thanks, LORD!" *(See entry on November 24)*

I can tell you that millions have prayed these kinds of shotgun prayers in times of trouble...BOOM!!

<u>Random thoughts for today</u>:

Let your steadfast love comfort me according to Your promise to Your servant. (Psalm 119:76 ESV)

Advertising has us chasing cars and clothes, working jobs we hate so we can buy stuff we don't need.

If we're not right with others, we're probably not right with God.

Never hesitate to tell the truth...And never ever give in or give up.

Good morning, Lord...I love You! What are you up to today? I want to be a part of it.

"Oh, God!" *(The most honest prayer I ever prayed—Rich Mullins)*

I have a couple of very special places to pray. I suppose you can refer to them as my quiet time places. One is in the living room, on the couch in front of our fireplace. The other is on our deck, overlooking the backyard (See June 16 entry). So, I have both cold weather and warm weather days covered. On in-between days I have used our kitchen table. But of course, this is not to say that I can't pray in other places. *Pray without ceasing* is a call and permission to pray anyplace, anytime. I remember hearing Edith Schaeffer speak years ago. She made a statement that I wrote down in my journal, word for word—"God has given us prayer to have a realistic work that can be done in prison, in a wheelchair, in bed, in a hospital, in a hovel, in a palace, on the march, in the midst of battle, or in the dark of a chalet when everyone else is asleep." Ephesians 6:18 (in the context of that spiritual battle) tells us that we are to be *praying at all times* (and that means in all places) *in the Spirit with all prayer and supplication for all the saints.* I gave pause a few years ago when I read in the Koran— "The earth is a mosque for thee; therefore, wherever the time of prayer reaches thee, there pray." Wherever we are, whenever that may be, the purpose of prayer is to be alone in the presence of our God.

Random thoughts for today:

I do not cease to give thanks for you, remember you in my prayers... (Ephesians 1:16 ESV)

We cannot die on every cross...Pick your battles.

Don't fall victim to the "Ready-Aim-Aim" syndrome...Be willing to fire...Be ready to make choices.

Today, if I encounter someone who seems sad or troubled, I will be understanding.

Character is a by-product of walking with Jesus.

Most of the time my prayers are not neat and tidy, nor are they particularly religious...They are, as one writer puts it, "graffiti scrawled on the walls of heaven." *(written in my journal; don't know who said it)*

September 12   Social Media Rules

I love the paraphrase I came across recently of Proverbs 11:9— *Evil words destroy one's friends; wise words rescue the godly.* Remember that statement I made at the beginning of the year (See January 3 entry)—"I want to be a seed-sower, not a crap-thrower"? With what we've experienced in the last two years, I'd like to include this entry:

<u>Rules for Christians on Social Media</u>

1. Be kind.
2. Don't say, "I'll bet you won't re-post this."
   Upon what do you base that statement? By the way, if I see this on a post, I automatically refuse to re-post it.
3. Don't preach to unbelievers...They're not reading your posts anyway.
4. Be kind.
5. Drop the arrogance of the "I'm right, you idiot" attitude.
6. Be kind.

7. Use scripture sparingly.
8. Watch your politics...What are you a contender for---The Kingdom or a political party?
9. Be kind.
10. *Love your neighbor as yourself*...Check with Jesus on this one.
11. Do your homework; check what you pass along to the hoards.
12. Oh yeah, I almost forgot—BE KIND.

Let me close with Proverbs 16:24—*Gracious words are like a honeycomb, sweetness to the soul and health to the body.* Oh wait! Perhaps I should close with Matthew 12:36--...*people will give account for every careless word they speak* (post). Jesus said that.

Random thoughts for today:

A soft answer turns away wrath, but a harsh word stirs up anger. (Proverbs 15:1 ESV)

The heart is always happiest when it beats for others.

Character may be tested in the great moments, but it is made in the small ones. *(Phillips Brooks)*

It is only in later years, that I have become enough of a disciple to say honestly, "Lord, teach me to pray."

Almost a year ago, our youngest daughter was preaching at her church, speaking on the truth that God will always be much better than what we conceive Him to be. It was a message on Daniel of the Old Testament. She shared much food for thought, and I have regularly meditated on the lessons she shared. I have compared some of these lessons as they have applied to my own life. When discussing Daniel's successful ministry for the Lord, she made a statement that has stayed with me since—"Daniel didn't start with a plan to face a bunch of lions; he started with vegetables." This refers to the account in the first chapter of Daniel—*But Daniel resolved that he would not defile himself with the king's food or the wine that he drank* (Daniel 1:8 ESV). The servant in charge of Daniel was fearful because the king had ordered Daniel and his Israelite friends to eat certain foods and drink certain beverages. Daniel proposed a 10-day test. *Let us be given vegetables to eat and water to drink; then compare our appearance with the appearance of the youths who eat the king's food* (Daniel 1:13 ESV). The test was successful in that the diet of Daniel and his friends was healthier than the king's rich diet. This was just one step in Daniel growing into a trust relationship with his captors. In time he was promoted to a high position and served faithfully kings Nebuchadnezzar and Belshazzar of Babylon, Darius the Mede, and was there until the first year of King Cyrus of Persia after the Babylonians were overthrown (at the end of the 70-year captivity). Daniel was dragged into captivity from Judah to Babylon, not having a clue as to his future. He did not plan on having a significant influence upon the leaders of that powerful nation that destroyed Jerusalem. He never imagined a dramatic confrontation in the lions' den.

He began with vegetables—Obedience—not to the conquering king of Babylon, but to what God was leading him to do. During these 70 years of transition, kings (and nations) come and go, but Daniel remains. He followed his own convictions, no matter what, true to his beliefs. And we think the last many months have been rough. No matter what the months ahead may bring, what are my "vegetables?" Stay strong in the Lord – Obedience to His direction – Stay true to your convictions – FAITHFULNESS!!

Random thoughts for today:

...And no kind of harm was found on Daniel because he had trusted in his God. (see Daniel 6:24)

The eyes are the window of the soul. *(Ancient Proverb)*
Many Christians end up acting like pagans in a crisis.
If there is no struggle, there is no progress. *(Frederick Douglas)*

September 14   Out of Habit

I've heard it said, "I don't want to just pray out of habit." Seriously? That's precisely what we need to be praying out of. If you want a regular daily prayer life, you have to begin...Now...Today. You can't mature in your prayers and grow in your discipline if you don't have a regular prayer life. The major difficulty in forming a habit is that we don't discipline ourselves. Our "whatever" culture doesn't lend itself to that. Psychology professor, William James writes, "The trick is to make our nervous system our ally instead of our enemy." He suggests three keys in helping you to do that.

1. BE DETERMINED to do it, whether you feel like it nor not. Prove to yourself that you can do it.
2. Never allow an exception until that habit is securely rooted in your life and daily routine.
3. DO IT NOW!! Not tomorrow.

I've always struggled with the sacred/secular dichotomy of life. God has given us one body, one personality. You know, I've learned that the method and discipline I used to learn a secular skill, many times is the way I learn any spiritual discipline as well."

Random thoughts for today:

Watch and pray that you might not enter into temptation. The spirit indeed is willing, but the flesh is weak. (Matthew 26:41 NIV)

It's never too late to have a happy childhood...Be a kid again!!

Say very little about yourself...Be content to act and leave the talking to others.

Do I love ALL people and look at all of them as people He loves and died to save?

There isn't anyone you couldn't love once you've heard their story.

There is no place where our lives bear a clearer witness than in the disciplines of generosity. *(Albert E. Day)*

Worrying about the next minute is so much beyond our control. It really is. A hard lesson I've learned (and I seem to have to keep learning it) is that every moment I spend worrying about tomorrow is a moment I lose from enjoying today. It robs me of my strength, not to mention my peace, to do what God wants me to do now. Three times in the Sermon on the Mount, Jesus says, *Take no thought.* It literally means "take no worry." A friend of mine sent me a little-known truth that is appropriate for the past years of pandemic.

"In 1606, William Shakespeare's theater was forced to close because of the plague. So he wrote *Macbeth, King Lear,* and *Antony and Cleopatra.* So friends, wash your hands, be grateful, and get better at what you do."

Instead of worrying about what might transpire tomorrow, I DO what I can do today, in the Lord's strength. George McDonald, Scottish pastor and writer and mentor to Lewis Carroll, used to say, "Care for the next minute is just as foolish as care for the morrow, or for a day in the next thousand years—In either case can we do anything; in both, God is doing everything." Ah, the ongoing war with worry and anxiety. If the Lord isn't present, I've discovered that I absolutely cannot win that battle. Exercising my prayer muscle has been my greatest weapon in this war; my worry muscle needs no more gym-time. I WAS planning to dedicate today to worrying about the year 2025, but I think I'll pass!

Random thoughts for today:

...*casting all your anxieties on Him, because He cares for you.* (1 Peter 5:7 NIV)

Example moves the world more than doctrine.

Don't walk in front of me; I may not follow...Don't walk behind me; I may not lead...Walk beside me and be my friend.

The beginning is always today.

Prayer has become the gymnasium of my soul.

When I read Robert Frost's poem, "The Road Not Taken," I feel the support of someone who is on my side.

September 16   The Ultimate Transition
                                 From Mourning to Dancing

You might want to reread the June 24 entry—"Remember the Journey." But what about the end of the journey? Hebrews 9:27 ESV says that *it is appointed for men to die once, and after that comes judgment.* The statistics on death are quite impressive— one out of one people die. And we don't have a handbook that tells us when the journey will end. A little guy named Alan (age 7) said, "God doesn't tell you when you are going to die because He wants it to be a big surprise!" Remember the words of Emily Dickinson—

"I could not stop for Death - He kindly stopped for me –
The Carriage held just Ourselves - And immortality."

There's a good chance that I have already lived over three-quarters of my life here on earth. James tells me that life is *a mist that appears for a little while and then vanishes* (James 4:14).

Where am I now on my journey? How much further? I passed the three-fourths mark, maybe. Am I five-sixths complete? How much longer? My body tells me that it's getting older; my glasses and hearing aids are evidence of that. I begin each day with my pill organizer purchased from Wal-Mart. Helen and I are taking advantage of the benefits of Medicare and Social Security, which we paid into for so many years. By the way, regardless of what the politicians tell you, they are NOT entitlements. How much further? But wait. The journey doesn't end with death. The cessation of life on this planet is transitional. It is the ULTIMATE evolving from GROANING TO DANCING. Bask in the sunlight of scripture—*If Christ has not been raised, then our preaching is in vain and your faith is in vain...If Christ has not been raised, your faith is futile and you are still in your sins...If in this life only we have hope in Christ, we are of all people to be pitied...The gift of God is eternal life through Jesus Christ our Lord...Whoever believes in Him shall not perish, but have eternal life* (1 Corinthians 15:14; 17; 19; Romans 6:23; John 3:16 - ESV). How much further? Eternity is a long time...Forever, baby!!

Random thoughts for today:

Death is swallowed up in victory. O death, where is your victory. O death, where is your sting. (I Corinthians 15:54-55 ESV)

Mix a little foolishness with your prudence; it's good to be silly at the right moment. *(Horace)*

Good-byes always make my throat hurt...I need more hellos. *(Charlie Brown)*

Sometimes I wonder if I'm not too chummy with the world. I wonder if I try too hard to *be all things to all people* (1 Corinthians 11:22). How many compromises have I made in the name of relevancy to the culture? But I have been "successful," whatever that means. I have had a distinguished and respectable career as a pastor. Have you spent much time in 1 Corinthians 4? Verses 9-13, specifically? Paul describes his life as an apostle; we could call it God's exhibit "A," *last of all, like men sentenced to death* (V 9). Apostles of Jesus on exhibit, as described in I Corinthians 4:

- Made a spectacle for all
- Fools for Christ
- Weak
- Dishonored
- Hungry, thirsty, in rags
- Brutally treated
- Homeless
- Cursed – Persecuted – Slandered
- Looked upon as scum of the earth; refuse of the world

Why am I not treated this way? I don't have all the answers here, but it is something to think about and discuss. Younger seminarians seem to be more willing to talk about this than we older "clergy" appear to be, but "they" have so much to learn. Which ones, the younger or the older? You decide. Now it's true that in a recent Gallup survey, the respect Americans have in clergy members has dropped to a record low. I'm not celebrating this fact that we are looked down upon by more people than ever, but I'm pretty sure it has nothing to do with our preaching the gospel without compromise.

<u>The apostle Paul's distinguished career:</u>

...far more imprisonments, with countless beatings, and often near death. Five times I received at the hands of the Jews the forty lashes less one. Three times I was beaten with rods. Once I was stoned. Three times I was shipwrecked; a night and a day I was adrift at sea; on frequent journeys, in danger from rivers, danger from robbers, danger from my own people, danger from the Gentiles, danger in the city, danger in the wilderness, danger at sea, danger from false brothers; in toil and hardship, through many a sleepless night, in hunger and thirst, often without food, in cold and exposure. And then, apart from other things, there is the daily pressure on me of my anxiety for all the churches. (2 Corinthians 11:23-28 ESV)

September 18   Homecoming

You may have heard the old story of the missionary and his wife, who had served faithfully for many years in Asia. This was in the day that you did international travel by steamship. When they got off the boat in San Diego, there was no one there to greet them. On the same ship, a famous statesman was greeted by a throng of people cheering him with a rousing welcome home. The old missionary turned to his wife with tears brimming up in his eyes and said, "Faithfully serving the Lord for all these years, and this is our homecoming." His wife took his hand and responded, "I know dear, but remember, we're not home yet." Ernest Boyer said, "As we mature in our walk with the Lord, we need to recognize the fulfillment of the 'not yet'; the fulfillment of God's total gift." It's surprising how often we Christians expect every prayer to be answered in this lifetime. Maybe...Maybe not. We really should know better. What does scripture tell us? *Humble yourselves, therefore, under the mighty hand of God so that at the proper time He may exalt you, casting all your anxieties, on Him, because He cares for you...And after you have suffered a little while, the God of all grace, who has called you to His eternal glory in Christ, will Himself restore, confirm, strengthen, and establish you. To Him be the dominion forever and ever. Amen* (1 Peter 5:6-7; 10-11). I have learned, or I guess I should say I am learning, that I have to listen carefully for God's voice and leading and be ready to walk through any doors He opens. My path needs to be the one He has set for me. If He takes a detour in the road, I have to be ready and willing to take it, wherever that might be. It's not always a plan that I create that brings fulfillment; it's what I let Him do in the plan of His choosing.

Random thoughts for today:

And we know that for those who love God, all things work together for good, for those who are called according to His purpose. (Romans 8:28 ESV)

There are two lasting things we can give our kids...One is roots...The other is wings.

If you desire wisdom, you must seek the Creator of wisdom.

The best things in life are not things.

It seems I have become a specialist in the "let's make a deal" school of prayer.

Jesus said, *I am truth*...Sinful men do not like this kind of truthfulness...That's why they persecute it and crucify it.

September 19   Spirit of the Age

Johann von Goethe, German writer and statesman, once said, "At least once every day one ought to hear a song, read a good poem, see a fine painting, and if possible, speak a few reasonable words." I think that perhaps that advice could be helpful in battling the spirit of our age. I could be mistaken, but I can't remember in my lifetime a period of so much negativism, complaining, criticism, and in many cases, out and out hatred toward our neighbor. It's become a lot easier because now we can cowardly make our pronouncements in our private spaces via social media. It would seem that everyone should be able to see daily instances of those who complain from a mere habit of complaining. When I complain, I do it because "it's good to get things off my chest." When you complain, I will remind you that griping doesn't help anything. No one sings or shouts or fills the pages of the internet over things that are *true or honorable or just or pure or lovely or commendable* (Philippians 4:8 ESV). We only scream about our offenses, those things that REALLY tick us off. I read something from Julia Seton years ago, and although we would differ theologically in many ways, her words impacted me. She said, "we have no more right to put our discordant states of mind into the lives of those around us and rob them of their sunshine and brightness than we have to enter their houses and steal their silverware." Daily watch out for the joy-stealers; gossip, criticism, complaining, faultfinding, and a negative, judgmental attitude. I love what a teacher-friend said to me years ago—"If you feel led to correct, make sure that you have a gentle heart to help."

Random thoughts for today:

But no human being can tame the tongue. It is a restless evil, full of deadly poison. (James 3:8 ESV)

Try to say nothing negative about anybody for three days; for 45 days; for three months...See what it does to your life.

It's not the years in your life that count...It's the life in your years. *(Abe Lincoln)*

It takes God a long time to get me out of the way of thinking that unless everyone sees as I do, they must be wrong.

Don't confuse excellence with perfection...Striving for excellence is my choice...Perfection is God's business.

September 20   Monasticism?

Monasticism = the devotional practice of Christians in ascetic and typically cloistered lives; the word "monk" originated from the Greek word, *monachos,* from the root, *monos, meaning "alone."* Because of several of entries in both of my prayer devotional volumes, I've been asked if I tend toward monasticism (or as some like to call it, "hermit Christianity"). I strongly believe that personal prayer, silence, and meditation are important disciplines to foster spiritual growth, but this is only one segment in our daily walk with the Lord. You may have heard the quote from Oliver Wendell Holmes, "Some people are so heavenly minded that they

405

are no earthly good." Without casting stones at the monastic ascetics throughout history, I have to confess that I cannot relate in any way whatsoever to that kind of lifestyle. It seems to fly in the face of the KOINONIA (the community drawn together by common belief and sharing—Acts 2:42) of the New Testament church. I have enjoyed personal retreats for a couple of days, and my early morning quiet time is beneficial to my spiritual life. Still, I cannot imagine a total lifestyle of monasticism. I desire to be a spiritual man, but not a monk. M. Basil Pennington, who himself was an American Roman Catholic monk, advocated balance. He wrote, "Intimate union with God is to be sought not only in seclusion but in the everyday life of the community." Thomas Merton, also a Catholic monk said, "If we want to be spiritual, let us first of all live our lives." Life is to be lived, and if we desire to make a difference in our world, we definitely need to get a life. Merton went on to say, "Love is our true destiny. We do not find the meaning of life by ourselves alone; we find it with one another." How vital it is that I live out my relationship to Christ in the world in which I live. It dawns on me...It would be quite difficult to honor and obey the Great Commission as a monk.

Random thoughts for today:

Go therefore and make disciples of all nations, baptizing them in the name of the Father and of the Son and of the Holy Spirit. (Matthew 28:19 ESV)

Have you ever noticed that to be rich usually means an impoverishment on another level.

You are not just the age you are; you are all the ages you have ever been.

Don't just believe the Bible...Believe in the One the Bible reveals.

Man needs difficulty...They are necessary for our health. *(Carl Jung)*

September 21   Celebrate the Fall

The scripture below in the random thoughts section talks about the Feast of Tabernacles or Feast of Booths celebrated in September or October each year or that time that James Whitcomb Riley (the "Hoosier Poet") describes as the time "when the frost is on the pumpkin and the fodder's in the shock." The Feast of Tabernacles (or "shelters" in some translations) was when the Israelites remembered back to their wanderings in the desert and God providing shelter for them. It is at this time of year that I celebrate the Fall, not the autumnal equinox, but the season of harvest and gratitude it represents. CELEBRATE THE FALL!! Cooler weather – Fires (inside and out) – pumpkins (that's the "Hoosier" in me) – Kids trick or treating – Leaves and color – First frost – Apples – Thanksgiving – First snow – Pre-Christmas stuff – I LOVE IT!! *This is the (SEASON) that the LORD has made; rejoice and be glad in it* (Psalm 118:24 ESV). It's not only a season of all the above but certainly a season of change. Things change. Through the years, I've learned that well. Just when I think I'm holding onto something solid, it moves or evaporates. Relationships, jobs, finances. Hopefully, we all learn that we risk disappointment if we put our trust in anything except the Lord. His Kingdom cannot be shaken! I thank my Lord for the changes in the season, for the changes in me, and He reminds me that everything around me changes, EXCEPT HIM!!

Random thoughts for today:

...when you have gathered in the produce from your threshing floor and your winepress, you shall rejoice in your feast...The LORD your God will bless you in all your produce and all the work of your hands, so that you will be altogether joyful. (Excerpts from Deuteronomy 16:13-15 ESV)

Those who deny freedom to others deserve it not for themselves. *(A. Lincoln)*

If we were supposed to talk more than we listen, we would have two mouths and one ear.

The devil will let a preacher prepare a sermon if it will keep him from preparing himself.

The problem is not to find the answer; it's to face the answer.

Often when you think you are at the end of something, you're at the beginning of something else.

September 22   I Am Many People
                              Guest Entry by Helen Jones

In a recent tweet on Twitter, a gentleman, commenting on another tweet, said, "We're talking about a description of a woman who proudly introduces herself as 'Mrs. (Husband's Last Name)'. That always made me sad that they never had their own identity outside the marriage." This Twitter exchange prompted a discussion between my wife and me and her subsequent writing of this

entry. I thought it appropriate that we include this on her birthday. *(RWJ)*

My name is Helen Marie Sims Jones. I was given most of that name when I was born. Who was I? Who am I? I was and am the daughter of a farm couple from LaPorte County, Indiana. Yup, I was a Hoosier country kid. Some years later, I was a high school graduate who went on to college. During my years in that Illinois college, I met and became the wife of Richard Jones. I became a "pastorette," as I liked to call myself, and I worked alongside my husband as a partner in our ministry. The bottom-line—I was Helen, nothing less. A couple of years went by, and we had two special daughters. I became "Mom." A few years later, I became "Grandma." During that time, I did choose to work outside the home. In the last number of years, I have worked in a bookstore, was a receptionist for a physician, and have been a substitute teacher. With each new title, each new "identity," I never lost sight of being an individual. I had and do have my own opinions, which sometimes differ from my husband. And by the way, that's OK. I know in this day of women struggling with identity (many times a struggle not of their making), I've never had to grapple with proving who I am. God made each of us unique; I've never felt otherwise about myself. I make no apologies for who I am or what identity or title by which I am known. Every individual, whether woman or man, has the privilege to choose their identity as they mature. So ultimately, which title is my favorite? I am a child of God, and I continue to strive to be obedient to Him wherever He has chosen to place me. *(Helen Marie Sims Jones)*

I can testify that Helen is not sad in any of her identities, and I know of no one who is sad for her. And I can also say truthfully that after 55 years plus of marriage with her, she is unique. That's our Helen!! Happy Birthday, Sweetheart. *(RWJ)*

An excellent woman, who can find? She is far more precious than jewels. *(Proverbs 31:10)*

September 23   Romans 12:9

Romans 12:9 tells us that we are to *let love be genuine* (sincere). How do we demonstrate genuine love to everyone, I mean everyone? The apostle Paul gives some pretty good advice.

- Bless those who mistreat you (that one's pretty hard, isn't it?)
- Rejoice with those who rejoice
- Mourn with those who mourn
- Live in harmony with each other (even when you disagree)
- No pride; no conceit
- Genuine association with those of "lowly" positions
- Never repay evil with evil
- Do the right thing for the right reason
- Live at peace with everyone (that's always easy to do)
- No revenge...NEVER!
- Overcome evil with good
                    (Romans 12:14-21)

How are you doing in living out this advice? Daily assessment is often necessary. It probably helps to digest Luke 6:46 when Jesus says, *Why do you call Me "Lord, Lord," and not do what I tell you?* So, Jones, you're saying that these are not suggestions... You mean scripture actually says this...YUP!! The good news is that we are not called to do this on our own. Our helper, the Holy Spirit, is always ready to help us *love as He first loved us* (1 John 4:19).

Random thoughts for today:

Love never ends... (1 Corinthians 13:8)

If you can bring one moment of happiness into the life of a child, you are a co-worker with God.

Those having torches will pass them on to others. *(Plato)*

The object of teaching a child is to enable him to get along without a teacher.

Don't wait...The time will never be "just right."

September 24   Elections

I've learned the hard way that it's probably a mistake for a pastor to get involved in politics. When I taught high school, my students used to try and coax it out of me as to who I voted for, even to the point of tricking me into letting it slip out. I've never endorsed a candidate from the pulpit, nor have I ever tried to influence anyone concerning their vote. I'm not convinced that who I think should be elected is of any consequence. The more I study Romans 13:1—*Everyone must submit himself to the governing authorities, for there is no authority except that which God has established. The authorities that exist have been established by God.*

It is He who changes the times and the epochs; He removes kings and establishes kings; He gives wisdom to wise men and knowledge to men of understanding. (Daniel 2:21 NASB1995)

I could be wrong, and forgive a judgmental spirit (I DO struggle with that), but from the many posts on social media that I've read this past year, it would seem that many of us believers are more concerned with who my neighbors voted for, rather than if he has a relationship with the Lord. As soon as an election is decided (some results take longer than others), that candidate-elect goes in my prayer journal--...*supplications, prayers, intercessions, and thanksgivings made for all people, for kings and all who are in high positions* (1 Timothy 2:1-2 NASB). I may not like the result of an election; I may even question how the result came about, but I am cautious to rebel against that result and lest I find myself rebelling against God (Romans 13:2). It also troubles me that scripture places rebellion in the same category as witchcraft (1 Samuel 15:23). Something to ponder.

Random thoughts for today:

Submit yourselves for the Lord's sake to every human institution, whether to a king as one in authority. (1 Peter 2:13 NASB)

'Tis better to be alone than in bad company; associate yourself with men of good quality. *(George Washington)*

Reflect upon your blessings of which every man has many; not on your past misfortunes of which all men have some. *(Charles Dickens)*

For the believer, eternal life has already started.

First say to yourself, what would you be; then do what you have to do. *(Epictetus)*

September 25   Lessons from Rabbi Heschel

Polish-born Abraham Joshua Heschel once wrote, "Faith will come to him who passionately yearns for ultimate meaning." He authored numerous books, including *God in Search of Man* and *Man's Quest For God,* both written in the 1950s. Here are some of his suggestions for finding that "ultimate meaning."

- Be alert
- Suspend trivial thinking
- Beware of standardized notions (following the crowd)
- Don't be content with half-truths or half-realities
- Embrace solitude
- Widen your thinking to the whole of reality
- Hold small things great; take light matters seriously
- Witness a holy within the world's affairs; look for those God-things
- Seeking God is a life-long pursuit
- God might have a direct hand in those things that upset you

Rabbi Herschel wrote, "God is of no importance unless He is of supreme importance." Seeking Him must also be of supreme importance. I cannot help but zero in on that scripture from Hebrews—*Without faith it is impossible to please God, for whoever would draw near to Him must believe that He exists and that He rewards them WHO SEEK HIM* (11:6). Quoting the late rabbi, I have discovered that I am closer to God when I ask the questions rather than think I have all the answers.

Random thoughts for today:

You will seek Me and find Me. When you seek Me with all your heart, I will be found by you, declares the LORD... (Jeremiah 29:13-14 NASB)

Maturity = A new lack of self-consciousness
Every day is like a bank account and time is your currency.
The oldest habit in the world for resisting change is to complain. *(Winston Churchill)*
A good laugh is sunshine in a house.

September 26   Wake Up!

Ephesians 5:14 ESV admonishes us, *Awake, O sleeper, and arise from the dead, and Christ will shine on you.* John addresses the church at Sardis with the warning, *Wake up! You have the reputation of being alive, but you are dead. Strengthen what remains and is about to die* (Revelation 3:1-2 ESV). Many respected leaders/men of God have proposed the questions to the church of today. Is the church of 2021 awake? As we see the secular culture taking over the globe, is the church failing? Are we busy playing church while the world is turning its back on the gospel? Are we alive? It's been estimated that the church has lost approximately 20% of its people due to the pandemic and subsequent closings of in-person services. The Barna organization tells us that if we continue to conduct the business of the church as usual, they won't be coming back. Just because a congregation has cool music and worship leaders, strobe lighting and smoke machines, and all the technology money can buy doesn't mean it's alive. I'm not saying that there is anything necessarily wrong with these things (well, I'm not sure about the smoke machine), but they are not the benchmarks of a living church. We live in an exciting time; we really do. I believe that this is the most exciting hour in the history of the church. You who are younger, how fortunate you are to be here right now. I believe kids today are the most privileged youth who walk the face of the earth; what an exciting time to be a part of the kingdom. And those of you who are older, hang in there. Things are happening, and God is in control. You "patriots" who are expending ample amounts of energy to save the republic, get busy full-time broadcasting the kingdom of God. You retirees, if you got one foot in the grave, hurry up and take it out, this is no time to be dying. WE HAVE WORK TO DO!! And it begins with allowing the Holy Spirit to fulfill God's purposes in our lives. What will you live for? Just like one guy recently told me, "I'm tired of playing games...I want to spend the rest of my life significantly for the Lord!"

Random thoughts for today:

You know the time, that the hour has come to wake up from sleep. For salvation is nearer to us now than when we first believed. (Romans 13:11 ESV)

It's hard for Americans to understand that Christianity is not a democracy.

God's tenderness never says, "I love you, but I don't like you."

415

Whatever is churning in my heart must either be prayed out or left to fester.

Try not to be a man of success...Rather be a man of value.

September 27   Time Alone

The longer I've been at this, the more I realize why time alone with my Abba Father is so important to me in the early hours of the day. On many mornings, I sit alone by the fireplace, wrapped in a blanket, a cup of coffee on the table next to me, along with Bible and journal. My role model is Jesus. *In the early morning, while it was still dark, Jesus got up, left the house, and sent away to a secluded place, and was praying there* (Mark 1:35 ESV). It is a time that I can block out all noise and distractions; technology is put on hold. I set aside all of the bothersome chaos surrounding all of us and focus on being alone with God. I need these moments, these pauses in time, to examine my life openly and honestly. This time with the Lord allows my mind and my spirit the opportunity to renew and create order. I'm a busy guy, but I prioritize my quiet time every morning to keep balance in my day ahead and be centered on His path. Some of the most powerful times of my day are when I'm quiet. It's in the quiet that I know that I am blessed. And ironically, it is during this so-called "alone time," I know that I am not alone. There are certainly days that I struggle in my journey, when I can feel the enemy's icy grip on my heart and doubt seems to be winning. My alone time with the Lord can be like that warm blanket wrapped around me. Troubling thoughts can be replaced with conviction as my Abba Father is present with me, wrapping His warm arms around me, and many are the mornings that I sense I am being enveloped in the warmth of His love.

Random thoughts for today:

I rise before dawn and cry for help; I hope in Your words. (Psalm 119:147 ESV)

What are we for? What do we support? Micah 6:8 says we are to act justly, love mercy, and walk humbly with our God.

The more I wonder, the more I love.

I believe that unarmed truth and unconditional love will have the final word.

Celebrate together these days of Autumn.

What a good, good Father I have...I fall down...He picks me up.

September 28   My Editor Speaks

At the close of 2020, I listened to a message from my grandson (also my editor for this book). It was a blessing to me in the middle of the turmoil we're going through in our nation, and that includes the church. I was tremendously uplifted by his message on unity in the church. Timothy Keller made a statement in 2015—"I predict the church will be more divided than ever in politics." Here are some excerpts from Christian's message:

> "The basics of this message is NOT politics...It's about unity in EVERYTHING. The basis of our unity as believers is the fact that WE ARE IN CHRIST. Are we that self-centered? Do we live our lives as if we are the center of

the universe? What's the first thing you focus on when you rise in the morning? Is it the LORD? Self-absorption and vain conceit are destructive to the church. We can disagree on many things, but disagreement isn't what causes disunity in the church...It is selfishness. Philippians 2:5 says that *our attitude should be the same as that of Christ Jesus.* IT BEGINS WITH ME. We don't have unity because we don't agree about everything, but because we aren't maturing in selflessness. Few of us are masters at disagreeing, agreeably. I'm not talking about compromise of convictions. Universalism has no place in the gospel. The priority of the matter is this:

> *Therefore God has highly exalted Him and bestowed on Him the name that is above every name, so that at the name of Jesus every knee should bow, in heaven and on earth and under the earth, and every tongue confess that Jesus Christ is Lord, to the glory of God the Father.* (Philippians 2:9-11 ESV)

Why is the church so divided over everything? Not because of Jesus!!"

My response to this message—YUP!! Thanks, Christian.

Random thoughts for today:

So if there is any encouragement in Christ, any comfort from love, any participation in the Spirit, any affection and sympathy, complete my joy by being

***of the same mind, having the same love, being in full
accord and of one mind.*** (Philippians 2:1-2 ESV)

There are plenty to follow our Lord halfway, but not the other
half. *(Meister Eckhart)*

You don't get harmony when everyone sings the same note;
you get harmony when the body harmonizes.

September 29   Guile

Interesting word, guile. It originates from the late 12th, early
13th century French and Germanic. It means "insidious cunning
in attaining a goal, crafty or artful deception; duplicity." I started
thinking about this word and what it means when I read about
Nathaniel (also known as Bartholomew) in the first chapter of
John a few weeks ago. Jesus said of Nathaniel in John 1:47—
Behold, an Israelite indeed, in whom there is no deceit. The
King James Version translates it—*In whom there is no guile.* The
ultimate character reference from Jesus Himself. It would seem
that Nathaniel did not twist the Law as the Pharisees did, their
traditions becoming their doctrine, canceling out the purpose and
effectiveness of the Law and its power to reveal sin. Apparently,
Nathaniel didn't fit that pattern. So in this matter, Nathaniel
needs to be my role model. Is my heart without deceit? Are my
motives always pure before God? Do I ever use duplicity to further
my agenda or attain my goals? I love the description in Revelation
14:4-5 ESV—*They have been redeemed from mankind as first
fruits for God and the Lamb, and in their mouth no lie* (guile) *was
found, for they are blameless.* As one pastor said recently, "What

is childlike humility? It is not the lack of intelligence but the lack of guile. The lack of an agenda."

Lord, search my deceitful heart today...Show where and when I may be walking "in guile."

Random thoughts for today:

So put away all malice and deceit* (guile) *and hypocrisy and envy and all slander. (1 Peter 2:1 ESV)

May I become less and less a hypocrite in my relationship with the Lord so that I might become less and less a hypocrite in my relationship to others.

What is essential is invisible to the eyes. *(The Little Prince—Saint-Exupery)*

Reading maketh the full man...Conference a ready man... Writing an exact man. *(Sir Francis Bacon)*

"Broke" is what happens when your yearnings get ahead of your earnings. *(Southern Proverb)*

Fearing the Lord means giving Him proper place in our lives.

September 30   Lighten Up!

May I make a confession? For most of my life, I have struggled with taking myself too seriously. As a child, a teenager, a student, a husband and father, a pastor, I've wrestled with it in all of these roles. I've been told this by my parents, my teachers and pastors, my spouse, and my co-workers. My wife has told me many times through the years—"Lighten up!" I guess I need to share this confession because as I have read and reread many of my entries in this volume, I have, in so many words, been telling others to lighten up. Perhaps being honest here makes me less of a hypocrite. Maybe, maybe not. Part of this weakness comes from passion, but it is more of a battle with pride than anything else. I had a long discussion with my dad the night before I was ordained into the ministry. I don't remember all of what we talked about, but I do remember these words, "Pride is concerned with who is right; humility is concerned with what is right." Before I preached my first sermon (I was 16 years old), my pastor said to me—"If you enter the pulpit with your head bowed before the Lord, you will leave with your head held high." Sounds like a Proverbs 16:18 illustration to me. I came across a prayer years ago that is not only in my journal but has ministered to me again and again. I don't know the original author, so I've just credited God.

Remember, my child, don't take yourself too seriously. Your calling is about God's Spirit working in your life to draw them nearer to Jesus. You are called to serve them. Preach the Word faithfully, and then disappear into the background so that I will get the praise and honor and glory. Your Abba Father.

Random thoughts for today:

But He gives more grace. Therefore it says, "God opposes the proud, but gives grace to the humble. (James 4:6 ESV)

Better a humble garbage man than an arrogant philosopher.

We will not become a people of God without the presence of solitude.

What if God's word is really serious about love and grace and justice and mercy? *(Rebecca Crain)*

Friends are the family we choose for ourselves.

The home marks the child for life.

October

Are We Willing To Say Something Is Ok, Simply Because Our Culture Says It's Ok?

October 1   Enjoy the Journey

One of my earlier entries was entitled "Remember the Journey" (June 24). *Remember your journey that you may know the righteous acts of God* (Micah 6:5 ESV). That's important. But today, I want us to reflect on our enjoyment of that journey. Ecclesiastes says, *There is nothing better for a person than that he should eat and drink and find enjoyment in his toil. This also, I saw from the hand of God* (2:24 ESV). It's amazing how many Christians are running around looking like the most miserable people on earth. As I read scriptures on the fulness of joy, I can almost hear my Abba Father saying to me, "Let Me show you the path forward, moment by moment...Let me set the pace...Slow down...ENJOY THE JOURNEY...Remember, I am with you!" As I read and cogitate (I really love that word) on this matter, I hear the action clause again and again—"In the presence of the Lord." The result clause follows—"You will enjoy the journey." Living a productive life is good, but it's not all there is to the journey. I don't have to be doing every moment of the day. I don't have to be talking during every minute of my prayer time. Not too long ago, I prayed a simple prayer; it was the only thing I prayed that morning—"Lord, here I am this morning in the presence of my

Abba Father; in Your presence. I find myself doing nothing but sitting here in the presence of my Father." There is a little side note here to help us enjoy our journey: The apostle Peter says, *Whoever desires to love life and see good days, let him keep his tongue from evil and his lips from speaking deceit* (1 Peter 3:10 ESV). Oh yeah, I almost forgot.

Random thoughts for today:

You make known to me the path of life; in Your presence there is fulness of joy; at your right hand are pleasures forevermore. (Psalm 16:24 ESV)

We aren't just thrown on this earth like dice tossed across a table...We are lovingly placed here for a purpose.

Being honest with the Lord makes it a lot easier to be honest with others.

Lord, I have nothing to say out loud today...Thanks for sitting here with me.

It is the deep human condition—The need to love and be loved.

October 2   Freedom of Speech?

At the beginning of today (10-2-20), the news reported that President Trump and his wife, Melania, both tested positive for COVID-19. Within minutes, a radical left publication tweeted, "I hope they both die!" An acquaintance of mine commented, "I'm sad; it's a pretty dark world in which we live." While this inexcusable comment didn't come from a Christian, I have seen many posts on social media from good God-fearing church people that have been both embarrassing and definitely not in sync with the Sermon on the Mount. First amendment, right? The Constitution of the United States gives us the right to speak and be heard. Really. Do Christians have unbridled, unlimited freedom of speech? Hmmm...

> *Let no corrupting talk come out of your mouths, but only such as is good for building up, as fits the occasion, that it may give grace to those who hear* (Ephesians 4:29 ESV).

> *Let your speech always be gracious, seasoned with salt, so that you may know how you ought to answer each person* (Colossians 4:6 ESV).

> *It is not what goes into the mouth that defiles a person, but what comes out of the mouth that defiles the person* (Matthew 15:11 ESV).

> *Set a guard, O Lord, over my mouth; keep watch over the door of my lips* (Psalm 141:3 ESV).

> *Whoever keeps his mouth and his tongue keeps himself out of trouble* (Proverbs 21:23 ESV).

> *If anyone thinks he is religious and does not bridle his tongue but deceives his heart, this person's religion is worthless* (James 1:26 ESV).

> *Know this, my beloved brothers: let every person be quick to hear, slow to speak, slow to anger* (James 1:19 ESV).

And what you do, in word or deed, do everything in the name of the Lord Jesus, giving thanks to God the Father through Him (Colossians 3:17 ESV).

There are many, many more scriptures on the subject of our speech. It would seem that the counsel we receive from scripture trumps the First Amendment every time.

Random thoughts for today:

God's love is deeper than any depth to which we can sink.
We check social media more than we check in with the Lord.

October 3   YHWH

No offense, but Americans as a whole are not known to be great scholars of the Bible. Many of our ideas about the Lord come from paintings, songs, poems, works of art, and, God forbid, Hollywood. Not that there can't be some truth found in the medium of fine art, but by and large, we are not a nation of great knowledge when it comes to the God of scripture. There are many in the church who know quite a bit about the historical Jesus but know nothing about the Jesus who has said He desires to inhabit our hearts. I wonder how many of us are still only playing with religion." Don't you love it when people say, "Well, my God wouldn't say that or do that!" How about the God of scripture? And if we don't use the Bible as our authority in determining who God is, what He would do or say, what objective means do we have to make those kinds of decisions. Is my image of God biblical? Do I know the Lord of the whole scripture, or do I just accept

Him in part, you know, the parts I like or those with which I agree? Exodus 20:2 introduces the ten commandments by saying, *I am the LORD your God*...This verse is not concerned with the question, "Is there a God?" but with the question, "Who is God?" The word for LORD (when all caps are used) is literally YAHWEH. It is the personal name of God (four Hebrew consonants=YHWH, referred to by scholars as the tetragrammaton). Many scholars believe the most proper meaning is "He brings into existence whatever exists." Short version..."I am." Religious Jews did not (or do not) often say this name aloud; they believed it to be too holy to be spoken. So let me get this straight. God is not about my opinions or ideas about Him; it's about WHO HE IS. YAHWEH...*I am that I am* (Exodus 3:14).

<u>Random thoughts for today</u>:

I am the LORD, that is My name; I will not give my glory to another, nor my praise to any idol. (Jeremiah 42:8 ESV)

Now and again, it's good to pause in our pursuit of happiness and just be happy.

We check our phones more than we check in with the Lord.

To teach, to mentor, to disciple, is to touch lives forever.

When given the choice between being right or being kind, choose kind.

What you do every day matters more than what you do every once in a while.

I don't have to hide all the thoughts and feelings I have that aren't very pretty...He's perfectly aware of what I'm thinking and feeling anyway.

Isaiah 46:4 says *even to your old age I am He, and to gray hairs I will carry you. I have made, and I will bear, I will carry and will save.* As I grow older and find the shadows of life lengthening, I reflect and meditate on some meaning in the myriad experiences of my journey. Job says that *wisdom is with the aged, and understanding in length of days* (12:12 ESV). I've been asked more than once or twice, what is the key that will unlock the secret and meaning of the good days, the bad days, joy and sorrow, youth and old age, sickness and health, life and death? How do I separate that which is truly important with the trivia of day to day? How do you answer questions like that? We can't know everything, and that's OK. But as we continue to mature in our walk and trust of the Lord, more understanding comes. *For everything, absolutely everything, above and below, visible and invisible; everything got started in Him and finds its purpose in Him* (Colossians 3:16 ESV). I continue to find my purpose as the Word of God teaches me what on earth I'm here for. Dag Hammarskjold summarized it best (I mentioned him in my August 29 entry)—"On the day I first really believed in God, for the first time life made sense to me and the world has meaning."

"Grow old along with me!
The best is yet to be... *(Robert Browning)*

<u>Random thoughts for today:</u>

So we do not lose heart. Though our outer nature is wasting away, our inner nature is being renewed day by day. (2 Corinthians 4:16 ESV)

With mirth and laughter let old wrinkles come. *(William Shakespeare)*

It's always too early to quit.

Great works are performed not by strength but by perseverance. *(Samuel Johnson)*

How often has my hypocrisy been a barrier in my prayer life?

There are no lost causes.

I like to look at people by what they might be.

There is sufficiency in the world for man's need but not for man's greed.

October 5   Kids' Prayers - 3

Fyodor Dostoevsky said, "The soul is healed by being with children." Yeah, I have found that to be true. Then there's the other side of the coin from a southern philosopher—"Children are like mosquitoes. The moment they stop making noises, you know they're getting into something." Here's another edition of great prayers from kids.

> "Dear God, my Mom tells me that You have a reason for everything on earth. I guess broccoli is one of Your mysteries." *(Autumn – Age 7)*

> "Please make my parents understand that if I don't eat salad, I do better at school." *(Max – Age 8)*

> "Dear God, I saw my big brother walk out of the shower on accident. Could You please erase that from my brain?" *(Lilly – Age 6)*

"Dear God, I think about You sometimes even when I'm not praying." *(Elliott – Age 10)*

"God, I went to this wedding, and they kissed right in church. Is that OK?" *(Neil – Age 7)*

"Dear God, I am an American. What are You?" *(Robert – Age 6)*

"Dear God, my turtle died. Is she there with You? If so, she likes lettuce." *(Susie – Age 5)*

"Dear God, I think the stapler is Your greatest invention." *(Ruth M. – Age 8)*

I close this entry with a quote (unknown source); you can take it literally or philosophically—"Kids really brighten a household. They never turn off the lights."

Random thoughts for today:

Behold, children are a heritage from the LORD, the fruit of the womb a reward. (Psalm 127:3 ESV)

God doesn't comfort us to make us comfortable but to make us comforters.

Not getting what you want is sometimes a wonderful blessing.

Thank you for memories...I think I must be an emotional archaeologist.

A sister in the Lord whom I admire very much said, "My most spectacular answers to prayers have come when I was helpless, so out of control as to be able to do nothing at all for myself." There are times that I feel we become so enamored with good female writers of today like Beth Moore, Jen Hatmaker, Elizabeth Elliot, Sheila Walsh, Anne Graham Lotz, and Sarah Bessey, to name a few, we neglect the rich writings of women of faith of generations ago. How about the powerful words of women of faith like Evangeline Booth, Hannah Whitall Smith, Lettie Cowman, and of course, the late Catherine Marshall. I could say the very same thing about male authors. Modern-day authors have helped me immeasurably. But what about the writings of some of the "ancients," be it a book from the 19th century, or a prayer from the fourth century? We must not neglect the wisdom and insight that these authors (both men and women) have to offer us! I see a reoccurring theme among these writers of bygone days—prayerful dependence. Again and again I read of the belief that helplessness is a prerequisite of answered prayer. It would seem that in this 21st century, it is easier to delude ourselves into thinking that human resources can get the job done. Perhaps that is fading a bit during this pandemic. Maybe, maybe not. What did Jesus have to say about that? *Apart from Me you can do nothing* (John 15:5).

And we, too, being called by His will to Christ Jesus, are not justified by ourselves, nor by our own wisdom, or understanding, or godliness, or works which we have wrought in holiness of heart; but by that faith through which, from the beginning, Almighty God has justified all men; to

whom be glory forever and ever. Amen. (Clement of Rome – AD 35-99)

Random thoughts for today:

My grace is sufficient for you, for my power is made perfect in weakness... (2 Corinthians 12:9 ESV)

God's grace keeps pace with whatever we face.

There is a wisdom of the head and a wisdom of the heart. *(Charles Dickens)*

In prayer, trying to manipulate God is probably not the best way to get things done.

Nothing is so strong as gentleness; nothing so gentle as real strength.

Growing old isn't for wimps...But as the saying goes, "The old pipe gives the sweetest smoke."

October 7   COVID-19 Journal

In March of 2020, Helen and I began our attempt to follow CDC guidelines to protect ourselves and others from this new virus we were hearing about a hundred times a day—COVID-19. We went nowhere for three weeks. The self-imposed quarantine was our life for that brief period of time. I prayed the spirit of Psalm 91 over my family and loved ones every morning. During this time, a phrase kept creeping into my consciousness, more and more as each day passed—"No longer a slave to fear; I am a child of God." I told Helen, we're not going to live in fear. After three weeks, we began to venture out slowly. Helen made an occasional trip to the grocery store, and we began to order take-out and curbside. We weren't foolish; we followed the CDC protocols of masking and social distancing. Our first family gathering was at our house. The kids came over to surprise Helen on Mother's Day. No problems. We got through a weird and relatively unbusy summer, including the weddings of our grandson and granddaughter. We even went out to eat occasionally (following restaurant protocols all the way). In June, we began in-person worship at our little church in New Carlisle, practicing social distancing, of course (not difficult to do with 15-20 people). I made the following entry today in my prayer journal—"I have a strong suspicion that I have contracted the virus; extremely fatigued and no taste or smell."

> October 12 – Helen and I tested
> October 14 – Tests positive; self-quarantined for the next 15 days
> October 25 – Reopened our church after a two-week closure

We recovered quickly; actually, all of our symptoms were mild. No one has to tell me how fortunate we are. I have friends who have been "long-haul" victims of this virus and are still struggling with complications after many months. We are still practicing masking and social distancing and probably will continue to do so for some time to come. Our philosophy continues to saturate us daily—"No longer a slave to fear; I am a child of God." We are ready for a season of thanksgiving...Soon. It'll be a big deal...More later. HOW BLESSED WE ARE!!

> ADDENDA: Helen and I received our first vaccine dose on 2/18/21
> Second vaccine dose on 3/18/21

Do not fear the pestilence that stalks in darkness...
(Psalm 91:6 ESV)

The teacher is like the candle, which lights others in consuming itself. *(Italian Proverb)*

October 8   Another Prayer from Francis of Assisi

In my first prayer devotional, I submitted a prayer of Francis of Assisi—"O Lord, make me an instrument of Thy peace." Francis was never a priest though he was later ordained a deacon under his protest. He was not a reformer; he preached about returning to God and obedience to His word. Founder of the Franciscan orders, he is known as the patron saint of ecology and animals. Although the prayer found in my earlier book is probably more well-known, this prayer is just as meaningful, and I have used it often in my personal prayer times.

> **You are holy, LORD, the only God, and Your deeds are wonderful...**
> **You are Good, all Good, supreme Good, Lord God, living and true.**
> **You are love. You are wisdom. You are humility.**
> **You are endurance. You are rest. You are peace.**
> **You are joy and gladness. You are justice and moderation.**
> **You are all our riches, and You suffice for us...**
> **Amen.**

Random thoughts for today:

You are our epistle written in our hearts, known and read by all men; clearly you are an epistle of Christ... (2 Corinthians 3:2-3 - NKJV)

Francis of Assisi quotes:

Preach the gospel at all times and when necessary use words.

It is no use walking anywhere to preach unless our walking is our preaching.

If God can work through me, he can work through anyone.

All the darkness of the world cannot extinguish the light of a single candle.

Above all the grace and the gifts that Christ gives to his beloved is that of overcoming self.

While you are proclaiming peace with your lips, be careful to have it even more fully in your heart.

October 9   The Mind of God?

Life is messy...Reality is not neat. Romans 11:34 ESV says to us, *For who has known the mind of the Lord, or who has been His counselor?* Have you got God all figured out yet? I know theoretically and personally that He loves me deeply, but beyond that, no, I don't have Him all figured out yet. I believe Christianity is a religion and a lifestyle that I could never have made up. One theologian said (in the 1950s), "I find no rhyme nor reason (that we can see) in the structure of our universe; about either the sizes or distances or symmetry of the planets. Some (planets) have one moon, one has four, one has two, some have none, and one has a ring. The reality, in fact, is usually something you could not have guessed." Wait a minute...Solar system update. Saturn has 53 moons and counting. Jupiter has 79; Uranus has at least 27. Neptune has 14, and its moon, Triton, is as big as the dwarf planet Pluto. I've always considered this theologian to be a pretty intelligent guy. How could he be off by so much? Could it be that he is writing in the context of 1952? Is it possible that telescopes have become much, much more powerful in 70 years? I've been reflecting upon this for a few weeks. If my vision of God is blurred, could it be that I'm trying to view Him through a telescope with a dirty lens? Or maybe a stronger lens is needed? I have learned the power of many helpful tools in growing to know the mind of God. 1) Personal time spent with Him every day 2) Quality time spent in the Word of God 3) Maturing in my ability to have an honest and open dialogue with others, including those with whom I disagree. You will never reach perfection in knowing the mind of God. There are only three alternatives in this journey:

- To think you ARE God (That position has been filled)
- To grow in your intimate knowledge of Him (It can be a struggle to grow to be more like Him...How do we do that? What's He look like? Look at Jesus.)
- To go through life without a clue

Random thoughts for today:

For now we see in a mirror dimly, but then face to face. Now I know in part; then I shall know fully, even as I have been fully known. (1 Corinthians 13:12 ESV)

You don't stop laughing because you grow old...You grow old because you stop laughing.

Challenge your own perceptions...Labels belong on cans, not people.

The temple parents build shall endure while the ages roll, for that beautiful, unseen temple is a child's immortal soul. *(Unknown)*

Opportunity is missed by most people because it is dressed in overalls and looks like work. *(Thomas Alva Edison)*

October 10   Moderation?

Throughout this devotional, I've addressed the issue of balance in our walk with the Lord. It's all about balance (July 12) – Balanced theology (August 4) – Balanced worship (August 28) – Balanced praying (September 5). There are many areas of our lives where we struggle with balance instead of leaning toward irrational extremism. I've made the statement before that while my faith is not based upon emotionalism, I can get pretty emotional about my faith. When I speak of "balance," I am talking about stability, steadiness, and equilibrium. But when someone says that my faith is excessive (too much) or confronts me with "Hey, a little religion can be helpful, but moderation in all things," we're not on the same page. In our culture today, it's interesting that it's OK for me to be a passionate sports fan but not a fanatical Christian. The last time I checked, to be a fanatic is defined as being zealous, enthused, fervent, or passionate. Moderation is essential in issues such as whether to eat steak seven days a week (and I am pretty extreme about steak); it isn't a valid virtue to describe my walk with Jesus Christ. I remember a proper church lady saying to me as a teenager, "Religion is all very well up to a point, but don't be carried away." That's quite a contrast to the words of Jesus—*If anyone would come after Me, let him deny himself and take up his cross daily and follow Me* (Luke 9:23 ESV). As you wrestle with balance in many areas of your life, remember this —A moderated Christianity is as good for us as no Christianity at all.

Random thoughts for today:

I have been crucified with Christ. It is no longer I who live, but Christ who lives in me.... (Galatians 2:20 ESV)

When you get into trouble, a friend will not walk away and leave you there.

What comes from the heart, goes to the heart. *(Samuel Coleridge)*

When I plead, "Lord, have mercy on me, a sinner," I travel more steps into God's mercy.

Loving can cost a lot...But not loving always costs more.

Only base men and oppressors can rejoice in a triumph of injustice over the weak and defenseless. *(Frederick Douglass)*

The time is always right to do the right thing.

October 11   Tests & Trials

Charlie Brown used to say that it always looks darkest just before it gets totally black! Remember that scripture always quoted to you when times get dicey? *Blessed is the man who remains steadfast under trial, for when he has stood the test he will receive the crown of life, which God has promised to those who love Him* (James 1:12). What's a believer to do when faced with disappointment, disaster, and despair? Scripture teaches us that *all things work together for good to them that love God...*(Romans 8:28). When we encounter difficulties, our common question is "Why?" while life seems to mock us and respond, "Why not?" Definitions come into play here as well. Are all of my so-called trials, truly trials? Have I ever actually been persecuted for my faith? Searching for answers and learning to view bad things as good things in disguise are disciplines the Lord wants me to develop as I mature spiritually. This is a great topic for dialogue, and the Bible does seem to indicate that God does use tests and trials to build my character. James 1:2 tells me I should *count it all joy* when I meet trials of various kinds. I confess that I still struggle with that one. It's kind of like that old saying that the Lord doesn't take us into deep water to drown us but to develop us. Read through Psalm 44—*You are my King and my God; I do not trust in my own strength.* This was written during Judah's exile in Babylon, during times you call "trials." Every time I read that psalm, I'm confronted with a lot of questions. Is what I'm going through right now truly a tribulation? When Psalm 44 says, *I will praise Your name all day long and forever!* Is that my go-to response? Do I praise God more during times of blessing or times of trial? Hmmm...Too convicting... Let's move on. One thing I know from experience. When I thank God for the bitter things, I realize that they can become a friend to grace. How often they drive me to my secret place.

Random thoughts for today:

Rejoice in hope, be patient in tribulation, be constant in prayer. (Romans 12:12 ESV)

Never answer an angry word with an angry word...It's the second one that makes the quarrel.

Are you hot or cold for the Lord, or are you just so much warm, tepid water?

The person who says it can't be done should not interrupt the person who is doing it. *(Chinese Proverb)*

When I confess, "I believe; help my unbelief," my faith is made a little stronger.

No one ever wins a fight.

October 12   Praying by Grace

I used to think I had to have all of my "ducks in a row" and have all my motives in order before I could pray...I mean really pray. The truth of the matter is that I begin the day pretty disheveled with a mixed-up mess of intentions. I rarely jump out of bed early in the morning, ready to pray. Some days I feel compassionate; some selfish. Some days loving; some bitter. In times past, I have felt like many of the ancients who thought they needed to bathe before approaching God. It was liberating when I realized that I didn't have to "clean up" before my prayer time. What freedom it is to understand that my Abba Father is big enough to receive me with all of my messes and contradicting struggles. Only He can clean me up. God unravels the good and the bad, the genuine from the hypocritical. It can be a hard lesson to learn, and we have to relearn it. Through His grace, He helps me to sort out my motives when I pray. Sometimes there's a lot of praying FOR stuff...He often brings me to the place where I pray for qualities to BE—"Lord, help me to be a better lover of others." I can't do that on my own. I mentioned this before. To receive grace, we need only to love the Donor of grace. I don't even have to be filled with faith to approach my Father. That's grace—His grace. I've quoted Ephesians 2:8-9 ESV for years—*For by grace are we saved by faith. And this is not our own doing; it is the gift of God.* And then I realized the fulness of it. I am not only saved by grace, but I also live by it. And guess what? We pray by grace as well.

Random thoughts for today:

But God, being rich in mercy, because of the great love with which He loved us, even when we were dead in our trespasses, made us alive together with Christ— by grace you have been saved. (Ephesians 2:4-5 ESV)

Sometimes concentration on the problem redoubles the strength of the problem.

Am I more in love with Jesus today than I was yesterday?

Lord, may You help silence and solitude become precious friends to me.

Be bold enough to use your voice, brave enough to listen to your heart, and strong enough not to compromise the life you've been called to. *(Unknown)*

A good marriage is where both people feel like they're getting the better end of the deal.

October 13   A Supernatural Event

Worship is, in part, listening to what God might say to us, through music, through words, through fellowship. It is also our response to what He speaks. It means to recognize supreme worth.

I've stated it many times in my writing and speaking, "Wonder is the basis for worship." Many ancient writers talk about worship as a "supernatural event taking place." I often wonder how many worship services in our churches, how much worship in individual believers (myself included) is fueled by the amazement that God is allowing me to participate in a supernatural experience. When I speak of this phenomenon, I'm not referring to tongues or visions or words of prophecy, etc. I'm not anti-charismatic and have witnessed many positive things come out of this movement. Having spent three years fellowshipping with this branch of the church, including a month and a half trip to Asia with the Full Gospel Businessmen's Fellowship, I can also tell you that many of these "miraculous manifestations" were absolutely manipulated by men. When I speak of a supernatural event taking place, I am referring to being overwhelmed with the presence of God and the truth that I am allowed to worship the sovereign of the universe; an event that has nothing to do with the style of songs we sing or what personality is leading worship or how many people give prophetic messages or whether there are 20 people or 2000 people in the room. C. S. Lewis said that the perfect (worship) service would be one we were almost unaware of because our attention will be focused upon the Lord. Think back on the service you participated in this past weekend. Was it a supernatural event or just the same old story? Can you say with my friend, Augie, "I could go through that church service in a coma?" Was God there? Were you overwhelmed by that truth?

Random thoughts for today:

Holy, holy, holy is the LORD of hosts; the whole earth is full of His glory. (Isaiah 6:3 ESV)

Care for others is a spiritual discipline.

Words are a writer's tears. *(Arthur Plotnik)*

As if I can hear Him say to me, "Gaze at Me through the eyes of your heart."

In Christianity, the one vital thing is not speed or distance attained, but direction.

As I read through scripture, I get the idea that the fruit I produce is kind of important.

October 14   I Do Not Change

One pastor's wife said that trying to understand God is like swimming underwater to the deepest part of the ocean and then back to the surface with one deep breath. Even though there is so much I do not understand about Him; there is one characteristic that I find to be extremely comforting. In my college doctrine class, we called it immutability. It's a fancy theological word which means, GOD DOES NOT CHANGE. He doesn't change His character or His plan. I don't know about you, but I find that quite refreshing. There's a security there that I long for—Consistent, unconditional love. In Malachi 3:6, the LORD says, *I the LORD do not change...* This is the God we serve!! It's consoling to know that we believe in and follow a God who keeps His word. What He has said in His word is as true today as when He spoke it. I think of His many promises to us—

> *Everyone who calls on the name of the Lord will be saved.* (Romans 10:13 ESV)

> *My grace is sufficient for you.* (2 Corinthians 12:9 ESV)

Surely I am coming soon. (Revelation 22:20 ESV)

—To recall a few.

Random thoughts for today:

Have you not known? Have you not heard? The LORD is the everlasting God, the Creator of the ends of the earth. (Isaiah 40:28 ESV)

No duty is more urgent than that of returning thanks. *(Ambrose)*

Following Jesus is a daily discipline...A step at a time, a day at a time.

Lord, fill my mouth with worthwhile stuff; and nudge me hard when I've said enough.

We cannot attain the presence of God because we are already in the presence of God...What is absent is our awareness.

What's a friend? A single soul dwelling in two bodies. *(Aristotle)*

October 15   Short and Sweet

BE KIND OR BE QUIET!!

Random thoughts for today:

Watch your tongue and keep your mouth shut, and you will stay out of trouble. (Proverbs 21:23 – NLT)

By learning you will teach...By teaching you will learn. *(Latin Proverb)*

I develop godliness as I continue to make choices in accordance with the will of God.

Teaching kids to count is fine, but teaching them what counts is best. *(Bob Talbert)*

A successful marriage is an edifice that must be rebuilt every day.

The Holy Ghost doesn't just make you dance and speak in tongues...He also makes you shut up, apologize, and examine yourself. *(Unknown)*

October 16   Alternate Truth?

The whole concept of truth seems to have disappeared and ridden into the sunset. I've seen surveys that indicate approximately 75% of Americans do not believe in absolute truth. Recently a politician said, "There is truth, and then there is alternate truth." Seriously? In our age of cancel culture, we live in a time of facts and "alternate facts." If you don't like what you hear on the news, dismiss it by labeling it fake news. Only 11% of people, ages 18-29, have a high level of personal trust in anything, making Gen Z the least trusting generation in American history. Jim Estep, Academic Dean of one of the nation's Christian colleges, says, "We have demoted truth from something knowable and absolute to a circumstantial feeling, a matter for personal or public preference." One Christian musician has expressed dismay that too many modern believers are learning their theology from praise songs. It has become common practice in many churches today to replace the voice of scripture with our own voice—Or perhaps the voice of friends or family or an author or church tradition. Anything but scripture. Too many scholars have flippantly said with Pontius Pilate, "What is truth?" To some, "there is no truth" is the only true statement there is. And yet, my life continues to be founded upon Jesus' words, *I am the way, the TRUTH, and the life and no man comes to the Father but by Me* (John 14:6 ESV). Century after century, and generation after generation, scripture continues to be that "inconvenient truth" (in the words of Estep) that reminds us of our calling in the Lord and stands as a direct contradiction of the myths and lies and deceit of the world system. The teaching of scripture continues to keep "our paths straight (Proverbs 3:5)" and guards our hearts against fake truth. Abraham Lincoln once asked a denier of absolute truth, "How many legs does a cow have?" The cynic responded, "Four, or course." "Well suppose you call the cow's tail a leg," Lincoln pressed on, "now how many legs does a cow have?" "Five, of course," said the denier confidently. "Nope," said Lincoln. "Calling a cow's tail a leg doesn't make it a leg!"

Random thoughts for today:

If you abide in My word, you are truly my disciples, and you will know the truth, and the truth will set you free. (John 8:31-32 ESV)

Behold the turtle...He makes progress only when he sticks his neck out.

Only when we are no longer afraid do we continue to live.

Sometimes prayer is just sitting still in the presence of the LORD, being quiet enough to listen to Him

Have you ever come across a lyric or a poem or a prayer that plucks a particular string in your heart? Here's an anonymous prayer found in one of my journals:

> **Lord, simplify my life beginning with my desires and my appetites. Take Your rightful place within my heart so that I may see Your way and Your direction among the conflicting claims of the world in which we live. Help me never to be drawn aside by these things and to put away from my heart all useless anxiety and distress. When you feel that people let you down, know that I will never let you down. May I know what I ought to know, love what I ought to love, praise and honor that which delights You, value what's precious to You, and to hate that which breaks Your heart. Lord, You are my light in the darkness; You are my warmth in the cold; You are my happiness in sorrow. I trust in You now by relinquishing control into Your hands.**

Random thoughts for today:

If you are not firm in the faith, you will not be firm at all. (Isaiah 7:9 – ESV)

Justice is truth in action. *(Benjamin Disraeli)*
God's judgment comes from experience...Experience comes from bad judgment.

Love truth...Pardon error. *(Voltaire)*

It is today that your best work can be done and not some future day or future year.

What a joy when I remove all the clutter in my life and discover I just want Jesus.

Laughter is not at all a bad beginning for a friendship, and it's far the best ending for one.

October 18   Offended?

My wife told me once that she had a beef with me. She said, "Doesn't anything offend you?" I confess that there are a few things that can bring feelings of offense within, but it is indeed difficult to offend me. I've tried hard to live by Ecclesiastes 7 ESV—*Do not take to heart all the things that people say, lest you hear your (friend, co-worker, etc.) cursing you. Your heart knows that many times you yourself have cursed others* (Vv 21-22). I would guess that I hear or read the phrase, "I'm offended by that," at least 10-12 times a week. Proverbs says that *a brother offended is more unyielding than a strong city*...(18:19). One writer talks about our culture being filled with a "spirit of offense." Psychologists have found when people associate almost exclusively with those who agree with them, they suffer from group-think and confirmation bias and lose their ability to critically think and see events clearly. This is a problem on both sides of the left-right controversies. A more valid question should be, "Is what I'm doing offending the Lord that I claim to serve?" I hear many speak of how the words of Jesus offend them—*Blessed is the one who is not offended by Me* (Jesus, Luke 7:23 ESV). What about my offense to Him? Sometimes people say hurtful things to get attention. One

Christian sister said, "Before I comment, text, tweet, post, write, or act, I remember to ask five questions: Is it true? Is it helpful? Is it inspiring? Is it necessary? Is it kind?" As I look at my Savior's life and try to live out His example, I often wonder if I ever have the right to be personally offended. Paul does say, *The Lord's servant must not be quarrelsome but kind to everyone, able to teach, patiently enduring evil* (2 Timothy 2:24 ESV). And then there's this thought to ruminate upon—"If everything is offensive, nothing is offensive."

Random thoughts for today:

Good sense makes one slow to anger, and it is his glory to overlook an offense. (Proverbs 19:11 ESV)

We live, my dear soul, in an age of trial...What will be the consequences, I know not. *(John Adams, a letter to his wife, Abigail)*

In our faith, we follow in Someone's steps...Then we leave footprints to guide others...It's the principle of discipleship.

For the Christian, it's all good in the end. If it's not good, it's not the end.

The greatest thing we can do is to let people know that they are loved.

October 19   Whose Morality?

My mother used to tell me that you cannot legislate morality. And my response was always, "Every law on the books legislates somebody's morality!" My mom and I had many intense discussions, usually from opposite points of view. Our morality discussion probably missed some deeper issues, but I believe my mother was probably more accurate than I. The problem with morality tests is the many definitions of morality. Who defines it? There are those in our culture today who even deny the existence of any morality. Indian author, Isha Sadhguru, says that morality is necessary when spirituality is absent. But whose morality? I had a discussion a few years ago with a college sophomore about absolutes and morality. He was challenging some of the standards for the believer outlined in the New Testament. I asked him, "What's your authority?" He responded that my standards might be different than his standards. "Are there any absolute standards?" I asked. He hesitated. "Would it be alright if I raped my sister?" "Of course not!" "Why?" I said. "Who made up that standard?" It was a lengthy interchange and ended with his promise rethink some of his positions. But all of the rethinking of absolutes and reformation of our morality systems are meaningless unless men's hearts are changed. You cannot make men good by law, and without good men you cannot have a good society. Jeopardy question for today—Just who defines "good?" Jeopardy answer—WHO IS GOD? Once again, only God can change a heart. Theology and philosophical discussion can be interesting, but when we walk out into the real world of life, it is the indisputable proof of changed hearts that makes us believers.

Random thoughts for today:

If it had not been for the law, I would not have known sin. I would not have known what it is to covet if the law had not said, "You shall not covet." (Romans 7:7 ESV)

Life in Christ is bigger than any country, loftier than any civilization, broader than any human ideology.

This week, pour everything out to God—EVERYTHING!! *(Nathan Sloan)*

A friend is a gift you give yourself. *(Robert Louis Stevenson)*

You can't always keep trouble from coming, but you don't have to give it a chair to sit on. *(Southern Proverb)*

October 20   Whose Will on Earth?

In previous entries I've discuss several aspects of the Lord's model prayer (Feb 4 – Feb 5 – June 1 – July 10 – August 10). In just these past months I've been convicted by a new insight of a line I've prayed over and over again since I was a boy—*Your kingdom come, Your will be done, on earth as it is in heaven.* I've always thought that it was a prayer of submission to the kingdom of God and to God's will being done. "Yes, Lord, I agree with that. Let Your kingdom come and you know I always cast a vote for Your will to be done on earth!!" We all want the will of God, right? But is it all upon His shoulders? How does the will of God come about on earth as it is in heaven. Read carefully and slowly today, Ephesians 5:15-17 ESV. The passage ends with the words *understand what the will of God is.* Dietrich Bonhoeffer once wrote, "Being a Christian is less about cautiously avoiding sin than about courageously and actively DOING God's will." I believe this prayer is not only about submission to His will, but it is also absolutely about His will to be done on earth by ME. Always kingdom things to be done; neglected things to be caught up with. Hebrews 10:36 ESV says, *You need to persevere so that when you have done the will of God, you will receive what He has promised.* This line in the model prayer is all about MY daily application of these words. Is His will being done by me?

Random thoughts for today:

Now may the God of peace...equip you with everything good for doing His will, and may He work in us what is pleasing to Him... (Hebrews 13:20-21 ESV)

Hope and love are never cultivated by just being against things...What are we for?

Reflect on your present blessings of which all men have many... Not on your misfortunes of which all men have some. *(Charles Dickens)*

When you're on a horse gallopin' off a cliff, it's too late to shout, "Whoa!" *(Southern Proverb)*

Next time you feel fear or confusion or despair, remember Jesus has already won the victory for you.

The beauty of believers consists in their resemblance to Jesus Christ. *(Matthew Henry)*

October 21   Common Vice

There is one vice of which no man is free. Clive Hamilton called it the essential vice. It is a vice I've battled off and on in my life many times, beginning in my teen years. I'm talking about PRIDE. I'm talking about self-conceit, and the virtue opposite to it is humility. I love the old story of the man who was awarded a humility button, and was allowed to keep it until he wore it. It was through pride that Satan became the devil. I say "battled off and on" because there have been many periods of my life that I didn't battle it at all; I just allowed it to control me. Maybe that's why you find me discussing the whole pride conflict within many times in this book. In the middle of one of these battles years ago, a mentor said to me, "Rick, pride will always be the longest distance between two people; it will cost you everything and leave you with nothing." Pride has probably been the chief cause of problems and dissatisfaction in every family and in every nation. Some writers have called it the ultimate evil. I believe that pride leads to every other vice; it is the complete anti-God state of mind. Or as one brother told me some time ago, "A person who gets too big for his britches will be exposed in the end."

NOTE: Clive Hamilton was the pseudonym of C.S. Lewis (1919)

Random thoughts for today:

God opposes the proud but gives grace to the humble. (James 4:6 ESV)

Honesty leads to confession, and confession leads to change.

One of the reasons mature people stop growing and learning is that they become less and less willing to risk failure.

Today I will find beauty in everyday things.

The older I get I discover that I am in charge of nothing!!

How often does our happiness depend upon ourselves?

The longer we live the more we find that we are like other persons.

Proper morals and ethics, not force, are the basis of law.

The light is dark in his tent, and his lamp (candle) above him is put out (Job 18:6 ESV) These were the words of Bildad to his friend, Job. This past week has been a time of the flickering of my "candle."**(*)** In just a matter of days, Helen and I had to make a trip to Missouri for her brother's memorial service, our oldest daughter was going through a major crisis, a little girl in the small community of 2,000 where we minister was murdered by a teenager, and another teen formerly from the school where I taught committed suicide. Again, as I have asked many times, WHY? As I continue on my journey through life, I have more questions than answers. The stillness of this morning brings weight and sadness. All of us have those times in our lives when we waver and our candles flicker; perhaps you've felt that your candle was even snuffed out! In the Old Testament, candles and lamps were lit before God in the tabernacle and later, in the temple (Leviticus 24:3-4). The candles represented the presence of God and the way He illuminates life, reveals hidden things, and knows the intentions of the heart. I often use candles in my quiet time. The power, of course, was not in the candles, but in the Lord. Google "candles in scripture" and do a mini-study on their significance in the believer's life. The greatest strength I have had through the years is the claiming of the promise that God is present with me, even when I don't feel that presence. And there certainly have been times I haven't felt the presence of God. Thank You for Your promise, LORD—*For you light my candle; the LORD my God illuminates my darkness* (Psalm 18:28)

LORD, light a candle in me today.

(*)Written in the morning of March 23, 2021...It's been quite a week, Lord...Thank You for turning my mourning into morning.

Random thoughts for today:

The Lord's lamp (candle) shone upon my head, and by His light I walked through darkness. (Job 29:3 ESV)

The child is in me still, and sometimes not so still.
Readers are plentiful...Thinkers are rare.
I wonder if part of our problem in praying is that we have made prayer into something entirely unnatural, something that doesn't really fit into our lives.

October 23   Worship Leadership

In the late 1990s, Matt Redman wrote a moving worship song (speaking of worship) that said, "I'm sorry, Lord, for the thing I've made it, when it's all about You, it's all about You, Jesus." The song was born from a period of apathy within Matt's home church. His church was struggling to find meaning in their worship offerings. The pastor did a pretty brave thing. He got rid of the sound system and the worship band for a season, in other words, "unplugged." My August 28 entry was about balanced worship. I led a devotional time with the worship team of my home church about priorities for worship leaders. Here is a summary of that time together.

1. Relationship to my LORD
    This includes honest and frequent communication with Him and much confessed sin.

2. Building relationship with others on the team
   Love God, Love others...No barriers between
3. Connection to the SOURCE
   Remember: Worship is a supernatural event; we easily forget that...Rely on the SOURCE and not on my own ability.
4. Personal preparation
   Includes spiritual preparation and musical preparation (balance)
5. Group preparation
   Balance your connection to the SOURCE to the technology connection.
6. Intercession before and during the worship service
   O Lord, <u>Forgive</u> what I have been, <u>Sanctify</u> what I am, and <u>Order</u> what I shall be. Amen. (Our team prayed this prayer together after devotional time)

<u>Random thoughts for today</u>:

Let everything that has breath praise the LORD! Praise the LORD! (Psalm 150:6 ESV)

Never too old to learn something new.
We are conductors of light. *(Sir Arthur Conan Doyle)*
Strong people don't put other people down...They lift them up.
Never say that you have no time...What we lack is not time, but rather heart.

Pandemic-Fatigue...I hear that term a lot lately. I use that term with shame, knowing that there are genuine heroes out there who know what it truly is. My oldest daughter, as I've shared before, is an RN in a large hospital in the Chicago area. She knows what it is. I am also aware that I can be a closet cynic, and occasionally the cynic gets out. This entry is probably not appropriate for a prayer devotional; but then again maybe it is. So, just for a few moments, I am coming out of the closet. It is what it is. I entitle this "Ode to My World."

- Thank you, Americans, for your personal scientific research and expertise determining that COVID-19 is a hoax and masks are silly (this hoax quarantined my wife and I for a couple of weeks after we tested positive; it also put my grandson in the hospital for a week).
- Thank you, politicians, for making our national crisis a political football.
- Thank you, CDC, for telling us "to follow the science," and changing the "science" every other week.
- Thanks you, many of our churches, for making COVID a human rights issue instead of a *love thy neighbor* issue.
- Thank you, for all of state and local health departments, for published infection and death rates daily (even though no one has any idea of what the true numbers are any more).
- Thank you, medical bureaucrats, for falsifying numbers for the purpose of receiving more financial reimbursement.
- Thank you, news-media, for daily reminding us that we're all gonna die...We appreciate the hope that you generate.

- Thank you, all of you purveyors of social media posts and tweets, for being the masterful idiots that you are.

Random thoughts for today:

Scripture (?) – I won't justify this entry with a Bible verse.

Hate breeds more hate...Love breeds love...LOVE WINS!!
I am a child again; joy holds me fast. *(Lizette Woodworth Reese)*

My favorite childhood prayer:

Thank You for the world so sweet, Thank You for the food we eat;
That You for the birds that sing, Thank You, LORD, for everything!!

October 25   Honest Prayers

Teresa of Avila was a Spanish noblewoman who felt called to convent life in the 16th century. Historians record her as a woman "for God," a woman of prayer, discipline, and compassion. She is called an energetic reformer, a holy woman, a womanly woman. The following is a conversation she wrote over 500 years ago (most of it with God):

"I had some fun with God today. I dared to complain to Him. I said, Lord, explain to me, please, why you keep me in this miserable life. Why do I have to put up with it? Everything here interferes with my enjoyment of You. I have to eat and sleep and work and talk with everyone. I do it

all for the love of You but it torments me. And how is it that when there is a little break and I have some time with You, You hide from me? I honestly believe, Lord, that if it were possible for me to hide from You the way You hide from me, You would not allow it. But You are with me and see me always. Stop this, Lord! It hurts me because I love You so much. I said these and other things to God. Sometimes love becomes foolish and doesn't make a lot of sense. The Lord puts up with it. May so good a King be praised! We wouldn't dare say these things to earthly kings."

Have you ever had a conversation with God anything like that? If you haven't, how much of your prayer life is filled with honest praying?

Random thoughts for today:

An honest answer (or prayer) *is like a kiss on the lips.* (Proverbs 24:26 ESV)

Quotes from the writings of Teresa of Avila:

Be gentle to all and stern with yourself.

I know the power obedience has of making things easy which seem impossible.

There are some tears shed over answered prayers than over unanswered prayers.

I do not fear Satan half so much as I fear those who fear him.

We can only learn to know ourselves and surrender our will and fulfill God's will in us.

There's a lot of conversation happening across the land about "getting back to normal." The "new normal" has become a catch-phrase for many. What does that mean? How does the new normal differ from the old normal, or does anybody have clue. The dictionary says that normal is conforming to the standard of the common type; not abnormal—That's helpful! It has also been defined as approximately average. Isn't that exciting? Do I really desire normal in my life? When we discuss normalcy, I think that a lot of us mean the way things used to be before the pandemic. Or we equate the normal with some kind of "good-old-days" philosophy. How many times in my life has normalcy and consistency been interrupted because my routine was ambushed? If I'm honest, I have to admit that going back to the way it used to be doesn't excite me all that much, no matter what you're considering. Same old, same old doesn't seem to correspond with *What no eye has seen, nor ear heard, nor the heart of man imagined, what God has prepared for those who love Him* (1 Corinthians 2:9 ESV). My prayer is that I WON'T return to normal when the super-spread evolves into a whimpy-spread (speaking of course of COVID). My prayer is that the Church won't return to normal when we're back to full on in person worship services. I guess my major purpose in this entry is to make all of us totally dissatisfied with the norm. I mean, bored with it!! Do you have vision for something beyond normal? Do you ever pray for something like that? Duke Ellington said that vision is like rhythm. If you have it, you don't need a definition. If you don't have it, no definition in the world will help you.

Random thoughts for today:

Where there is no vision, the people perish... (Proverbs 29:18 ESV)

I guess our most important prayer is just two words— "Thank You!"

If you miss the little things in life, you miss the vast majority of life.

Let us dare to read, think, speak, and write. *(John Adams)*

I pray for the Lord to draw me closer to Him...That's what's most important to me...I do not desire a "normal" relationship with the Lord.

What a difference it would make if every Christian in our nation were to begin to live as a child of God should live.

October 27   Why I Oppose the Death Penalty

Whoever takes a human life shall be put to death (Leviticus 24:17 ESV). In my February 2 entry I shared that I am pro-life all the way which includes opposition to the death penalty. Some might think this a strange topic for a devotional. Perhaps. My purpose continues to be to stimulate discussion and dialogue, but I think that a greater purpose in this entry is to show how we can evolve through the years of our journey, if we are brave enough to be open-minded. In my younger years I was a staunch supporter of capital punishment; you know, *an eye for an eye* all the way. My goal is not to convince or to win anyone over to my position, but rather to share the evolution of my excursion from one side of the issue to the other. I once asked a friend of mine who worked death row at Indiana State Prison, "Do you believe the death penalty is really a deterrent?" His response, "Statistically, I'm not sure, but it's certainly a deterrent to the person we've executed." I read periodically of individuals who have been convicted and sentenced and spent many years in prison, and then were exonerated and released. The problem with the death penalty is that you cannot undo the sentence after it's been carried out. *National Geographic* reports that since 1973, more than 8700 people have been sentenced to death and more than 1500 have been executed. 182 of those sent to death row actually were innocent. During the past 50 years, an average of four people a year have been exonerated of all charges. DNA has played a role in this, but 68% of the cases were eventually dismissed over official misconduct, such as concealing evidence, or a witness who lied under oath. 25% of the cases involved inadequate legal defense. Facts like these have served as a proverbial "rock in my shoe" for quite some time. Then there are the words of Jesus as He changes the "eye for eye" principle—*Here's an old saying that deserves another look: "Eye for eye, tooth for tooth." Is that going to get us anywhere? No more tit-for-tat stuff. Live generously* (Matthew 5:36-42/The Message paraphrase).

Random thoughts for today:

You have heard that it was said, "You shall love your neighbor and hate your enemy." But I say to you, "Love your enemies and pray for those who persecute you." (Matthew 5:43-44 ESV)

Faith will come to him who passionately seeks after his God.

Quiet time is often disdained by men because it reveals our inward poverty.

Lord, I believe...Help me with my unbelief.

One characteristic of maturity is a new lack of self-consciousness.

October 28   Shoulder Taps

My friend, Roger Ash, sent me a post not too long ago entitled, "Shoulder Taps." It was a brief testimony from a brother who was having lunch with his wife, and he felt a "tap" on the shoulder regarding an older woman sitting in the next booth. "Tell her she really looks nice today," said the inner urging. While his wife went to pay the bill, he approached the woman and said, ""I don't know if anyone else has told you this today, but you really look lovely." The elderly woman paused for a brief moment, tearing up. She responded, "My husband died a year ago, and that's exactly, word for word, what he often said to me." That account really grabbed my heart. I don't know how often stuff like that ever happens to you, but I'm convinced that there are many God-happenings all around us. As a young man I heard the phrase, "nudging from the Spirit" many times, but wasn't sure what that was all about. Through the years of my journey the Lord has been teaching me regarding these so called shoulder taps. Henri J. Nouwen talks about a gentle "interiority"—a heart of flesh and not of stone, "a room with some spots on which one might walk barefooted. God can work that way in us. He can descend with our minds into our hearts, if we are open to it. Ah, there's the key. Are we open to Him nudging us? Is your heart ready to receive a nudge from the Lord? Or are we so busy and consumed by the chaos of the culture around us that we fail to notice when God is trying to get our attention? A great biblical example of this principle is in Acts 8:26-39 (the account of Philip and the Ethiopian eunuch). Read it. Hmmm...Shoulder taps.

Random thoughts for today:

If we live by the Spirit, let us also walk by the Spirit. (Galatians 5:25 ESV)

We struggle daily to keep in mind what we are here for and to not forget we're all about.

See a lot...Over-look some things...Correct where I can make a difference.

When given the choice between being right or being kind... Be kind.

More men fail for lack of purpose than lack of talent. *(Billy Sunday)*

There must be always remaining in every man's life some place for the singing of angels. *(Ancient writer)*

Live your individuality to the full, but always for the good of others.

Help us to be attentive to all You have prepared for us.

October 29   Who Do Worship Leaders Lead?

In my October 23 entry I shared some important lessons I've learned over the years concerning worship leadership. Recently the Lord has given me some very real convictions regarding the individuals we are leading in worship on a weekly basis. Basic question—WHO DO I LEAD IN WORSHIP? On any given Lord's Day there may be (probably are) in our congregation:

- Those who have all their "ducks in a row"; they have all their doctrine in order
- Those who know nothing (I like to refer to them as "pre-born")
- Those who know everything
- Those who don't want to be here
- Cynics
- Those sick in body
- Those sick in heart (because of marriage problems, kid problems, job problems, someone has betrayed them)
- Those burdened by secrets eating them alive
- Someone considering taking their own life
- Those on the verge of financial ruin
- Those suffering from depression
- Those wrestling with decisions that could affect the rest of their lives
- Those close to committing their life to Jesus Christ

Prepare well. Lead them well. Lead them to Jesus who says, *Come, you who are burdened and heavy-ladened, broken hearted, and I will give you rest* (Matthew 11:28 ESV).

Random thoughts for today:

Let the word of Christ dwell in you richly, teaching and admonishing one another in all wisdom, singing psalms and hymns and spiritual songs, with thankfulness in your hearts to God. (Colossians 3:16 ESV)

Giving praise is for all who know that they owe their joy to someone else.

Fall down seven times...Get up eight. *(Japanese Proverb)*

There are always flowers for those who see them.

Education is a great thing...If you couldn't sign your name you would have to pay cash.

October 30   Drifting?

I was listening to a TV commercial the other day. I don't remember what the product was, but the opening line was, "There is a compass in each one of us; and it always points true north." I've been thinking a lot about that. As I look at all that is happening around us in our world today, it would seem that there are a lot of broken compasses, and everyone's compass doesn't seem to point true north. Of course, we can't come to an agreement as to the definition of true north, even in the body of Christ. Our culture receives very little guidance today from the church as we continue to make less and less difference. It would appear that the church itself has been drifting. One influential theologian said, "We must continue to test traditional and orthodox doctrines. We are outgrowing many and others survive only as fairy tales." Others in the church have proclaimed that we must trust in the guidance of the Holy Spirit (I agree with that), but we can't seem to nail down exactly what that means. Maybe we've outgrown Him as well. I don't think we've done a very good job *teaching all nations... teaching them to observe all that (He) has commanded us* in these current times (Matthew 28:20 ESV). Meanwhile the church continues to lose more and more of the trust of more and more people in the midst of our prosperity (worship leaders wearing

$800 sneakers) and holy scandals of the month. Oh, Lord, we've dropped the ball!! The Pontius Pilate in us asks, "What IS truth?"

Random thoughts for today:

For the time is coming when people will not endure sound teaching, but have itching ears that they will accumulate for themselves teachers to suit their own passions, and will turn away from listening to the truth and wander off into myths. (2 Timothy 4:3-4 ESV)

We always expect every prayer to be answered in this lifetime... Maybe...Maybe not.

God will honor me more when I admit that I am wrong than for claiming that I know everything.

I've never been able to bring myself to pray for a better standard of living...I guess I've always left my standard of living up to the Lord.

May you experience the powerlessness and poverty of a child and sing and dance in the love of the Father. *(A different kind of benediction)*

The final word is LOVE.

October 31   Hopelessly Devoted

How do I measure my devotion to Christ? What does it mean when I say, "I am devoted to Jesus?" When my two daughters were growing up, one of their favorite movies was the 1978 film, *Grease.* Their favorite musical number was John Travolta and Olivia Newton John singing, "Hopelessly Devoted to You."

Remember? "I'm outta my head; hopelessly devoted to you." How do you define it? My dictionary says that devotion is a zealous or ardent attachment, loyalty, affection. The original New Testament Greek word means "to be steadfastly attentive to; to give relentless care to; tenaciously clinging to." Acts 2:42 ESV tells us that the early church were *devoting themselves to the apostles' teaching and fellowship, to the breaking of bread and the prayers.* In 1609, St. Francis de Sales wrote in his volume, *Introduction to the Devout Life,* "True devotion presupposes love of God; rather, it is nothing else than the true love of God." Isaiah writes in scripture, *But they who wait upon the LORD shall renew their strength, they shall mount up with wings like eagles, they shall run and not be weary, they shall walk and not faint* (Isaiah 40:31). One brother of mine said, "I love Him not only for what He is and what He has done for me, but I love Him for what I am when I am with Him and what He is making of me." How do we sum that all up? How do I define being hopelessly devoted to Jesus? John 14:15 does a nice job doing it—*If you love Me, you will keep my commandments.*

Random thoughts for today:

You shall love the Lord your God with all your heart and with all your soul and with all your strength and with all your mind... (Luke 10:27 ESV)

Hope is being able to see that there is light despite all the darkness.

Look to the experience of others who have gone before you... They are there to offer comfort as well as guidance.

There are two ways of exerting strength...One is pushing down; the other is pulling up. *(Booker T. Washington)*

"Being nice" is not the same thing as "choosing kind."

We should not only use the brains that we have, but all that we borrow. *(Woodrow Wilson)*

Prayer is not just putting my needs and problems before the Lord, but first and foremost, putting my SELF before the Lord.

November

Thanks, Lord, For The Change Of Seasons...Reminds Me That Everything Around Me Changes, Except You!

November 1   All Must Be Thanksgiving

Supposedly, a global season of thanks is to begin very soon. I know that we are to be thankful all year long, but God's people have always had SPECIAL times and celebrations for thanksgiving, and it's always been a big deal. A Jewish rabbi said, "Thanksgiving! Thanksgiving! All must be thanksgiving!" Our national Thanksgiving Day is 25 days away at this writing, and I would suggest that we need a big deal, month-long celebration just to give our thanks to the Lord. I have recently spent some time on social media (too much time, I admit). I would like to say to all my friends and brothers and sisters in the Lord to cease and desist all the jabbering about politics, and COVID, and masks, and individual liberties, and elections and instead dedicate this coming month to THANKS UNTO THE LORD. If you're going to post or tweet anything for the next few days, give thanks to the Lord. Two years ago, my youngest daughter proposed a project for anyone interested. She encouraged a "Thanks Journal." Those participating were to jot down <u>three things</u> each day in November for which they were thankful. I accepted that challenge and found it to be a tremendous blessing. I'm finding myself needing a gratitude attitude adjustment even more this year. So I begin this week. I've used the following anonymous piece of verse in previous postings: "Last night I started to count my blessings, it wouldn't take me very long. But oh how I misjudged the grace of God, for tonight I'm still going strong."

Random thoughts for today:

Oh give thanks to the LORD, for He is good; His steadfast love endures forever. (1 Chronicles 16:34 ESV)

Growing in transparency in my prayer life WILL LEAD to greater transparency in my relationships with others around me.

Never use words when action is required.

Never say, "Don't cry!"...Instead say, "Go ahead and cry; I'm here to be with you.

November 2   On Death and Dying

It happened a year ago today...Seems so much longer. It was time for my precious Dad to step across from here to there. *The time of his departure was at hand* (2 Timothy 4:6 NKJV). He passed away on the couch of his weakness (a hospital bed in the living room of his condo), surrounded by his stuff which he would need no longer, on hangers, in drawers, in little boxes on the bureau, until my siblings and I would later clear them out. It seems that our exit from this life should be surrounded with more dignity and grace at the end of our time on earth and the completion of all of our accomplishments. But here we are, rumpled, faded, gasping, dressed in our pajamas, and lying on this plastic-covered mattress. Thomas Howard said, "We arrive in a mess (as we are born); and we leave in a mess." And after the flurry of all that has transpired in that death chamber, we feel we must DO something, so we have a funeral. But does a memorial service fully accomplish summarizing a life like Dad's? Then I remember all that has happened has been from my perspective on this side of the crossing. I'm still "here" and not "over there" where Dad is. What did that crossing bring to my father as he experienced it? What did he see? What did he hear? I dreamed the other night of Jesus carrying my Dad in His arms as they crossed over together. And I heard Jesus say to him, *Well done, good and faithful servant!*" The summary of saved by <u>grace</u>. It doesn't get any more <u>dignified</u> than that.

(Written on the first anniversary of my father's passing)

<u>Random thoughts for today</u>:

I tell you this, brothers: flesh and blood cannot inherit the kingdom of God, nor does the perishable inherit the imperishable...Death is swallowed up in victory!! (1 Corinthians 15:50; 54 NKJV)

It is always on the backside of the desert that we come to the mountain of God. *(Vance Havner)*

Better to live a holy life than to talk about it...Lighthouses don't fire cannons to advertise they are lighthouses—They just shine.

Don't strive for love...BE LOVE.

If a friend is in trouble, don't annoy him by asking if there's anything you can do...Think of something appropriate and do it.

Leadership is not being in charge...It's about taking care of people in your charge.

In the acknowledgment section, I've given credit to Jacqueline Osborn for allowing me to use her beautiful painting for the cover of this book. This painting of her son and her granddaughter has long been a favorite of mine. I call it a legacy picture. This work of art touched my heart because I used to pick up my daughters when they were little and dance with them. Every time I look at the picture, I think of legacy. I'm reminded of that scripture in Zephaniah 3:17 NKJV—*My God...will rejoice over you with gladness. He will quiet you with His love. He will dance over you with singing.* I've talked a lot about legacy in this book. I've shared that one of my daily prayer goals is to leave behind a godly legacy. What is the foundation of what I am building in my life? I often wonder what the mention of my name will bring to people's minds after I have died. In ancient times a person's name represented his character. My best personal models for life have been people who have left lasting impressions upon me, embodying godliness. I wonder if my character and faith will continue on in the lives of my kids and my grandkids (and great-grandkids). Parents, have you ever pondered how your family's faith will look a hundred years from now? I can't expect anyone (children, grandchildren, students, people in my congregation) to treasure what I don't think is valuable enough to demonstrate in my life. As one modern-day philosopher said, "We need to live so that our children won't have to edit their heritage."

<u>Random thoughts for today</u>:

We will not hide them from our children, but tell to the coming generation the glorious deeds of the LORD, and His might, and the wonders He has done. (Psalm 78:4 ESV)

To live without hope is to cease to live.

The opposite of love is indifference.

The two lasting legacies we can hope to give our children—One is roots; the other is wings. *(Hodding Carter)*

Anger is never without reason, but seldom with a good one.

God loved us even before He made us...But He had to make us to prove it. *(6-year-old kid)*

The world changes...God's word does not!!

November 4   Amazon.Soul

It's amazing how much more Helen and I have ordered online during the pandemic. And because we have an *Amazon Prime* account with free delivery, it was so easy; click a few times, and we are the proud recipients of next-day transport. At least once a day, one of us would ask, "Are we expecting any packages today?" What a great life!! I've been thinking. Isn't it interesting how much busyness and information we have allowed to be delivered to our existence, our inner lives? And the internet has significantly contributed to this. With what shabby riches do the shopping centers and marketplaces of this world fill my soul? Has my life become a vast warehouse of stuff? German theologian Karl Rahner describes the process. He says, "Day after day, the trucks unload their crates without any plan or discrimination, to be piled helter-skelter in every available corner and cranny, until it is crammed full from top to bottom with the trite, the commonplace, the insignificant, the routine." The "amazon.soul delivery truck" makes daily stops in our lives. My time with the Lord in the morning has been helpful in not being overwhelmed with this ongoing process, to battle the trivia, if you will. This time alone with my Abba Father has helped me to discern the few precious moments when the grace of God's love has succeeded in taking root into a corner of my inner life. Bit by bit, when we discover the treasures that God has to offer us, we realize that those shabby riches filling up our everyday routine will never measure up.

Random thoughts for today:

The kingdom of heaven is like treasure hidden in a field, which a man found...In his joy he goes and sells all that he has and buys that field. (Matthew 13:44 ESV)

Do not lose heart or be afraid when rumors are heard in the land—Lesson from Jeremiah 51:46.

There is no old age; there is, as there always was, just you.

It's so easy to be solemn; it's so hard to be frivolous. *(G.K. Chesterton)*

I'm not afraid to ask my teacher stuff because he has a "yes" face. *(Small boy)*

The best things in life are the people we love, the places we've been, and the memories made along the way.

Disappointments should be cremated, not embalmed.

Years ago, we used to sing a song by Jimmy Owens—"Turn the hearts of the children to their parents; turn the hearts of the parents to their young; turn the hearts of us all to one another; turn the hearts of the people to the Lord." We used that song a lot in our meetings when I pastored a youth group in the 70s. The song is based upon Malachi 4:6. Even today, I find myself humming that tune from time to time. Goethe shared his philosophy almost 200 years ago—"He is the happiest, be he king or peasant, who finds peace in his home." It's also been said that home is where life makes up its mind. A child is like a mirror; a mirror that reflects happiness, or lack of it, in the home. When homes have nothing to give in the early years of a child's life, there will be many complications later in life. With the direction that our society has taken in the last hundred years, it should come as no surprise that the fabric of our families is unraveling. The church should be extremely concerned with what is happening in our Christian homes. Hardly a week goes by that I don't read of young men and women leaving the church and denouncing the faith of their parents, or of moms and dads disowning their children because of choices they have made in life—you know, the ancient "you are dead to me" philosophy. The teaching of unconditional love seems to have been laid aside. I have personally done family counseling and witnessed attitudes of bitter hatred in a teenager toward their parents, and many times that hatred has vicariously been transferred toward Jesus. What's happened, Mom and Dad? When a home comes apart, rarely has it begun with the child. What are you teaching, and how are you teaching it? Most importantly, what are you modeling? By the way, the last 13 words of Malachi sum up the result of NOT turning our hearts to one another—*Turn the hearts of the fathers to their children and the hearts of the children to their fathers, LEST I come and strike the land with a decree of utter destruction.*

Random thoughts for today:

Children, obey your parents in the Lord, for this is right. "Honor your father and your mother" (this is the first commandment with a promise), **"that it may go well with you and that you may live long in the land." Fathers, do not provoke your children to anger, but bring them up in the discipline and instruction of the Lord.** (Ephesians 6:1-4 ESV)

Sometimes I need to inject more honesty in my talks with the Lord.

Isn't it interesting that in the same culture, children are neglected, and animals are pampered and cared for?

November 6   No Law

Saved by grace!! I didn't hear a lot about grace in my walk with the Lord until later in life. I was out of college and in the pastoral ministry before the light came on in understanding Ephesians 2:8-9, understanding that grace was something I sorely needed but did not deserve. *Not a result of works, so that no one may boast.* If we spend any time at all in scripture, how can we miss it? The grace of God has two dimensions. One dimension (we've heard all about that since childhood) is the forgiveness of all our sins. If I really believe that, why do I strive so relentlessly to live in such a way that God will accept me? The second dimension is, *I will give you a new heart, and a new spirit I will put within you. And I will remove the heart of stone from your flesh and give you a heart of flesh. And I will put my Spirit within you, and cause you to walk in my statutes...*(Ezekiel 36:26-27 ESV). In Galatians, Paul lists the fruit of that Spirit (Vv 22-23), and at the end of that listing, he says, *against such things there is no law.* One who has a new heart (and remember only God can change a heart) doesn't need any law because the Holy Spirit makes the law unnecessary in my life. Jesus Himself taught us that the greatest commandment is to love God with all we got; the second is to love others. Galatians 5:14 ESV tells us that all commandments *are summed up in this word: You shall love others as you love yourself.* God's Spirit working in us causes us to do what the law intended to do, plus a great deal more. What does that old hymn say?

> **Grace, grace, God's grace; Grace that will pardon and cleanse within**
>
> **Grace, grace, God's grace; Grace that is greater than all our sin.**

Random thoughts for today:

> ***The fruit of the Spirit is love, joy, peace, patience, kindness, goodness, faithfulness, gentleness, self-control; against such things there is no law.*** (Galatians 5:22-23 ESV)

There is joy in seeing how good God is "right now"...The pleasure of the "now" moments.

Be sure to put your feet in the right place, and then stand firm. *(Abraham Lincoln)*

Wise people, even though all laws were abolished, would still lead the same life. *(Aristophanes)*

If prayer were school, I'd flunk praying...But prayer isn't school; it is a mystery.

When life hands you lemons, make orange juice...Be unique!!

November 7   Thirsty?

Are you tired lately? I've heard that a lot in recent days (or weeks, or months). Weariness, fatigue, reluctance to see or experience any more of something. The years 2020-2021 have been dubbed by many as the Years of the Weary. Tired of COVID-19 reports. Tired of wearing masks. Tired of social distancing. Tired of Zoom meetings and broadcasts. Tired of virtual anything. It's no surprise that much of the rebellion in our country against mandates and shutdowns is a result of weariness. Scripture promises you that you aren't alone in these kinds of feelings. I often confess to the Lord my weariness, and many times He does send comfort. That comfort doesn't always come in the form of a change in my circumstances. Still, it is often a supernatural peace that motivates me to forge on in the face of weariness. Psalm 73:26 ESV says, *My flesh and my heart may fail, but God is the strength of my heart and my portion forever.* Recently, I began to realize that a lot of my weariness is more about THIRST than it is about being tired. I write this during the year 2021 and recognize a great thirst within me. I'm not tired so much; I'm thirsty!! I'm thirsty for peace in our land and in our communities. I'm thirsty for truth in our culture; for selflessness to replace selfishness. I'm thirsty for people to be kind to each other. I'm thirsty for integrity and character to replace ratings and popularity in the media. I'm thirsty for churches across the land to be more concerned about honesty and transparency than image and style over substance. And then I remember the words of Jesus—*Whoever drinks of the water that I will give him will never be thirsty forever. The water that I will give him will become in him a spring of water welling up to eternal life* (John 4:14 ESV). So are you just tired, or is your weariness caused by thirst? What kind of water are you using to quench that thirst?

Random thoughts for today:

My peace I leave with you; my peace I give to you. Not as the world gives do I give to you. Let not your hearts be troubled, neither let them be afraid. (John 14:27 ESV)

No matter how much you do, you'll feel it's not enough.

Do you have a "me-centered" view of scripture or a "Christ-centered" view?

Turn your wounds into wisdom.

There's no shame in not knowing...The shame lies in not finding out. *(Russian Proverb)*

There is as much danger from false brethren as from open enemies. *(Matthew Henry)*

Prayer is never just asking. Nor is it merely a matter of asking for what I want. Dallas Willard said, "God is not a cosmic butler or fix-it man." The aim of the universe is not to fulfill my desires and needs. It's been said that we need to learn to pray our hearts. Have you noticed that your most passionate prayers are when you lift up the things that are closest to your heart? I often find myself fumbling through words, sometimes of willful demands and childish "gimmes." I want to hear His voice and pray within His will. To do that, I have to let myself go (yes, get myself out of the way), releasing myself into His arms. I've shared in the past writing those times I picture myself being embraced by my Abba Father or laying my head on His breast. Sometimes I have to work through self to get to Him. The way to build a meaningful prayer life is to pray for those things that I am genuinely drawn to, not just good words. I often pray that God will change me and shape me so that my heart beats more and more in tune with the Lord's. How often do we truly pray our hearts? You may be surprised as to how much such a practice can enlarge your circle of interest. Silence and solitude have a lot to do with that practice. They are excellent aids to conversation, especially with the Lord. My greatest heart prayers have come during those periods of silence.

Lord, I have no words today to express the things that stir within me, so I bow before You in silence.

Random thoughts for today:

To You, O LORD, I lift up my soul. O my God, in You
I trust. (Psalm 25:1 ESV)

A mature disciple reflects Jesus Christ.

Virtue untested is really no virtue at all.

Contentment is the state of mind and heart in which you would be at peace if God gave you nothing more than He already has.

Joy is not in things...It is in us.

Am I not destroying my enemies when I make friends with them. *(A. Lincoln)*

The first resistance to change in my life is to say it's not necessary.

November 9   Heart for People

Unlike Muhammed or Siddhartha Gautama (Buddhism) or Bhaktivedanta (Hinduism), Jesus had no desire to set Himself up above the crowds and initiate them into an esoteric system of religion or ethics. He had come and worked and suffered for the sake of His people. He came to feed the flock, lead them to fresh waters to quench their thirst, and protect them from the wolf. *I came that they might have life and have it abundantly* (John 10:10 ESV). He had a heart for all people. I often read and love to preach the "Good Shepherd" passages in the tenth chapter of John. I came across this prayer years ago and have made it my personal plea when I catch myself being arrogant or taking myself too seriously:

Gracious Lord, I exalt You, I lift Your holy name and give you all the thanks and the glory. You alone are worthy; only in You am I worthy. Continue to show me what it means to walk humbly with You. Help guide me not to have a spirit that is filled with pride but a spirit of humility. Teach me not to be arrogant but to recognize that You fill me and use me in my childlike faith. Lord, melt and mold my heart in true humility before You.

At times I wonder if shepherds in the church today are most like Jesus or more like Siddhartha?

Random thoughts for today:

Those who are well have no need of a physician, but those who are sick. I came not to call the righteous, but sinners. (Mark 2:17 ESV)

There is no shame in not knowing...The shame lies in not finding out. *(Russian Proverb)*

Bad theology hurts real people!!

The way up is always down.

We are so concerned with the "doing" rather than concentrating on the "being." *(Rebecca Crain)*

Thank You, Father, for the peace that comes from You as I daily lean into the palm of Your hand.

Comfort emanates from finding truth...Are you seeking comfort, or are you seeking truth?

Have you ever read through the Old Testament book of Habakkuk? It was probably written between 640 – 615 BC, just before the fall of Assyria and the rise of Babylon. The major theme of Habakkuk is, how can God use a wicked nation like Babylon for His divine purpose. Read the scripture below in the "Random Thoughts." Ever felt that way? Sure we have. If you read through the book in one sitting, you will discover many questions of the ages.

- Why do You tolerate wrong?
- Why do You put up with the treacherous who do violence all around us?
- Why are You silent while the wicked swallow up the righteous?
- Why is justice on earth so perverted?
- How long must this go on?
- Of what value are their idols; their images that teach lies?
- Will their false guidance ever give guidance and peace?
- WHY??
- Are You, Lord, not from everlasting?

Now take a few minutes and meditate on Habakkuk 2:20—*But the LORD is in His holy temple; let all the earth keep silence before Him.* But, Lord, how long must we stay silent as politicians lie and evil men around us are killing vulnerable people right and left (I wrote this in the aftermath of a mass shooting in Indianapolis two days ago)? Why? How long? In Habakkuk 1:5, the Lord answers—*I am doing a work in your days that you would not believe if I told you.* And in 2:4, he goes on to say—*The righteous shall live by his faith.* In chapter three, we find a lengthy prayer of Habakkuk. Set some time aside soon and study over that prayer. He concludes Habakkuk and his prayer with these words—*Yet I will rejoice in the LORD; I will take joy in the God of my salvation. God, the Lord, is my strength; he makes my feet like the deer's; He makes me tread on my high places* (Vv 18-19). By the way, this oracle was written to be sung with stringed instruments. Why not?

Random thoughts for today:

O LORD, how long shall I cry for help, and You will not hear? (Habakkuk 1:2 ESV)

The small routine tasks that fill every day may be, in fact, turned into one of the finest of spiritual disciplines, a special sacrament. *(Ernest Boyer Jr.)*

November 11   Lesson From a Veteran

Out of the furnaces of war come many true stories of sacrifice and honor. One account tells of two friends in World War I, who were inseparable. They had enlisted together, trained together, were shipped overseas together, and fought side-by-side in the trenches. During an attack, one of the men was critically wounded in a field filled with barbed wire obstacles, and he was unable to crawl back to his foxhole. The entire area was filled with enemy crossfire, and it was suicidal to try and reach him. Yet his friend decided to try. Before he could get out of his trench, his sergeant yanked him back inside and ordered him not to go. "It's too late.

You can't do him any good, and you'll only get yourself killed." A few minutes later, the officer turned his back, and instantly the man was gone after his friend. Shortly, he staggered back, mortally wounded, with his friend, now dead in his arms. The sergeant was both angry and deeply moved. "What a waste," he blurted out. "He's dead, and you're dying. It just wasn't worth it!" With almost his last breath, the dying man replied, "Oh, yes, it was, Sarge. When I got to him, the only thing he said to me was, "I knew you'd come, Jim." Without heroes we are all plain people and don't know how far we can go. I share this story on this Veteran's Day in tribute to my own hero...my veteran...my Dad.

Random thoughts for today:

Greater love has no one than this, that someone lay down his life for his friends. (John 15:13 ESV)

The character of your life many times is determined by how you handle Plan B.

I go down on my knee today, not to protest, but to pray for those who have and are faithfully serving.

Regardless of our circumstances, we who are in Christ should keep our heads...God has not given us a spirit of fear, but of power and of love, and of a sound mind. *(The apostle Paul)*

When our devotionals or teachers speak more about finding our lives than losing them, we miss out on the wonder of the Christian life.

I stop and give thanks today for our veterans and their service and for the freedoms I possess.

November 12   Speak Up!!
                        Social Media Post from my daughter

Speak up, I told myself, speak up
For the poor and the hurting and oppressed
Speak up, I promised myself, speak up
As the world spit out more hatred and unrest
And I did.
For a while.
But it got hard.
And I got tired.
And my voice became quieter as I was told in no uncertain terms...
that it should.
Those considered friends making known that love was conditional.
Those with shared experience deeming me dangerous or heretical
or unworthy
Making clear that to remain in the club, words must not be spoken
about things that might disrupt
Making it clear that to speak up is simply not allowed for a middle-
aged white girl who's expected to follow the rules.
But who is making these rules....
These rules that exclude and always seem to be about what we
should be against, but never about what we are for.
Rules that speak in veiled terms about "love" but look nothing like
'love your neighbor'
Absolutely nothing like 'love your neighbor.'
I want new rules....
Rules that are for
For nuance and generosity and the ability to not be so easily
offended
For mercy and kind words and hearing someone's story

For inclusion and belonging and community
I want new rules
So I try
Because I have to
And God nudges
while I try to sleep
Speak up, I tell myself, speak up
And I beg myself to comply
Not today, I'm too tired; I'm too sad
But I promise myself again...and again
To Speak up
(Posted April 20, 2021, by pastor Rebecca Crain)

Rather, speaking the truth in love... (Ephesians 4:15)

November 13   Trustworthy Testimony

C.S. Lewis said, "Though I cannot see why it should be so, I can tell you why I believe it is so." I first read that statement in the 1970s, and I've thought a lot about it numerous times since. Why was I baptized? Why do I pray? Why do I spend much time in scripture? Why does the Lord's Supper still draw me close to the Lord? And I parrot Lewis' words, "I don't always understand why it should be so, but I believe with all I am that it IS so." I believe that Jesus is the Christ, the Son of the living God. I believe that He is everything He claimed to be and did for me everything scripture says He did. I believe it on His authority. Lewis said 99% of the things we believe are believed on authority (although in this age of social media, that probably isn't true). I believe the accounts of scripture because the people who saw and experienced them left testimony. I have invested my life on that testimony (as many others before me have done). I have based all on that testimony because I believe the testifiers to be trustworthy, as I would hope that people who know me well would find me trustworthy. Because of this trustworthy testimony, I repeat, I believe that Jesus is the Christ, the Son of the living God. I believe that He died in my place upon the cross. I believe that on the third day, He arose from the dead, proving He was everything He claimed to be (seen by over 500 eyewitnesses). I believe He sent His Holy Spirit to empower the church and guide us in His absence. I believe that the Church throughout the world is His body, commissioned to preach the good news to all nations. I believe that He will return, as He promised, to gather His people to Him at the end of the age. And in the words of that chorus I learned as a toddler,

**"Yes, Jesus loves me; Yes, Jesus loves me;
Yes, Jesus loves me, the Bible tells me so."**

Random thoughts for today:

What you have heard from me in the presence of many witnesses entrust to faithful men who will be able to teach others also. (2 Timothy 2:2 ESV)

Courage is fear holding on a minute longer. *(George S. Patton)*
A humble mind is the soil out of which thanks naturally grows.
When I can't think of anything to say, HE says what I can't say.

Good morning, Lord...I come before You to refresh myself in the peace of Your presence. *(Prayer from my personal journal – 2020)*

Why is peace such an elusive inner quality in me? In one of my journals I wrote down quite a few years ago—"Peace is that calm of mind and soul that is not ruffled by adversity, overclouded by a remorseful conscience, or disturbed by fear...Sounds good... When do I start practicing it?" It seems that peace is an antithesis of everything that exists in our culture today. H.G. Wells once said, "I cannot adjust my life to secure any fruitful peace. Here I am at sixty-four, still seeking peace. It is a hopeless dream." Is it? One guy said, "When somebody gets arrested for disturbing the peace these days, I'm surprised he found any." Peace within is something I've struggled with for a lot of years. Stress and worry have won many battles in my life. It seems to be a little easier to win that war in these later years, but it certainly is not a complete victory. I haven't found the pastoral ministry to be the ideal place to discover it. It's not hiding in the annals of social media. Jesus has told me again and again, *My peace I leave with you; my peace I give to you. Not as the world gives do I give to you. Let not your hearts be troubled, neither let them be afraid* (John 14:27 ESV). And sometimes I listen. Often, I discover (or rediscover) the peace that is found in my walk with Christ, and then I forget and have to relearn the truth that peace is the deliberate adjustment of my life to the will of God. The result of my asking God will be my peace of mind. What does that old song from 1955 say? "Let there be peace on earth; and let it begin with me."

<u>Random thoughts for today</u>:

And the peace of God which surpasses all understanding, will guard your hearts and your minds in Christ Jesus. (Philippians 4:7 ESV)

Seasons of gratitude for God's people are always to be a big deal!!

Sometimes when we get overwhelmed, we forget how big God is.

Complaining expresses the accusations of the enemy. *(International House of Prayer, Kansas City))*

I have found that writing something down often works as a magnet for other thoughts. *(One of many reasons I journal.)*

November 15   Falling Rain

What has God taught you lately that has truly lifted you up, maybe even in the midst of despair? Some days I feel as vulnerable as the grass of the field or the questionable quality of grass in my yard being choked out by many weeds. I feel like that touching song we sing in church,

> **"All who are thirsty; all who are weak. Just come to the fountain, dip your heart in the stream of life. Let the pain and the sorrow be washed away, in the waves of His mercy...As deep cries out to deep."**

I love the New Living Translation of the Deuteronomy scripture listed below—*Let my teaching fall on you like rain; Let my words fall like rain on tender grass.* The Lord's words are life to those who are thirsty. They're like a drink of freshwater when we are weary. Aren't you glad that He doesn't dump all that He has for you all at once? He doesn't drown us in a flood of insight, but rather He saturates us with His teaching when we are in need, like a gentle rain. His word always seems to be there for me when I need it. At those times, this is my prayer:

> **"Let your Spirit come, fall upon me now**
> **And let the rain fall down, fall upon my soul**
> **Come and wash me now, come and make me whole."**

Random thoughts for today:

May my teaching drop like the rain, my speech distill as the dew, like gentle rain upon the tender grass, and like showers upon the herb. (Deuteronomy 32:2 ESV)

A friend walks in when others walk out.

When in interpretive doubt, we should always default to following the grace and mercy of Jesus Christ. *(Nate Loucks)*

A spiritual leader can't nourish others if he has not allowed the Word of God to be born within.

Never cut what you can untie.

My faith is personal, but not private.

November 16   Nationalism

Putting it perhaps too simply, nationalism is an ideology based on the premise that the individual's loyalty and devotion to the nation-state surpass all other individual or group interests.

Patriotism, on the other hand, is a commitment to a nation, love of country, if you will. The two terms are often incorrectly used synonymously. However, patriotism had its origins some 2000 years prior to the rise of nationalism in the 19th century. Greek and Roman antiquity provides the roots for political patriotism, a loyalty to a republic. It is associated with the love of law and common freedom, the belief in the common good, and behaving justly toward one's country. If you study the two terms and their history carefully, you'll see a great difference. One historian has said nationalism is basically concern for a nation above concern for individuals who live there and can easily evolve into believing that one's nation should be more powerful than any other nation. It's always been interesting to notice that most churches have an American flag in a prominent place in their worship rooms. Nothing wrong with that, I guess. Many congregations have special recognitions on Memorial Day, Veteran's Day, and Independence Day. Nothing wrong with that. I found myself feeling proud when my father was honored and received special honor as a WW2 veteran. I love my country. I have stated in a previous entry (February 2), "But let us be cautious that we don't equate nationalism with faithful allegiance to Jesus Christ. I am not called by God to save a republic." I can't help but remember a poster I saw not too long ago—"Not for societies or states Christ died, but for men."

Random thoughts for today:

Let every person be subject to the governing authorities, for there is no authority except from God, and those that exist have been instituted by God. (Romans 13:1 ESV)

494

Patriotism consists not in waving the flag but in striving that our country shall be righteous as well as strong. *(James Bryce)*

The foundation of my prayer life is not that I change the Lord... But rather that He changes me.

The eating will give you the appetite. *(Columbian Proverb)*

One of the deepest longings a person can have is to feel needed and essential.

You may never know what results come from your actions, but if you do nothing, there will be no results.

November 17   Christian?

Who do You say that I am? Peter answered Him and said, "You are the Christ, the Son of the living God."

What IS a Christian? What's the definition? As an adjective, the dictionary says it is relating to or professing the teachings of Christianity. That was helpful. As a noun, the Webster crowd says it is a person who has received Christian baptism or believes in Christianity. One source says that Christianity is an Abrahamic monotheistic religion based on the life and teachings of Jesus of Nazareth. It is the world's largest religion, with about 2.4 billion followers. So, are you one of those? It is Peter's confession of faith—*I believe that Jesus is the Christ, the Son of the living God* (Matthew 16:16). It is believing that Jesus is everything He claimed to be and did everything He said He would do. Jesus is the Christ, the Son of the living God...because He is the Christ, the Son of the living God. If everyone on the planet rejected this statement, He would still be the Christ, the Son of the living God!! If you do not embrace this truth, then you may be a "follower" of Jesus of Nazareth as a great man and an extraordinary teacher (Muhammad proclaimed Him to be a prophet), and you may attempt to live a life based on his teaching, but you are NOT a Christian.

(*)If you are a seeker, one who is honestly studying the claims of Christianity, *Mere Christianity,* by C. S. Lewis is a volume that I recommend.

Random thoughts for today:

For I delivered to you as of first importance what I also received: that Christ died for our sins in accordance with the Scriptures, that He was buried, that He was raised on the third day in accordance with the Scriptures... (1 Corinthians 15:3-4 ESV)

Thankfulness is the seed of faith.
People are people, nothing more...God is God, nothing less.
Why are we generous—Because we care...Some lives are like one grand selfie!!
Lord, help me develop those times of doing nothing.
The devil can quote scripture for his own agenda.
Pie makes everybody happy.

November 18   Red-Letter Christians

When I graduated from the Junior Department of my Sunday School, my church gave me a World Publishing Company Holy Bible, King James Version, copyrighted in 1945. It was a "red-letter" edition (first published in 1899). The front page of the

New Testament says, "With all the words recorded therein as having been spoken by our Lord printed in red." If you're not familiar with this kind of Bible, it means that anytime Jesus spoke, it is printed in red ink. Somewhere along the line, I lost track of that Bible, but I recently inherited my dad's Bible, same edition. I've been using that version this year in my personal time in scripture. I go through my New Testament each morning and study the words in red ink. It's been a great exercise. As a result, I've started a sermon series on the Sermon on the Mount from Matthew, chapters 5-6-7. This is something you may want to try in the future. There are lots and lots of "red" in the Gospels. You can also find a few red verses in the Book of Acts (chapters 1, 9, 11, 18, 20, 22, 23, 26), I Corinthians 11, II Corinthians 12, and the Book of Revelation (chapters 1, 2, 3, 16, 21, 22). There are several devotional books available on the red-letter words of Jesus. You can still purchase red-letter editions in other translations. It can be a helpful practice if we understand that *all scripture is breathed out by God and profitable for teaching, for reproof, for correction, and for training in righteousness* (2 Timothy 3:16 ESV). This recent devotional study has also helped me when I'm asked the question, "Did Jesus really say that?" I must be honest and confess that I have asked that question numerous times myself. Understanding this has made a big difference in my continuing journey. Did Jesus really say that? Yup!! He really did.

Random thoughts for today:

You have heard it said to those of old, "You shall not murder, and whoever murders will be liable to judgment." But I say to you that everyone who is angry with his brother will be liable to judgment...

(Jesus - Matthew 5:21-22 ESV) ***Also check out Matthew 5:27-28; 31-32; 33-34; 38-39; 43-44

Sometimes my ministry lies more in powerlessness than in power, and I can only give my tears.

A very important thing my dad taught me is that there are many more important things than me.

Quit saying, "Marriage is just a piece of paper."...So is money, but you get up every morning to work for it.

Is it time to D.T.R. with Jesus?—"Define the Relationship" (Kyle Idleman)

November 19   Funerals

It seems that I have been attending funerals a lot lately. They say that this is a part of the life of someone like me who is getting older. I recently conducted the memorial service for one of my closest friends of over 50 years (May-2021 *). Have you ever wondered where our funeral practices come from? A brief look backward would seem to establish that there is no resemblance between the funeral/burial practices of today and those of even 50 to 100 years ago. On the contrary, the significant features of the contemporary American funeral (beautification of the corpse, metal casket and vault, and banks of store-bought floral arrangements are all newer practices in this country). One friend of mine said, "The current price of funerals is enough to make you glad that you're alive!" I believe that there are three purposes for a Christian funeral: 1) To honor the loved one who has passed on; 2) To remember that loved one; memories can be precious gifts from the Lord; 3) To comfort and be comforted. Most memorial services contain sudden unanimous praise and the miraculous disappearance of criticism and reservation of the dearly departed. I believe that there is a place for a memorial service and even a time of visiting with the grieving family, but I have absolutely no desire to have numerous people file by my caskets saying, "Don't they look good." (My wife and I have both agreed and we vote for cremation). I love the sign on a casket of a funeral I attended when I was in college that said, "Please don't grieve over this shell I've left behind; I moved out four days ago." Perhaps the greatest purpose of a funeral service is proclaiming the answer to the question in the scripture listed below. Read John 11:25-26 below. Did you notice the last four words of that verse? Jesus said, *DO YOU BELIEVE THIS?* The purpose of the memorial service is to declare it loudly—YES, WE BELIEVE IT!!

(*) Written three days after the memorial service of my friend, Bob McMonigal...I have used the scripture below in every memorial service I have conducted.

Random thoughts for today:

I am the resurrection and the life. Whoever believes in Me, though he dies, yet shall he live, and everyone who lives and believes in Me shall never die. Do you believe this? (John 11:25-26 ESV)

O Lord, that lends me life, lend me a heart replete with thankfulness. *(William Shakespeare)*

"Stay" is a charming word in a friend's vocabulary. *(Louisa May Alcott)*

We are made kind by being kind.

On St. Werburgh Street, in Chester, Cheshire, England, is an ancient cathedral, construction dating back to 1093, having been modified several times through history. The site has been used for Christian worship since Roman times. It is currently a Church of England cathedral and the mother church of the Diocese of Chester. It was formerly the abbey church of a Benedictine monastery, and since 1541, it has been the seat of the Bishop of Chester. Closed because of the pandemic, it has recently opened again to the public, including tours of the 216-step tower. It is many things to many people: a vibrant community of worship, an ancient abbey, an archaeological treasure, a center of excellent music, and a unique blend of medieval and modern history. Recently, an anonymous prayer was discovered in the cathedral:

> **"Give me good digestion, Lord, and also something to digest.**
>
> **Give me a healthy body, Lord, with sense to keep it at its best.**
>
> **Give me a healthy mind, good Lord, to keep the good and pure in sight, which seeing sin is not appalled, but finds a way to set it right.**
>
> **Give me a mind that is not bored, that does not whimper whine, or sigh.**
>
> **Don't let me worry over so much about the fussy thing called "I."**

Give me a sense of humor, Lord; give me the grace to see a joke, to get some happiness from life and pass it on to other folk. Amen."

Devote yourselves to prayer, being watchful and thankful. (Colossians 4:2 ESV)

Gratitude beget generosity!!
I dwell in possibility. *(Emily Dickinson)*
No one has ever become poor by giving.
You have to expect things of yourself before you can do them.

November 21   Tribute to a Best Friend

On May 22, 2021, I got a call from Greg Weiler's wife, Lynn. He had just passed away. When Helen and I got over to the house, Greg was still on the kitchen floor. We waited and prayed together for the funeral director to arrive. How do I sum up a relationship of over 35 years? In my first prayer devotional published ten years ago, I stated, "I have someone who goes beyond the 'normal' levels of friendship, someone with whom I can be totally open and vulnerable. Someone who loves me enough to ask me the hard questions. The rigorous demands of that kind of friendship, the gift of oneself, one's time, one's preferences, the nakedness and honesty, are beyond the price many are willing to pay. Anyone who has been graced with a true friendship like that knows the cost and the value." Greg and I were accountability partners. We believed that true loving friendship was not being afraid to ask the hard questions. Like what? Like, how's your prayer life? How's your walk with the Lord going? Are you spending time in the Word? Are you honest in your actions and your words? Are you living out the gospel in your daily life? Has anything taken priority in your life this past week that shouldn't be there? How are you progressing with the pride struggle in your life? I have many relationships but few true friends that I trust without reservation. I'm not talking about perfection. All men are flawed and have the potential to let me down, but I trust them anyway. I have few friends like that. Thomas Jefferson said, "True friendship is precious, not only in the sunshine of life but in the dark shadows of life as well." A true friend is one who knows the worst and dark side of me and doesn't turn his face away. Do you have a friend like that? I did. I guess friendship doesn't have anything to do with how many "friends" you have on Facebook, does it?

(Written 5-23-21...I conducted Greg Weiler's memorial service on 5-29-21)

Random thoughts for today:

A man of many companions may come to ruin, but there is a friend who sticks closer than a brother. (Proverbs 18:24 ESV)

Wishing to be friends is quick work, but friendship is a slow ripening fruit. *(Benjamin Franklin)*

Friendship is a union of spirits; a marriage of sorts of two hearts." *(William Penn)*

You've got a friend in me...You've got troubles; I've got 'em too... There isn't anything I wouldn't do for you. *(Randy Newman—Toy Story)*

November 22   Loving the People

I was re-watching the old *West Wing* TV series. In one of the earlier episodes, a hot debate ensues between members of the progressive Bartlett administration and a very conservative young lawyer over gun control. It's very obvious that the Bartlett people are very anti-gun, which is understandable after an assassination attempt that wounded President Bartlett. The conversation gets pretty heated when the young lawyer makes a statement that I haven't forgotten. She says, "You don't just hate the guns; you don't like the people who have the guns." It made an impression on me that really doesn't have anything to do with gun control. I remember the old sarcastic pun of my Bible college days, "The church would be great if it weren't for the people!" I've thought about that a lot lately, especially in the last number of months. It has dawned on me, or at least it seems, that much of the church today really doesn't care much for people—those outside the church and even some inside the church, especially if they are different than we are. Through the years, I've participated in many conversations (I guess you call them that), sarcastically putting down other denominations, making pronouncements about their erroneous doctrinal positions. Of course, we always did it in "love;" you know, truth in love. I think those kinds of discussions reveal more truth in us than we would like to admit. We forget that in talking about people who differ from us (doctrine, ethnicity, sexual preference, etc.), we are speaking of people. We don't just hate the belief systems; we don't like the people who believe them. Sarah Bessey said it best—"Lord, teach us to love the world again!"

Random thoughts for today:

You shall love your neighbor as yourself. (Jesus - Matthew 22:39 ESV)

A thankful heart is the parent of all other virtues.

Nothing speaks louder or more powerfully than a life of integrity.

I ask not for a lighter burden but for broader shoulders. *(Jewish Proverb)*

Laws control the lesser man...Doing the right thing controls the greater man. *(Mark Twain)*

Lord, may I not be one who "understands" everything too soon.

What our nation needs right now is a gratitude attitude!!

November 23   Expressions of Thanks
                                                 From 3 Sources

My wife grew up on a farm in northern Indiana. Because of harvest time, it was one of the busiest times of their year. Helen's mom, Lillian Edith, didn't use the term thanksgiving as much as she did, "harvest time." She told me once that her favorite hymn this time of the year was "We Gather Together," not just because people and families gathered together, but because it reminded her of the gathering of the harvest (both physically and spiritually). Maybe you've never thought of Leviticus containing thanksgiving stuff. Leviticus 19:9-10 ESV says, *When you reap the harvest of your land, do not reap to the very edges of your field or gather the gleanings of your harvest. So go over your vineyard a second time or pick up the grapes that have fallen. Leave them for the poor and the alien. I am the LORD your God.* Perhaps it is no accident that the very next verse says, *Do not steal.* I've been thinking about that. Martin Luther wrote, "If our goods are not available to the community, they are stolen goods." Hmmm...

A Disciples of Christ pastor from Indianapolis shared this prayer years ago:

> "O God, when I have food, help me to remember the hungry;
>
> When I have work, help me remember the jobless;
>
> When I have a home, help me to remember those who have no home at all;
>
> When I am without pain, help me to remember those who suffer.
>
> And remembering, help me to destroy my complacency;
>
> Bestir my compassion to be concerned enough to help;
>
> By word and deed for those who cry out for what we take for granted. Amen." (Samuel F. Pugh)

Three sources...Three expressions of thanks. Moses, Samuel Pugh, and third from Lillian Edith—"Harvest time is thanks time...Gratitude begets generosity!"

Random thoughts for today:

Generosity is giving more than you can, and pride is taking less than you need. *(Khalil Gibran)*

You do not have to be rich to be generous.

November 24   Spirit of Generosity

Psalm 69:36 says *I will praise God's name in song and glorify Him with thanksgiving.* There is no place where our lives bear a more evident witness than in the discipline of generosity and the practice of daily thanksgiving. One writer defines generosity as "the quality of being kind and liberal in what you give to others." I often pray that the Lord may open me up to others and free me from my self-centeredness; that He will lead me into specific ways of generosity to others, for releasing and for sharing. Because everything I am and have, I owe to the Lord and to others, there is an urgency within me to give thanks and praise to the Lord. William Jennings Bryan has said, "When we give thanks, we acknowledge our dependence." I like that. As you continue along your journey, do you take things for granted or take them with gratitude? May I encourage you to get up every morning and focus on what you do have in life. Do you want to turn your life around? Try thankfulness; it will change your life!! The spirit of true thanksgiving will build a spirit of generosity within you.

Being generous often consists of simply extending a hand. And don't forget, the most important prayer in the world is just two words long—"Thank You!"

Are you still engaged in your thanks journal experiment?

Random thoughts for today:

...for God loves a cheerful giver. (2 Corinthians 9:7 ESV)

We rarely have time to do everything we want to do...Make good choices.

No duty is more urgent than that of returning thanks. *(Ambrose)*

This day I pray in the name of Your Son, O Lord, who loved children and flowers and people.

Generosity is an activity that loosens us up.

Be kind, for everyone you meet is fighting a hard battle.

The gifts we treasure most over the years are often small and simple.

Family traditions make occasions feel special and exciting. They mark the passage of time in a happy way, and they provide a sense of anticipation, security, and continuity.

November 25   Give Thanks

Don Moen's chorus some time back has resonated in my spirit for many years. "Give thanks with a grateful heart..." so the chorus goes. It has blessed me and taught me and convicted me all at the same time. I find it difficult not to tear up when I sing it. "Give thanks to the Holy One..." I sit here by the fire on a cold, crisp morning, realizing how blessed I am to be living in a nation where the average American misplaces more money each year than the majority of people on the planet earn. That leaky faucet in our kitchen represents, in one day, more water than the average Asian family in a drought-stricken area will drink or use in a month. The chorus continues: "And now, let the weak say, 'I am strong;' let the poor say, 'I am rich'..." Am I strong? It depends upon how you define strength. Am I rich? My retirement income is 4-5 times the average per capita income worldwide. The average per capita in Sub-Saharan Africa is under $2000. I cringe when a member of the US Congress says, "Our generation of youth has never known prosperity." This chorus we sing in church tells us the weak are strong, and the poor are rich because of what the Lord has done for us. My life changed when I finally realized that my God was for me. "Give thanks to the Holy One; because He's given Jesus Christ, His Son." I find myself saying over and over and over again, "Thank You, Lord...Thank You...Thank You!!" Ambrose, archbishop of Milan, wrote, "No duty is more urgent than that of returning thanks." And why wouldn't we want to do that duty?

Random thoughts for today:

Give thanks to the LORD; sing to Him, sing praises to His name. (Psalms 105 ESV)

What qualifies me most to pray?...My helplessness!!
We must keep ourselves in touch, not with theories, but with people.

Last night I decided to count my blessings, it wouldn't take me very long...But O how I misjudged the grace of God for tonight, I'm still going strong.

God has given us a life...It's a gift...Enjoy it!!

Reading Recommendation: *The Remarkable Ordinary* (Frederick Buechner)

November 26   Duck and Cover

Have you ever heard the old line, "Living in a garage doesn't make you an automobile, any more than being in church doesn't make you a Christ-follower?" Preachers used to say that a lot when I was growing up. The Jews of Jesus' day believed that they had their backs covered, no matter what, because they were related to Abraham—"We're good because we're descended from Abraham." Through the years, I've met many professed believers who sincerely believed that if they were members of a church and attended faithfully, they automatically possessed a spiritual get-out-of-jail-free card. I've known others who believed that their good works would get them entrance into the kingdom of heaven. Some of you (depends upon whether you were in school in the 1950s) may remember the old "duck and cover" drills we practiced so that we would be ready for any potential nuclear attack. When the signal was given, we all immediately crawled under our desks, bowed down, and covered our heads with our hands. I understood some of the logic behind that, but no one really believed that a sheet of plywood over us would save us from the atom bomb. As a boy, I memorized Ephesians 2:8-9—*For by grace you have been saved through faith, and this is not your own doing, it is the gift of God, not a result of works, so that no one may boast.*

I was in elementary school attending Vacation Bible School, and it was the beginning of great impact upon my life—SAVED BY GRACE!! Do you believe it? I sometimes wonder if we get sucked into accepting our membership or participation in the church as our duck and cover?

Random thoughts for today:

Just as Abraham believed God, and it was counted to him as righteousness, know then that it is those of faith who are sons of Abraham. (Galatians 3:6-7 ESV)

Thanksgiving! Thanksgiving! All must be thanksgiving!
How do I describe the "well-lived" life? Look at Jesus*!!*
Always keep my heart ready to give itself away.
It's easier to think of everyone as your friend so that hate doesn't get in the way.

November 27   Petitions Not Granted

Have you ever had anyone tell you that a prayer was not answered because you didn't have enough faith? There are congregations and movements out there that will drill that message home. I remember speaking with a young woman in Australia years ago who was told by her church that she continued to be blind because she just didn't believe enough for a healing. Mark 11:24-25 says *I tell you, whatever you ask in prayer, believe that you have received it, and it will be yours. And whenever you stand praying, forgive....*Jesus said that. Does that scripture say that <u>whatever</u> I ask for, with faith, I shall receive? I've been told this many times by many Christians. With enough faith, can I actually pick up mountains and throw them into the sea? Does the context of Jesus addressing the withered fig tree or the caveat of my forgiving others have anything to do with it? Perhaps? I don't know. I believe in miracles. I've seen some remarkable answers to prayer. But when I don't receive the response I prayed for, is this indicative of an imperfect faith on my part? In every war, every plague, every famine, every death (I've attended the funerals of two 15-year-olds in the last two months—I heard lots of prayers from lots of believers), we see testimonies of ungranted petitions. We have knocked, but the door is unopened. How do I reconcile Mark 11:24-25 with personal experience in my ministry? Perhaps I need to temper my questions with the prayer of Jesus in Gethsemane—*"If it be Your will, Father?"* Did Jesus lack faith when he prayed, "Father, can this cup of suffering pass from Me?" What about God answering one guy's prayer, which involves refusing another guy's prayer? I know that my faith is strong enough to trust my Father, even when His response is not what I desire. God may not always respond in a way I expect, but I believe He is always listening...My Listener is always present. As I grow older, I have more questions than answers. Know what? I was much more comfortable when I had all the answers. Maybe it's not about my comfort.

Random thoughts for today:

Hear my prayer, O LORD, and give ear to my cry; hold not Your peace at my tears. (Psalm 39:12 ESV)

O Lord, that lends me life, lend me a heart replete with thankfulness.

He preaches well who lives well...That's all the theology I know. *(Cervantes)*

Love isn't a state of perfect caring—It's an active noun, like struggle.

They are well guided that God guides. *(Scottish Proverb)*

November 28   Advent

This day (in the year 2021) is the first Sunday of Advent. Advent begins four Sundays before Christmas and ends on Christmas Eve. Each week in the Catholic Mass, the phrase is used, "we wait in joyful hope for the coming of our Lord Jesus Christ." The word advent means "coming." The lighting of advent candles was not a part of the tradition in which I was raised, but we began it as a family tradition when our kids were quite young. We began to incorporate it into our weekly December worship services at our church in the 1970s. Today, I have a small advent wreath in my personal devotional area. The tradition continues in the congregation where Helen and I serve. Through the years, we have seen the Christmas story from different perspectives—the prophets, Elizabeth, Mary, Joseph, the shepherds. When our children were still at home, we would have our special advent time on Sunday evening. Each member of the family would bring something to the table to share—a scripture, a song, a poem, a devotional thought. Then we would light a candle. Special times, special memories. As a family, we were reminded that while Christmas is a glorious time, it was our human sinfulness and separation from God that made it necessary for Jesus to come to earth. We remember the greatest part of the Christmas story again: the self-sacrificing love of God for the people of the world, for all of us—*For God so loved the world that He gave His one and only Son...*(John 3:16). Paul tells us that in the fulness of time, God sent His Son to us. What a moment that was when the Word became flesh. Advent is the name of that moment.

Random thoughts for today:

And the Word became flesh and dwelt among us, and we have seen His glory, glory as of the only Son from the Father, full of grace and truth. (John 1:14 ESV)

Lots of talk this season (2020) about "canceling" Christmas because of the pandemic...Kind of comical when you think about it.

Being nice is not the same as choosing kind. *(5ᵗʰ-grade girl)*

Always keep your heart ready to give itself away.

Thank God for the gardeners around you who make your soul blossom.

There's nothing so absurd but some philosopher has said it. *(Cicero)*

November 29   Open My Heart

In my February 22 entry, I discussed the concept of guarding our hearts (Also, read the entries from November 8-9). Have you picked up on the tension and balance between the concepts of *Guard your heart, for everything you do flows from it* (Proverbs 4:33), and *I will remove the heart of stone from you and will give you a heart of flesh* (Ezekiel 36:27)? And Jeremiah 17:9 explains why that tension exists—*The heart is deceitful above all things and desperately sick; who can understand it?* Is guarding my heart important? Of course it is. Have you noticed that Satan often attacks when your guard is down? Many times, the attack comes through those you trust and to whom you have opened your heart. So, yeah, guard your heart! But Jesus teaches that we are to keep our hearts open to others. How do we do both? Ah, there is the conundrum. I contend that it is impossible to pull it off apart from the Holy Spirit. If we're not careful, we can find ourselves in the same boat as the woman who said, "I've been hurt by love, so I quit loving. I will not entrust my heart to anyone else ever again." I have learned, and am still learning, that my ability to entrust my heart to the Lord is the secret and foundation of my opening my heart to others around me. A lyric has come from Hillsong that beautifully describes that entrusting—

> **"This is my desire, to honor You, Lord with all my heart I worship You**
>
> **All I have within me I give You praise, All that I adore is in You."**

As I have previously stated, only the Lord can change a heart. The Holy Spirit is my primary tool in guarding my heart and keeping me fiercely faithful. And it is the Spirit that guides me through that labyrinth of keeping my heart open through it all and being fiercely and unconditionally loving to others.

Random thoughts for today:

Create in me a pure heart, O God, and renew a steadfast spirit within me. (Psalm 51:10 ESV)

What I kept, I lost...What I spent, I had...What I gave, I have. *(Persian Proverb)*

Allow your opinions to be enriched by the insights of others.

When it's dark, be the one who turns on the light.

I have discovered the reason for my praying is not receiving things, but instead, it is the intimacy of relationship with my Lord.

As a general rule, teachers teach more by what they are than by what they say.

November 30   What Do You Miss Most as a Kid?

In both of my prayer devotionals, I've often used the prayer, "Lord, keep the kid alive in me." I love that prayer, and I love that concept. There are three previous entries in this volume sharing actual prayers prayed by real kids. I was probably in my forties when I was first introduced to the concept of "growing down." That's part of the reason I'm still such a Christmas junkie. I was listening to talk radio a few days ago, the host asked a question and asked for call-ins—"What do you miss most about being a kid?" Feeling a bit nostalgic today, I worked on the list of my own kid memories:

- Playing sandlot baseball with other kids in the neighborhood
- Riding my bike with my best friend, and especially through flooded streets after a big rain
- Catching fireflies and putting dozens of them in a Mason jar (after punching holes in the top, of course) and pretending it was a lantern
- Singing simple choruses in Sunday school

- Getting neighborhood kids together and putting on a show
- Getting my dog all fired up by simply shouting, "Squirrel!"
- The excitement of Christmas morning (My brother and I were usually awake at three or four am)
- Going to the beach; building stuff in the sand
- Going to Grandma Jones's house in Modoc, Indiana; sleeping in a feather bed
- Going anywhere with my Dad
- The childlike faith and awe of my first-time taking communion

This, of course, is not anywhere near an exhaustive list. I Corinthians 13 says, *When I was a child, I spoke like a child, I thought like a child, I reasoned like a child. When I became a man, I gave up childish ways* (V 11). I have no problem with giving up childish ways. But may the CHILDLIKE ways of my past always stay with me—Keep the kid alive in me!! How about creating your own list today?

Random thoughts for today:

Train up a child in the way he should go; even when he is old, he will not depart from it. (Proverbs 22:6 ESV)

Bring love into your homes...Your family is a gift from God.

December

Carve Your Name On Hearts...Not Marble
(C.H. Spurgeon)

December 1   The Eyes of My Heart

The scripture near the bottom of the page in Random Thoughts is one that I have used several times in this book. I appreciate the paraphrase by Eugene Peterson in *The Message* that simply says, "We are going to love—love and be loved. First, we were loved, now we love. He loved us first." Isn't that great? God not only is love, God not only loves us, but He loves us unconditionally! Our love for others around us is born out of that love; it continues to mature because of that love. There are some mornings when I am spending time with the Lord that I can almost hear Him say, "You must gaze at me, Rick, through the eyes of your heart." And I can hear the words of the chorus I've sung many times in worship, "Open the eyes of my heart, Lord, I want to see You." It continues to bring peace to me as I reflect and claim that promise of His absolute and total love for me. So why do I struggle so much to see others around me through the eyes of my heart? Am I loving without reservation the friend who betrayed me, turned his back on me? How about the individual who told lies about me? Or the ones who hate me because of my personal beliefs? And then there was the guy who flipped me off last week in traffic. Why do I struggle with those people? Why do I wish negative things for them when they cause me to lose my composure and "Christian" countenance? Why can't I just see them through the eyes of my heart as You see me? Maybe, just maybe, it comes down to the condition of my heart.

Random thoughts for today:

We love because He first loved us. (1 John 4:19 ESV)

When your heart aches for those no longer with you at the holidays, transform your pain into a prayer of thanksgiving.

An eye for an eye leaves everybody blind.

In war you can only be killed once...In politics, many times. *(Winston Churchill)*

December 2   The Social Media Verse

Have you ever given any thought to a scripture like Psalm 4:4?—*Be angry, but do not sin; ponder in your own hearts, on your beds, and be silent.* One writer said anonymously, "I was born with my heart on my sleeve, a fire in my soul, and a mouth I can't control." To quote the Eugene Peterson paraphrase of this verse—"Keep your mouth shut, and let your heart do the talking." I like to call this scripture the social media sacred scripture. There seem to be many folks who have no idea this scripture exists, or maybe don't care that it exists. By the way, SEVERAL scriptures address this same concept. I can't help but remember the words of Mark Twain when he wrote, "Better to keep your mouth shut and appear stupid than to open it and remove all doubt." Yeah!! How beautiful it is to stay silent when someone expects you to be enraged. One guy said, "I should get an award for being silent; I mean, how can I keep my mouth shut when there is so much that needs to be said?" Read that scripture at the top of the page again. I'm ready to call for a moratorium encouraging all Christians to get off social media. Contrary to what you think, there isn't much witnessing going on there; not a great amount of truth being shared in love. I believe the church would benefit more if we fasted from Facebook, Twitter, and all the rest (perhaps for a long, long time). Keep your mouth shut and let your heart (and your lives) do the talking...I love it. And oh yes, keeping your tongue includes the control of your fingers on the keyboard. My daily prayer...

Lord, keep your arm around my shoulder and your hand over my mouth.

Random thoughts for today:

Whoever keeps his mouth and his tongue keeps himself out of trouble. (Proverbs 21:23 ESV)

I love the Messianic prophecy of Isaiah 9—People walking in darkness have seen a great light... Christmas is coming!!

Think once before you act, twice before you speak, and three times before you post on Facebook. (*Paul Carrick Brunson*)

Remember me in your prayers as you do in your gossip.

Turn your wounds into wisdom.

I often say that life was a lot more fun when I had all the answers. The older I get, the more questions I have. I recently jotted down a number of questions in my mind that I would like to ask the Lord in a sit-down over coffee. Lord...

- How am I doing in balancing priorities in my life and my ministry?
- How much of what we do in our churches actually worships and pleases You?
- How much of our agendas in our churches today coincide with Your agenda?
- What dishonors You in the evangelical church? What dishonors You in the progressive church today?
- How do You feel about the many theological doctrines that divide Your church?
- Is Your definition of social justice the same as my definition?
- How do You really feel about the LBGTQ+ movement? What should our response be?
- Do You really care about politics? Do you care who I vote for? Would Jesus vote in an election?

These are not meant to be "stir-the-pot" questions; I ponder them often. I'd love to have honest discussions over them. And each year, I have more questions than answers. QUESTIONS?? Even though I have fewer answers, I love You, Lord; I trust you!! You are still my rock and my refuge. Lord, no matter what, make me love as I ought to love.

Random thoughts for today:

Why do you pass judgment on your brother? Or you, why do you despise your brother? For we will all stand before the judgment seat of God...Each one of us will account of himself to God. (Romans 15:10; 12)

Where do we draw the line between legitimate use and extravagant accumulation?

When I'm tempted to judge someone today, I'll look over my own life and bite my tongue.

I keep forgetting that the Holy Spirit can't be manipulated or regulated.

The one who forgives ends the quarrel. *(African Proverb)*

The tragedy of life is not in the fact of death but in what dies inside of us while we live. *(Norman Cousins)*

Today's church needs once again to see the glory of God.

December 4   Revisiting Big or Little Church

In my first prayer devotional (written over ten years ago), I discussed the pros and cons of "big church" vs. "small church." I recently reread that entry and began thinking about my first ministry in central Indiana vs. my ministry in northern Indiana during the 1980s and 1990s. The former was a church of about 30 people; the latter, around 1200+ at the height of that ministry. Again I was reminded of a statement I made ten years ago—"What matters is not how many people are showing up, but how active and vibrant their faith is in the God they serve." So it would appear that Helen and I have come full-circle. When we decided to step down from school teaching, I prayed that the Lord might open the door to minister to a small congregation, possibly part-time. That same summer of my retirement, I received a call to help a little flock very close to closing their doors after ministering for over 150 years (See July 3 entry). At this writing, we have been with this congregation for over two years. There have been a few who discouraged us from getting involved with this little church. I was even told by two pastors, "You're wasting your time!" We had 55 precious souls this last Easter Sunday and just over 30 people this past week. Again, it's not how many are showing up; but it's exciting that Helen and I are no longer the youngest in the building. I have no idea what the Lord has in mind for this small flock, but I pray each morning that the Lord's will be done at New Carlisle Community Church (And that prayer has nothing to do with how many people are there). A month or so ago, a seasoned pastor approached me and asked me how I was doing. I shared with him what was happening in our ministry at New Carlisle. He put his hand on my shoulder, looked me in the eye and said, "Remember, Rick, every church, no matter how small, needs a pastor."

Random thoughts for today:

Where two or three are gathered in my name, there am I among them. (Matthew 18:20 ESV)

If you have one true friend, you have more than your share.

God is always trying to give good things to us, but many times our hands are too full to receive them. *(Augustine)*

The work can wait while you show the child the rainbow, but the rainbow won't wait while you do the work.

How much time do we focus on what we don't have rather than what we do have?

We make a mistake in ministry by always measuring achievement and neglecting smallness.

December 5 — The Problem with Buzzwords

We are a culture of buzzwords. A few years ago, I would hear the word "awesome" at least a dozen times a day. The word would be used to describe God or a taco. It would seem to me that the major problem here has to do with definition. Buzzwords mean so many different things to different people. At present, the word "amazing" seems to have replaced awesome. My pastor is amazing!! It doesn't really tell me anything, except that you like him/her. The two years of the pandemic have brought its own buzzword vocabulary—social distancing, masking, Zoom (is it a verb or a noun?), in-person worship, virtual worship, trying times (I feel like quoting Dickens), and my favorite, the new normal. In our 2021 culture, we use words or phrases like dope, rad, iconic (a favorite of celebrities), legend, white privilege, outrage (I see this in the media at least 10-12 times a day; it seems like everyone is outraged about something), synergy, viral (not talking about COVID), AI, data visualization, BOPIS (that's Buy Online, Pick Up In-Store, for you who are not buzzword savvy), retargeting, and think outside the box (I'm not always sure what the box is). The church has its share of buzzwords and phrases as well—Spirit-filled, biblical (again, different definitions as to what that means), anointed, love on, missional, a God thing, reach out, THE baptism, let's unpack this, social media fasting, do life together, hedge of protection—You get the idea; any word or phrase we use in the church that leaves the unchurched puzzling. But after all, using buzzwords is much easier than honest dialogue about vital issues, either sacred or secular. Come to think of it, those two words are hard to nail down and define as well. I'm reminded of a prayer I read long ago by Eugene Peterson—"Lord, help me not to go "shopping" for a church or a god; may I never treat god-names like brand names." Words are free; it's how you use them that may cost.

Random thoughts for today:

The words of a man's mouth are deep waters, the fountain of wisdom is a bubbling brook. (Proverbs 18:4 ESV)

I wonder if the pandemic is providing us the opportunity to step out of the chaos of the normal holiday season (written in 2020) and spend more quiet moments with the Lord.

Make understanding your priority before trying to be understood.

Isn't it interesting how unpopular the subject of the fear of the Lord is in our churches today?

December 6   Mystic Sweet Communion

C.S. Lewis once said, "I've never written anything about the Holy Communion for the very simple reason that I'm not good enough at theology." Isn't it ironic that a sacrament given to us by Jesus meant to unify the body of Christ has ended up dividing the church even more? Do the emblems literally become the body and blood of Jesus when we partake? Are these elements of bread and wine simply symbolic of His body and blood? Do we partake daily, weekly, monthly, yearly, whenever? I'm not saying that your belief is wrong; I'm saying that your explanation for your belief leaves the mystery for me still a mystery. In the great hymn of the church, *The Church's One Foundation,* there is a line that talks about "mystic sweet communion with those whose rest is won." While the verse is not talking about the Lord's Supper (or perhaps it is), I love the sentiment when applied to the eucharist. Cicero, Ovid, Horace, Pliny the Elder, and Seneca often used a Latin phrase, *favete linguis,* literally, "facilitate with your tongues." In other words, hold your tongue; facilitate the ritual acts by being silent. Quit studying it. Stop debating it. In silence and awe, partake of it (because maybe we're not good enough at theology). To me, it is still a mystery; magic, in a sense. That last word just turned some of you off, didn't it? It is so much more than a realm of objective facts. It is tearing up when I partake of the elements, remembering the instruction of my own dad when he said, "Just close your eyes and focus on the cross, Rick." I refuse to lay down eucharist rules. Lewis said, "I will not take the act of communion and treat it like a red coal taken out of the fire to examine it and watch it become a dead coal." But I will push back against those enlightened people who want to eliminate this "magical" element. A pastor friend of mine at a community communion service handed me a piece of bread and said, "Take it; it's for sinners." The command is *Take, eat*...Not, take, understand.

Random thoughts for today:

For as often as you eat this bread and drink the cup, you proclaim the Lord's death until He comes. (1 Corinthians 11:26 ESV)

Do we always let our Christmas lights shine, consistently shining the light of Christ? Christianity is not seasonal.

Things can be different only if you make them different.

Critical thinking is not a lost art, but regard for it is a lost tradition.

Never be afraid to sit awhile and think.

Teach me the glorious lesson that occasionally it's possible that I may be mistaken. *(A nun's prayer)*

December 7   My Weak Prayer Life

A theologian once said, "A good instruction book on prayer may be much needed, but I shall never try to write it." I believe that discussion on the subject can be helpful, but I think I agree with that theologian that an "instruction manual," as it were, would be rather condescending. In both of my prayer devotionals, I have tried not to do that and I'm sure I've probably failed a few times. The only "how-to" instruction we have in scripture is the model prayer of Jesus when He said, *Pray then like this...* (Matthew 6:9-13ESV). Through the years, I've shared a few of my personal "prayer rules."

- No rules
- Begin where you are

- Don't be afraid to be spontaneous
- Better to have a heart without words than words without heart.
- Practice prayer more than you talk about prayer
- Trust God to cover you when your prayer life has crashed

C. S. Lewis, in discussing his own prayer life, said he hadn't language weak enough to depict the weakness of his spiritual life. Yup!! I am uncomfortable when someone calls me a prayer warrior. Not me. I pray. Sometimes I succeed in praying well; sometimes I fail. I don't have all the answers to successful praying. I only know that Jesus told me to pray. Paul instructed me to *pray without ceasing.* So I pray.

Random thoughts for today:

When you pray, say: "Father, hallowed be Your name. Your kingdom come. (Luke 11:2 ESV)

I believe that it is appropriate to "return" to Jesus' birthplace every year to honor and celebrate the coming of the Child of Bethlehem.

Keeping open to change is one secret to staying young—Lord, keep changing me!

The smallest good deed is far better than the grandest intention.

Beware of posing as a profound person...God became a baby.

Many of the psalms are much more like confused cries to make some sense out of tragedy than they are stately prayers.

Fred Rogers used to say that often when you think you're at the end of something, you're at the beginning of something else. I was reminded recently that I was in my sixties when I started a second career in school teaching. So far, I have "retired" twice in the last sixteen years. In reality, I was only retired for a week or so. I'm often asked, "How do you like retirement?" My response is, "I'll let you know when I retire." I've had two retirement parties (2006 and 2019), and my kids have let it be known that there will be no more coming. It would seem that the Lord always had other plans for Helen and me. I've never been the kind of person who could sit around and do nothing, and that's good because I've yet to find anything about retirement in scripture anyway. Mark Twain said, "Age is an issue of mind over matter; if you don't mind, it doesn't matter." The concept of "retirement," whatever that may mean to you, is not the end of the road. It's the beginning of the open highway in life. My problem with retirement is I never really have a day off. But I do mostly get to spend time doing what I enjoy doing. It's a chance to redesign my life into something new and different. Many churches today would have a surplus of workers and volunteers to serve if many senior citizens realized that they retired from work, not from life. I've known servants of God in their sixties and seventies who have begun new careers in the mission field. Retirement can be a catastrophe or a commencement, a rocking chair or a launching pad. I love a quote I saw years ago by Vince Lombardi—"A lot of my friends complain about their retirement...I tell 'em to get a life!"

<u>Random thoughts for today</u>:

Is not wisdom found among the aged? Does not long-life bring understanding? (Job 12:12 ESV)

The first "Christmas carol" was not a quiet sentimental tune, but royal pageantry on that Judean hillside, heralding the arrival of a king...*Glory to God!!*

If you don't care about what hurts me, how can you truly love me? *(Hassidic rabbi)*

It would seem that much of the modern church is a lot more talk than power.

Before you embark upon a journey of revenge, dig two graves. *(Confucius)*

You have to put off being young until you can retire. *(Unknown)*

December 9   "Witnessing" Hats

It's interesting how many are watching me when I blow it! There is no shortage of "concerned" brothers, as well as unbelievers who have no problem calling me out when I fail to exhibit Christ in my life. Have you ever heard the statement, "Make no judgments where you have no compassion?" I love it! I remember not too long ago snapping at someone in a store while forgetting that I was wearing one of my "witnessing" hats. Yes, I own a few witnessing hats. I have a "Thankful" hat, and I have a "Love Anyway" hat. I won't even talk about my Victory Christian Academy sweatshirt and other athletic jackets. Ironically, when I was rude to a guy in the store that day (you know, just a little rude; not evil rude), I happened to be wearing my "Be Kind" hat. His response to me was, "Merry Christmas, Buddy!" Go back and read the October 15 entry. As I get older, it becomes a little more challenging to be kind. If I'm going to honor my October 15 entry, I should probably substitute my "Old Guys Rule" hat for witnessing apparel. Maybe that's why kindness has become a repetitive theme in this book. And maybe that's why I wear my "Be Kind" hat the most. I just have to remember that I'm wearing it.

Random thoughts for today:

But take care that this right of yours does not somehow become a stumbling block to the weak. (1 Corinthians 8:9 ESV)

Christmas is a time to be thankful for what is past and to contemplate what will come.

Christianity is not always complicated...But it is often very hard. *(Nate Loucks)*

I'm not afraid of storms, for I am learning how to sail my ship. *(Louisa May Alcott)*

My most precious possession—The ability to be in the presence of the Lord, to just be with Him.

Reveal your heart and heal a soul. *(Unknown)*

Father, forgive me for the times I have desired a seat at the table that you would have overturned.

You cannot change the culture around us unless you change men's hearts.

If everything becomes offensive, nothing is offensive.

Up to this entry, I have talked about the model prayer of Jesus eight or nine times in this book. During my quiet time recently, some insights came to me while comparing the Lord's Prayer with Jesus' entire teaching on prayer in the Sermon on the Mount *(Matthew 6:5-13)*. The first part of this section of the sermon describes what can be called "showtime praying." I've mentioned in previous writing that I pray the model prayer each morning during my quiet time. It's so easy to get caught up in the <u>form</u> of the prayer and "babble," that's the word Jesus uses in His lesson; the King James Version translates it "vain repetitions." The word literally pictures a process of repeating empty phrases over and over again. This scripture is a caution for congregations like ours that pray the Lord's Prayer together in our service weekly. On our board meeting Sundays at our church, I end up praying that prayer three times before lunch—My private time, in our worship service, and closing the board meeting after church. Am I just saying words with this kind of repetition? Possibly. Can I pray this prayer three times and truly mean it? Of course. It's all about our focus. In Tibet, they hollow out large logs making drum-like cylinders. Then they put prayer requests inside and roll the drum around on the theory that for every revolution the drum makes, those prayers are automatically prayed up to God. If that's true, our modern computers could turn out millions of prayers per second. Just think of it...Talk about vain repetitions. My grandson recently said, "The Sermon on the Mount is about our motives!" What's our motive in following Jesus? Why do we pray? Get your focus off of yourself and the "form" and put it back on the Lord.

<u>Random thoughts for today</u>:

When you pray, go into your room, close the door and pray to your Father, who is unseen. Then your Father, who sees what is done in secret, will reward you. (Matthew 6:6 ESV)

Cliché, but valid...What gifts will you bring this season to honor our Lord and King?

When was the last time I tried to see an issue from God's perspective rather than ask Him to see it from mine?

It is all right, believe it or not, to be people.

No man has the authority to divide the truth and preach only part of it.

John Wesley's three rules: 1) Do no harm 2) Do good 3) Stay in love with God

December 11   Covid Fear

***This entry was actually written in August 2021

Psalm 112:6 tells us that the righteous will never be moved. I believe that. At this writing, COVID-19 (the Delta variant) has surged in our world and new infections are again on the rise. Please know that I do have concerns over where this will all lead. I'm not a conspiracy theorist. The threat is real. Add to this a confusion caused by media gearing up their "fear-machine" again and medical experts flip-flopping about every other week. I have no idea where we'll be when this book comes out. I don't have a clue as to the specifics of the resolution phase of this thing. I DO know if I react to bad news in fear or panic, it just adds to the problem. I DO know that God is not sitting up in heaven wringing His hands, saying, "Well, I never expected this to happen!" I DO know that the promise of scripture is as valid as it ever was—*When I am afraid, I put my trust in YOU, LORD* (Psalm 56:3). Bad news doesn't change who God is; rather, it challenges us to trust WHO He is. Notice that David does not say, "I am never afraid." God knows the future and is not surprised by sudden disappointments or even crises. He prepares our hearts to handle them. For this reason, we live in freedom, not fear. Our hearts are steady because we trust in Him, and He has given us His peace. My heart knows peace because I know Him. I don't know what lies ahead (whether COVID is here or not), but I know my Abba Father, and that is enough.

Random thoughts for today:

He is not afraid of bad news (the man who fears the LORD); ***his heart is firm, trusting in the LORD.*** (Psalm 112:7 ESV)

The intent of early Christmas cards was to send God's blessings to those we love...Blessings to all of you!!

What prayer am I trying to answer in my own strength today?

If you're lucky enough to be different, don't ever change.

6-year olds laugh an average of 300 times a day...Adults only laugh from 15 to 100 times a day...Be six again. *(Unknown)*

Sometimes I pray, "Lord, I don't know what's going on, but I trust You."

If you're reading this in 2021, this is the third Sunday in Advent (See entry on November 28). Just thirteen more days until Christmas. If you've read any of my stuff in the past, you know that I AM a Christmas junkie; so at this point in the year, I'm pretty pumped. We light the third candle in worship service today and continue to enjoy the old carols of yesterday and the newer choruses of today. Every year I try to find an interesting daily devotional with a Christmas theme for daily reading. Many are available online. Whether you celebrate the day or not, it's interesting how this time of year often brings about a state of mind; one of reflection, gratitude, and goodwill. Here are few thoughts to ponder during this season.

> "Christmas is not a time nor a season, but a state of mind. To cherish peace and goodwill, to be plenteous in mercy, is to have the real spirit of Christmas." *(Calvin Coolidge)*

> "He who has not Christmas in his heart will never find it under a tree."

> "'Maybe Christmas,' the Grinch thought, 'doesn't come from a store.'" *(Dr. Seuss)*

> "Love the giver more than the gift."

> "I will honor Christmas in my heart and try to keep it all the year." *(Ebenezer Scrooge)*

When we were children, we were grateful for those who filled our stockings at Christmas time. Why are we not grateful to God for filling our stockings with legs?" *(G.K. Chesterton)*

"A Christmas candle is a lovely thing. It makes no noise at all, but softly gives itself away." *(Unknown)*

May PEACE be your gift of Christmas and your blessing all year through.

Random thoughts for today:

Glory to God in the highest, and on earth peace among those with whom He is pleased. (Luke 2:14 ESV)

Our role model, Jesus, goes beyond the manger...*Surely, He took up our pain and bore our suffering.* (Isaiah 53:4)

December 13   Old Buildings

Occasionally, I feel a bit overwhelmed with change. On our 55th wedding anniversary, Helen and I drove over to the church where we were married to take some pictures. We knew that the building was in the process of being demolished. This was the same building that housed the church where I grew up, was baptized, and made a commitment to the ministry. After college, I served as a youth pastor there for seven years. Helen and I started reminiscing about buildings. Both of our elementary schools have been razed. Our high school buildings are gone. The church where I first preached beginning in 1964 has been torn down (although I still possess a brick from that building). Things never stay the same, do they? As I stood on the corner of 11th and Cedar Streets watching the large crane loading up rubble to be transported to a landfill somewhere, I was surprised that I didn't feel a lot of emotion. I thought that I would, but I discovered some time ago that my well-being is not contingent upon physical structures. My memories are just as sweet and authentic as I reflect on events of the past. My walk with the Lord is not dependent upon any building. Memories are indeed gifts from God, and as time passes, they become sweeter and sweeter. Helen and I still have and rehearse beautiful memories of our wedding at First Christian Church in Michigan City. The demolishing of that building does not diminish those memories one iota. Paul wrote in 2 Corinthians 4:16—*So we do not lose heart. Though our outer self is wasting away, our inner self is being renewed day by day.* I love that scripture. Things change...But Jesus never does!!

Random thoughts for today:

He will wipe away every tear from their eyes, and death shall be no more, neither shall there be mourning nor crying nor pain anymore, for the former things are passed away. (Revelation 21:4 ESV)

The impact of Christ's birth is not limited to one day...His arrival changed history and our eternal destiny.

This is what I know of prayer...It's best done often and on my knees.

A promise is a cloud; fulfillment is the rain. *(Arabian Proverb)*

To teach is to learn twice.

I think that true joy is a connection to what matters.

Prayer changes things. Does it though? Depends upon what you mean by that. I've struggled for years with the "name-it-claim-it" theology that many Christians seem to embrace. I just can't picture the supreme Lord of the universe as an eternal vending machine waiting for my beck and call. The late Donald Barnhouse, American pastor and author, once said from his pulpit, "Prayer changes nothing!" You can imagine the pin-drop silence in that auditorium that morning. What a great way to open a sermon on prayer. His comment, of course, was designed to make believers realize that we don't control God. He is sovereignly in charge of everything. We control nothing! I heard one preacher a few years ago say, "No puny human being takes charge of events and changes them by uttering a few words of prayer." God does the shaping and the changing. He is in control. Our times are literally in His hands. I think quite a few of us have used that statement, "God is in control," almost as a mantra, but I'm not sure we believe that. Of course, God can and has answered specific prayers through the ages; He has certainly answered many of mine, but it is not because we have wrested control out of His hands. Of all the changes prayer can bring into my life, the greatest change takes place in my heart. When I pray, I change. How many times has my anxiety been erased by time alone with the Lord? That time with Him has brought peace into my spirit again and again. So, it's really not correct to say prayer changes nothing. PRAYER DOES CHANGE ME!!

*Some prayer thoughts continued in tomorrow's entry

Random thoughts for today:

... pray without ceasing... for this is the will of God in Christ Jesus for you. (1 Thessalonians 5:16-18 ESV)

Let's be careful not to let cultural Santa Clauses tempt us to forget about Jesus and settle for a jolly old man.

Your descendants shall gather your fruits.

I have learned that there is more power in a good strong hug than in a thousand meaningful words.

Am I dependent upon myself to do what only God can do? *#Notetomyself*

December 15   According to His Will

*Some thoughts continued from yesterday

1 John 5:14 says, *This is the confidence that we have toward Him, that if we ask anything according to His will he hears us.* I've come to realize in my maturing spiritual years (I hope) that the aim of prayer is not to force God's hand or make Him do our will as opposed to His will. Sometimes it seems scriptures on prayer contradict each other. Still, as I deepen my knowledge of Him and my fellowship with Him, I discover that prayer is more about embracing His goals for my life. My prayer life is to be driven by my being taught by His word and by the Spirit of God. I want my desires to line up with His desires. I want my will to line up with His will. My praying then must be according to God's will and in the name of Jesus. To ask in Jesus' name is not to become some kind of mantra, but rather to make petitions to

God, which J.I. Packer says, "petitions which Christ can endorse and put His name to." Wilbur Culbertson writes, "Be thankful that God's answers are wiser than your prayers." Very simply, prayer is fellowship with God. It's communion with the Lord through praising Him, rehearsing His promises, and then sharing our needs, certainly not demanding God's performance. I love the little piece of verse by Ruth Harms Calkin—"Lord, Day after day I've thanked You for saying yes; but when have I genuinely thanked You for saying no." The heart of my prayer life is to be *not my will, Father, but Your will be done.*

Random thoughts for today:

Rejoice in hope, be patient in tribulation, be constant in prayer. *(Romans 12:12* ESV*)*

The name of Immanuel/"God with us" is a title indicating choice...He chose to come down to us... That's Christmas!!

The future begins today, not tomorrow.

Carefully water your children like you water a tree. *(Hopi Proverb)*

How would it be if God struck me silent like He did Zachariah every time I doubted Him?

Lord, dismiss with Your peace, except for those who don't know You; keep them miserable until they come to know the Prince of Peace. *(Donald Barnhouse)*

In my life and experience, this season of the year has always been a tender time. Maybe that's because the foundation of the season is *Behold, the virgin shall conceive and bear a son, and they shall call His name, Immanuel (which means, God with us)*—Matthew 1:23). It would seem that character traits such as gentleness and tenderness have been sadly missing in the evangelical church, especially among men. Why is that? Men, why do we balk at exhibiting a tender heart? I think this may be why I have become increasingly uncomfortable with the evangelical church. Is this lack of tenderness and gentleness one of the reasons so many are leaving the church today, especially young people? Jean Vanier writes, "Love doesn't mean doing extraordinary or heroic things; it means knowing how to do ordinary things with tenderness." Recently, I was led to begin rereading a book in my library by Brennan Manning, *The Wisdom of Tenderness*. It's been quite a few years since I first read it. I'm not sure "God told me to read it," but then again, maybe He did. The Jerusalem Bible (I was surprised to learn that this translation is in the top five of most widely used) was first translated from the original texts into French. From the French, it was translated into English. The French noun, *la tendresse,* is richer in meaning than the English, "tenderness." It literally pictures one stretching out one's arms in a gesture of welcoming love. I love that. Manning addressed was how difficult it is to dialogue with a person who considers it unthinkable that they might be wrong on any given subject. Have I ever been one of those? One of my favorite quotes of his, is "The way of tenderness affects our manner of *being* in the world rather than our manner of *doing* in the world." I don't have all the answers here gang. I am learning in these latter years of my life that in my experiences of warm, caring, affectionate relationships, my heart grows more and more tender. May this year's Christmas season be for you a greater season of tenderness. Henri Nouwen wrote, "When we honestly ask ourselves which person in our lives means the most to us, we often find that it is those who, instead of giving much advice, solutions, or cures, have chosen rather to share our pain and touch our wounds with a gentle and tender hand."

Random thoughts for today:

Be kind to one another, tenderhearted, forgiving one another as God in Christ forgave you. *(Ephesians 4:32*—4th time I've used this scripture in Random Thoughts...I detect a theme)

Why did Jesus come to us? Because He loves to be with the ones He loves.

It costs nothing to be kind.

December 17   Ancient vs. Contemporary Authors

"So, you have difficulty with wandering thoughts in prayer. That's nothing new! You have lots of company." Can you relate to that quote? I've learned that if I'm interested, I pay attention. If I'm bored, my mind wanders. But how can I be bored in the presence of the Lord? Do I genuinely believe that He is at my side? When I am spending time with Him, I work hard to make it my business to keep my mind in His presence. But I still struggle. I've found one way is to admit to God that I am struggling. It's a daily discipline to think often of Him during the day. If I think of Him a lot, I find it easier to keep my mind clear in my prayer time. And when I fail, as I often do, I don't beat myself up as a pathetic disciple of Jesus; and I don't worry about a "down-tick" of my spiritual life. I take a deep breath and bring my thoughts back to Him. So let's go back to the opening quotation of this entry. Max Lucado or Chuck Swindoll or Sarah Bessey did not say that, although they all have probably experienced it. It was written by an ancient 17th-century monk, Brother Lawrence of the Resurrection. I have mentioned him previously (January 5 – April 22 – May 11). May I state once again a sentence from the acknowledgment section at the beginning of this book—"I believe it to be arrogant to assume that only our generation or our era has anything valid to say to the church of today." On quite a few occasions, men and women of the past have come to my rescue with their writings. Thanks again, Brother Lawrence. Thank you for helping to open my eyes that I might see the Lord here with me.

"Lord, always be shaping me according to Thy heart." (Brother Lawrence)

Random thoughts for today:

What has been is what will be, and what has been done is what will be done, and there is nothing new under the sun. Is there a thing of which it is said, "See, this is new?" It has been already in the ages before us. There is no remembrance of former things... (Ecclesiastes 1:9-11 ESV)

There was not one person who was reluctant to approach Jesus for fear of being rejected.

Technology is a good servant but a bad master.

I don't necessarily understand life any better at 77 than I did at 20, but now I have no problem admitting it.

Our greatest gift to one another should be our love for others.

December 18   Psalm 37

Psalm 37:3-4 says, *Trust in the LORD and do good...Delight yourself in the LORD and He will give you the desires of your heart.* In recent days, I have found myself pouring over the words of Psalm 37. It's a rich psalm of David with a theme of trust, regardless of circumstances, and not getting all worked up because of evildoers. There seems to be much stress and anxiety these days over all the wickedness that surrounds us. I have reflected on many of the verses in this chapter—*Commit your way to the LORD; trust Him and He will act* (We pray to a God who acts) – *The meek shall inherit the land and delight themselves in abundant peace* (Pray first, rendering worry unnecessary) – *Be still before the LORD and wait patiently for Him; fret not yourself; it tends only to evil* (Help me, Lord, with my churning places; I've got a lot of those) – *Better is the little that the righteous has than the abundance of many.* And these are just a few tidbits from the 40 verses of this psalm. There's an interesting little phrase I left out of the Psalm 37:3 quote above. It simply says, *befriend faithfulness.* It literally translates, "feed on faithfulness." It's a pastoral picture of finding a safe pasture in which to eat. And the greatest example of faithfulness we have before us is found in the faithfulness of the Lord (More about this tomorrow). The *steps of a man are established by the LORD when he delights in His way* (Psalm 37:23 ESV).

Random thoughts for today:

The LORD helps them and delivers them; He delivers them from the wicked and saves them, because they take refuge in Him. *(Psalm 37:40* ESV —The "they" and "them" referring to the righteous in the Lord)

The Word becoming flesh can make us uncomfortable... There's something about keeping Jesus divine that keeps Him distant, packaged, predictable.

Depth, not length, in our prayers is important...Don't underestimate a few minutes with God in prayer.

Make understanding your priority before trying to be understood. *(Unknown)*

Help me see prayer as communication with Someone I love.

Help me never forget that the trust of a child is to be cherished.

December 19   Befriend Faithfulness

The Lord would have us FEED ON FAITHFULNESS!! Am I "befriending" faithfulness by trusting in Him and doing good (Psalm 37:3)? I find it interesting that volumes are written about faith, but not so much about being faithful. I've often prayed, "Lord, thank You for being faithful, even when I am not." Do we understand that we will not naturally drift into becoming faithful disciples of Jesus, faithful spouses, or faithful parents? We must be intentional. Our level of faithfulness is to be found in our priorities:

- Involvement in the body of Christ
- Worship
- Giving
- Prayer and the Word
- The words you speak; promises made and words spoken
- A good reputation
- Moral standard

When faithfulness is most difficult, it is most necessary. Brothers and sisters, faithfulness is our business!! And by the way, it is impossible to be faithful to Jesus Christ and not incur the opposition of the world.

Random thoughts for today:

Let us hold fast the confession of our hope without wavering, for He who promised is faithful. *(Hebrews 10:23 ESV)*

Do you suppose Gabriel had questions about his message to Mary? Seriously, a baby? That's OK for humans...But God?

Prayer is not a substitute for work, thinking, watching, suffering, or giving...It's a support for all the efforts.

There are few things as uncommon as common sense.

Determining who's to blame is like slicing pudding...It's just best to share it all.

It's friends you can call up at 4:00 am that matter.

The prophet Malachi proclaimed that the Day of the Lord was coming. Part of Ezra and Nehemiah's ministry was to prepare their people for that day. All was ready for the coming of the Messiah...Or was it? Not quite. The era between the Old and New Testament begins, called the "silent years" of biblical history. 400 years. During those years, Aristotle is born, Alexander the Great begins his reign in Greece, and Hannibal is defeated. In the last hundred years before the birth of Jesus, Buddhism begins to rise in China, Rome begins to conquer the known world, Julius Caesar is assassinated, and in BC 31, Caesar Augustus becomes emperor. Why a 400-year interlude from the close of the Old Testament up to the birth of Christ? Galatians 4:4 says that the Day of Lord would come *in the fulness of time*. What would bring about this "fulness of time" In other words, when the time was just right? I remember how anxious I was as a kid waiting for Christmas to come; sometimes, from the 7-year old perspective, it seemed like 400 years. Why was the end of this 400-year historical gap just the right time? This "fulness of time" was just right because of:

- Intensive ministry of prophets in the years before, much of it Messianic.
- The Jewish culture influenced by a dispersed people.
- A renewed interest and knowledge of the Law because of Ezra.
- The influence of Greek Hellenism upon the Jews (Koine Greek became an international language and became the original language of the New Testament).

- The influence of Roman rule (Pax Romana and an extensive system of Roman roads, the very roads Christian missionaries used after the church began).

God's master plan comes together...Right time...Right place...No random throw of the dice here.

Random thoughts for today:

When the fulness of time had come, God sent forth His Son, born of a woman, born under the law... (Galatians 4:4 ESV)

Joseph swapped his Torah studies for a pregnant fiancée and an illegitimate son...He placed God's plan ahead of his own.

The great man is one who does not lose his child's heart. *(Mencius)*

Our lives can be frittered away by detail...Simplify! Simplify!

I've never really had a point of view, Lord, until my life was filled with You.

December 21   Promise Keeping

A day doesn't go by that someone forgets the promises they made—to their employees, to the ones who elected them, to their friend, to their mate or their children...People fail us right and left, and one of the reasons is because they forget their promises...Wait, no, that's not right. They BREAK their promises. It just sounds better when we say, "We forgot." But that's not true with God—our never-forgetting, always promise-keeping God. I'll tell you what.

That's something over which I jump up and down with joy. In Luke, chapter one, that is precisely what Mary is doing. She sings about her joy over what her never-forgetting, always promise-keeping God has told her—*My soul glorifies the Lord and my spirit rejoices in God, my Savior* (Luke 1:46-47 ESV). So here we are toward the end of this Advent season. Our never-forgetting, always promise-keeping God has provided us the forgiveness of sins, release from shame and guilt, and blessing in this life and the next. If that's not reason enough to join Mary this Christmas season in jumping up and down with ecstatic, overflowing, soul-bursting joy, then I don't know what is. Praise be to our God for remaining faithful, even when we are not.

Never-forgetting, always promise-keeping Lord... May we join with Mary this Advent in overflowing with praise and thanks and joy to You for Your limitless mercies and love.

Random thoughts for today:

Blessed be the Lord God of Israel, for He has visited and redeemed His people. (Luke 1:68 ESV)

The authentic experience of Christmas gives us lasting hope in the midst of a hopeless world.

My relationship with my Abba Father is like a blanket just out of the dryer wrapped around me.

I've never lost the wonder!! *(Gipsy Smith)*

How often do we hope like a child on Christmas morning? It seems as adults, we hope less and less. *(Maddie Bailey, former VCA Student)*

Max Lucado asks the question, "What must it have been like for Mary to carry God in her womb? The virgin birth is a picture of how close Christ will come to you. The first stop in his itinerary was a womb." John 1:14 tells us that *the Word* (that would be Jesus) *became flesh and dwelt among us, and we have seen His glory, glory as of the only Son from the Father, full of grace and truth.* In other words, He literally moved in right next door. One 20th century expositor put it this way—"He pitched His tent right next to ours." I love camping metaphors. Remember when the angel told Mary that she was going to be pregnant with the Son of God. She offered no excuses or resistance. "Maybe I can do that later, Lord?" No, she responded, *Behold, I am the servant of the Lord; let it be to me according to your word* (Luke 1:38). One preacher said, "Christ grew in Mary until He had to come out." Are we that pregnant with Christ in us? What was it Paul said? *Christ IN you, the hope of glory* (Colossians 1:27). We have the same promise as did Mary. The Lord offers to us a Mary-level invitation. Paul accepted that invitation without reservation. Remember what he said in Galatians 2:20—*I have been crucified with Christ. It is no longer I who live, but Christ who lives in me. And the life I now live in the flesh I live by faith in the Son of God, who loved me and gave Himself for me.* What's the invitation? "IF YOU'LL LET ME, I'LL MOVE IN!!"

Random thoughts for today:

So that Christ may dwell in your hearts through faith... (Ephesians 3:17 ESV)

Immanuel—"God with us"...Even in the bad times.

How appropriate the angel should appear to poor shepherds that night. *(Lil-Lee-Ann)*

No act of kindness, no matter how small, is ever wasted. *(Aesop)*

Do exactly what your "Yeah, but" says you shouldn't...Write that book – Adopt that kitty – Resist oppression...Keep the "yeah" and kick the "but."

Almost Christmas...The world may not, but I anticipate the coming the King!!

December 23   Christmas Ramblings

I'm in a contemplation mood today. A little Christmas nostalgia has overtaken me. LORD, on this December 23, two days before Christmas, may I treasure and ponder all of the things in my heart *(Luke 2:19* ESV). Here are a few ramblings from my journals:

> For the Lord omnipotent reigneth...King of kings and Lord of lords. *(Handel)*

> Thank You, Lord, for this festival of praise and celebration of *the Word becoming flesh and dwelling among us* (John 1:14).

> Christmas is a time to be thankful for what is past and to contemplate what will come.

> Freshly cut Christmas trees smelling of stars and snow and pine resin—inhale deeply and fill your soul with wintry night. *(John J. Geddes)*

Christmas is the day that holds all time together. *(Alexander Smith)*

Let us have music for Christmas...Sound the trumpet of joy and rebirth; let each of us try, with a song in our hearts, to bring peace to men on earth. *(Unknown)*

May you never be too grown up to search the skies on Christmas Eve. *(Anonymous)*

Christmas isn't just a day; it's a frame of mind.

God bless us, everyone. *(Tiny Tim)*

Random thoughts for today:

For unto you is born this day in the city of David, a Savior, who is Christ the Lord. (Luke 2:11 ESV)

It's not what's under the Christmas tree that matters...It's who's around it.
There's no delight in owning anything unshared.

December 24   Naughty or Nice?

I was participating in a communion service some time ago. What does that have to do with Christmas? EVERYTHING!! The pastor took the bread and took the cup, and held it out toward the congregation, and said, "Take it...It's for sinners." Tears immediately began to well up in my eyes. I have talked with many in the body of Christ through the years who would not take the Lord's Supper because they felt they were unworthy (misunderstanding and misinterpreting 1 Corinthians 11:27-29, which talks about partaking unworthily). There was a time that I felt I had to have everything in order and settled in my life before I could partake; I sure hoped that there wasn't a sin lurking out there I had forgotten to confess. Then my pastor said, "If you are in the family, it's for you." Dietrich Bonhoeffer said that a pious fellowship permits no one to be a sinner. So, maybe it's not a Santa Claus principle at work here. Perhaps he's not "checking his list and checking it twice; to see if I've been naughty or nice." (A coal in your stocking tonight.) It truly IS for sinners...That's me*!!* I've discovered that in the presence of my Lord, anxious thoughts fade. Judgmental criticism is diminished as I claim His unconditional love. I pray my daily prayer of hope— "In You, Lord, I have hoped; let me never be confounded." I came across a quotation in my journal the other day; I don't remember where I got it. "Take away the pomp of religion. Dissipated is the fog of theology. Momentarily lifted is the opaque curtain of controversy and opinion and bickering. Erased are our own binding errors and egotism and selfishness. And there He stands...JESUS*!!*" God bless you this Christmas Eve.

Random thoughts for today:

She will bear a son, and you shall call his name JESUS, for he will save his people from their sins. (Matthew 1:21 ESV)

Hope is not, "I wish that would happen"...Hope is a certainty. *Unto us a child is born.*

Lord, on this day before Christmas, may I treasure and ponder all these things in my heart.

Lord, help me not to be so busy that I miss the small pleasures sprinkled throughout this day.

Thank You, Lord, for this silent, holy night.

May we hear the sound of snow tonight...Do you know that snow falling can make a sound?

December 25   All Are Welcome

So, you need to understand my wife. She's different. Most of the reasons that make her different are the reasons I married her. Every December, Helen sets up a nativity scene in our living room, but it's not like any other nativity scene. It does have the traditional Mary and Joseph, the baby Jesus, and the shepherds. It also has the typical sheep, cattle, and of course, a donkey. But it also has lots and lots of other animals surrounding the manger. It has giraffes, llamas, zebras, a turtle, rabbits, dogs, cats, pigs, a rooster, and, oh yeah, elephants. The angel overhead is a snowman with a silver halo. One of the shepherds is holding a lamb. We're talking about a ceramic figurine with two broken legs—not the lamb, the shepherd (our granddaughter broke the legs years ago). Helen titles her nativity scene, "All Are Welcome." You've heard the quotation, "The gospel of Jesus Christ is good news, but if it's not for everyone, it's not good news." The good news is for the strange, the slow, the big, the small, the broken...It's for everybody! The thing that I love the most about this nativity scene is that right next to the manger is a black sheep. That's me! The good news is for sinners like me. I've learned through the years that what's important is not how you're dressed or whether you're weird. What's important is whether you are willing to listen and to believe and to follow...Because followers follow. From one silent night long ago, to a forever future with our Immanuel—God with us...GOOD NEWS!! Thanks, Helen, for your sweet, weird, beautiful nativity scene. MERRY CHRISTMAS!!

Random thoughts for today:

And while they were there, the time came for the baby to be born, and she gave birth to her firstborn, a son. She wrapped him in cloths and placed him in a manger, because there was no room for them in the inn. (Luke 2:6-7 ESV)

Let there be peace on earth and let it begin with me.

Make my heart your manger, I pray.

Thank You, Father, that I have never lost the wonder of Christmas*!!*

Merry Christmas, world...Whether you believe it or not... Merry Christmas anyway*!!*

December 26   Boxing Day

Happy Boxing Day!! Every 26th of December is designated as Boxing Day; not only a day for Santa Claus to catch his breath, but a public holiday in the United Kingdom and other British Commonwealth countries such as Australia, New Zealand, and Canada. You've probably noticed it on your calendar, or maybe not. This year I decided to do a little research as to what it was all about. I discovered that there are two sides to the day—what it used to be about and what it is all about today. Despite of its peculiar name, Boxing Day has nothing to do with slugfests or the return of unwanted gifts to department stores. The Oxford English Dictionary traces its earliest print attribution to 1833, four years before Dickens referred to it in *The Pickwick Papers*. Many historians think that December 26 was the day centuries ago when the lords of the manor typically distributed Christmas boxes filled with small gifts, money, and food to their household servants and employees, a kind of early version of the Christmas bonus, if you will. Another theory is that it represents boxes placed in churches for monetary donations to be distributed to the poor on December 26, which is also the feast of St. Stephen, the first Christian martyr and a figure known traditionally for acts of charity. Today, the 26th (one of the most popular days of the year for shopping in our country), is still a popular holiday in the Commonwealth countries for watching sports such as soccer and cricket, shopping, and partying with friends. Wait a minute; I thought that was Thanksgiving Day. Hmmm...Quite a difference between then and now, huh?

Random thoughts for today:

Whoever is generous to the poor lends to the LORD, and He will repay him for his deed. (Proverbs 19:17 ESV)

This day, take your rest in the embrace of your Abba Father.
In a gentle way, you can shake the world. *(Gandhi)*
We are made kind by being kind.
Pride is the thing I will miss least when my earthly life comes to an end.

A kid's description of Jesus—"He's the most beautifulest person on earth...for a baby."

It's a mystery why adults expect perfection from children...I can't get through one day without making a mistake.

December 27   Truth Be Told

Matthew West has written a song entitled "Truth Be Told." It introduces two lies that we so often tell—1) We've got it all together; we're fine; 2) Everyone's life is perfect (except mine). The problem is, of course, that we're not okay and no one's life is perfect. The lyric in West's song that grabs me is, "Truth be told; the truth is rarely told, now." But what about this world of ours in which we journey and struggle? We live in a world where truth is mostly absent. We are overwhelmed by a world system that is based upon lies. We listen to our politicians, celebrities, and news sources and end up trusting no one. Many churches and their well-known leaders have broken their promises. I remember the counsel given to me by my father the night before I was ordained into pastoral ministry—"Rick, always be honest with yourself and with others. Don't just preach the truth; always personally tell the truth." The day before I assumed the role of interim principal at Victory Christian Academy, I met with my dad, a former high school principal, for some advice. He said, "Be consistent, be fair, and always tell the truth." There's another line in Matthew's song that says, "Being honest is the only way to fix it." How about refusing to edit the truth according to fashion or popular opinion? C'mon guys!! Don't bend. Don't water it down. Don't make it logical. Shades of Mark Twain—"When in doubt, tell the truth!" In our world of falsehood, confusion, phoniness, spin, "alternate truths," and compromise, the question of defining truth

always comes up. What is truth anyway? Whose truth? My truth may differ from your truth. Philosophers through the ages have asked, "What is truth?" Pontius Pilate asked the question of Jesus. And His response, *I am the way, and the truth, and the life, and no man comes to the Father but by Me* (John 14:6). I learned that truth from my dad as well.

Random thoughts for today:

You will know the truth, and the truth will set you free. (John 8:32 ESV)

Change always brings fear before it brings faith.

Inspiration exists…But it must find you working.

Prayer—Depth, not length…Away with our blah-blah-blah prayer lives.

Attitude of heart can rob us of loving people.

Sin is the great equalizer.

If only we'd stop trying to be happy, we'd have a pretty good time. *(Edith Wharton)*

December 28   Friendships - 2

At the beginning of the year, I wrote an entry on friendships (January 17). As we come to the end of this year, I'd like to share a follow-up. Not too long ago, my daughter told of a staff meeting at her church. Members of their ministry team were sharing concerning friendships recently ended (some relationships of many years) over disagreements and differences of opinion. Each staff member had experienced a break-up of a friendship over

theological issues, the vax/anti-vax debate, or who one supported for President in the last election. Paul writes in Colossians 3:12-13—*Put on then, as God's chosen ones, compassion, kindness, humility, meekness, and patience, bearing with one another, and if one has a complaint against another, you must end the friendship.* Oh, wait...I think I got that wrong. I believe the last phrase says, *forgiving each other, as the Lord has forgiven you. You also must forgive.* Reading the account of that church staff meeting pretty much bummed me out for the rest of the day. Seriously, people!! The spirit of enmity, anger, resentment, and judgmentalism seems to be alive and well in the church today. This same spirit continues to divide our nation, and the church is involved in perpetuating it. How are we different? Perhaps the greatest challenge for believers in the 21st century is to make the church of Jesus Christ great again. Maybe we've been debating so much about "following the science" that we've forgotten how to follow the scriptures—*Be kind to one another, tenderhearted, forgiving one another as God in Christ forgave you* (Ephesians 4:32 ESV). I believe I've used that verse quite a few times in this book. Hopefully, our churches will keep on teaching it until we get it right. We can have more impact on others for Christ if we choose to love and live peaceably rather than standing staunchly in our ideas. *If possible, so far as it depends on you, live peaceably with all* (Romans 12:18).

Random thoughts for today:

Greater love has no one than this, that someone lays down his life for his friends. (John 15:13 ESV)

I reread the nativity story today—Summary: Majesty in the midst of the mundane.

Sometimes courage is the quiet voice at the end of the day saying, "I will try again tomorrow." *(Unknown)*

When life is difficult, it's always good to have people we love next to us.

The pious fellowship permits no one to be a sinner. *(Dietrich Bonhoeffer)*

A big heart is determined to make other hearts grow.

Do your little bit of good where you are.

December 29   Christmas Over?

My most unfavorite Christmas song is *The 12 Days of Christmas*...You know the one—"On the first day of Christmas, my true love gave to me..." It's kind of like the song that never ends. Its "secular" counterpart could be "99 Bottles of Beer on the Wall." Perhaps you're not aware that the actual 12 Days of Christmas are the 12 days AFTER Christmas, not before. I've confessed before that I am a Christmas junkie, and I still believe that there is magic in this season of the year. Even last year, during the holidays, when we discovered that my wife had cancer, there was still a wonder in the month that lifted our spirits and kept us going. After 76 Christmases, I still have been able to keep a childlike spirit after all these years. May I suggest that even though this is after Christmas, the "magic" needs to continue. Don't be in such a hurry to tear down the Christmas stuff around the house. Keep the tree up a little longer (unless it has become a fire hazard). Why are we in such a hurry to get back to "normal," whatever that means. We ought to be used to the "not normal" by now. The message of Christmas is presenting HOPE amid the darkness of the normalcy of our world. Hope is coming! Hope has come! Even in the brokenness, Emmanuel is here with us (that is, of course, what Emmanuel means). In Matthew 2, we read of the magi, Gentile astrologers from Babylon (outsiders, mind you), proclaiming that the King of the Jews has come! How about that— Outsiders proclaiming to religious insiders. The advent of Jesus Christ brings CLARITY into the dark and complicated world in which we live. Why are we in such a hurry for it to be over?

Random thoughts for today:

Where is the One who has been born king of the Jews? We saw His star in the east and have come to worship Him. (Matthew 2:2 ESV)

Whatever you dream you can do, begin it...Boldness has power and magic in it.

Idolatry is anything we put before the Lord. *(Faith Linden, former VCA Student)*

There is no delight in owning anything unshared. *(Seneca)*

My life was changed when I realized that God was for me.

December 30   I Am A Writer?

It's been said, there's no agony like having an untold story inside you. I am, among other things, a writer. I attempt to exercise my writing muscle every day; I am constantly writing, most of which will never be published. I don't consider myself a great writer, maybe a notch above mediocre, maybe not. I know that I want to write. I need to write. I have to write. I write, not as an expert in much of anything, but as a fellow traveler who has more questions than answers on this journey, we call life. And I write out of what I have experienced and am experiencing on this journey. I do know that if God is not present, I cannot raise a peep out of anything that isn't me. It has been my daily prayer that this volume is a reflection of God's presence in the project and not just a compilation of "Jones ramblings." W. Somerset Maugham said it well, "There are three rules for writing a book. Unfortunately, no one knows what they are." In this volume, I've tried not to be distrustful of the reader's intelligence or be patronizing. At the same time, I desire that there has been some content that has caused you to pause and think or rethink some issues in your life. I always prefer the plain, direct word to the long, vague one. Most of all, I have desired that this writing be a labor of love to the body of Christ and any others who might be open to its message. Logan Pearsall Smith says that what he likes in a good author isn't always what he says but what he whispers. Perhaps in your reading this book, you've picked up on a few of my whispers. Yes, I am a writer. How do I write? One word at a time.

Random thoughts for today:

You yourselves are our letter of recommendation, written on our hearts, to be known and read by all. (2 Corinthians 3:2 ESV)

This year is almost gone. Not all of our friends and family made it. Never take for granted the people you love. Be thankful for today because, in one moment, your entire life could change.

Lord, grant that I may always desire more than I can accomplish.

To be ignorant of what occurred before you were born is to remain forever a child. *(Cicero)*

With all the data compiled on our kids today, I find a sense of relief that all that data is not compiled on me.

The danger in not praying is the loss of one's capacity to pray.

December 31   Year End Prayer

Isn't it funny how day by day nothing changes, but when you look back, everything is different? I found the following in one of my journals, not sure of its origin—"To hold on to the past, wanting God to move as He has formerly done, is at the risk of finding yourself out of the mainstream of His moving forward. The flow of divine activity sweeps from generation to generation." What legacy am I leaving behind? How am I investing my life for eternity? The following is a prayer that I have used often at the end of each year.

"Father, we surrender this past year and give it up to You. We give you our failures, our regrets, and our disappointments, for we have no more use for them.

Make us now a new people, forgetting what lies behind and pressing on toward that which lies ahead of us. We give you all our hopes and dreams for the future. Purify them by Your Spirit so that our wills shall truly reflect Your will for us.

As we stand on the threshold of another year, encourage us by our successes of the past, challenge us by the power of Your Word, and guide us by the presence of Your Holy Spirit."

Thank You, Lord, for Your presence and Your blessing throughout this past year!!

<u>Random thoughts for today</u>:

May the LORD bless you and keep you...May the LORD shine His face and His smile down upon you... May the LORD turn His countenance upon you, looking you full in the face...And give you peace! (Numbers 6:24-26 ESV)

(This is my paraphrase of the Aaronic Blessing...I use it often in congregational blessing)

Every moment is a fresh beginning. *(T.S. Eliot)*

New year coming...the grace of God never fails me; may I not fail His grace so often in the coming year.

God provides the wind; man must raise the sails.

The closer one is to God, the more deeply human one becomes.

Epilogue

"Oh, (2020-21), we hardly knew ye..."
(Joseph B. Geoghegan - 1867)

Until the year 2020, you probably didn't say "in-person gatherings," "social distancing," "flatten the curve," or "the new norm," but now you do. Many moons ago, you would have asked me what mask wars, Zoom, the Cubs playing to an empty stadium, defunding the police, and America—the land of homeschooling all had in common. Would you have guessed the years 2020-2021? But here we are. 2022 is about to begin.

You've probably read these excerpts from Joshua, chapters 1 and 24, but read them again:

> *Only be strong and courageous, being careful to do that which was commanded you...Be strong and courageous. Do not be frightened, and do not be dismayed, for the LORD your God is with you wherever you go...Only be strong and courageous... Serve the LORD in sincerity and in faithfulness... Choose you this day who you will serve...But as for me and my house, we will serve the LORD.*

"What a wonderful thought it is that some of the best years of our lives haven't even happened yet." *(Anna* Frank)

Fear does not necessarily keep us from dying...But it certainly can keep us from living*!!* Who gets to decide what's normal? I'm not always sure we've got the right people doing it.

Let the journey continue...Let's Dance!!